# Lecture Notes in Artificial Intelligence 10077

Subseries of Lecture Notes in Computer Science

More information about this series at http://www.springer.com/series/1244

Alberto Abad · Alfonso Ortega
António Teixeira · Carmen García Mateo
Carlos D. Martínez Hinarejos · Fernando Perdigão
Fernando Batista · Nuno Mamede (Eds.)

# Advances in Speech and Language Technologies for Iberian Languages

Third International Conference, IberSPEECH 2016
Lisbon, Portugal, November 23–25, 2016
Proceedings

 Springer

*Editors*

Alberto Abad
INESC-ID/IST
Universidade de Lisboa
Lisbon
Portugal

Alfonso Ortega
I3A/University of Zaragoza
Zaragoza
Spain

António Teixeira
DETI/IEETA
University of Aveiro
Aveiro
Portugal

Carmen García Mateo
AtlantTIC Research Center
Universidad de Vigo
Vigo
Spain

Carlos D. Martínez Hinarejos
Universitat Politècnica de València
Valencia
Spain

Fernando Perdigão
University of Coimbra
Coimbra
Portugal

Fernando Batista
INESC-ID/ISCTE-IUL
Lisbon
Portugal

Nuno Mamede
INESC-ID/IST
Universidade de Lisboa
Lisbon
Portugal

ISSN 0302-9743 ISSN 1611-3349 (electronic)
Lecture Notes in Artificial Intelligence
ISBN 978-3-319-49168-4 ISBN 978-3-319-49169-1 (eBook)
DOI 10.1007/978-3-319-49169-1

Library of Congress Control Number: 2016956496

LNCS Sublibrary: SL7 – Artificial Intelligence

Printed on acid-free paper

This Springer imprint is published by Springer Nature
The registered company is Springer International Publishing AG
The registered company address is: Gewerbestrasse 11, 6330 Cham, Switzerland

# Preface

The Spanish Thematic Network on Speech Technology (RTTH) and the International Speech Communication Association (ISCA) Special Interest Group on Iberian Languages (SIG-IL) are pleased to present a selection of papers from the IberSPEECH 2016 conference—*IX Jornadas en Tecnologías del Habla* and the V Iberian SLTech Workshop—that was held in Lisbon, Portugal, during November 23–25 2016.

The IberSPEECH series of conferences have become one of the most relevant scientific events for the community working in the field of speech and language processing of Iberian languages. This is demonstrated by the increased interest and success of previous editions, starting in Vigo 2010 with FALA and continuing in Madrid 2012 and Las Palmas de Gran Canaria 2014 with the new denomination: IberSPEECH. Prior to these past joint editions of the *Jornadas en Tecnologías del Habla* and the Iberian SLTech Workshop, separate events were held. The former ones have been organized by the RTTH (http://www.rthabla.es) since 2000. This network was created in 1999 and currently includes over 200 researchers and 30 research groups in speech technology all over Spain. The latter (Iberian SLTech) have been organized by the SIG-IL (http://www.il-sig.org/) of the ISCA since 2009. Overall, these events have attracted the attention of many researchers over the years, mainly from Spain, Portugal, and from other Iberian-speaking countries in Latin America, but also from several other research groups from all around the world. These previous efforts have contributed to the consolidation of a strong and active community addressing the problems of speech and language automatic processing of Iberian languages.

The IberSPEECH 2016 conference –the third of its kind using this name– brought together the *IX Jornadas en Tecnologías del Habla* and the V Iberian SLTech Workshop events, and it was co-organized by INESC-ID Lisboa, the RTTH, and the ISCA SIG-IL. Maintaining the identity of previous editions, this new event represented not only a step forward for the support of researchers in Iberian languages, but also a new challenge for the community, since it was the first edition to be held outside Spain. In order to promote interaction and discussion among all the members of the community, the Organizing Committee planned a three-day event with a wide variety of activities, such as technical paper presentations, keynote lectures, evaluation challenges, presentation of demos and research projects, and recent PhD thesis.

This *Lecture Notes in Artificial Intelligence* volume contains only a selection of the full regular articles presented during the IberSPEECH 2016 conference. To ensure the quality of all the contributions, each submitted article was reviewed by three members of the Scientific Review Committee, who provided feedback to improve the final article version, in addition to acceptance/rejection recommendations for the Technical Program Committee. Authors of the accepted papers had time to address the comments before submitting the camera-ready versions. We had 48 regular full papers submitted and only 27 of them were selected for publication in this volume. This selection was based on the scores and comments provided by our Scientific Review Committee, which includes over 66 researchers from different institutions mainly from Spain, Portugal, and Latin America, but also from France, Germany, Hungary, Italy, Norway, Sweden, UK, and the USA, to whom we also would like to express our deepest gratitude. The selected articles in this volume are organized into four different topics:

- Speech Production, Analysis, Coding and Synthesis
- Automatic Speech Recognition
- Paralinguistic Speaker Trait Characterization
- Speech and Language Technologies in Different Application Fields

The Organizing Committee of IberSPEECH is extremely proud of the contents of this volume. We trust that we have achieved and delivered the scientific quality standards that the researchers in the field of speech and language technologies for Iberian languages value.

As mentioned previously, besides the excellent research articles included in this volume, the conference included a wide variety of scientific activities that are worth mentioning in more detail, particularly, the ALBAYZIN Technology Competitive Evaluations, the Special Session contributions, and the keynote lectures.

The ALBAYZIN Technology Competitive Evaluations have been organized alongside the conference since 2006, promoting the fair and transparent comparison of technology in different fields related to speech and language technology. In this edition we had two different challenge evaluations: Speaker Diarization and Search on Speech. The organization of each one of these evaluations requires the preparation of development and test data, which is released along with a clear set of rules to the participants, and gathering and comparing results from participants. This organization was carried out by different groups of researchers with the support of the ALBAYZIN Committee. Although article contributions and results from the evaluations are not included in this volume, we would like to express our gratitude to the organizers and also to the participants of these evaluation challenges.

In addition to full articles, a subset of which are represented here, and to system description papers of the ALBAYZIN participants, Special Session papers were also included in the conference program. These were intended to describe either progress in current or recent research and development projects, demonstration systems, or PhD Thesis extended abstracts to compete in the PhD Award.

Moreover, we had the pleasure of hosting three extraordinary keynote speakers: Prof. Elmar Nöth (University of Erlangen-Nuremberg, Germany), Dr. Bhuvana Ramabhadran (IBM T.J. Watson Research Center, USA) and Prof. Steve Renals (University of Edinburgh, UK). We would like to acknowledge their extremely valuable participation that helped to elevate the quality of the overall event.

Finally, we would like to thank all those whose effort made possible this conference, including the members of the Organizing Committee, the Local Organizing Committee, the ALBAYZIN Committee, the Scientific Reviewer Committee, the authors, the conference attendees, the supporting institutions, and so many people who gave their best to achieve a successful conference. We would also like to thank Springer for the possibility of publishing another volume of selected papers from an IberSPEECH conference.

November 2016

Alberto Abad
Alfonso Ortega
António Teixeira
Carmen García Mateo
Carlos D. Martínez Hinarejos
Fernando Perdigão
Fernando Batista
Nuno Mamede

# Organization

## General Chair

Alberto Abad                 INESC-ID/IST, University of Lisbon, Portugal
Alfonso Ortega               Universidad de Zaragoza, Spain
António Teixeira             Universidade de Aveiro, Portugal

## Technical Program Chair

Carmen García Mateo          Universidad de Vigo, Spain
Fernando Perdigão            Universidade de Coimbra, Portugal
C.D. Martínez-Hinarejos      Universitat Politècnica de València, Spain

## Publication Chair

Nuno Mamede                  INESC-ID/IST, University of Lisbon, Portugal
Fernando Batista             INESC-ID/ISCTE-IUL, Portugal

## Special Session and Awards Chair

Juan Luis Navarro Mesa       Universidad de Las Palmas de Gran Canaria, Spain
Doroteo Torre Toledano       Universidad Autónoma de Madrid, Spain
Xavier Anguera               ELSA Corp., USA

## Plenary Talks Chair

Isabel Trancoso              INESC-ID/IST, University of Lisbon, Portugal

## Evaluations Chair

Luis J. Rodríguez Fuentes    Universidad del País Vasco, Spain
Rubén San-Segundo            Universidad Politécnica de Madrid, Spain

## Publicity and Sponsorship Chair

Helena Moniz                 INESC-ID/FL, University of Lisbon, Portugal

## Albayzin Committee

Luis J. Rodríguez Fuentes    Universidad del País Vasco, Spain
Rubén San-Segundo            Universidad Politécnica de Madrid, Spain

Alberto Abad                 INESC-ID/IST, University of Lisbon, Portugal
Alfonso Ortega               Universidad de Zaragoza, Spain
António Teixeira             Universidade de Aveiro, Portugal

## Local Organizing Committee

Alberto Abad                 INESC-ID/University of Lisbon, Portugal
Fernando Batista             INESC-ID/ISCTE-IUL, Portugal
Nuno Mamede                  INESC-ID/IST, University of Lisbon, Portugal
David Martins de Matos       INESC-ID/IST, University of Lisbon, Portugal
Helena Moniz                 INESC-ID/FL, University of Lisbon, Portugal
Rubén Solera-Ureña           INESC-ID, Portugal
Isabel Trancoso              INESC-ID/IST, University of Lisbon, Portugal

## Scientific Review Committee

Alberto Abad                 INESC-ID/IST, University of Lisbon, Portugal
Plinio Barbosa               University of Campinas, Brazil
Jorge Baptista               INESC-ID/University of Algarve, Portugal
Fernando Batista             INESC-ID/ISCTE-IUL, Portugal
José Miguel Benedí Ruiz      Universitat Politècnica de València, Spain
Carmen Benitez               Universidad de Granada, Spain
Antonio Bonafonte            Universitat Politecnica de Catalunya, Spain
German Bordel                University of the Basque Country UPV/EHU, Spain
Alessio Brutti               FBK, Italy
Paula Carvalho               INESC-ID/Universidade Europeia, Portugal
Diamantino Caseiro           Google Inc., USA
Maria Jose Castro-Bleda      Universitat Politecnica de Valencia, Spain
Ricardo Cordoba              Grupo de Tecnologia del Habla, Spain
Conceicao Cunha              IPS Munich, Germany
Carme De-La-Mota             Universitat Autònoma de Barcelona, Spain
Laura Docío Fernández        University of Vigo, Spain
Daniel Erro                  University of the Basque Country UPV/EHU, Spain
David Escudero               University of Valladolid, Spain
Ruben Fernandez              Universidad Politécnica de Madrid, Spain
Javier Ferreiros             GTH, Universidad Politécnica de Madrid, Spain
Julian Fierrez               Universidad Autonoma de Madrid, Spain
Ascension Gallardo           Universidad Carlos III de Madrid, Spain
Carmen Garcia Mateo          Universidade de Vigo, Spain
Juan I. Godino Llorente      Universidad Politécnica de Madrid, Spain
Javier Hernando              Universitat Politecnica de Catalunya, Spain
Lluís Felip Hurtado Oliver   Universitat Politecnica de Valencia, Spain
Irina Illina                 LORIA, France
Eduardo Lleida               University of Zaragoza, Spain
José David Lopes             KTH, Sweden
Paula López Otero            Universidade de Vigo, Spain

## Organizing Institutions

INESC-ID Lisboa
Spanish Thematic Network on Speech Technology (RTTH)
ISCA Special Interest Group on Iberian Languages (SIG-IL)

## Support and Partner Institutions

Instituto Superior Técnico, University of Lisbon
Ministerio de Economía y Competitividad, Gobierno de España
FCT, Fundação para a Ciência e a Tecnologia
Cámara Municipal de Lisboa
TAP Portugal

# Contents

**Paralinguistic Speaker Trait Characterization**

## Speech and Language Technologies in Different Application Fields

# Speech Production, Analysis, Coding and Synthesis

# Study of the Effect of Reducing Training Data in Speech Synthesis Adaptation Based on Frequency Warping

Agustin Alonso[1(✉)], Daniel Erro[1,2], Eva Navas[1], and Inma Hernaez[1]

[1] AHOLAB, University of the Basque Country (UPV/EHU), Bilbao, Spain
{agustin,derro,eva,inma}@aholab.ehu.es
[2] Basque Foundation for Science (IKERBASQUE), Bilbao, Spain

**Abstract.** Speaker adaptation techniques use a small amount of data to modify Hidden Markov Model (HMM) based speech synthesis systems to mimic a target voice. These techniques can be used to provide personalized systems to people who suffer some speech impairment and allow them to communicate in a more natural way. Although the adaptation techniques don't require a big quantity of data, the recording process can be tedious if the user has speaking problems. To improve the acceptance of these systems an important factor is to be able to obtain acceptable results with minimal amount of recordings. In this work we explore the performance of an adaptation method based on Frequency Warping which uses only vocalic segments according to the amount of available training data.

**Keywords:** Speech adaptation · Statistical speech synthesis · Frequency warping · Dysarthric voice

## 1 Introduction

The voice is the principal way that humans have to communicate with each other. Sadly, in some cases people lose totally or partially the ability to speak due to an illness or an accident. In these cases speech technologies can provide a partial solution, in particular Text-to-Speech (TTS) systems [1] can be used by these people as an alternative communication tool. The rise of the use of smartphones together with the emergence of statistical parametric TTS [2], which requires few resources, have made possible that anybody can bring his/her own TTS in the pocket. However, conventional TTS systems produce a generic and personality-less voice, so an important desired characteristic is the ability to provide personalized voices to the users. There are several initiatives to achieve this goal using voice adaptation [3]: with some recordings of a human target voice it is possible to change the acoustic properties of the synthetic voice.

Although conventional adaptation methods are valid when the user knows that he or she will suffer some impairment (e.g. a planned surgery) and he or she can make the necessary recordings, it is not an option if the user's voice

A. Abad et al. (Eds.): IberSPEECH 2016, LNAI 10077, pp. 3–13, 2016.
DOI: 10.1007/978-3-319-49169-1_1

already exhibits severe symptoms of a given pathology. In this case two different approaches exist. One of them consists in using the recordings made by a "donor". In other words, the user will obtain a TTS system with the acoustic properties of another person [4]. This solution is the most reasonable when the user has completely lost the ability of speaking. The other approach applies when the user is able to produce partially intelligible speech with only some sounds are correctly pronounced, i.e. dysarthric voice. In this case it is possible to extract characteristics from the healthy fragments and try to extrapolate this information to adapt the whole voice [5,6].

When the second approach is followed two aspects must be evaluated. First, the usable segments have to be selected, e.g. in dysarthric voices the vowels are usually the best pronounced sounds. Then, enough usable data should be collected. On the one hand, if there are few data the adapted voice will not adequately mimic the target one. On the other hand, it is not practical to ask too many recordings to people who have troubles speaking. If we want to improve the system's acceptance and make it more accessible, the process of obtaining the adaptation information should be as friendly as possible. So, an important factor to determinate is how many recordings are necessary to collect the data for the adaptation process. In order to resolve this question in this paper we present the analysis of the performance of the method presented in [7]. This method has already shown to obtain good results in terms of quality and similarity to the target speaker when it works with sufficient data using only vocalic segments. We gradually reduce the data used to train the transforms and study how the performance of the system is affected.

Although the final goal of our work is to provide personalized synthesizer to people with dysarthric voice, in this first steps of the research we used healthy voices. In this way we can obtain an indicator of the performance in the most favourable conditions. Moreover, the comparison with state of the art adaptation methods is only possible with healthy voices.

The rest of the paper is structured as follows. In Sect. 2 a brief description of statistical parametric synthesis and some adaptation techniques are introduced. Section 3 summarizes of our previous work and the method we used in the experiments. In Sect. 4 the experiments carried out are presented. Finally in Sect. 5 the conclusions of this work are summarised.

## 2    Statistical Parametric Synthesis and Adaptation

In a HMM-based synthesizer, a set of HMMs are trained using a database containing audio utterances from one (or more) speaker(s) and their transcription. Text is converted into labels that describe it phonetic, prosodic and linguistically, and audio is parameterised into acoustic features using a vocoder. State-of-the-art vocoders [8,9] consider three different acoustic streams: logarithm of fundamental frequency (log-$f_0$), Mel-Cepstral (MCEP) or linear prediction related representation of the spectral envelope, and a degree of harmonicity of different spectral bands. The context-dependent HMMs learn the correspondence between the labels and the acoustic parameters, together with their first and second derivatives over time. Since the transition probabilities between states don't model correctly the actual durations, a variant of HMM called Hidden Semi-Markov Models (HSMM) [10] is used. In this model the state durations are characterized by explicit Gaussian distributions.

In the synthesis phase any arbitrary text is translated into labels in the same way as the transcriptions from the training dataset. Given these labels and the model, the system generates the most likely sequence of acoustic parameters [11] and feeds the vocoder, which builds the synthetic waveform.

The main idea behind the adaptation consists in changing the mean vectors and covariance matrices from the set of HSMM using a new small database from another speaker to obtain a new voice which sounds similar to the target. If the database used to train the initial model contains utterances from more than one speaker the result is called average model [12]. This average model is suitable for adaptation because it does not convey peculiarities from any particular speaker, so it is easier to adapt.

Usual adaptation techniques, such us Constrained Maximum Likelihood Linear Regression (CMLLR) [13] or Constrained Structural Maximum a Posteriori Linear Regression (CSMAPLR) [14], uses unconstrained linear transforms, to project the acoustic space of the source into the acoustic space of the target. These kind of transforms are capable of capturing the source-target correspondence, but they are not directly interpretable. There is another kind of transform, namely Frequency Warping (FW) plus Amplitude Scaling (AS), which has a direct physical interpretation [15] but is not as flexible as the free linear one. FW maps the frequency axis from a source spectrum onto that of a target spectrum, without eliminating any spectral detail from the source. AS compensates the amplitude differences between the warped-source spectrum and the target spectrum. FW+AS transforms were originally used in the voice conversion field [16–19], where they obtained satisfactory conversion scores without degrading the quality of the speech significantly. Also it has been proved that, in cepstral domain, FW is equivalent to a multiplicative matrix [20] and AS can be implemented as an additive term. This means that FW+AS can be seen as a linear transform in cepstral domain, so it can be applied to adapt the HSMM state distributions as:

$$\hat{\boldsymbol{\mu}} = \hat{\mathbf{A}}\boldsymbol{\mu} + \hat{\mathbf{b}}, \quad \hat{\boldsymbol{\Sigma}} = \hat{\mathbf{A}}\boldsymbol{\Sigma}\hat{\mathbf{A}}^{\top} \tag{1}$$

where $\boldsymbol{\mu}$ and $\boldsymbol{\Sigma}$ are the mean vector and covariance matrix of the HSMM state, $\hat{\boldsymbol{\mu}}$ and $\hat{\boldsymbol{\Sigma}}$ are their transformed counterparts, and

$$\hat{\mathbf{A}} = \begin{bmatrix} \mathbf{A} & 0 & 0 \\ 0 & \mathbf{A} & 0 \\ 0 & 0 & \mathbf{A} \end{bmatrix}, \quad \hat{\boldsymbol{b}} = \begin{bmatrix} \mathbf{b} \\ 0 \\ 0 \end{bmatrix} \tag{2}$$

$\mathbf{A}$ representing the FW, $\mathbf{b}$ the AS, and $\hat{\mathbf{A}}$ and $\hat{\boldsymbol{b}}$ are used to modify simultaneously the static and the dynamic features.

## 3   Description of the Adaptation Method

The FW+AS-based adaptation methods require a set of paired source-target vectors as input. In our case, the vectors from the target speaker are taken selecting the vowels from the uttered sentences where: (i) all the frames are voiced, which avoids artifacts related to $f_0$ misdetection; (ii) the duration is greater than 55 ms, which ensures that there are enough samples for an accurate spectral analysis and also that there is a sufficiently wide stable zone free of co-articulation. From the vowels that fulfil both requisites we only take the central frame. The corresponding source frames are selected from the original voice model: first we generate labels from the text of the adaptation utterance; using these labels, we select the p.d.f. of the central state of each vowels and extract the static part of the mean vector which is used as source frame.

The method we proposed in [7] is an evolution of the method explained in [17], which is based on Dynamic Frequency Warping (DFW) [21] procedure. DFW calculates the FW function that should be applied to a set of $(N + 1)$-point log-amplitude semi-spectra, $\{X_t\}$, to make them maximally close to the paired counterparts, $\{Y_t\}$. It is based on an accumulative cost function $D(i, j)$ that indicates the log-spectral distortion obtained when the $i^{th}$ bin from the source is mapped onto the $j^{th}$ bin from the target following the optimal path from $(0, 0)$ to $(i, j)$. The mathematical expression of $D(i, j)$ can be describes as follows

$$D(i,j) = \min \left\{ \begin{array}{l} D(i-1,j) + d(i,j) \\ D(i-1,j-1) + w \cdot d(i,j) \\ D(i,j-1) + d(i,j) \end{array} \right\} \tag{3}$$

where $i, j = 0...N$, $w$ is an empirical control parameter to manage the penalty of the horizontal and vertical paths, and $d(i, j)$ is the distance between the source's $i^{th}$ bin and target's $j^{th}$ bin. In our case $d(i, j)$ is calculated simultaneously from all the paired source-target vectors using the following equation:

$$d(i,j) = \sum_{t=1}^{T} (X_t[i] - Y_t[j])^2 + \sum_{t=1}^{T} \alpha_t (X_t'[i] - Y_t'[j])^2 \tag{4}$$

where $T$ is the total amount of training paired vectors, $X_t'$ and $Y_t'$ are the derivatives over frequency of $X_t$ and $Y_t$ respectively, and $\alpha_t$ is an empirical factor that stands for the relative weight of the derivatives of the spectra. The frequency warping path $P$ is defined as a sequence of points,

$$P = \{(0,0), (i_1, j_1), (i_2, j_2), \ldots (N, N)\} \tag{5}$$

where the presence on the point $(i, j)$ indicates that the $i^{th}$ bin from the source should be mapped into the $j^{th}$ bin from the target. The points of $P$ are computed backward from $(N, N)$ to $(0, 0)$ using the recursive formula expressed in (3).

Since the DFW works in the log-spectral domain, the adaptation data must be converted from $p^{th}$-order MCEP into $(N + 1)$ point discrete log-amplitude semispectra. Using a traditional MCEP definition this can be done multiplying the MCEP vectors by a matrix $\mathbf{S}$ defined as follows

$$\mathbf{S}[n, i] = \cos(i \cdot mel(\pi n/N)), \;\; 0 \leq n \leq N, \;\; 0 \leq i \leq p \tag{6}$$

In a similar way, the MCEP representation of a discrete log-amplitude spectrum of $(N+1)$ points can be calculated through the technique known as regularized discrete cepstrum [22], i.e. multiplying the semispectra in vector form by

$$\mathbf{C} = \left(\mathbf{S}^T\mathbf{S} + \lambda\mathbf{R}\right)^{-1}\mathbf{S}^T \tag{7}$$

where $\mathbf{S}$ is given by (6), $\mathbf{R}$ is a regularization matrix that imposes smoothing constraints to the cepstral envelope,

$$\mathbf{R} = 8\pi^2 \cdot diag\left\{0, 1^2, 2^2, \ldots p^2\right\} \tag{8}$$

and $\lambda$ is an empirical constant typically equal to $2 \cdot 10^{-4}$ [22]. Since the $0^{th}$ cepstral coefficient, related to energy, and the $1^{st}$ cepstral coefficient, mainly related to glottal spectrum, are not relevant in terms of FW [17], they are set to zero before the multiplication by $\mathbf{S}$. With the training vectors translated from MCEP domain into log-semispectra domain using $\mathbf{S}$, the optimal warping path P is obtained via DFW. The matrix which implements the frequency warping operation can be defined as follows

$$\mathbf{W}[j, i] = \frac{m_{i,j}}{\sum_{k=1}^{N} m_{i,k}} \tag{9}$$

where $m_{i,j} = 1$ when $(i,j) \in P$ and $m_{i,j} = 0$ otherwise. Once $\mathbf{W}$ has been determined the matrix $\mathbf{A}$ which implements the same operation in the MCEP domain is calculated as:

$$\mathbf{A} = \mathbf{C} \cdot \mathbf{W} \cdot \mathbf{S} \tag{10}$$

In our work we calculated a unique FW matrix $\mathbf{A}$ for the whole training dataset, regardless of the vowel the vectors belong to. Using its block replicated version $\check{\mathbf{A}}$ (2), this curve can be applied to all the distributions of the model without altering their phonetic content.

The additive MCEP term that implements the AS operation is calculated as the difference between the target and source-warped MCEP vectors:

$$\mathbf{b} = \frac{1}{T}\sum_{t=1}^{T}\left(\mathbf{y_t} - \mathbf{A} \cdot \mathbf{x_t}\right) \tag{11}$$

where $\mathbf{x_t}$ and $\mathbf{y_t}$ are the $t^{th}$ pair of source and target vectors respectively, and $\mathbf{A}$ is given by 10. Unlike the FW matrix, we don't assume a single bias vector for all the distributions. We compute one $\mathbf{b}$ vector per vowel and then we apply a different AS vector to each distribution according three cases:

– Distributions that correspond to only one vowel are modified by the specific AS vector of that vowel.

- When a distribution is shared by more than one vowel, we use a weighted average of the AS vectors of these vowels. The weights are the proportion of times the current distribution belonged to each vowel when the original voice model was trained.
- The remaining distributions are modified using the average of the AS vectors of all vowels.

Not only the spectral information but also the fundamental frequency is a very important acoustic feature that defines the identity of the speaker. For this reason we also perform a single mean normalization as follows: First, we take the log-$f_0$ values at the central frame of the previously selected vowels. From these values, we calculate the target average log-$f_0$. Then, similarly as in the spectral case, a source average log-$f_0$ is calculated from the static parts of the means of the p.d.f. in the central state of the vowels. Finally the adaptation is carried out applying a linear transform similar to 1 to all the distributions of the log-$f_0$ model where $\mathbf{A}$ is set to 1 and $\mathbf{b}$ is equal to the difference between source and target average log-$f_0$:

The experiments carried out in [7] showed that the method above explained presents a good performance in terms of quality and similarity when it is compared with a state-of-the-art adaptation algorithm. However in our first experiments we used as training data all the available vocalic segments from an adaptation dataset of 100 utterances per speaker. The need of collecting this amount of recordings can be troublesome and tedious, so be able to reduce the number of required vocalic segments, and therefore the number of recordings, is an important task. Our final goal is to be able to provide a personalized synthesizer to people with disarthric voice, thus an important factor to ensure the acceptance of this system is making it easy and friendly.

## 4    Experiments

### 4.1    Experimental Setup

To determine the minimal amount of adaptation data required by our method for an acceptable performance, we used recordings made through a voice-banking dedicated web-portal [23]. This is the most suitable kind of data for our experiments because we plan to include adaptation functionalities in the web-page in order to provide speaking aids to impaired people. We collected 100 phonetically balanced utterances from 6 non-professional Spanish speakers (3 male and 3 female). Because all of them were recorded using the speaker's own equipment over a variable number of sessions in a non-controlled environment the recordings exhibit medium/low quality. Therefore, the signals were normalized in order to maximize dynamic range, and were passed through a Wiener filter to reduce noise. Phonetic segmentation was carried out automatically using HTK [24]. Table 1 shows the amount of vowels available when the segments are selected according to the method described in Sect. 3. As expected this is different for each speaker.

**Table 1.** Number of available vowels per speaker.

|    | /a/ | /e/ | /i/ | /o/ | /u/ | Total |
|----|-----|-----|-----|-----|-----|-------|
| M1 | 256 | 154 | 111 | 153 | 66  | 740   |
| M2 | 451 | 239 | 182 | 249 | 63  | 1184  |
| M3 | 261 | 185 | 160 | 163 | 72  | 842   |
| F1 | 317 | 201 | 169 | 186 | 74  | 1530  |
| F2 | 453 | 364 | 244 | 334 | 135 | 1123  |
| F3 | 283 | 139 | 206 | 147 | 68  | 843   |

In order to avoid a too long perceptual test we first limited the number of different adaptations to compare. According to informal perceptual tests carried out in the laboratory, we decided to use three adaptations with a varying amount of training data in the test: the first one using all available vowels, the second one using 10 % of samples of each vowel and finally the extreme case of using only one sample per vowel. In the second and third cases the used samples where randomly selected.

As source we used a standard HTS [2] speaker-dependent voice trained with 1962 utterances from a female speaker in Spanish. The use of an average voice model was discarded because we do not have enough training data from different speakers with the quality necessary to obtain a good average model. The audio signals for the target and the source voices were sampled at 16 kHz and parameterised using Ahocoder [9], a high quality harmonic-plus-noise based vocoder. We extracted $39^{\text{th}}$ order MCEP coefficients, log-$f_0$ and Maximum Voiced Frequency (MVF) each 5 ms.

As baseline for comparison we used a state-of-the-art HTS-based speaker adaptive method that uses CMLLR+MAP [3]. For this method we use all the information from the utterances instead of only vowels. Although the baseline method adapts not only the spectral envelope but all of the acoustic features (log-$f_0$, MVF and duration), we restricted the comparison to the MCEP model adaptation. In synthesis, we used for each adaptation method the corresponding MCEP model. For the log-$f_0$ model, we used the proposed average correction explained in Sect. 3 in all the methods. The duration and MVF models used were those of the source voice.

## 4.2   Perceptual Test and Results

For the evaluation, 10 short sentences were synthesised for each adapted speaker and method, i.e. 240 sentences. A total of 11 evaluators took part in the evaluation. Two sentences per speaker and method were randomly selected from the whole evaluation set and presented to each evaluator, so each evaluator rated 48 sentences. For every synthetic sentence, a recording of the original voice was also given as reference. The evaluators were asked to rate both the quality of the adapted voice (regardless of the quality of the reference) and the similarity to the original target, both using a 1–5 scale. The mean opinion scores are shown in Figs. 1 and 2.

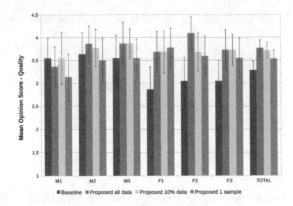

**Fig. 1.** Mean opinion scores for quality and 95 % confidence intervals.

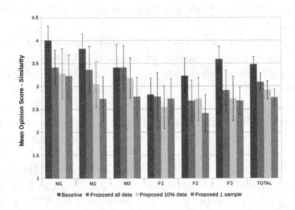

**Fig. 2.** Mean opinion scores for similarity and 95 % confidence intervals.

As we can observe, overall the experiments confirm that the proposed method is better in terms of quality, whereas it is not as good as the baseline method (which exploits the whole signal content) in terms of similarity to the target. In this regard, we have to admit that the gap has increased with respect to our previous experiment [7]. Among the possible reasons for this, the most likely is the replacement of M3 and F3 target voices in the experiments by other speakers. The recordings used previously presented worse recording conditions (noise, reverberation and other artifacts). We decided to use recordings from new users of the voice bank and, therefore the scores are different. In any case, this test shows more clearly the limitations of the suggested approach. We can also observe difference in term of similarity score between male and female target voices. We believe this is due to the specific characteristics of the source voice. To overcome this limitation, an appropriate source voice could be selected from a voice bank.

As for the behaviour of the method under training data reduction, overall performance degradation is little when the amount of data is reduced by factor 10. However, for a single randomly-selected sample for each vowel the differences are significant. There are two alternative ways of interpreting this. First, it could be an indicator that a single vowel is not enough to train the system. Second, the problem could be an "unfortunate" random selection, i.e. the selection of a strongly co-articulated vowel. To clarify this point, we trained the system using sustained vowels recorded in the laboratory from several speakers instead of fragments of continuous speech. We found that for some of these voices the performance of the method dropped substantially. More specifically, we observed that under these non-spontaneous articulation conditions some of the resulting FW curves were too irregular and produced annoying artifacts during synthesis. This leads us to the conclusion that FW-based adaptation must be reinforced by means of a proper source speaker selection algorithm. Moreover, we are currently exploring alternative speaker interpolation based approach, assuming the availability of multiple donors.

## 5    Conclusions and Future Work

In this paper we have studied the effect of reducing the amount of training data in an adaptation method that uses only vocalic segments, which was already proved to obtain good results when it has enough samples. We found that if we carry the system to the limit case of having only one sample per vowel the performance in terms of quality and similarity deteriorates. However the method supports quite well the lack of training data and we obtain similar results when we use all the available data and when we use only 10 % of them. With this knowledge we are now capable of designing a more specific corpus to record by people with speech impairments. For these people the request of recording too many sentences may be annoying. If we can reduce the amount of necessary recordings, these systems could be more easily accepted. The next step is building this specific corpus and using the recordings made by people with dysarthric voices for adaptation. Future works will also tackle the automatic detection of useful vocalic segments from pathological voice recordings. Furthermore, we will address the main limitation of this method, namely the need of correctly articulated vowels. Preliminary experiments in this direction have shown that for severe dysarthria it is convenient to repair the vocalic triangle of the recorded utterances before adaptation to avoid unnatural warping trajectories.

**Acknowledgments.** This work has been partially supported by MINECO/FEDER, UE (SpeechTech4All project, TEC2012-38939-C03 03 and RESTORE project, TEC2015-67163-C2-1-R), and the Basque Government (ELKAROLA project, KK-2015/00098).

# References

1. Taylor, P.: Text-to-Speech Synthesis. Cambridge University Press, Cambridge (2009)
2. Zen, H., Tokuda, K., Black, A.: Statistical parametric speech synthesis. Speech Commun. **51**(11), 1039–1064 (2009)
3. Yamagishi, J., Nose, T., Zen, H., Ling, Z.H., Toda, T., Tokuda, K., King, S., Renals, S.: Robust speaker-adaptive HMM-based text-to-speech synthesis. IEEE Trans. Audio Speech Lang. Process. **17**(6), 1208–1230 (2009)
4. Yamagishi, J., Veaux, C., King, S., Renals, S.: Speech synthesis technologies for individuals with vocal disabilities: voice banking and reconstruction. Acoust. Sci. Technol. **33**(1), 1–5 (2012)
5. Creer, S., Cunningham, S., Green, P., Yamagishi, J.: Building personalised synthetic voices for individuals with severe speech impairment. Comput. Speech Lang. **27**(6), 1178–1193 (2013)
6. Lanchantin, P., Veaux, C., Gales, M.J.F., King, S., Yamagishi, J.: Reconstructing voices within the multiple-average-voice-model framework. In: Proceedings of the 16th Annual Conference of the International Speech Communication Association (Interspeech), Dresden, Germany, pp. 2232–2236 (2015)
7. Alonso, A., Erro, D., Navas, E., Hernaez, I.: Speaker adaptation using only vocalic segments via frequency warping. In: Proceedings of the 16th Annual Conference of the International Speech Communication Association (Interspeech), Dresden, Germany, pp. 2764–2768 (2015)
8. Kawahara, H., Masuda-Katsusue, I., de Cheveigne, A.: Restructuring speech representations using a pitch-adaptive time-frequency smoothing and an instantaneous-frequency-based F0 extraction: possible role of a repetitive structure in sounds. Speech Commun. **27**, 187–207 (1999)
9. Erro, D., Sainz, I., Navas, E., Hernaez, I.: Harmonics plus noise model based vocoder for statistical parametric speech synthesis. IEEE J. Sel. Top. Signal Process. **8**(2), 184–194 (2014)
10. Zen, H., Tokuda, K., Masuko, T., Kobayashi, T., Kitamura, T.: A hidden semi-Markov model-based speech synthesis system. IEICE Trans. Inf. Syst. **E90-D**(5), 825–834 (2007)
11. Tokuda, K., Yoshimura, T., Masuko, T., Kobayashi, T., Kitamura, T.: Speech parameter generation algorithms for HMM-based speech synthesis, vol. 30, pp. 1315–1318 (2000)
12. Yamagishi, J.: A training method of average voice model for HMM-based speech synthesis using MLLR. IEICE Trans. Inf. Syst. **86**(8), 1956–1963 (2003)
13. Gales, M.J.F.: Maximum likelihood linear transformations for HMM-based speech recognition. Comput. Speech Lang. **12**(2), 75–98 (1998)
14. Yamagishi, J., Kobayashi, T., Nakano, Y., Ogata, K., Isogai, J.: Analysis of speaker adaptation algorthims for HMM-based speech synthesis and a constrained SMAPLR adaptation algorithm. IEEE Trans. Audio Speech Lang. Process. **19**(1), 66–83 (2009)
15. Erro, D., Alonso, A., Serrano, L., Navas, E., Hernaez, I.: Interpretable parametric voice conversion functions based on Gaussian mixture models and constrained transformations. Comput. Speech Lang. **30**, 3–15 (2015)
16. Erro, D., Moreno, A., Bonafonte, A.: Voice conversion based on weighted frequency warping. IEEE Trans. Audio Speech Lang. Process. **18**(5), 922–931 (2010)

17. Zorila, T.C., Erro, D., Hernaez, I.: Improving the quality of standard GMM-based voice conversion systems by considering physically motivated linear transformations. Commun. Comput. Inf. Sci. **328**, 30–39 (2012)
18. Godoy, E., Rosec, O., Chonavel, T.: Voice conversion using dynamic frequency warping with amplitude scaling, for parallel or nonparallel corpora. IEEE Trans. Audio Speech Lang. Process. **20**(4), 1313–1323 (2012)
19. Erro, D., Navas, E., Hernaez, I.: Parametric voice conversion based on bilinear frequency warping plus amplitude scaling. IEEE Trans. Audio Speech Lang. Process. **21**(3), 556–566 (2013)
20. Pitz, M., Ney, H.: Vocal tract normalization equals linear transformation in cepstral space. IEEE Trans. Speech Audio Process. **13**, 930–944 (2005)
21. Valbret, H., Moulines, E., Tubach, J.P.: Voice transformation using PSOLA technique. Speech Commun. **11**(2–3), 175–187 (1992)
22. Cappé, O., Laroche, J., Moulines, E.: Regularized estimation of cepstrum envelope from discrete frequency points. In: IEEE ASSP Workshop on Applications of Signal Processing to Audio and Acoustics, pp. 213–216 (1995)
23. Erro, D., Hernáez, I., Navas, E., Alonso, A., Arzelus, H., Jauk, I., Hy, N.Q., Magariños, C., Pérez-Ramón, R., Sulír, M., Tian, X., Wang, X., Ye, J.: ZureTTS: online platform for obtaining personalized synthetic voices. In: Proceedings of eNTER-FACE 2014 (2014)
24. Young, S., Kershaw, D., Odell, J., Ollason, D., Valtchev, V., Woodland, P., et al.: The HTK Book, version 3.4 (2006)

# A Dynamic FEC for Improved Robustness of CELP-Based Codec

Nadir Benamirouche[1], Bachir Boudraa[2], Angel M. Gomez[3],
José L. Pérez-Córdoba[3(✉)], and Iván López-Espejo[3]

[1] Laboratoire de Génie Electrique, Faculté de Technologie,
Université de Bejaia, 06000 Bejaia, Algeria
benam_nadir@yahoo.fr
[2] Faculty of Electronics and Computer Science,
University of S.T.H.B, Algiers, Algeria
b.boudraa@yahoo.fr
[3] Department of Signal Theory, Networking and Communications,
University of Granada, 18071 Granada, Spain
{amgg,jlpc,iloes}@ugr.es

**Abstract.** The strong interframe dependency present in Code Excited Linear Prediction (CELP) codecs renders the decoder very vulnerable when the Adaptive Codebook (ACB) is desynchronized. Hence, errors affect not only the concealed frame but also all the subsequent frames. In this paper, we have developed a Forward Error Correction (FEC)-based technique which relies on energy constraint to determine frame onset which will be considered for sending the FEC information. The extra information contains an optimized FEC pulse excitation which models the contribution of the ACB to offer a resynchronization procedure at the decoder. In fact, under the energy constraint the number of Fixed Codebook (FCB) pulses can be reduced in order to be exploited by the FEC intervention. In return, the error propagation is considerably prevented with no overload of added-pulses. Furthermore, the proposed method greatly improves the CELP-based codec robustness to packet losses with no increase in coder storage capacity.

**Keywords:** Speech coding · VoIP · Forward error correction · Lossy packet networks · Error propagation · ACB resynchronization

## 1 Introduction

Media streaming services such as Voice over Internet Protocol (VoIP) is an emerging technology which has become a key driver in the evolution of voice communications. Unfortunately, the quality of service (QoS) of VoIP does not yet provide toll-quality voice equivalent to that offered by the traditional public switched telephone network [1]. Indeed, another critical issue for media streaming applications such as VoIP, is its vulnerability to end-to-end performance [2,3]. Some packets may be delayed or lost due to network congestion. Hence, the missing packets have to be regenerated at the decoder side using packet

© Springer International Publishing AG 2016
A. Abad et al. (Eds.): IberSPEECH 2016, LNAI 10077, pp. 14–23, 2016.
DOI: 10.1007/978-3-319-49169-1_2

loss concealment techniques. In Code Excited Linear Prediction (CELP)-based codecs [4] a long-term predictor (LTP) is used to encode the excitation signal through its past samples. Since such speech parameters are not efficiently estimated by the concealment approach, it is reported that this mismatch on the obtained excitation introduces error propagation through the properly received frames [6]. A wide variety of error concealment techniques have been proposed as solutions for the above problems in order to mitigate the effect of lost frames, especially in the context of voice over packet networks [1–7]. These alternative solutions are based on considering some side information sent as extra bit-rate. In the same direction, recent approaches are focused on limiting the inter-frame dependencies using forward error correction (FEC) [8], where additional information are used to reinitialize the decoder in presence of packet loss. This redundancy provides an alternative representation of the previous excitation samples to prevent error propagation [7].

In this paper, we propose a decoder resynchronization method based on dynamically adding FEC information to improve the robustness of CELP-based codecs. As a solution to the error propagation problem, the proposed method sends side information replacing the Adaptive Codebook (ACB) contribution with a set of pulses as memoryless codebook. The developed FEC-based technique relies on energy ratio constraint to determine voiced subframes (frame onset) which side information will be considered for. Through the proposed method, a higher reduction in bit-rate is achieved when the extra information is sent for only the first two subframes ($SF_0$ and $SF_1$) of a voiced frame, since the pitch component of the subsequent subframes ($SF_2$ and $SF_3$) can be estimated using the previous two subframes. The proposed method is a subframe-based technique which uses the Least Square Error (LSE) criterion over the synthesized speech domain to optimize the FEC pulses. Hence, at the decoder side when the previous frame is erased, this set of pulses is added to the Fixed Codebook (FCB) vector to form the total excitation. The synthesized speech signal is finally obtained as the LP filter response to this excitation. Through this approach the ACB resynchronization pulse search does not significantly increase the overall complexity of the CELP-based codec.

This paper is organized as follows. In Sect. 2, we present the ACB resynchronization approach using reduced-FCB pulse compensation and the applied criterion for its optimization. Subsequently, in Sect. 3, we describe the experimental framework applied to simulate lossy packet channels, the used speech database and objective quality measure to assess the quality of the proposed method. In Sect. 4, we discuss the effectiveness of the proposed method, where the obtained results under the FEC method intervention are shown. Finally, conclusions of this work are summarized in Sect. 5.

## 2   ACB Resynchronization Approach Using Reduced-FCB Pulse Compensation

Under the CELP model, a segment of synthesized speech for each subframe is obtained by filtering an error signal (1), by means of a short-term linear prediction (LP) filter, $1/A(z)$. After removing the contribution of the LP filter memory, the new version of the error signal, $\widehat{e}(n)$, can be expressed as follows,

$$\widehat{e}(n) = x(n) - \widehat{x}(n),$$
$$= x(n) - \sum_{j=0}^{N-1} h(j) \cdot \widehat{e}(n-j), \tag{1}$$

where $x(n)$ indicates the target signal once the contribution of the LP filter memory has been removed, $\widehat{x}(n)$ is the synthesized one, $h(j)$ the impulse response of the LP filter and $N$ is the subframe length. Similar for most CELP-based codecs, the excitation signal given in (1) consists of two components, the FCB (Fixed Codebook) excitation $e_f(n)$, and ACB (Adaptive Codebook) excitation $e_a(n)$ also known as Long-Term Prediction (LTP) contribution. Formally, the total excitation signal, $\widehat{e}(n)$, is obtained as

$$\widehat{e}(n) = \sum_{j=-(l-1)/2}^{(l+1)/2} b(j) \cdot e(n - (T+j)) + g_f \cdot e_f(n)$$
$$= e_a(n) + g_f \cdot e_f(n), \tag{2}$$

where $T$, $b(j)$ and $g_f$ are the pitch lag, LTP filter and fixed vector gain respectively, and $l$ is the order of the LTP filter. The goal of the innovative codebook contribution $e_f(n)$ is to model the residual signal remaining after removing the long-term redundancy.

## 2.1   Frame Onset Detection

In order to determine the onset frames, an energy ratio is continuously computed for subframes $SF_0$ and $SF_1$. This energy ratio is based on the ACB excitation energy and the target signal energy. Let us suppose that $Q$ is the quotient of ACB contribution energy noted $E_{ACB}$, over the target signal energy noted $E_x$, that is

$$Q = \frac{E_{ACB}}{E_x} \tag{3}$$

where, $E_{ACB} = \sum_{n=0}^{N-1} e_a^2(n)$, and, $E_x = \sum_{n=0}^{N-1} x^2(n)$. Then, the energy ratio, $Q$, is compared to a predefined energy threshold, $Q_c$. If $Q$ is greater than or equal to $Q_c$, implies the corresponding subframe is judged as important (voiced), otherwise, the subframe is not important (unvoiced).

To set the value of $Q_c$, we performed multiple tests under different values of the energy ratio threshold in the range of [0.1, 1] with respect to three lossy channels of 6 %, 13 % and 18 % loss rate. Figure 1 shows the obtained PESQ (Perceptual Evaluation of Speech Quality) scores [9] as a function of the energy ratio threshold $Q_c$ with respect to different channel erasure conditions. In regard to the depicted curves in Fig. 1, we can notice that the coding robustness is

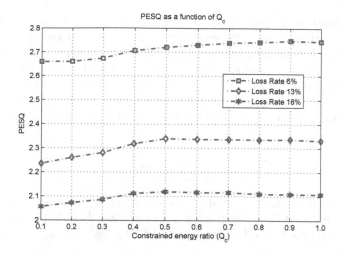

**Fig. 1.** Obtained PESQ scores of FEC method by varying the energy ratio threshold with respect to different channel erasure conditions and without any reduction of FCB pulses.

significantly improved around $Q_c$ equal 0.5. Obviously, under this constraint $(Q \geq Q_c)$, more than a half of synthesized speech signal energy is within the ACB contribution, which means the FCB contribution has lower energy contribution from the total excitation energy.

$$\frac{E_{ACB}}{E_x} \geq 0.5, \Rightarrow E_{ACB} \geq \frac{E_x}{2}. \tag{4}$$

## 2.2 Applied Least Square Error Criterion

The proposed method uses the Least Square Error (LSE) criterion in order to provide the minimum error between the synthesized speech signal $\widehat{x}(n)$ and the original speech signal $x(n)$, where $h(n)$ is the impulse response of the LP filter and $N$ is the subframe length. For this purpose, the error is given by

$$\Delta = \sum_{n=0}^{N-1} (x(n) - \widehat{x}(n))^2 = \sum_{n=0}^{N-1} (x(n) - h(n) * \widehat{e}(n))^2. \tag{5}$$

To take into account the human auditory perception, the error signal is commonly weighted by a perceptual filter, $W(z)$, so that

$$\Delta_w = \sum_{n=0}^{N-1} (w(n) * (x(n) - \widehat{x}(n)))^2,$$

$$= \sum_{n=0}^{N-1} (x_w(n) - h_w(n) * \widehat{e}(n))^2. \tag{6}$$

The CELP excitation $\hat{e}(n)$ can be considered as a summation of two signals, namely, the zero state and the zero input excitation. On one hand, the zero state excitation is computed by considering that the samples before the current frame are zero (i.e., no samples on the memory). On the other hand, the zero input excitation is obtained by considering that the fixed vector is zero for the current frame (i.e. the input is null). To resolve the LSE optimization problem, we can redefine the excitation signal as the resulting signal of the filter $P(z)$,

$$P(z) = \frac{g_f}{1 - \sum\limits_{j=-(l-1)/2}^{(l-1)/2} b(j)z^{-(T+j)}}. \tag{7}$$

Therefore, the excitation signal can be obtained as the sum of the zero state $\hat{e}_{zs}(n)$ and zero input $\hat{e}_{zi}(n)$ responses from the filter $P(z)$. Under this assumption, the quadratic error to be minimized can be expressed as

$$\Delta_w = \sum_{n=0}^{N-1} (x_w(n) - h_w(n) * (\hat{e}_{zs}(n) + \hat{e}_{zi}(n)))^2. \tag{8}$$

## 2.3  FEC Size Reduction

Firstly, in order to reduce the binary payload introduced by coding the FEC pulses, the second part of (2) is modified, so that the number of FCB pulses, $M$, is reduced to $(M - \alpha)$ and the new expression for the fixed codebook is

$$e_f(n) = \sum_{i=1}^{M-\alpha} g_f \cdot \delta(n - m_i), \tag{9}$$

where $(1 \leq \alpha \leq K)$ is the number of the subtracted pulses from FCB codebook, $K = 3$, $m_i$ indicates the pulse position 'm' with index 'i' in the FCB excitation, with $i = 1, ..., M - \alpha$ and $M$ is a legacy number of FCB pulses which is greater than $\alpha$. Secondly, the contribution of the reduced FCB pulse vector $e_f(n)$ in (9), can be removed from the optimization to deal with its introduced complexity. In this new context, the quadratic error to be minimized can be expressed as

$$\Delta_w = \sum_{n=0}^{N-1} (x_w(n) - x_{zs}(n) - h_w(n) * \hat{e}_{zi}(n))^2, \tag{10}$$

where $\hat{e}_{zs}(n)$ is the zero state contribution introduced by the reduced-FCB and $x_{zs}(n)$ is the LP response to the fixed vector excitation. As a result, the excitation signal can be defined as a recursion of only adaptive contributions which finally depends on a set of initial pulses placed on the ACB memory. Since the zero-state does not depend on previous samples by definition, we can remove it from the optimization so the final square error to be minimized is given by

$$\Delta_w = \sum_{n=0}^{N-1} (t(n) - h_w(j) * \hat{e}_{zi}(n))^2. \tag{11}$$

Hence, the problem is now simplified to optimize the Least Square Error (LSE) criterion between the modified target signal $t(n)$ and the weighted-synthesis filter response $h_w(n)$, excited with an optimized FEC pulse excitation signal, (seen as a zero input response). Therefore, the zero input excitation $\widehat{e}_{zi}(n)$ that we are searching for is,

$$\widehat{e}_{zi}(n) = \sum_{k=1}^{K} g_{m_k} \delta(n - m_k), \qquad (12)$$

where $g_{m_k}$ is the amplitude of the pulse, $\delta(n - m_k)$ is the unit pulse, $m$ its position, $k$ is the index of each pulse to be set, while $(K= 1, 2, 3)$. Thus, the pulse positions and amplitudes are optimized using the MP-MLQ algorithm [4].

### 2.4 The Proposed ACB Resynchronization Scheme

Figure 2 shows the modified encoder scheme for FEC pulse optimization. The dashed boxes in Fig. 2 represents the added functions to perform this optimization. It must be pointed out that the resynchronization parameter search is applied only if the imposed condition on the energy ratio is satisfied. Subsequently, at the decoder side, the ACB resynchronization procedure takes place once the previous frame is erased. In this case, the added FEC pulses are used to replace the desynchronized ACB codebook then the generated total excitation $\hat{e}(n)$ is used to resynchronize the ACB memory.

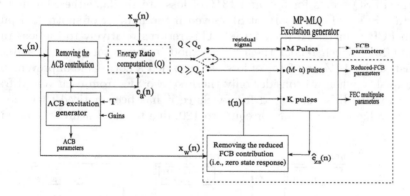

**Fig. 2.** Modified encoder scheme for FEC side information optimization.

## 3 Experimental Framework

We have used the standard codec G.723.1 [4] as a CELP codec for carrying the experiments to check the improvements of our proposed technique. Likewise, for performance evaluation, we have considered an objective test performed by means of the ITU Perceptual Evaluation of Speech Quality standard (PESQ) [9]. In order to provide an objective quality measure, PESQ is applied over a subset of the well-known TIMIT database which contains broadband recordings from 630 speakers of eight major dialects of American English [10,11]. To this end, testing and training utterances from the TIMIT database are down-sampled to 8 kHz and their lengths artificially extended to approximately 14 s. For each used utterance, the PESQ algorithm provides a score within a range from −0.5 (bad) to 4.5 (excellent). In order to obtain an overall score for each channel condition, the score of each sentence is weighted by its relative length.

During these simulations, packet loss rates of 6, 8, 10, 13, 16, 18, 20, 21 and 23 % were generated by the Gilbert-Elliot model defined in [12]. Under these frame loss channels, the burst of consecutive frame losses is varying from 1 up to 3 frames. Likewise, for our study the larger size of burst losses cannot be considered since the used CELP-based codec design does not support more than 3 successive frame losses [4] and the error propagation effects are usually noticed.

## 4    Experimental Results

To assess the efficiency of sending side information only for the first two sub-frames instead of all the four subframes Fig. 3 illustrates a comparison between PESQ scores obtained from both cases, relative to the variation of reduced FCB pulse $(M - \alpha)$ under loss rate conditions (6 %, 13 %, 18 % and 23 %) with a constrained energy ratio $Q_c$ at 0.5. We can notice from the obtained figures in Fig. 3 that the PESQ scores for 6 % and 13 % of loss are similar either, for first two important SFs or four important SFs, even if the number of subtracted pulses $\alpha$ from FCB is increased from 1 to 3. This returns relatively to the loss rates, 6 % and 13 % which render the FEC method intervention very restricted. In contrast, under 18 % and 23 % of loss, we recorded a noticeable improvement of PESQ quality when we consider only the first two SFs from each voiced frame relative to four SFs per voiced frame. Since it has been noticed that most of pitch-lag values are less than or equal to 120, due to this feature, the obtained

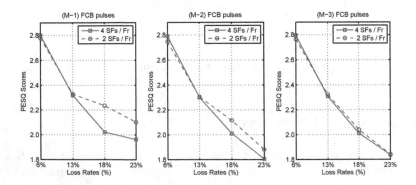

**Fig. 3.** PESQ Scores as a function of loss rate and reduced FCB pulse number $(M - \alpha)$ for 2 important SFs and 4 important SFs per frame, respectively.

results confirm the efficiency of our choice to send extra information for only first two subframes. Accordingly, the obtained results confirm once again the effectiveness of ACB in modeling the glottal pulses when this latter is updated. In other words, it is more efficient to use the resynchronized ACB for $SF_2$ and $SF_3$ instead of FEC pulses since it has been updated by the recovered first two subframes. In return, in case of $(M-3)$ for 18 % and 23 % of loss rate, the recorded equality in PESQ values between 2 SFs and 4 SFs, returns to the limits of the established tradeoff between reduced-FCB and pulse compensation efficiency to model the ACB. This feature led us to restrict the variation of $\alpha$ up to $K$, which means that the targeted performance of the proposed method is not guaranteed for a higher value of $\alpha$. To emphasize on the proposed method robustness, a wide range of channel conditions based on Gilbert-Elliot model is tested, including frame erasure ratios of 6 %, 8 %, 10 %, 13 %, 16 %, 20 %, 21 % and 23 % in order to exhaustively evaluate the efficiency of this latter against error propagation. Therefore, Fig. 4 shows the obtained PESQ results related to the performance of the proposed method by varying the number of subtracted pulses $\alpha$ from FCB codebook. In addition, the results from a complete LTP restoration (Restore memory) and those obtained from legacy standard G723.1 codec [4] are also shown in this figure. As expected, reducing FCB pulse $(M-\alpha)$ for important subframes does not strongly affect the quality of synthesized speech signal. This can easily be explained by the fact that most of the excitation energy is within the ACB contribution. Indeed, as we can see in Fig. 4 under high loss rates, there is a great improvement of PESQ quality offered by the proposed FEC method while it is approaching the quality of complete memory restoration compared with the legacy G723.1 codec.

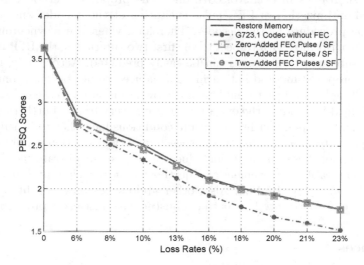

**Fig. 4.** PESQ scores obtained from legacy G723.1 codec, G723.1 with complete ACB restoration and from FEC based technique intervention relative to two, one or zero added-pulse under different lossy channel conditions.

**Table 1.** PESQ results obtained by FEC multi-pulse relative to the number of added-pulses at multiple loss rate conditions.

| Added pulses | Packet loss ratio | | | | | | | | Avg. |
|---|---|---|---|---|---|---|---|---|---|
| | 6 % | 8 % | 10 % | 13 % | 16 % | 18 % | 20 % | 23 % | |
| 0 P. | 2.7596 | 2.5977 | 2.4561 | 2.2693 | 2.1018 | 1.9937 | 1.9194 | 1.7601 | 2.2322 |
| 1 P. | 2.7651 | 2.6041 | 2.4598 | 2.2704 | 2.1035 | 1.9997 | 1.9251 | 1.7696 | 2.2372 |
| 2 P. | 2.7664 | 2.6052 | 2.4638 | 2.2720 | 2.1062 | 2.0011 | 1.9278 | 1.7602 | 2.2378 |

Table 1, lists the obtained PESQ results corresponding to different cases of reduced-FCB ($M-1$, $M-2$ and $M-3$), with respect to the packet loss conditions. The results show a very small variation of PESQ averages although the value of $\alpha$, is increased from 1 to 3. It has also been proved that reducing FCB pulses under certain limits does not really affect the quality of the proposed method. Thus, the subtracted pulses from FCB are replaced by FEC pulse insertion which offers the opportunity to improve the decoder robustness with no overload of extra pulses, particularly when $\alpha$ is equal to 3.

## 5   Conclusions

In this paper, we have proposed a FEC method to offer a resynchronization step for CELP-based G732.1 codec which relies on dynamically adding side information. In particular, a constrained energy ratio is applied to determine the important subframes in each voiced frame. The proposed method consists of constrained optimization of FEC pulse excitation at the encoder and a resynchronization procedure at the decoder. Therefore, when the resynchronization procedure is performed with respect to the first two subframes, the LTP parameters of the subsequent subframes can be easily predicted. Accordingly, the aim behind the proposed method is to achieve a reduced computational complexity with a resulting bit-rate that would be much lower compared to the increase that can be obtained by sending the extra information every frame. Furthermore, the objective quality tests under frame erasure conditions have shown the suitability of the proposed technique. Finally, the speech quality evaluation confirmed that the pulse compensation of ACB, introduces a very small bit-rate increase and achieves a noticeable improvement of objective quality which approaches a complete ACB memory restoration. Also, other approaches may benefit from this method and can contribute to a better robustness against error propagation.

## References

1. Toral, C.H., Pathan, A.K., Ramirez, P.J.C.: Accurate modeling of VoIP traffic QoS parameters in current and future networks with multifractal and Markov models. Math. Comput. Model. **57**(11), 2832–2845 (2013)

2. Bhebhe, L., Parkkali, R.: VoIP performance over HSPA with different VoIP clients. Wirel. Pers. Commun. **58**(3), 613–626 (2011)
3. Kim, B.H., Kim, H.G., Jeong, J., Kim, J.Y.: VoIP receiver-based adaptive playout scheduling and packet loss concealment technique. IEEE Trans. Consum. Electron. **59**(1), 250–258 (2013)
4. ITU Rec.: G.723.1, dual rate speech coder for multimedia communication transmitting at 5.3kbit/s and 6.3kbit/s (1996)
5. Oh, S.M., Kim, J.H.: Application-aware retransmission design for VoIP services in BWA networks. In: 14th International Conference on Advanced Communication Technology (ICACT), pp. 122–131. IEEE (2012)
6. Gomez, A.M., Carmona, J.L., Peinado, A., Sanchez, V.: A multipulse-based forward error correction technique for robust CELP-coded speech transmission over erasure channels. IEEE Trans. Audio Speech Lang. Process. **18**(6), 1258–1268 (2010)
7. Gomez, A.M., Carmona, J.L., Peinado, A., Sanchez, V.: One-pulse FEC coding for robust CELP-coded speech transmission over erasure channels. IEEE Trans. Multimed. **13**(5), 894–904 (2011)
8. Ehara, H., Yoshida, K.: Decoder initializing technique for improving frame-erasure resilience of a CELP speech codec. IEEE Trans. Multimed. **10**(3), 549–553 (2008)
9. Perceptual Evaluation of Speech Quality (PESQ): An objective method for end-to-end speech quality assessment of narrow-band telephone networks and speech codecs. ITU-T P.862 Recommendation (2001)
10. Lamel, L., Kassel, R., Seneff, S.: Speech database development: design and analysis of the acoustic-phonetic corpus. In: Proceedings of Speech Recognition Workshop (DARPA), pp. 100–110 (1986)
11. Garofolo, J.S.: The Structure and Format of the DARPA TIMIT, CD-ROM Prototype, Documentation of DARPA TIMIT
12. Jiang, W., Schulzrinne, H.: Modeling of packet loss and delay and their effect on real-time multimedia service quality. In: Proceedings of NOSSDAV 2000 (2000)

# Objective Comparison of Four GMM-Based Methods for PMA-to-Speech Conversion

Daniel Erro[1,2(✉)], Inma Hernaez[1], Luis Serrano[1],
Ibon Saratxaga[1], and Eva Navas[1]

[1] Aholab, University of the Basque Country (UPV/EHU), Bilbao, Spain
derro@aholab.ehu.es
[2] IKERBASQUE, Basque Foundation for Science, Bilbao, Spain

**Abstract.** In silent speech interfaces a mapping is established between biosignals captured by sensors and acoustic characteristics of speech. Recent works have shown the feasibility of a silent interface based on permanent magnet-articulography (PMA). This paper studies the performance of four different mapping methods based on Gaussian mixture models (GMMs), typical from the voice conversion field, when applied to PMA-to-spectrum conversion. The results show the superiority of methods based on maximum likelihood parameter generation (MLPG), especially when the parameters of the mapping function are trained by minimizing the generation error. Informal listening tests reveal that the resulting speech is moderately intelligible for the database under study.

## 1 Introduction

Breaking the communication barriers of the speaking impaired is one of the most challenging research problems in speech technologies. In the case of laryngectomees, i.e. patients whose larynx has been removed for one reason or another, speech can be well articulated but, in the absence of vocal folds, the phonation consists of pushing air from the esophagus. This is known as *alaryngeal* speech, which includes purely *esophageal* speech and *tracheoesophageal*, i.e. speech produced with the help of a prosthesis that connects the trachea with the esophagus. It requires a huge effort from the patient to learn how to produce alaryngeal speech and, even after a successful rehabilitation and learning, it is less intelligible than modal speech.

Existing technological solutions aiming at enhancing the naturalness and intelligibility of alaryngeal speech can be classified into two groups: signal processing approaches and statistical mapping approaches. In signal processing approaches [1–5], alaryngeal speech signals are analyzed and their acoustic features (pitch trajectories, formants, spectral envelope) are processed in a knowledge-driven manner to match the patterns of normal speech. In statistical mapping approaches [6–8], the patological voices are projected onto healthy ones by means of transformation functions typical from the voice conversion field. A different possible approach, given that the articulation capabilities of the patient remain unaltered, is establishing a mapping between measured articulatory features and their corresponding acoustic realization [9,10]. Similarly, any other

© Springer International Publishing AG 2016
A. Abad et al. (Eds.): IberSPEECH 2016, LNAI 10077, pp. 24–32, 2016.
DOI: 10.1007/978-3-319-49169-1_3

biosignal related to the speech production process, such as electromyographic or electroencephalographic signals, can be mapped onto speech, thus enabling the so-called silent speech interfaces [11]. Recently, the Universities of Hull and Sheffield [12–14] have suggested the use of PMA signals, i.e. the magnetic field produced by several implants properly placed on relevant articulators, as input for a silent speech interface.

Using parallel PMA+speech recordings collected by the Universities of Hull and Sheffield, this work compares the performance of four state-of-the-art voice conversion algorithms when applied to PMA-to-speech conversion. The algorithms, all based on GMMs, are the following:

- Joint density modeling by means of a GMM [15].
- GMM-weighted linear regression [16], as formulated in [17].
- The MLPG algorithm proposed in [10,18].
- MLPG with minimum generation error (MGE) training, as formulated in our recent work [19].

This work extends that in [10] in the sense that it studies a different type of data, i.e. PMA, and it includes one more method for evaluation which turns out to exhibit the best objective performance.

The remainder of this paper is structured as follows. Section 2 describes the pre-processing applied to the input PMA vectors to make them more tractable. The different parts of Sect. 3 contain the theoretical fundamentals of the four listed methods, as well as some practical configuration details. Section 4 compares the four methods in terms of objective measures and discusses the results. Section 5 presents the main conclusions of this study.

## 2 Data Preparation

The dataset used in this work contained 420 parallel PMA+speech recordings from a British male speaker. Each recording corresponded to a short utterance from the CMU Arctic database [20]. All of them were recorded in a single session. A total of 9 sensors were used to capture the PMA signals. The sampling rate was 16 kHz for speech recordings and 100 Hz for each of the PMA channels. This dataset was split into two parts: a training set of 212 utterances and a test set of 208 utterances.

First, speech was analyzed every 5 ms by means of Ahocoder [21]. As a result, we obtained three acoustic streams: Mel-cepstral (MCEP) coefficients, logarithm of the fundamental frequency ($\log f_0$), and maximum voiced frequency (MVF). Only MCEP is considered in this work, as $f_0$ prediction from PMA signals is far from straightforward and excitation features like MVF are relatively less important. MCEP vectors, i.e. the *target* vectors, will be referred to as $\{\mathbf{y}_t\}$.

The raw PMA signals captured by the sensors were processed as follows:

- First, every PMA channel was normalized in terms of mean and variance.
- As the sampling period of the PMA signals was twice that of a standard vocoder, we interpolated them by factor 2.

- To overcome the spurious fluctuations of the PMA signals, each PMA vector was combined with the two adjacent ones on the left and also on the right, which increased the dimension up to 45.
- The dimension was reduced by means of principal component analysis (PCA). The final dimension, equal to 15, was found to capture 99.93 % of the variability.

The resulting PMA vectors, i.e. the *source* vectors, will be referred to as $\{\mathbf{x}_t\}$. Note that these vectors contain, implicitly, some information about the variation of the PMA signals over time. In that sense, it would be redundant to consider their derivatives over time during processing.

Finally, a joint GMM of $G$ Gaussian components was trained from the training dataset. We built a set of concatenated vectors $\mathbf{z}_t = [\mathbf{x}_t^\top \ \mathbf{y}_t^\top]^\top$ and then, using the expectation-maximization (EM) algorithm, we trained a GMM given by the weights $\{\alpha_g\}$, mean vectors $\{\boldsymbol{\mu}_g^{(z)}\}$ and full covariance matrices $\{\boldsymbol{\Sigma}_g^{(zz)}\}$, for $1 \le g \le G$. As stated in [15], the elements of the GMM can be decomposed into their source and target parts as follows:

$$\boldsymbol{\mu}_g^{(z)} = \begin{bmatrix} \boldsymbol{\mu}_g^{(x)} \\ \boldsymbol{\mu}_g^{(y)} \end{bmatrix}, \quad \boldsymbol{\Sigma}_g^{(zz)} = \begin{bmatrix} \boldsymbol{\Sigma}_g^{(xx)} & \boldsymbol{\Sigma}_g^{(xy)} \\ \boldsymbol{\Sigma}_g^{(yx)} & \boldsymbol{\Sigma}_g^{(yy)} \end{bmatrix} \tag{1}$$

In the remainder of this document, the probability that a source vector $\mathbf{x}_t$ belongs to class $g$, calculated from $\{\alpha_g\}$, $\{\boldsymbol{\mu}_g^{(x)}\}$ and $\{\boldsymbol{\Sigma}_g^{(xx)}\}$, will be denoted as $\gamma_g(\mathbf{x}_t)$.

## 3   GMM-Based Feature Mapping Methods

### 3.1   Joint-Density Modeling (JDM)

This method, originally proposed in [15], transforms the source vectors on a frame-by-frame basis according to the following expression:

$$F(\mathbf{x}_t) = \sum_{g=1}^{G} \gamma_g(\mathbf{x}_t) \left[ \boldsymbol{\mu}_g^{(y)} + \boldsymbol{\Sigma}_g^{(yx)} \boldsymbol{\Sigma}_g^{(xx)^{-1}} (\mathbf{x}_t - \boldsymbol{\mu}_g^{(x)}) \right] \tag{2}$$

where the necessary matrices and vectors are those in Eq. (1), which means no extra training steps are needed.

### 3.2   GMM-Weighted Linear Regression (WLR)

This method was originally proposed in [16]. In this paper we use the formulation in [17], where the mapping function was described as

$$F(\mathbf{x}_t) = \sum_{g=1}^{G} \gamma_g(\mathbf{x}_t) \left[ \mathbf{A}_g \mathbf{x}_t + \mathbf{b}_g \right] \tag{3}$$

The unknown matrices $\{\mathbf{A}_g\}$ and vectors $\{\mathbf{b}_g\}$ of $F(\cdot)$ are calculated by minimizing the error given by $\sum_t \|F(\mathbf{x}_t) - \mathbf{y}_t\|^2$ over the whole training dataset. If we group the unknowns into a single matrix,

$$\boldsymbol{\Omega} = [\mathbf{A}_1 \, \mathbf{b}_1 \, \ldots \, \mathbf{A}_G \, \mathbf{b}_G]^\top \tag{4}$$

then the problem can be formulated as system of linear equations:

$$\mathbf{U} \cdot \boldsymbol{\Omega} = [\mathbf{y}_1 \, \ldots \, \mathbf{y}_T]^\top \tag{5}$$

where

$$\mathbf{U} = \begin{bmatrix} \gamma_1(\mathbf{x}_1)\hat{\mathbf{x}}_1^\top & \cdots & \gamma_G(\mathbf{x}_1)\hat{\mathbf{x}}_1^\top \\ \vdots & \ddots & \vdots \\ \gamma_1(\mathbf{x}_T)\hat{\mathbf{x}}_T^\top & \cdots & \gamma_G(\mathbf{x}_T)\hat{\mathbf{x}}_T^\top \end{bmatrix}, \quad \hat{\mathbf{x}}_t^\top = [\mathbf{x}_t^T \, 1] \tag{6}$$

The solution that minimizes the conversion error can be obtained via least squares:

$$\boldsymbol{\Omega} = (\mathbf{U}^\top\mathbf{U})^{-1}\mathbf{U}^\top[\mathbf{y}_1 \, \ldots \, \mathbf{y}_T]^\top \tag{7}$$

### 3.3 Maximum-Likelihood Parameter Generation (MLPG)

The MLPG algorithm in [18] was originally proposed in the context of statistical parametric speech synthesis [22]. Let us assume a sequence of $2p$-dimensional mean vectors $\{\boldsymbol{\mu}_1, \ldots, \boldsymbol{\mu}_T\}$ and $2p \times 2p$ covariance matrices $\{\boldsymbol{\Sigma}_1, \ldots, \boldsymbol{\Sigma}_T\}$ which model not only the acoustic features within an utterance but also their 1st-order derivatives. The goal is to calculate the most probable sequence of $p$-dimensional acoustic vectors $\{\mathbf{y}_1, \ldots, \mathbf{y}_T\}$. It is normally assumed that the relationship between acoustic vectors and derivatives is governed by the following expression:

$$\Delta\mathbf{y}_t = (\mathbf{y}_{t+1} - \mathbf{y}_{t-1})/2 \tag{8}$$

The problem is formulated in terms of supervectors. The supervector containing the unknowns, of dimension $Tp \times 1$, is

$$\bar{\mathbf{y}} = [\mathbf{y}_1^\top \, \cdots \, \mathbf{y}_T^\top]^\top \tag{9}$$

Similarly, we build a $2Tp \times 1$ mean supervector $\bar{\mathbf{u}}$ and a $2Tp \times 2Tp$ block-diagonal covariance supermatrix $\bar{\bar{\mathbf{D}}}$:

$$\bar{\mathbf{u}} = \begin{bmatrix} \boldsymbol{\mu}_1 \\ \vdots \\ \boldsymbol{\mu}_T \end{bmatrix}, \quad \bar{\bar{\mathbf{D}}} = \begin{bmatrix} \boldsymbol{\Sigma}_1^{-1} & & 0 \\ & \ddots & \\ 0 & & \boldsymbol{\Sigma}_T^{-1} \end{bmatrix} \tag{10}$$

Neglecting an additive term which does not depend on $\bar{\mathbf{y}}$, the log-likelihood of a candidate $\bar{\mathbf{y}}$ given $\bar{\mathbf{u}}$ and $\bar{\bar{\mathbf{D}}}$ can be expressed as

$$L = -\tfrac{1}{2}(\mathbf{W}\bar{\mathbf{y}} - \bar{\mathbf{u}})^\top \bar{\bar{\mathbf{D}}}(\mathbf{W}\bar{\mathbf{y}} - \bar{\mathbf{u}}) \tag{11}$$

where $\mathbf{W}$ is a matrix that adds derivatives to all the individual vectors contained in $\bar{\mathbf{y}}$. According to Eq. (8), $\mathbf{W}$ can be mathematically described as

$$\mathbf{W} = \mathbf{V} \otimes \mathbf{I}, \quad \mathbf{V} = \begin{bmatrix} 1 & 0 & \cdots \\ 0 & 1/2 & \cdots \\ 0 & 1 & 0 & \cdots \\ -1/2 & 0 & 1/2 & \cdots \\ \cdots & 0 & 1 & 0 & \cdots \\ \cdots & -1/2 & 0 & 1/2 & \cdots \\ & & \vdots & \vdots & \vdots \end{bmatrix} \tag{12}$$

where $\otimes$ denotes the Kronecker product and $\mathbf{I}$ is an identity matrix of order $p$. It can be shown that the solution that maximizes Eq. (11) is

$$\bar{\mathbf{y}} = (\mathbf{W}^\top \bar{\bar{\mathbf{D}}} \mathbf{W})^{-1} \mathbf{W}^\top \bar{\bar{\mathbf{D}}} \bar{\mathbf{u}} \tag{13}$$

For the sake of efficiency, the covariance matrices (and the resulting supermatrix) are frequently forced to be diagonal. In these conditions, the acoustic vector components are mutually independent and the problem can be solved separately for each component:

$$\bar{\mathbf{y}}^{(i)} = (\mathbf{V}^\top \bar{\bar{\mathbf{D}}}^{(i)} \mathbf{V})^{-1} \mathbf{V}^\top \bar{\bar{\mathbf{D}}}^{(i)} \bar{\mathbf{u}}^{(i)}, \quad 1 \leq i \leq p \tag{14}$$

where $\bar{\mathbf{u}}^{(i)}$ and $\bar{\bar{\mathbf{D}}}^{(i)}$ contain the statistics of the $i^{\text{th}}$ component and its derivatives.

In the specific mapping problem we are addressing, the mean vectors and covariance matrices used for generation are obtained as:

$$\begin{aligned} \boldsymbol{\mu}_t &= \boldsymbol{\mu}_{\hat{g}}^{(y)} + \boldsymbol{\Sigma}_{\hat{g}}^{(yx)} \boldsymbol{\Sigma}_{\hat{g}}^{(xx)^{-1}} (\mathbf{x}_t - \boldsymbol{\mu}_{\hat{g}}^{(x)}) \\ \boldsymbol{\Sigma}_t &= \mathrm{diag}\left( \boldsymbol{\Sigma}_{\hat{g}}^{(yy)} - \boldsymbol{\Sigma}_{\hat{g}}^{(yx)} \boldsymbol{\Sigma}_{\hat{g}}^{(xx)^{-1}} \boldsymbol{\Sigma}_{\hat{g}}^{(xy)} \right) \end{aligned}, \quad \hat{g} = \arg\max \gamma_g(\mathbf{x}_t) \tag{15}$$

In this case, the vectors and matrices needed to compute (15) cannot be directly taken from the decomposition in Eq. (1) because the GMM has been trained from the acoustic vectors without derivatives. Therefore, using $\{\gamma_g(\mathbf{x}_t)\}$ as EM initialization, we reestimate the parameters of the GMM after appending derivatives to the target acoustic vectors $\{\mathbf{y}_t\}$.

It is worth remarking that the MLPG algorithm proposed in [18] considers not only the likelihood of the acoustic features but also their global variance (GV), i.e. their variance within the utterance. However, it is a common practice to ignore the GV for an objective assessment of the method.

## 3.4   MLPG with Minimum Generation Error Training (MGE)

We recently proposed an algorithm where the mean vectors used for MLPG are estimated by minimizing the error between the generated vectors and the target data [19]. We basically keep the covariance matrices of the previous method while the mean vectors are obtained as

$$\mu_t = \sum_{g=1}^{G} \gamma_g(\mathbf{x}_t) \left( \begin{bmatrix} \mathbf{A}_g \\ \mathbf{A}'_g \end{bmatrix} \mathbf{x}_t + \begin{bmatrix} \mathbf{b}_g \\ \mathbf{b}'_g \end{bmatrix} \right) \tag{16}$$

Similarly as in Sect. 3.2, the unknowns can be grouped into a single matrix $\check{\mathbf{\Omega}}$ given by

$$\check{\mathbf{\Omega}} = [\mathbf{A}_1 \ \mathbf{b}_1 \ \mathbf{A}'_1 \ \mathbf{b}'_1 \ \ldots \ \mathbf{A}_G \ \mathbf{b}_G \ \mathbf{A}'_G \ \mathbf{b}'_G]^\top \tag{17}$$

The $i^{\text{th}}$ column of $\check{\mathbf{\Omega}}$, denoted as $\check{\mathbf{\omega}}_i$, is related to the $i^{\text{th}}$ acoustic vector component. Given the constraints in Eq. (16), it can be shown that the MLPG Eq. (14) becomes

$$\bar{\mathbf{y}}^{(i)} = \mathbf{Q}^{(i)} \check{\mathbf{\omega}}_i, \quad \mathbf{Q}^{(i)} = (\mathbf{V}^\top \bar{\bar{\mathbf{D}}}^{(i)} \mathbf{V})^{-1} \mathbf{V}^\top \bar{\bar{\mathbf{D}}}^{(i)} \check{\mathbf{U}}, \quad 1 \le i \le p \tag{18}$$

where

$$\check{\mathbf{U}} = \begin{bmatrix} \gamma_1(\mathbf{x}_1)\check{\mathbf{X}}_1^\top & \cdots & \gamma_G(\mathbf{x}_1)\check{\mathbf{X}}_1^\top \\ \vdots & \ddots & \vdots \\ \gamma_1(\mathbf{x}_T)\check{\mathbf{X}}_T^\top & \cdots & \gamma_G(\mathbf{x}_T)\check{\mathbf{X}}_T^\top \end{bmatrix}, \quad \check{\mathbf{X}}_t^\top = \begin{bmatrix} \mathbf{x}_t^\top & 1 & \mathbf{0} & 0 \\ \mathbf{0} & 0 & \mathbf{x}_t^\top & 1 \end{bmatrix} \tag{19}$$

In a generic scenario with $N \ge 1$ adaptation utterances (we now include the utterance index $n$ in the notation), the solution that minimizes the generation error with respect to the training data is

$$\check{\mathbf{\omega}}_i = \left( \sum_{n=1}^{N} \mathbf{Q}_n^{(i)^\top} \mathbf{Q}_n^{(i)} \right)^{-1} \left( \sum_{n=1}^{N} \mathbf{Q}_n^{(i)^\top} \bar{\mathbf{y}}_n^{(i)} \right), \quad 1 \le i \le p \tag{20}$$

## 4    Evaluation

To assess the relative performance of the four methods under comparison, we trained the respective mapping functions for a GMM with variable number of Gaussian components: $G = \{16, 32, 64, 128\}$. Then, using the parallel test dataset (see Sect. 2 for details), we computed the Mel-cepstral distortion (MCD) between the target MCEP vectors and those obtained by converting the input PMA vectors. This measure is reliable only in certain conditions. It has been shown, for instance, that GV enhancement is detrimental in terms of MCD while it produces a substantial perceptual improvement. However, it is commonly accepted that MCD can be used to compare the accuracy of several variants of a given method. In this paper, MCD is formulated as:

$$\text{MCD}(\{\mathbf{c}_t\}, \{\hat{\mathbf{c}}_t\}) = \frac{10}{\log 10} \cdot \frac{1}{T} \sqrt{2 \sum_{t=1}^{T} \|\mathbf{c}_t - \hat{\mathbf{c}}_t\|^2} \tag{21}$$

The $0^{\text{th}}$ element of the MCEP vectors was removed before MCD computation. The results are shown in Fig. 1 (the curve labeled as MGE(b) will be explained later in this section). It can be seen that the optimal $G$ depends on the specific method. In their optimal point, the two algorithms based on MLPG, i.e. those labeled as MLPG and MGE, exhibit a better performance than frame-by-frame mapping algorithms. This is consistent with the findings in previous works [10,18]. Also, though they are more prone to overfitting, methods based on error minimization, WLR and MGE, outperform their maximum likelihood counterparts. This is logical because they are trained by optimizing almost the same metrics that we are using for assessment.

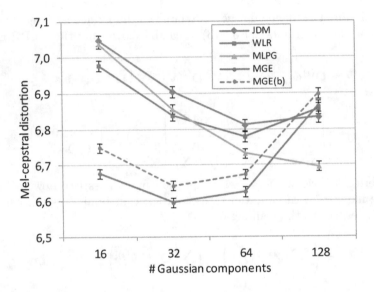

**Fig. 1.** Average Mel-cepstral distortion scores [dB] and 95 % confidence intervals for different GMM orders and mapping methods.

Overall, the MGE method we proposed recently [19] achieves the best MCD scores. In comparison with the method that ranked second, namely MLPG, it also requires a smaller number of Gaussian components, which means it brings a reduction of the computational cost of the GMM-based soft classification. It may be argued, however, that the computation of the mean vectors is much lighter in MLPG's Eq. (15) than in MGE's Eq. (16). This is an important issue, since a commercial PMA-to-speech converter should be able to operate in real time. For this reason, we retrained the MGE method by considering only the transform of the most probable Gaussian as in MLPG. The resulting curve, labeled as MGE(b) in Fig. 1, shows that although this simplification implies a slight penalty in terms of MCD, MGE(b) is still significantly better than others. Therefore, MGE provides a very interesting trade-off between accuracy and efficiency.

At the time of writing this document, no formal listening tests had been completed. Istead, informal listening tests were conducted in which we kept the original $f_0$ and excitation features and replaced the spectrum by the output of the PMA-to-spectrum converter. A few examples can be found in the following website: http://aholab.ehu.es/users/derro/demopma.html. For the two MLPG-based methods under study, we enabled GV enhancement. We observed that the identity of the speaker is well preserved despite having totally discarded the original spectral information, at least for the MLPG-based methods with GV enhancement. The intelligibility of the signals was found to be moderate. Nevertheless, we would like to emphasize that the recordings in the dataset had been made in a mid-low degree of articulation. In other words, better articulated recordings would possibly result in a more intelligible synthetic speech signal. In principle this is not an important limitation of the framework, as it is reasonable to assume that users (laryngectomees) would be careful in this regard. In any case, these results are promising given the enormous difficulty of the task.

## 5    Conclusions

We have addressed the PMA-to-spectrum mapping problem by comparing the accuracy of four transformation algorithms based on GMMs. We have shown that MLPG in combination with an MGE training criterion achieves the best objective scores while exhibiting interesting computational advantages as well. Informal listening tests lead to the conclusion that the identity of the speaker is well preserved, whereas there is still room for improvement in terms of intelligibility. Future works should address aspects such as better PMA vector designs, modern nonlinear mapping methods based on deep neural networks, and pitch prediction in the absence of related biosignals.

**Acknowledgements.** This work has been partially funded by the Spanish Ministry of Economy and Competitiveness (RESTORE project, TEC2015-67163-C2-1-R MINECO/FEDER, UE) and the Basque Government (ELKAROLA, KK-2015/00098). We would like to thank the Univeristy of Hull and the University of Sheffield, especially Dr. Jose A. Gonzalez, for the permission to use the PMA data in this work.

## References

1. Qi, Y., Weinberg, B., Bi, N.: Enhancement of female esophageal and tracheoesophageal speech. J. Acoust. Soc. Am. **98**, 2461–2465 (1995)
2. Matsui, K., Hara, N.: Enhancement of esophageal speech using formant synthesis. In: Proceedings of the ICASSP, pp. 81–84 (1999)
3. del Pozo, A., Young, S.J.: Continuous tracheoesophageal speech repair. In: Proceedings of the EUSIPCO, pp. 1–5 (2006)
4. Türkmen, H.I., Karsligil, M.E.: Reconstruction of dysphonic speech by MELP. In: Ruiz-Shulcloper, J., Kropatsch, W.G. (eds.) CIARP 2008. LNCS, vol. 5197, pp. 767–774. Springer, Heidelberg (2008). doi:10.1007/978-3-540-85920-8_93
5. Mantilla-Caeiros, A., Nakano-Miyatake, M., Perez-Meana, H.: A pattern recognition based esophageal speech enhancement system. J. Appl. Res. Tech. **8**(1), 56–71 (2010)

6. Doi, H., Nakamura, K., Toda, T., Saruwatari, H., Shikano, K.: Esophageal speech enhancement based on statistical voice conversion with Gaussian mixture models. IEICE Trans. Inf. Syst. **E93–D**(9), 2472–2482 (2010)
7. Nakamura, K., Toda, T., Saruwatari, H., Shikano, K.: Speaking-aid systems using GMM-based voice conversion for electrolaryngeal speech. Speech Commun. **54**(1), 134–146 (2012)
8. Doi, H., Toda, T., Nakamura, K., Saruwatari, H., Shikano, K.: Alaryngeal speech enhancement based on one-to-many eigenvoice conversion. IEEE/ACM Trans. Audio Speech Lang. Process. **22**(1), 172–183 (2014)
9. Kello, C.T., Plaut, D.C.: A neural network model of the articulatoryacoustic forward mapping trained on recordings of articulatory parameters. J. Acoust. Soc. Am. **116**(4), 2354–2364 (2004)
10. Toda, T., Black, A.W., Tokuda, K.: Statistical mapping between articulatory movements and acoustic spectrum using a Gaussian mixture model. Speech Commun. **50**(3), 215–227 (2008)
11. Denby, B., Schultz, T., Honda, K., Hueber, T., Gilbert, J.M., Brumberg, J.S.: Silent speech interfaces. Speech Commun. **52**(4), 270–287 (2010)
12. Hofe, R., Ell, S.R., Fagan, M.J., Gilbert, J.M., Green, P.D., Moore, R.K., Rybchenko, S.I.: Speech synthesis parameter generation for the assistive silent speech interface MVOCA. In: Proceedings of the INTERSPEECH, pp. 3009–3012 (2011)
13. Cheah, L.A., Bai, J., Gonzalez, J.A., Ell, S.R., Gilbert, J.M., Moore, R.K., Green, P.D.: A user-centric design of permanent magnetic articulography based assistive speech technology. In: Proceedings of the BioSignals, pp. 109–116 (2015)
14. Gonzalez, J.A., Cheah, L.A., Gilbert, J.M., Bai, J., Ell, S.R., Green, P.D., Moore, R.K.: A silent speech system based on permanent magnet articulography and direct synthesis. Comput. Speech Lang. **39**, 67–87 (2016)
15. Kain, A., Macon, M.W.: Spectral voice conversion for text-to-speech synthesis. In: Proceedings of the ICASSP, pp. 285–288 (1998)
16. Stylianou, Y., Cappé, O., Moulines, E.: Continuous probabilistic transform for voice conversion. IEEE Trans. Speech Audio Process. **6**(2), 131–142 (1998)
17. Ye, H., Young, S.J.: Quality-enhanced voice morphing using maximum likelihood transformations. IEEE Trans. Audio Speech Lang. Process. **14**(4), 1301–1312 (2006)
18. Toda, T., Black, A., Tokuda, K.: Voice conversion based on maximum-likelihood estimation of spectral parameter trajectory. IEEE Trans. Audio Speech Lang. Process. **15**(8), 2222–2235 (2007)
19. Erro, D., Alonso, A., Serrano, L., Tavarez, D., Odriozola, I., Sarasola, X., DelBlanco, E., Sanchez, J., Saratxaga, I., Navas, E., Hernaez, I.: ML parameter generation with a reformulated MGE training criterion participation in the voice conversion challenge 2016. In: Proceedings of the INTERSPEECH (2016)
20. Kominek, J., Black, A.W.: The CMU arctic speech databases. In: Proceedings of the 5th ISCA Speech Synthesis Workshop, pp. 223–224 (2004)
21. Erro, D., Sainz, I., Navas, E., Hernáez, I.: Harmonics plus noise model based vocoder for statistical parametric speech synthesis. IEEE J. Sel. Top. Sig. Process. **8**(2), 184–194 (2014)
22. Tokuda, K., Masuko, T., Miyazaki, N., Kobayashi, T.: Multi-space probability distribution HMM. IEICE Trans. Inf. Syst. **E85–D**(3), 455–464 (2002)

# Adding Singing Capabilities to Unit Selection TTS Through HNM-Based Conversion

Marc Freixes[✉], Joan Claudi Socoró, and Francesc Alías

GTM – Grup de Recerca en Tecnologies Mèdia, La Salle - Universitat Ramon Llull,
Quatre Camins, 30, 08022 Barcelona, Spain
{mfreixes,jclaudi,falias}@salleurl.edu

**Abstract.** Adding singing capabilities to a corpus-based concatenative text-to-speech (TTS) system can be addressed by explicitly collecting singing samples from the previously recorded speaker. However, this approach is only feasible if the considered speaker is also a singing talent. As an alternative, we consider appending a Harmonic plus Noise Model (HNM) speech-to-singing conversion module to a Unit Selection TTS (US-TTS) system. Two possible text-to-speech-to-singing synthesis approaches are studied: applying the speech-to-singing conversion to the US-TTS synthetic output, or implementing a hybrid US+HNM synthesis framework. The perceptual tests show that the speech-to-singing conversion yields similar singing resemblance than the natural version, but with lower naturalness. Moreover, no statistically significant differences are found between both strategies in terms of naturalness nor singing resemblance. Finally, the hybrid approach allows reducing more than twice the overall computational cost.

**Keywords:** Unit-selection TTS · Speech-to-singing · Text-to-singing · Harmonic plus Noise Model · Prosody modification

## 1 Introduction

The main challenge speech synthesis research community faces is to produce natural voices able to resemble all the range of human voice expressions, covering from regular speech, through emotions to expressive speech. Among those expressions, singing entails specific challenges, which have been addressed through several approaches, resulting in very popular applications as for example Vocaloid [10]. In the literature, we can find techniques based on the speech production model [22], which are very flexible but difficult to control in order to obtain natural results. Concatenative approaches [3,11] are able to produce good synthetic quality, but they lack of expressive context as the units are recorded individually. To overcome this drawback, the unit-selection (US) approach [12] is based on the recording of singing phrases. However, recording singing phrases to cover all phonetic and musical combinations becomes almost unfeasible. In contrast, statistical parametric methods based on Hidden Markov Models (HMM) allow

© Springer International Publishing AG 2016
A. Abad et al. (Eds.): IberSPEECH 2016, LNAI 10077, pp. 33–43, 2016.
DOI: 10.1007/978-3-319-49169-1_4

for more scalable singing systems, but achieving lower averaged naturalness due to its inherent statistical nature [2,13] (c.f. Sinsy [14] as a popular system).

From a different point of view, several works have addressed the production of singing from spoken speech. Some of them built on the so-called speech-to-singing approach [5,16,18]. These techniques transform spoken speech to singing by maintaining the speaker identity. Moreover, other works propose to integrate the singing synthesis in a text-to-speech (TTS) system in order to have systems capable of both speaking and singing, such as Flinger [11].

In order to take the most of these latter approaches, in this paper singing capabilities have been added to a US-TTS system by means of a Harmonic plus Noise Model (HNM) [20] speech-to-singing conversion to transform neutral speech to singing. The conversion is done following the approach described in [19], where duration, F0 and spectral control models were defined to convert a speaking voice reading the lyrics of a song in a synthetic singing voice. Moreover, it is worth noting that besides minimising the cost of collecting singing samples, this approach allows synthesising singing even if the original speaker was not a singing talent. Two different text-to-speech-to-singing synthesis strategies have been considered: applying the speech-to-singing conversion to the US-TTS synthetic output, or integrating the transformation within a hybrid US+HNM synthesis framework. These approaches are compared in terms of perceptual tests and their computational costs.

The paper is structured as follows. In the next section different approaches to generate singing from speech are reviewed. Then, Sect. 3 details the proposed text-to-speech-to-singing strategies. After that, Sect. 4 describes the conducted perceptual assessment experiments, the computational cost analysis and the results. Finally, the conclusions of this work are presented in Sect. 5.

## 2   Related Work

Even though the significant differences between speech and singing [21], both human voice manifestations share a common source. As a consequence, some works have tackled the synthesis of singing voices from speech, e.g. [5,16,18].

One of the first works that combined speech and singing synthesis was Flinger [11], which allows the Festival TTS [1] to sing by providing several modules including a residual LPC synthesiser and some diphone voices.

Later, from the analysis of the features unique to singing voice Saitou et al. [18] proposed a method to transform speech to singing, by modifying the pitch contour, phoneme duration and spectrum. Target phoneme durations are obtained by applying speech-to-singing duration conversion rules derived from the analysis of actual performances. Pitch contour is derived from the stepwise melody curve by applying a filtering that models the behaviour of the singing F0 dynamics: preparation, overshoot, fine fluctuation and vibrato. Finally, two spectral control models are applied to the spectral envelope: one to add the singing formant and the other to apply a formant amplitude modulation synchronised with the vibrato. Analysis, transformation and synthesis are carried out using STRAIGHT [9], allowing a higher synthesis quality than the Flinger approach.

In order to obtain more natural contours, other approaches have used real singing performances, but at the expense of needing parallel singing realizations. In [16] a set of phrases was recorded by a female singer to get a spectral envelope database. The same speech sentences, recorded by an actor, were time-stretched, transposed and aligned to the singing phrases. Finally, the spectral envelope from the female database was transferred to the speech signal. The transformation was performed by a phase vocoder, but improved signal models have been presented recently [8,17]. In [5] a system able to convert a speech or singing of poor quality input into high-quality singing was presented, using a template-based conversion [4] with professional singing as a reference model. Parallel singing templates are aligned to the speech input in a 2-step Dynamic Time Warping-based method. Thus, the pitch contour can be derived from actual singing voice and applied to the input speech through STRAIGHT.

# 3   System Description

## 3.1   Synthesis Framework

The proposed system is built upon the US-TTS system of La Salle - Universitat Ramon Llull, which includes a Case-Based Reasoning prosody prediction module, trained with prosodic patterns from the speech corpus, and a unit selection module that obtains the optimal sequence of speech database diphones (see [7] for more details). The speech corpus is a Spanish female voice of 2.6 h (with neutral expressivity).

In this work two main approaches have been considered in order to enable the US-TTS to generate singing speech: (i) a direct chaining of the original US-TTS with an HNM-based transformation module that performs the speech-to-singing conversion, and (ii) a hybrid US+HNM synthesis framework in which, following a similar approach that in [20], the processing is done on the HNM parameters of the speech units selected sequence. The later (referred as *HybSing* henceforth) allows to save computational resources at synthesis time because the speech corpora can be parametrised beforehand. Thus, obtaining the speech HNM parameters for the speech-to-singing conversion only requires the parameters concatenation instead of the TTS synthesis and the HNM analysis needed in the direct chained approach (referred as *VTSing* from here on). In both scenarios, the incorporation of HNM allows higher flexibility (e.g. to match the pitch curve to the musical score) than the Time-Domain Pitch Synchronous Overlap and Add (TD-PSOLA) technique that performed prosody variations and synthesis in the original US-TTS system. Time-scale and pitch modification algorithms [6] have been used to transplant the singing pitch contour to the speech units and modify their durations. Moreover, HNM allows an easy and direct control of spectral variations (e.g. the singing formant) which are hard to implement using TD-PSOLA.

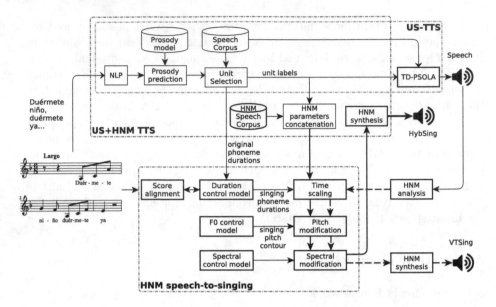

**Fig. 1.** Block diagram of the proposed synthesis system.

## 3.2   System Overview

The block diagram of the proposed system is depicted in Fig. 1. Firstly, lyrics are extracted from the score and input to the TTS system. The unit selection module gets the speech units that better fit the song lyrics, and their HNM parameters are concatenated, ready to be transformed. The TD-PSOLA synthesised speech (*Speech*) is analysed to get its HNM parameters. It should be noted that no transformation is applied to the units to fit the predicted prosody.

The speech-to-singing conversion is performed following the method described in [18]. Phoneme singing durations are obtained from the score note times and the phoneme original durations by applying conversion rules (duration control model). On the other hand, a stepwise melody contour is obtained from the score notes and durations, and this contour is filtered to reproduce the dynamics of a singing pitch contour (F0 control model). Finally, after applying time scaling and pitch modifications on the HNM speech parameters, the spectral control model modifies the spectral envelope reproducing the singing formant.

In Fig. 1 the two compared approaches can be easily devised in the signal flow: (i) the *VTSing* version is generated by firstly producing the *Speech* (up right) with the original US-TTS system, performing its HNM analysis and applying the speech-to-singing conversion and subsequent HNM synthesis; (ii) instead, in *HybSing* HNM parameters are concatenated just after the unit selection process within the TTS, and then the same speech-to-singing conversion and HNM synthesis used for the *VTSing* generation are also applied.

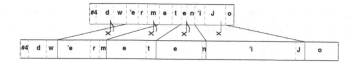

**Fig. 2.** Example of phonemes alignment with the score.

### 3.3  Speech-to-Singing

**Score Alignment.** The score interface extracts the lyrics and its relation with the notes from a MusicXML score. These relationships are used to align the speech phonemes to the notes, considering that a note onset always coincides with a vowel (see Fig. 2). Pitch and duration of each note are also obtained from the same score.

**Singing Phoneme Durations.** The duration of each note and their assigned speech phonemes have been retrieved in the score alignment, but a specific duration for each of the phonemes must be established. By applying Saitou et al. rules [18] phoneme singing durations can be obtained from the notes and the phoneme original durations. They considered three parts in the boundary between a consonant and a vowel: a consonant part, a boundary part (from 10 ms before the boundary to 30 ms after the boundary) and a vowel part. The consonant part is lengthened according to fixed rates (1.58 for a fricative, 1.13 for a plosive, 2.07 for a semivowel, 1.77 for a nasal, and 1.13 for a /y/). The boundary part is not lengthened and the vowel part is lengthened until the phonemes fit the note duration.

**Singing Pitch Contour.** From the score notes and the singing phoneme durations a stepwise melody contour is built. In this case transitions are set to syllable boundaries. Following the approach in [19] this contour is filtered to obtain the four types of F0 fluctuations present in singing: overshoot, vibrato, preparation and fine fluctuation. In the case of the preparation (defined in [19] as a deflection in the direction opposite to a note change observed just before the note change) the filtering is done from the end towards the beginning, in order to guarantee that the intended effect appears before the note change. Overshoot and preparation fluctuations are dynamically mixed by applying a mask, taking into account that the overshoot occurs at the beginning of a note, the preparation at the end, and there is a transition period in between where a cross-fading of both generated pitch curves is performed.

In Fig. 3 an example of a generated pitch contour regarding overshoot and preparation is shown. Preparation is obtained through filtering (from the end towards the beginning) a slightly delayed version of the stepwise input function (the green dash-dot line of the upper left figure) while the original stepwise melody contour (the red dashed line) is used for the overshoot generation.

Below the preparation and the overshoot figures, their respective mask functions are shown, and at the bottom the pitch curve resulting of the mix is represented.

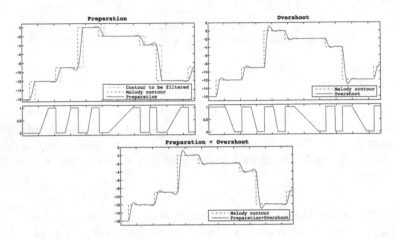

**Fig. 3.** Singing pitch curve generation: preparation (upper left), overshoot (upper right) and its final mix (bottom). (Color figure online)

**Spectral Control Model.** This control adds the singing formant to the speaking voice by emphasising the peak of the spectral envelope around 3 KHz, which in our system is implemented directly through HNM amplitude modification and using the same filter proposed in [19]. Furthermore, formant amplitude modulation is also applied if the singing pitch curve contains vibrato [19].

### 3.4   Time Scale and Pitch Modification

Time scaling and pitch modification are performed applying the phoneme singing durations and the singing pitch contour computed in the previous stage (see Sect. 3.3) and using the technique described in [6]. On one hand, the amplitudes of the new harmonics are calculated by linear interpolation in a logarithmic amplitude scale. On the other hand, the relative phases of the new harmonics are obtained by interpolating the real and the imaginary parts of the harmonic complex amplitudes at the new frequencies. Finally, the amplitudes are scaled to preserve the energy despite the variation in the number of harmonics.

## 4   Evaluation

In this section, we evaluate the synthetic quality of the proposal by means of a perceptual test and its computational cost in terms of analysing the execution time of the different modules that constitute the text-to-speech-to-singing approaches.

### 4.1   Subjective Evaluation

In order to evaluate the proposal, a perceptual evaluation has been conducted through the TRUE online platform [15] using a 5-point scale ($[-2, +2]$) Comparative Mean Opinion Score (CMOS). Three small excerpts of well-known Spanish songs for children ( *"Campana sobre campana", "Cocherito leré" and "Tengo una muñeca"*) have been chosen. For each excerpt the following versions have been generated: a synthetic spoken version of the lyrics by the original US-TTS system that includes the TD-PSOLA module (*Speech*); a natural singing version processed with the HNM analysis and resynthesis procedure (*Singing*); a sung version obtained by applying the chaining of the original US-TTS plus the HNM-based speech-to-singing transformation module (*VTSing*); and finally, the proposed hybrid US+HNM TTS approach (*HybSing*).

A total of 18 subjects took part in the perceptual tests, 11 of them having musical background. At the beginning of the test, the recorded performance of the songs was included as a reference. In each comparison, two utterances were presented to the evaluator (randomly ordered). All subjects were asked to relatively grade both utterances in terms of naturalness and singing resemblance.

The perceptual test was divided in two parts. In the first part, the speech-to-singing conversion was validated, especially assessing to what extent the generated singing (*VTSing*) quality is far from the original US-TTS spoken output (*Speech*), and how it compares with the actual singing versions (*Singing*) in terms of naturalness and singing resemblance (3 utterances x 3 methods = 9 comparisons). In the second part of the test, in order to validate the hybridisation, the evaluators were asked to compare the same excerpts synthesised through the hybrid approach (*HybSing*) with the ones obtained by directly transforming the spoken audios generated by the US-TTS (*VTSing*) (3 comparisons).

Figure 4 presents the results obtained from the perceptual test in terms of percentage scores. Moreover, the differences between the CMOS median (Mdn)

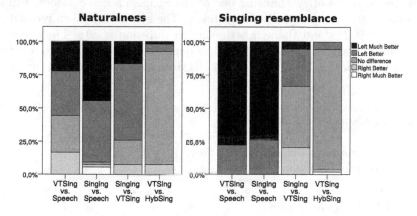

**Fig. 4.** Percentage bars representing the answers of the subjects for each evaluation (left stimuli in the answers legend is identified to the first technique in the evaluations labels and vice versa).

values are analysed by means of a one-sample Wilcoxon signed-rank test with significance level $p < 0.05$ in order to determine their statistical significance.

As it can be seen from Fig. 4, logically the synthetic speech is perceived less natural than the real singing (9 % *Speech* no difference/better). The synthetic singing (*VTSing*) even being significantly less natural than the real one (Mdn $= -1$; 26 % *VTSing* no difference/better) is considered much less natural than actual singing by only a 17 % of the subjects. Curiously, *VTSing* naturalness has been rated significantly better compared to the synthetic speech (Mdn $= -1$; 83 % *VTSing* no difference/better/much better). This could be due to the fact that some artifacts caused by pitch curve discontinuities in the synthetic speech are alleviated when transplanting the new singing pitch curve in the synthetic singing signal. Moreover, users' preferences could also be explained because it is possibly easier to emulate the singing pitch dynamics in an accurate manner than the real speech prosody.

Results also show that in terms of singing resemblance there is no significant difference between *VTSing* and actual singing (Mdn $= 0$; 67 % *VTSing* no difference/better). Finally the hybrid implementation (*HybSing*) has been validated against the voice transformation approach (*VTSing*), and no significant difference has been found regarding naturalness (Mdn $= 0$) neither singing resemblance (Mdn $= 0$). Thus, there is no preference between the hybrid approach and the former implementation from a perceptual point of view.

### 4.2   Computational Costs

The computational costs of the two proposed text-to-speech-to-singing approaches (*VTSing* and *HybSing*) have been evaluated in terms of time of execution. The technical specifications of the PC used for running the test are the following: CPU Intel(R) Core(TM) i7-4710HQ CPU @ 2.50 GHz and 16 GB of RAM, and Ubuntu 14.04LTS O.S.

The test consists of synthesising one of the Spanish songs considered in the perceptual test (*"Campana sobre campana"*). The synthetic spoken lyrics duration (*Speech*) is 21 s and the synthetic singing duration is 39 s. The execution time of each subprocess of each approach is depicted in the Table 1 (in seconds). As it can be seen, the TD+PSOLA and HNM analysis subprocesses run in the

**Table 1.** Computational costs in seconds (s) for each subprocess in each of the text-to-singing approaches.

| Voice transformation singing (*VTSing*) | | | | | |
|---|---|---|---|---|---|
| NLP+US | TD-PSOLA | HNM analysis | Transf | HNM synth | Total |
| 6.5 s | 1 s | 25 s | 1.8 s | 2.7 | 37 s |
| Hybrid singing (*HybSing*) | | | | | |
| NLP+US | - | HNM concat | Transf | HNM synth | Total |
| 6.5 s | | 3.3 s | 1.8 s | 2.7 s | 14.3 s |

*VTSing* approach are substituted by the HNM parameter concatenation sub-process in the hybrid proposal, producing a significant reduction of execution time.

From these results, we can conclude that the hybrid approach (*HybSing*) is more than twice faster than the baseline based on concatenating voice trans-formation at the US-TTS output (*VTSing*) (i.e., around a 258 % reduction of computational cost).

## 5   Conclusions

In this work, we have studied two HNM-based approaches to add singing capa-bilities to a unit selection TTS synthesis system: (i) directly chaining the origi-nal US-TTS with an HNM-based speech-to-singing conversion module and, (ii) integrating the speech-to-singing conversion within the TTS workflow, that is, a hybrid US+HNM TTS system.

On the one hand, the perceptual tests show that it is viable to produce singing by means of a unit selection TTS system without the need of explic-itly recording a singing corpus. On the other hand, although the two considered approaches obtain almost the same scores in terms of naturalness and singing resemblance in the perceptual tests, the hybrid approach dramatically outper-forms the concatenation of the US-TTS with the HNM-based speech-to-singing conversion module when comparing both text-to-singing strategies in terms of computational costs.

Future work will be focused on improving the naturalness of the singing out-put by studying new approaches for the transformation module, besides taking into account the prosody imposed by the melody in the unit selection process. Furthermore, new ways of customising the speech-to-singing conversion could be proposed so as to obtain even more flexibility while preserving good singing resemblance.

**Acknowledgements.** Marc Freixes thanks the support of the European Social Fund (ESF) and the Catalan Government (SUR/DEC) for the pre-doctoral FI grant No. 2016FI_B2 00094. This work has been partially funded by SUR/DEC (grant ref. 2014-SGR-0590). We also want to thank the people that took the perceptual test and Raúl Montaño for his help with the statistics.

## References

1. The fstival speech synthesis system (2016). http://www.cstr.ed.ac.uk/projects/festival/
2. Babacan, O., Drugman, T., Raitio, T., Erro, D., Dutoit, T.: Parametric represen-tation for singing voice synthesis: a comparative evaluation. In: IEEE International Conference on Acoustics, Speech, and Signal Processing (ICASSP), pp. 2564–2568, May 2014
3. Bonada, J., Serra, X.: Synthesis of the singing voice by performance sampling and spectral models. IEEE Sig. Process. Mag. **24**(2), 67–79 (2007)

4. Cen, L., Dong, M., Chan, P.: Template-based personalized singing voice synthesis. In: IEEE International Conference on Acoustics, Speech, and Signal Processing (ICASSP), pp. 4509–4512 (2012)
5. Dong, M., Lee, S.W., Li, H., Chan, P., Peng, X., Ehnes, J.W., Huang, D.: I2R Speech2Singing perfects everyone's singing. In: 15th Annual Conference of the International Speech Communication Association (INTERSPEECH), pp. 2148–2149 (2014)
6. Erro, D., Moreno, A., Bonafonte, A.: Flexible harmonic/stochastic speech synthesis. In: 6th ISCA Workshop on Speech Synthesis (SSW), Bonn, Germany, pp. 194–199, August 2007
7. Formiga, L., Trilla, A., Alías, F., Iriondo, I., Socoró, J.: Adaptation of the URL-TTS system to the 2010 Albayzin evaluation campaign. In: Proceedings of FALA 2010, Jornadas en Tecnología del Habla and Iberian SLTech Workshop, vol. 1, pp. 363–370, November 2020
8. Huber, S., Roebel, A.: On glottal source shape parameter transformation using a novel deterministic and stochastic speech analysis and synthesis system. In: 16th Annual Conference of the International Speech Communication Association (INTERSPEECH), pp. 289–293 (2015)
9. Kawahara, H., Masuda-Katsuse, I., De Cheveigné, A.: Restructuring speech representations using a pitch-adaptive time-frequency smoothing and an instantaneous-frequency-based F0 extraction: possible role of a repetitive structure in sounds. Speech Commun. 27(3), 187–207 (1999)
10. Kenmochi, H.: Singing synthesis as a new musical instrument. In: IEEE International Conference on Acoustics, Speech, and Signal Processing (ICASSP), pp. 5385–5388 (2012)
11. Macon, M., Jensen-Link, L., George, E.: Concatenation-based MIDI-to-singing voice synthesis. In: 103rd Audio Engineering Society Convention, pp. 1–10 (1997)
12. Meron, Y.: High quality singing synthesis using the selection-based synthesis scheme. Ph.D. thesis, University of Tokyo (1999)
13. Nose, T., Kanemoto, M., Koriyama, T., Kobayashi, T.: HMM-based expressive singing voice synthesis with singing style control and robust pitch modeling. Comput. Speech Lang. 34(1), 308–322 (2015)
14. Oura, K., Mase, A.: Recent development of the HMM-based singing voice synthesis system-sinsy. In: 7th ISCA Workshop on Speech Synthesis (SSW), pp. 211–216 (2010)
15. Planet, S., Iriondo, I., Martínez, E., Montero, J.A.: TRUE: an online testing platform for multimedia evaluation. In: Workshop Corpora for Research on Emotion and Affect Marrakech, Morocco (2008)
16. Röbel, A., Fineberg, J.: Speech to chant transformation with the phase vocoder. In: 8th Annual Conference of the International Speech Communication Association (INTERSPEECH), pp. 2–3 (2007)
17. Roebel, A., Huber, S., Rodet, X., Degottex, G.: Analysis and modification of excitation source characteristics for singing voice synthesis. In: IEEE International Conference on Acoustics, Speech, and Signal Processing (ICASSP), pp. 5381–5384, March 2012
18. Saitou, T., Goto, M., Unoki, M., Akagi, M.: Speech-to-singing synthesis: converting speaking voices to singing voices by controlling acoustic features unique to singing voices. In: IEEE Workshop on Applications of Signal Processing to Audio and Acoustics (WASPAA), pp. 215–218 (2007)

19. Saitou, T., Goto, M., Unoki, M., Akagi, M.: Vocal conversion from speaking voice to singing voice using STRAIGHT. In: 8th Annual Conference of the International Speech Communication Association (INTERSPEECH), pp. 2–3 (2007)
20. Stylianou, Y.: Applying the harmonic plus noise model in concatenative speech synthesis. IEEE Trans. Speech Audio Process. **9**(1), 21–29 (2001)
21. Sundberg, J.: The Science of the Singing Voice. Northern Illinois University Press, DeKalb (1987)
22. Sundberg, J.: The KTH synthesis of singing. Adv. Cogn. Psychol. **2**(2), 131–143 (2006)

# A Novel Error Mitigation Scheme Based on Replacement Vectors and FEC Codes for Speech Recovery in Loss-Prone Channels

Domingo López-Oller$^{(\boxtimes)}$, Angel M. Gomez, and José L. Pérez-Córdoba

Departamento de Teoría de la Señal, Telemática y Comunicaciones,
University of Granada, Granada, Spain
{domingolopez,amgg,jlpc}@ugr.es

**Abstract.** In this paper, we propose an error mitigation scheme which combines two different approaches, a replacement super vector technique which provides replacements to reconstruct both the LPC coefficients and the excitation signal along bursts of lost packets, and a Forward Error Code (FEC) technique in order to minimize the error propagation after the last lost frame. Moreover, this FEC code is embedded into the bitstream in order to avoid the bitrate increment and keep the codec working in a compliant way on clean transmissions. The success of our recovery technique deeply relies on a quantization of the speech parameters (LPC coefficients and the excitation signal), especially in the case of the excitation signal where a modified version of the well-known Linde-Buzo-Gray (LBG) algorithm is applied. The performance of our proposal is evaluated over the AMR codec in terms of speech quality by using the PESQ algorithm. Our proposal achieves a noticeable improvement over the standard AMR legacy codec under adverse channel conditions without incurring neither on high computational costs or delays during the decoding stage nor consuming any additional bitrate.

**Keywords:** Speech reconstruction · Error propagation · MMSE · FEC · LPC-excitation signal concealment · Steganography · AMR

## 1 Introduction

During the last decade, the Voice over IP (VoIP) service has grown in importance around the world as it offers a cheaper and more efficient way for speech transmission than the traditional telephony systems. Moreover, due to the widespread development of IP networks, due to the "all IP" convergence, the quality of service (QoS) has improved and more natural speech is obtained. However, switched-packet networks are not prepared to guarantee the quality of service in a real-time service due to the delays and congestion in these networks generate errors during the transmission which degrade the perceptual speech quality.

J.L. Pérez-Córdoba—This work has been supported by an FPI grant from the Spanish Ministry of Education and by the MICINN TEC2013-46690-P project.

© Springer International Publishing AG 2016
A. Abad et al. (Eds.): IberSPEECH 2016, LNAI 10077, pp. 44–53, 2016.
DOI: 10.1007/978-3-319-49169-1_5

Moreover, this kind of errors are not isolated and they often lead to high rates of packet/frame losses and/or consecutive packet/frame losses (burst). Thus, speech codecs must conceal these losses in order to reduce the degradation in the synthesized speech signal.

One of the most known codecs for speech transmission is the Adaptive Multi-Rate (AMR) codec [1] which is based on the well known Code Excited Linear Prediction (CELP) paradigm [2]. This paradigm provides high quality synthesis at a remarkably low bitrate, making it suitable for bandwidth limited channels. In particular, AMR can operate at different bitrates from 4.75 Kbps to 12.2 Kbps. However, it is well known that CELP-based codecs are more vulnerable to frame erasures due to the extensive use of the predictive filters, in particular the long-term prediction filter (LTP), responsible for the error propagation [3–5]. This is obviously a major drawback of these codecs when they operate over packet-switched networks as a single lost frame can degrade the quality of many subsequent frames albeit these were correctly received.

In order to minimize this degradation, speech codecs try to conceal the lost frame by using a Packet Loss Concealment (PLC) algorithm during the decoding stage. In that way, most of the modern speech codecs typically implement repetition [6] or interpolation/extrapolation techniques [7,8] due to their simplicity and because they are efficient on short bursts. The success in short burst relies on the large amounts of short-term self-similarity that speech signals exhibit, but in large bursts this stationarity is compromised so the performance of the PLC algorithm decreases quickly and a muting process is applied in order to avoid artifacts. Thus, a more sophisticated technique, based on a speech signal model [9,10], is necessary.

In a previous work [11], we propose an error mitigation scheme that when a frame loss happens during the transmission, the speech parameters (the Linear Prediction Coding coefficients (LPC) and the excitation signal) are provided by a replacement super vector according to the past correctly received frames. It must be noted that in that work we focused on the quantization and estimation of both speech parameters while in other works, the authors focus on the LPC coefficients estimation [12–16]. Indeed, the success of this proposal relies on the novel VQ-quantization method of the excitation signal. This quantization method is a modified version of the well known Linde-Buzo-Gray (LBG) algorithm [17] which modifies the optimal cell and center criteria according to a synthesis-based distance metric. Despite of this improvement, it is not enough because although we can provide better replacements than the legacy codec, it must be noted that as the burst length is longer, less intra-frame correlations are retained in the estimates. As a result, a bad estimate could be provided for the last lost frame in the burst incurring an error propagation along the next correctly received frames.

In order to minimize this error propagation, we will consider a media-specific Forward Error Correction (FEC) code technique. In the bibliography, there are already proposed a number of techniques to minimize or even to avoid the error propagation by using a FEC technique [18–20]. However, the use of a FEC technique will increase the bitrate depending on the number of extra bits used to quantize the speech parameters. Moreover, the resulting bitstream format could be incompatible with the original codec standard, so in order to minimize this overhead, in this work we will use an steganographic algorithm which embeds this redundant information into the bitstream in order to avoid this bitrate increment and also keep it working in a compliant way.

Finally, our proposal is the combination of two different approaches which achieves a noticeable improvement over the PLC algorithm of the AMR speech codec under whatever erasure channel condition because it provides both speech parameters along the burst and it avoids error propagation after the burst. Thus, our proposal is more robust for transmissions under erasure conditions.

The remainder of this paper is organized as follows. In Sect. 2 we will describe our error mitigation scheme and we explain both techniques, the replacement super vectors technique and the FEC technique with the steganography method. In Sect. 3, we describe our experimental framework and the results obtained over the AMR codec with its own PLC algorithm and our proposal. Finally, the conclusions are summarized in Sect. 4.

## 2 Novel Error Mitigation Scheme to Restore Lost Frames and Minimize Error Propagation

Since the speech features change quite slow in a speech transmission, when a packet/frame erasure happens, the PLC algorithm tries to minimize the degradation on the perceptual quality from the last correctly received frame. However, in case of consecutive lost frames (burst), this technique could lead to artifacts as speech signal is not stationary. That is the main reason why traditional PLC algorithms gradually mute the speech signal in long bursts. Nonetheless, the information contained in the source can be exploited to get better estimates if the speech parameters (LPC coefficients and the excitation signal) are quantized in an efficient way.

In that way, in a previous work [11], we propose an error mitigation scheme based on a replacement super vector technique which provides both speech parameters (LPC coefficients and the excitation signal) according to the quantization indexes of the corresponding speech parameters in the last correctly received frames. However, although this proposal can alleviate the errors during the burst, it must be considered that as the burst length is longer, each estimate is less correlated with the first estimate. Thus, the last estimate could incur an error propagation.

In order to minimize this error propagation, the speech parameters (LPC coefficients and excitation signal) of the previous frame are provided from the next correctly received frame by using a FEC code. However, it must be taken into account that these speech parameters are transmitted in the form of media-specific FEC bits, causing an increment of the transmitted bitrate which could be unfeasible for the network due to bandwidth constraints.

As can be noted, the success of both techniques, the replacement super vector and the FEC techniques, deeply relies on how well quantized are the speech parameters to minimize the quantization error and to avoid bad estimates during the generation of the replacement super vectors. Thus, on the one hand, the LPC coefficients' codebook will be obtained by applying the well known Linde-Buzo-Gray (LBG) [17] algorithm under the Linear Spectral Frequencies (LSF) [21] representation. This representation was chosen because the LSF coefficients exhibit properties of ordering [22] and distortion independence [23] which make them more suitable for coding. On the other hand, due to the characteristics of the excitation signal we should not directly apply the LBG algorithm because the euclidean distance does not account whether the final synthesized signal is close to the original one or not. As a result, we propose in [11] several vector quantization methods which modify the optimal cell and center criteria of the LBG algorithm according to a synthesis-based distance metric. From all of them, we selected the Synthesis LBG algorithm with Fixed splitting (SLBGF) which will be described below.

In order to generate an efficient excitation signal codebook, we must consider the LP impulse response during the minimization in order to obtain a good approximation of the entire residual signal $\hat{e}(n)$ by using a unique codebook. That is, it is necessary to minimize the synthesis error $\epsilon$ with respect to the original speech signal. This synthesis error is defined as:

$$\epsilon = \sum_{n=0}^{N-1} (h(n) * \hat{e}(n) - s(n))^2 \qquad (1)$$

where $N$ is the length of the frame and $s(n)$ is the original signal.

Thus, for cell optimization, given the excitation signal $e_b(n)$ and the LPC impulse response $\mathbf{h}_b$ of the $b$-th speech frame in the training database, this excitation vector is assigned to the centroid $\mathbf{c}^{(i)}$ iff $\epsilon(\mathbf{e}_b, \mathbf{c}^{(i)}, \mathbf{h}_b) < \epsilon(\mathbf{e}_b, \mathbf{c}^{(j)}, \mathbf{h}_b)) \forall i \neq j$. The distance function $\epsilon(\mathbf{e}, \mathbf{c}, \mathbf{h})$ is defined as:

$$\epsilon(\mathbf{e}, \mathbf{c}, \mathbf{h}) = \sum_{n=0}^{N-1} (h(n) * (e(n)) - h(n) * (c(n)))^2. \qquad (2)$$

Then, an optimum center can be obtained as the excitation vector which minimizes the overall error in a set of frames $\mathcal{B}_i$ within the cell $i$:

$$c_{new}^{(i)} - \underset{\mathbf{c}}{\mathrm{argmin}} \left( \sum_{b \in \mathcal{B}_i} \epsilon(\mathbf{e}_b, \mathbf{c}, \mathbf{h}_b) \right) \qquad (3)$$

As we explain in [24], this expression can be minimized in the DFT domain and we obtain the corresponding optimal center by using Least Squares (LS) method as:

$$C_{new}^{(i)}(k) = \frac{\sum_{b \in \mathcal{B}_i} H_b^*(k) H_b(k) E_b(k)}{\sum_{b \in \mathcal{B}_i} H_b^*(k) H_b(k)} \qquad (0 < k < K - 1) \qquad (4)$$

where $\mathbf{H}_b^*$ denotes the Hermitian transpose of $\mathbf{H}_b$ and $\mathbf{C}$; $\mathbf{H}_b$ and $\mathbf{E}_b$ are the DFT of the zero-padded extension, with $K = 2N - 1$ components, of $\mathbf{c}$, $\mathbf{h}_b$ and $\mathbf{e}_b$ in (2). Finally, all the centroids $\mathbf{c}_{new}^{(i)}$ are retrieved via IDFT.

This procedure will be applied over the training database until convergence is achieved with the first two centroids. Then, the most populated cell is split if its size is bigger than an $\alpha$ value and again convergence is achieved over this cell. In that way, this procedure will be applied until $C$ centroids are obtained and the obtained codebook will be used to generate the replacement super vectors and obtain the quantization indexes of the FEC code.

### 2.1  A Replacement Super Vector to Minimize Errors Along the Burst

As we explain in [11,24], the replacement super vector for each quantization index $u$ is a set of estimates defined as $\mathbf{V}(u) = (\hat{\mathbf{c}}_1^{(u)}, \hat{\mathbf{c}}_2^{(u)}, ..., \hat{\mathbf{c}}_T^{(u)})$, where $T$ is the maximum replacement length in the burst and $\hat{\mathbf{c}}_\tau^{(u)}$ contains the replacement speech parameters (either LPC coefficients or the excitation signal) computed for the $\tau - th$ consecutive lost frame. These estimates are obtained by means of a Minimum Mean Squared Error (MMSE) estimation defined as [25]:

$$\hat{\mathbf{c}}_\tau^{(u)} = \sum_{v=0}^{C-1} \mathbf{c}^{(v)} P(u_{t+\tau} = v | u_t = u), \quad (1 \leq \tau \leq T), \tag{5}$$

where $\mathbf{c}_\tau^{(u)}$ is the estimation at instant $t + \tau$ for the $\tau - th$ lost frame in the burst provided that index $(v)$ was the last quantization index computed at instant $t$, $\mathbf{c}^{(v)}$ is the corresponding codebook center and $C$ is the size of the corresponding codebook. Therefore, Eq. (5) is defined according to the 1st-order data-source model but it can be extended to an estimation based on the two or more nearest correct frames [11].

In order to generate the replacement super vectors, on the one hand, the estimate $\mathbf{c}_\tau^{(u)}$ of the LPC super vector $\mathbf{V}_{\mathrm{LPC}}(u)$ is obtained by averaging the corresponding LSF coefficients found at time instant $t + \tau$ each time the center $u$ is observed at instant $t$ over the entire training database and finally, they are reverted to LPC coefficients. On the other hand, in the case of the excitation signal, this procedure will be modified. The corresponding estimates for each replacement super vector $\mathbf{V}_{\mathrm{EXC}(u)}$ are obtained by considering all the excitations in $t + \tau$ each time the center $u$ is observed at instant $t$, over the entire training database, in a set $\mathcal{B}$ and apply again the error minimization over it. In such a way, the conditional probability of (5) is not necessary (but implicitly used) and quantization errors can be alleviated.

### 2.2  A FEC Code to Minimize Error Propagation

Despite the replacement super vector technique can alleviate the errors during the burst, it must be considered that as the burst length is longer, each estimate is less correlated with the first estimate and the error between the original signal $(s_\tau(n))$, in the $\tau - th$ lost consecutive frame, and the synthesized one $(\hat{s}(n) = \hat{h}_\tau(n)*\hat{e}_\tau(n))$ will increase. Moreover, this error and the extensive use of the LTP filter in CELP-basd codecs generate a desynchronization during the decoding stage which causes an error propagation in the next correctly received frames until synchronicity is achieved again.

In this work, we propose the use of a media-specific FEC code which provides the quantization indexes to obtain the corresponding speech parameters of the last lost frame in the burst. These quantization indexes are given from the corresponding codebooks described above which must be transmitted. As a consequence, this technique requires an extra bitrate. However, in order to avoid this overhead and keep compatibility with the original standard codec, we will use an steganography technique [26] which was applied in a previous work [27]. This steganographic method allows us to embed various bitrates from 200 bps to 2 Kbps into the analysis-by-synthesis loop for the fixed codebook (FCB) search over the AMR codec. Nevertheless, it must be taken into account that this steganographic technique will modify some bits in the bitstream so the speech quality could be seriously degraded on clean transmissions. Hence in order to minimize this effect, in this work only the quantization index of the previous excitation signal will be embedded. The corresponding excitation signal will be selected as the excitation which minimizes the synthesis error defined in (1) of the previous frame.

Once both techniques have been presented, the combined error mitigation scheme is depicted on Fig. 1. As it can be seen, the replacement super vector technique will provide estimates of the LPC coefficients and the excitation signal along the burst until the last lost frame, where only the excitation signal is provided by using the FEC code. This FEC code is recovered from the next correctly received frame by using an steganographic method in order to avoid the error propagation.

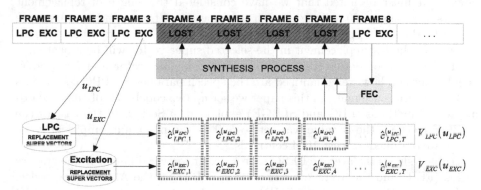

**Fig. 1.** Diagram of the error mitigation scheme. The envelope (LPC) and the excitation signal (EXC) are provided from the corresponding replacement super vector ($\mathbf{V}_{\mathrm{LPC}}$ and $\mathbf{V}_{\mathrm{EXC}}$) given the quantization indexes of the last frame before the burst ($u_{\mathrm{LPC}}$ and $u_{\mathrm{EXC}}$). In order to avoid the error propagation, the last excitation signal in the burst is provided by the first correctly received frame as a FEC code.

## 3  Experimental Framework and Results

In this paper, we have considered the AMR codec 12.2 mode to evaluate the performance of our proposal. Objective tests are performed by means of the ITU Perceptual Evaluation of Speech Quality (PESQ) algorithm [28] which results are consistent with subjective tests such as the MUlti-Stimulus test with Hidden Reference and Anchor (MUSHRA) [29] test.

During PESQ evaluation, we have considered a subset of the TIMIT database [30] downsampled at 8 KHz and composed of a total of 1328 sentences (928 sentences for training and 450 sentences for testing), where all the sentences' lengths are extended by concatenation to approximately 14 s, as lengths between 8 and 20 s are recommended for PESQ evaluation. Also, utterances from female and male speakers have been balanced. Our proposal will be tested under adverse conditions where the frame erasures will be simulated by a Gilbert channel, commonly used in the evaluation of PLC techniques, with an average burst length (ABL) from 1 to 12 frames and frame erasure ratios (FER) from 10 % to 50 %. Although this channel is not a realistic loss scenario, in order to provide long bursts, a high frame erasure ratio is required. Finally, the scores obtained for each test sentence, in the corresponding channel condition, are weighted according to their relative length in the overall score.

The replacement super vectors ($\mathbf{V}_{\mathrm{LPC}}$ and $\mathbf{V}_{\mathrm{EXC}}$) used during the reconstruction of the lost frames are precomputed off-line from the aforementioned TIMIT training set. In the case of the LPC coefficients the super vectors are arranged in a matrix of size $\mathcal{C} \times T \times p$, where $\mathcal{C}$ is the size of the codebook (1024 centroids), $T$ is the maximum number of replacement vectors and $p$ is the number of LPC coefficients (AMR codec uses 10 coefficients) and in the case of the excitation signal, the matrix size is $\mathcal{C} \times T \times N$, where $N$ is the number of samples in the frame (fixed to 160 in the 12.2 Kbps mode). Thus, it is required a considerable amount of memory but it is still affordable for currently available devices. It must be noted that we have considered the length of replacement vectors $T$ equals to 20 as long enough to recover lost frames in the worst case where FER = 50 % and ABL = 12. However, if during the tests a burst length exceeds $T$, the last replacement in the selected super vector will be repeated.

The success of both techniques, the replacements vector and FEC code, deeply relies on how well quantized are the speech parameters (LPC coefficients and the excitation signal). In this paper we set up two codebooks of 1024 according to the methods (LBG and SLBGF) explained in Sect. 2. In the case of the SLBGF method, the $\alpha$ value was set to 500 as the maximum empirical value where we obtained at least 1024 centroids.

Table 1 shows the average PESQ scores obtained over different frame erasure ratios (FER) and the average burst lengths (ABL) for the AMR legacy codec, with its own PLC algorithm (AMR), the replacement vector technique (RV) that we presented in [11] and our proposal where we also minimize the error propagation by using an embed FEC code (RVFEC). As can be observed, the RV results are better than the AMR in all the channel conditions. However,

**Table 1.** Average PESQ scores obtained over different frame erasure ratio (FER) and average burst lengths (ABL) for the AMR codec, with its own PLC algorithm (AMR), the replacement vector technique (RV) and our proposal (RVFEC) which minimize the error propagation by using a FEC code.

| | | Average burst length | | | | |
|---|---|---|---|---|---|---|
| | FER | 1 | 2 | 4 | 8 | 12 |
| AMR | 10 | 2,82 | 2,80 | 2,82 | 2,87 | 2,93 |
| | 20 | 2,27 | 2,25 | 2,22 | 2,23 | 2,30 |
| | 30 | 1,83 | 1,86 | 1,79 | 1,78 | 1,83 |
| | 40 | 1,35 | 1,54 | 1,46 | 1,45 | 1,45 |
| | 50 | 1,01 | 1,25 | 1,16 | 1,14 | 1,18 |
| RV | 10 | 2,99 | 2,99 | 3,01 | 3,06 | 3,08 |
| | 20 | 2,51 | 2,53 | 2,54 | 2,58 | 2,60 |
| | 30 | 2,01 | 2,08 | 2,14 | 2,19 | 2,24 |
| | 40 | 1,67 | 1,82 | 1,88 | 1,93 | 2.00 |
| | 50 | 1,32 | 1,54 | 1,60 | 1,64 | 1,69 |
| RVFEC | 10 | 3,15 | 3,18 | 3,20 | 3,23 | 3,26 |
| | 20 | 2,69 | 2,73 | 2,76 | 2,78 | 2,81 |
| | 30 | 2,14 | 2,21 | 2,27 | 2,31 | 2,35 |
| | 40 | 1,74 | 1.94 | 1,99 | 2,02 | 2,08 |
| | 50 | 1,39 | 1,60 | 1,65 | 1,70 | 1,74 |

our proposal (RVFEC) improves these results because the error propagation is reduced after the burst.

It must be noted that the FEC code, where each excitation signal is represented by an index of 10 bits, will increase the bitrate in an extra 0.55 Kbps, but through the use of a steganographic technique [26] this increment in the bitrate is avoided. Moreover, the proposed scheme which embed the FEC code does not incur a significant performance loss in comparison with the original standard codec on clean transmissions. This fact can be seen in [27] where we also embedded 10 bits into the bitstream and the performance was similar to the original codec (4,00 vs 3,99) on clean transmissions. Thus, our proposal is compatible with the original standard codec and also achieves a noticeable improvement under erasure channel conditions.

## 4    Conclusions

In this paper we have presented an error mitigation scheme which combines the advantage of two different approaches. The replacement vector technique which provides estimates of the speech parameters (LPC coefficients and the excitation signal) along the burst and a FEC code which minimize the error propagation by providing the excitation signal of the last lost frame. This FEC code will be embed into the bitstream by using an steganographic method in order to avoid an extra bitrate and keep compatibility with the original standard codec on clean transmissions.

The success of our proposal deeply relies on the quantization of the speech parameters in order to minimize the quantization error and avoid bad replacements during the decoding stage. In this work, the classical LBG algorithm is applied over the LPC coefficients while a modified version presented in [11] is applied over the excitation signal. As a consequence, the quantization error and the error propagation are minimized by using a codebook with only 1024 centroids.

The obtained PESQ scores have shown the suitability of our proposal for adverse channel conditions and without incurring on high computational costs or delays during the decoding stage nor consuming any additional bitrate.

# References

1. 3GPP TS 26.090: Mandatory Speech Codec speech processing functions; Adaptive Multi-Rate (AMR) speech codec (1999)
2. Schroeder, M., Atal, B.: Code-excited linear prediction (CELP): high-quality speech at very low bit rates. IEEE ICASSP **10**, 937–940 (1985)
3. Serizawa, M., Ito, H.: A packet loss recovery method using packet arrived behind the playout time for CELP decoding. IEEE ICASSP **1**, 169–172 (2002)
4. Chibani, M., Lefebvre, R., Gournay, P.: Fast recovery for a CELP-like speech codec after a frame erasure. IEEE Trans. Audio Speech Lang. Process. **15**(8), 2485–2495 (2007)
5. Carmona, J., Pérez-Córdoba, J., Peinado, A., Gomez, A., González, J.: A scalable coding scheme based on interframe dependency limitation. In: IEEE ICASSP, pp. 4805–4808 (2008)
6. Liao, W., Chen, J., Chen, M.: Adaptive recovery techniques for real-time audio streams. IEEE INFOCOM **2**, 815–823 (2001)
7. Merazka, F.: Packet loss concealment by interpolation for speech over IP network services. In: CIWSP, pp. 1–4 (2013)
8. Lindbrom, J., Hedelin, P.: Packet loss concealment based on sinusoidal extrapolation. IEEE ICASSP **1**, 173–176 (2002)
9. Hodson, O., Perkins, C., Hardman, V.: A survey of packet loss recovery techniques for streaming audio. IEEE Netw. **12**, 40–48 (1998)
10. Rodbro, C., Murthi, M., Andersen, S., Jensen, S.: Hidden Markov model-based packet loss concealment for voice over IP. IEEE Trans. Audio Speech Lang. Process. **14**, 1609–1622 (2006)
11. López-Oller, D., Gomez, A., Pérez-Córdoba, J.: Residual VQ-quantization for speech frame loss concealment. In: IberSPEECH, November 2014
12. Zhang, G., Kleijn, W.: Autoregressive model-based speech packet-loss concealment. IEEE ICASSP **1**, 4797–4800 (2008)
13. Ma, Z., Martin, R., Guo, J., Zhang, H.: Nonlinear estimation of missing LSF parameters by a mixture of Dirichlet distributions. In: IEEE ICASSP, pp. 6929–6933, May 2014

14. Boubakir, C., Berkani, D.: The estimation of line spectral frequencies trajectories based on unscented Kalman filtering. In: International Multi-Conference on Systems, Signals and Devices, pp. 1–6 (2009)
15. Chazan, D., Hoory, R., Cohen, G., Zibulski, M.: Speech reconstruction from MEL frequency cepstral coefficients and pitch frequency. IEEE ICASSP **3**, 1299–1302 (2000)
16. Merazka, F.: Differential quantization of spectral parameters for CELP based coders in packet networks. In: IECON, pp. 1495–1498, October 2012
17. Linde, Y., Buzo, A., Gray, R.: An algorithm for vector quantizer design. IEEE Trans. Commun. **28**(1), 84–95 (1980)
18. Gomez, A., Carmona, J., Peinado, A., Sánchez, V.: A multipulse-based forward error correction technique for robust CELP-coded speech transmission over erasure channels. IEEE Trans. Audio Speech Lang. Process. **18**, 1258–1268 (2010)
19. Gomez, A., Carmona, J., González, J., Sánchez, V.: One-pulse FEC coding for robust CELP-coded speech transmission over erasure channels. IEEE Trans. Multimedia **13**(5), 894–904 (2011)
20. Ehara, H., Yoshida, K.: Decoder initializing technique for improving frame-erasure resilience of a CELP speech codec. IEEE Trans. Multimedia **10**, 549–553 (2008)
21. Itakura, F.: Line spectrum representation of linear predictive coefficients of speech signals. J. Acoust. Soc. Am. **57**, S35 (1975)
22. Kondoz, A.: Digital Speech: Coding for Low Bit Rate Communications Systems. Wiley, Hoboken (1994)
23. Soong, F., Juang, B.: Line spectrum pair (LSP) and speech data compression. IEEE ICASSP **9**, 37–40 (1984)
24. López-Oller, D., Gomez, A., Pérez-Córdoba, J.: Source-based error mitigation for speech transmissions over erasure channels. In: EUSIPCO, pp. 1242–1246, September 2014
25. Gómez, A., Peinado, A., Sánchez, V., Rubio, A.: A source model mitigation technique for distributed speech recognition over lossy packet channels. In: Proceedings of EUROSPEECH, pp. 2733–2736 (2003)
26. Geiser, B., Vary, P.: High rate data hiding in ACELP speech codecs. In: IEEE ICASSP, pp. 4005–4008, April 2008
27. López-Oller, D., Gomez, A.M., Córdoba, J.L.P., Geiser, B., Vary, P.: Steganographic pulse-based recovery for robust ACELP transmission over erasure channels. In: Torre Toledano, D., Ortega Giménez, A., Teixeira, A., González Rodríguez, J., Hernández Gómez, L., San Segundo Hernández, R., Ramos Castro, D. (eds.) IberSPEECH 2012. CCIS, vol. 328, pp. 257–266. Springer, Heidelberg (2012). doi:10.1007/978-3-642-35292-8_27
28. ITU-T Recomendation P.862: Perceptual evaluation of speech quality (PESQ) (2001)
29. ITU-R BS.1534-1: Method for the subjective assessment of intermediate quality level of coding systems (2001)
30. Garofolo, J., et al.: The Structure and Format of the DARPA TIMIT CD-ROM Prototype (1990)

# Language-Independent Acoustic Cloning of HTS Voices: An Objective Evaluation

Carmen Magariños[1(✉)], Daniel Erro[2],
Paula Lopez-Otero[1], and Eduardo R. Banga[1]

[1] Multimedia Technology Group (GTM), AtlantTIC, University of Vigo, Vigo, Spain
{cmagui,plopez,erbanga}@gts.uvigo.es
[2] IKERBASQUE – Aholab, University of the Basque Country, Bilbao, Spain
derro@aholab.ehu.es

**Abstract.** In a previous work we presented a method to combine the acoustic characteristics of a speech synthesis model with the linguistic characteristics of another one. This paper presents a more extensive evaluation of the method when applied to cross-lingual adaptation. A large number of voices from a database in Spanish are adapted to Basque, Catalan, English and Galician. Using a state-of-the-art speaker identification system, we show that the proposed method captures the identity of the target speakers almost as well as standard intra-lingual adaptation techniques.

**Keywords:** HMM-based speech synthesis · Cross-lingual speaker adaptation · Polyglot synthesis · Multilingual synthesis · Voice cloning · I-vectors · Speaker identification

## 1 Introduction

The major drawback of the traditional speech synthesis techniques, such as unit-selection, is the costly process of recording new voices that needs to be performed to provide text-to-speech (TTS) systems with new speakers, speaking styles, emotions or languages. This process has been simplified thanks to the appearance of the statistical parametric speech synthesis [1], since it allows the modification of the voice characteristics by transforming the model parameters. This flexibility permits to obtain not only new speaker identities, but also voices with different speaking styles or emotions, avoiding the need for long additional recordings.

One of the most popular statistical parametric techniques is the so-called hidden Markov model (HMM)-based speech synthesis, where adaptation techniques [2,3] have been applied to obtain speaker-specific synthesis systems using a small amount of adaptation data. In this context, speaker adaptation can be defined as the transformation of acoustic models associated with one speaker (the source speaker) using adaptation data from another speaker (the target speaker). The transformation is made by applying adaptation techniques in such a manner that the resultant model produces synthetic speech that is perceived as the voice of

A. Abad et al. (Eds.): IberSPEECH 2016, LNAI 10077, pp. 54–63, 2016.
DOI: 10.1007/978-3-319-49169-1_6

the target speaker. We can distinguish between *intra-lingual* and *cross-lingual* speaker adaptation. In the case of intra-lingual adaptation, the source and the target speaker speak the same language, while in the cross-lingual situation the languages are different. However, heretofore most efforts in this field have focused on intra-lingual adaptation while only a few publications deal with the cross-lingual problem.

Some related work was presented in [4], where an HMM-based polyglot synthesizer is proposed. First, a speaker and language-independent (SI) model is trained using data of several speakers in different languages. Then, a speaker dependent (SD) model may be obtained by adapting the SI model to a specific speaker. Finally, using the SD model it is possible to synthesize speech in any language in the training set. In [5], the authors propose a method based on state-level mapping for cross-lingual speaker adaptation in HMM-based speech synthesis. In this work, the minimum Kullback-Leibler divergence (KLD) is used as the criterion to estimate the state mapping between voice models in source and target languages. Besides, two different approaches to use the mapping information are presented: data mapping and transform mapping. In [6,7], the same KLD-based method (transform mapping approach) is integrated in a mobile device that implements personalised speech-to-speech translation. Another method that enables polyglot speech synthesis is described in [8]. This method first factorizes the speech into language-specific and speaker-specific characteristics and, then, individual transforms are trained for each factor. Thus, speaker and language transforms can be independently applied.

In earlier work [9], we proposed a new method for cross-lingual speaker adaptation, that we refer to as *language-independent acoustic cloning*. Within the standard HMM-based synthesis framework [10], the proposed method takes two HTS voice models as input, one for the desired language (source speaker model) and another for the intended speaker identity (target speaker model), and builds a third model that combines the linguistic structure of the first model with the acoustic properties of the second model. The method uses the INCA algorithm [11,12] to estimate a mapping between the emission distributions of both models. Then, the distributions of the first model are projected onto those of the second model. As a result, the new model is able to produce speech in the target language while sounding like the target speaker. It is important to note that, unlike conventional adaptation techniques where the source model is modified to fit some input data from a target speaker, the proposed technique transforms the source model to be acoustically closer to another model that conveys the target speaker's identity. The proposed method was evaluated through a perceptual listening test, considering synthetic voice models in four different languages: Basque, Castilian Spanish, Galician and English. We used one voice per model (two females and two males) and the source-target pairs were selected to cover all the possible gender combinations. Although this subjective evaluation showed a satisfactory performance of the method, more extensive experiments (using a greater number of voices) were left for further research.

This paper intends to give a more exhaustive evaluation of the proposed adaptation method detailed in [9]. Since an evaluation through perceptual listening tests has certain limitations (it is not viable to use a large number of voices), in this work we decided to perform an objective evaluation by means of a speaker identification (SID) system. Therefore, this paper has a double goal: (1) to check to what extent it is possible to fool an SID system by cloning the target speaker's voice with the proposed method; and (2) to perform a more complete evaluation, with a higher number of voices, using a technology that has demonstrated its validity during the last years.

The rest of this paper is organized as follows: Sect. 2 gives an overall description of the proposed adaptation method; Sect. 3 presents the SID approach used for evaluation; the experimental framework is defined in Sect. 4; and, finally, some conclusions are summarized in Sect. 5.

## 2   Adaptation Method

Figure 1 represents the idea of the proposed adaptation method. Given two HTS voice models in two different languages (model 1 and model 2 in the figure), the objective is to obtain a new model that merges the language-dependent structure of model 1 with the acoustic characteristics of model 2. To do this, the method estimates a state-level mapping between both models, and then projects the emission distributions (Gaussian p.d.f's) of model 1 onto those of model 2.

Three separate streams of acoustic parameters compose each of the input models: fundamental frequency ($\log F0$), Mel-cepstrum (MCEP) and excitation parameters. The current version of the method focuses on transforming the cepstral part of the source model, in order to make it closer to that of the target speaker model. Regarding $\log F0$, a simple mean normalization is applied, while

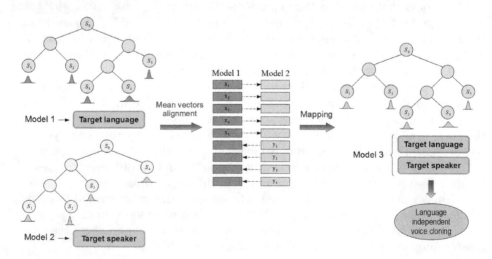

**Fig. 1.** Cloning of HTS voices. ©[2016] IEEE. Reprinted, with permission, from [9].

the excitation, the durations and the global variance statistics of the source voice model are not modified.

Figure 2 shows the block diagram of the MCEP adaptation process. We can distinguish two stages: one initial stage for the alignment of the distributions of both models, and a second one for estimating the final mapping between them.

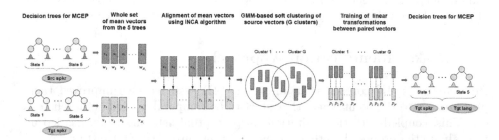

**Fig. 2.** Block diagram of the MCEP adaptation. ©[2016] IEEE. Reprinted, with permission, from [9].

### 2.1 Alignment of Mean Vectors

Standard HTS configuration considers 5 emitting states per phone, which are organized in 5 different decision trees. The first step of this stage, is to pack the whole set of Mel-cepstral distributions of the 5 trees for both the source and the target speaker model. In fact, only the static part of the mean vectors of the distributions are considered in the next steps, along with an assigned weight to capture the relative importance of the distributions within the model. As shown in Fig. 1, the static part of the source and target mean vectors are referred to as $\{\mathbf{x}_i\}_{i=1...N_x}$ and $\{\mathbf{y}_j\}_{j=1...N_y}$, respectively, while their corresponding weights are $\{w_i\}$ and $\{v_j\}$.

Then, in order to find an acoustic correspondence between the states of both models, vectors $\{\mathbf{x}_i\}$ and $\{\mathbf{y}_j\}$ are paired using a modified version of the INCA algorithm [9,11].

### 2.2 Final Mapping

In this stage, after compensating for one-to-many alignment and eliminating duplicate pairs, the final set of $N_x$ vector pairs, $\{\mathbf{x}_n, \mathbf{y}_n\}$, is employed to train a transformation function.

Previously, a soft classification of the source vectors $\{\mathbf{x}_n\}$ is performed using a Gaussian mixture model (GMM) of $G$ components, denoted as $\Theta$. Then, the following probabilistic combination of linear transforms

$$F(\mathbf{x}) = \sum_{g=1}^{G} P(g/\mathbf{x}, \Theta)[\mathbf{A}_g \mathbf{x} + \mathbf{b}_g] \tag{1}$$

is trained via error minimization:

$$\{\mathbf{A}_g, \mathbf{b}_g\}_{g=1...G} = \operatorname{argmin} \sum_{n=1}^{N} p_n \|\mathbf{y}_n - F(\mathbf{x}_n)\|^2 \qquad (2)$$

where $p_n = w_n + v_n$. Similar transforms are also trained for the dynamic parts of the source and target mean vectors, $\{\Delta\mathbf{x}_n, \Delta\mathbf{y}_n\}$ and $\{\Delta^2\mathbf{x}_n, \Delta^2\mathbf{y}_n\}$. Finally, the output voice model is obtained by replacing the mean Mel-cepstral vectors of all the distributions in the source model by their transformed counterparts.

## 3    Speaker Identification Approach

Recent studies [13] confirm that automatic SID systems have improved their performance to the point where they start to be comparable with human listeners. This, coupled with the limitations of perceptual listening tests, has led us to evaluate the proposed method by means of an automatic SID system.

The SID system used in this paper is a state-of-the-art i-vector approach combined with dot-scoring [14]: the i-vector technique defines a low dimensional space, named total variability space, in which speech segments are represented by a vector of total factors, namely i-vector [15]. Given a speech utterance, its corresponding GMM supervector $\mathbf{M}$, obtained by concatenating the means of the GMM, can be decomposed as:

$$\mathbf{M} = \mathbf{m} + \mathbf{T}\mathbf{w} \qquad (3)$$

where $\mathbf{m}$ is the speaker and channel-independent supervector, $\mathbf{T}$ is a low rank total variability matrix, and $\mathbf{w}$ is the i-vector corresponding to the GMM supervector. A comparison of two i-vectors can be simply performed by computing their dot-scoring:

$$\operatorname{score}(\mathbf{w}_i, \mathbf{w}_j) = \mathbf{w}_i \cdot \mathbf{w}_j \qquad (4)$$

Hence, given a test utterance, its i-vector $\mathbf{w}_{\mathrm{utt}}$ is extracted and compared by dot-scoring with the $n_{\mathrm{spk}}$ enrolment i-vectors $\mathbf{w}_{\mathrm{spk}_i}$, $i \in \{1, \ldots, n_{\mathrm{spk}}\}$ and the utterance is assigned to the enrolled speaker that maximizes this score:

$$\operatorname{speaker}(\mathbf{w}_{\mathrm{utt}}) = \arg\max_{i \in 1, \ldots, n_{\mathrm{spk}}} \operatorname{score}(\mathbf{w}_{\mathrm{utt}}, \mathbf{w}_{\mathrm{spk}_i}) \qquad (5)$$

## 4    Experimental Framework

### 4.1    Database

To evaluate the proposed method, we used the FP subset of the Albayzin phonetic database [16], which is composed by 40 Spanish speakers (20 male, 20 female) of different ages (18–55) with 50 phonetically-balanced sentences each.

## 4.2 Adaptation

The aim of this experiment was to obtain synthetic voices in different languages for each of the 40 speakers mentioned in the previous subsection. For this purpose, first a Spanish voice model was obtained for each speaker by means of standard adaptation techniques (intra-lingual adaptation), and then all the speakers were cloned into the rest of the languages using the proposed method (cross-lingual adaptation).

Speech databases in 5 different languages (Basque, Catalan, English, Galician and Spanish) took part in the experiment. Regarding the gender, all the voices correspond to female speakers except for English, which belongs to a male speaker. The approximate number of training utterances per language was: 2000 (Spanish), 4000 (Basque and Catalan), 2800 (English) and 10000 (Galician). Language-specific text analysers were used for each voice [17–20], while Ahocoder [21] was employed for parameter extraction. It is worth clarifying that the Spanish voice was employed as the base model for intra-lingual adaptation (using the 50 available utterances per speaker as the adaptation data), while the others worked as source models (target languages) for cross-lingual adaptation.

## 4.3 SID System Configuration

The SID system used for performance evaluation requires a universal background model (UBM) and a total variability matrix. Hence, a GMM of 1024 mixtures was trained using 19 Mel-frequency cepstral coefficients (MFCCs) augmented with their energy, delta and acceleration coefficients. Then, the total variability matrix was trained [15], and the dimension of the i-vectors was empirically set to 100. The data included in the DS1 partition of Biosecure database [22] were used for training, which was carried out using the Kaldi toolkit [23].

It must be noted that the aforementioned system achieved an identification accuracy of 99.2 % when performing an SID experiment using the FP subset of Albayzin database, which means that the system is suitable and correctly tuned to perform the proposed SID experiments.

## 4.4 Evaluation

After adaptation, we have five models per speaker: the Spanish model, obtained by intra-lingual adaptation, and the models resulting from cloning the corresponding speaker into each of the target languages (Basque, Catalan, English and Galician). An SID experiment was performed in order to find out whether the speaker identity remains in the cloned speech. To do so, 5 utterances of natural speech from the 40 test speakers were used for enrolment (18 s on average), and then the test utterances obtained with the aforementioned models were assigned to one of those speakers as described in Sect. 3. The test data was obtained by synthesising and concatenating a series of sentences, which were subsequently divided into 19 segments of 10 s duration per speaker and language, in order to obtain the same amount of test data for all cases.

**Table 1.** SID accuracy per language and percentage of sentences in which the true speaker is among the two highest scores (Accuracy (2)).

|              | Basque  | Catalan | English | Galician | Spanish |
|--------------|---------|---------|---------|----------|---------|
| Accuracy     | 82.50 % | 85.39 % | 86.84 % | 85.92 %  | 96.97 % |
| Accuracy (2) | 90.39 % | 92.37 % | 91.05 % | 93.16 %  | 99.87 % |

## 4.5   Results and Discussion

Table 1 shows two different measures per language: the SID accuracy, i.e. the percentage of utterances that were correctly assigned to their corresponding speaker; and the percentage of utterances for which the true speaker has the highest or the second highest score (accuracy (2)), both calculated by considering the 40 target speakers in the corresponding language. The best accuracy was achieved for the Spanish models (96.97 %), obtained by intra-lingual adaptation, while it decreased by a percentage between 10.1 % (English) and 14.5 % (Basque) for the models obtained by cross-lingual adaptation. Since the Spanish models were used as the target speaker models for the cross-lingual adaptation, a loss of accuracy with respect to them was expectable due to the adaptation method itself. Despite the perceptual results presented in [9] seemed to indicate that the quality of the models used as source played an important role in both the similarity and the quality of the adapted models, the objective results obtained in this experiment did not confirm that claim. In fact, the quality of the original Galician voice was higher than that of the other voices used as source (English, Catalan and Basque) and, however, only significant improvements were observed with respect to the Basque model (85.92 % of accuracy for Galician versus 82.5 % for Basque). This might be due to the influence of the voice quality in the perception of similarity by listeners, which may not affect in the same way to an automatic SID system. In other words, it is possible that the quality of the source model affects only the quality of the adapted model, which influenced the similarity perception, but not the accuracy of the SID system. Besides, as commented in [9], the prosody of the output speech could have also caused an overall reduction of the subjective similarity scores, since the linguistic and suprasegmental characteristics of the source voice were kept unmodified, and the output voice was presented to the listeners preceded by the same utterance in the source speaker's voice (in addition to a sample of the target speaker's voice). Moreover, certain characteristics of the source and target speakers (such as large differences in the variance of $F0$), could lead to a poorer performance of the method in terms of similarity. Finally, if we also consider as correct the sentences for which the true speaker reached the second place (accuracy (2)), all the languages achieve a performance higher than 90 %.

Figure 3 shows the confusion matrices per language, obtained when running the SID experiments. In these matrices (of dimension $40 \times 40$), darker cells represent more sentences assigned to that cell, and diagonal matrices stand for a perfect performance (accuracy of 100 %). Consistently with the results in Table 1,

Fig. 3 shows a very good performance of the Spanish models, where only 23 utterances (out of the 760) of 6 different speakers were assigned to an erroneous speaker. In the case of the English models, utterances of 12 out of the 40 speakers were not correctly identified (giving a total of 100 misidentifications), while Galician models presented a total of 107 misidentified utterances spread over 15 different speakers. Finally, for Catalan and Basque models, misidentifications were given in 13 out of the 40 speakers, which came to a total of 111 and 133 misidentified utterances, respectively. From these results, it is worth pointing out the case of the English models, which present a very good accuracy, despite the differences in the phoneset with respect to the Spanish language.

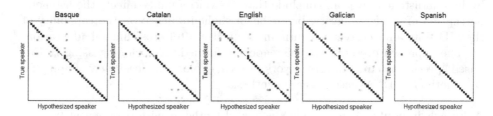

**Fig. 3.** Confusion matrices per language.

Table 2 presents the number of speakers per language with 100 % and more than 50 % of utterances assigned to an incorrect speaker. Once more, the best performance is given by the Spanish models, which do not have any speaker with 100 % of misidentification and only one speaker with more than 50 %. Based on this measure, the worst performance is offered by Basque and English models, which present 3 speakers with 100 % of misidentified utterances, while the number of speakers with more than 50 % is 6 and 5, respectively. However, it must be mentioned that if we consider the sentences in which the true speaker ranks among the top 5, all these speakers with 100 % of misidentification obtain more than 70 % of successes, except for one of the speakers in Basque. Overall, it can be concluded that the proposed method was able to fool an SID system in nearly all the studied cases, which demonstrates a competent performance, especially given the complexity of the task under consideration.

**Table 2.** Number of speakers per language with 100 % and more than 50 % of misidentified utterances.

|       | Basque | Catalan | English | Galician | Spanish |
|-------|--------|---------|---------|----------|---------|
| 100 % | 3      | 0       | 3       | 1        | 0       |
| >50 % | 6      | 6       | 5       | 4        | 1       |

## 5    Conclusion

This paper have conducted an objective evaluation of the cross-lingual adaptation method proposed in [9] using voices in four different languages (Basque, Catalan, English and Galician) as source models and 40 different target speakers in Spanish language. The target speaker models were obtained by means of standard HTS intra-lingual adaptation, and an SID system based on the state-of-the-art i-vector approach combined with dot-scoring was used for the evaluation. The results show a satisfactory performance of the method for the four considered target languages and the vast majority of the target speakers. Comparing the objective results presented in this paper with a subjective test performed by human listeners, we can conclude that the voice quality affects the listeners' perception of voice similarity, but it has a slight influence on the capability of the SID system for correctly identifying a speaker after cross-lingual adaptation.

The approach presented in this paper performed voice cloning using HMM-based speech synthesis. In future work, we will explore the feasibility of applying this method to DNN-based speech synthesis.

**Acknowledgments.** This research was funded by the Spanish Government (project TEC2015-65345-P and BES-2013-063708), the Galician Government through the research contract GRC2014/024 (Modalidade: Grupos de Referencia Competitiva 2014) and 'AtlantTIC' CN2012/160, the European Regional Development Fund (ERDF) and the COST Action IC1206.

## References

1. Zen, H., Tokuda, K., Black, A.W.: Statistical parametric speech synthesis. Speech Commun. **51**(11), 1039–1064 (2009)
2. Yamagishi, J.: Average-voice-based speech synthesis. Ph.d. dissertation, Tokyo Institute of Technology, Yokohama, Japan (2006)
3. Yamagishi, J., Nose, T., Zen, H., Ling, Z.H., Toda, T., Tokuda, K., King, S., Renals, S.: Robust speaker-adaptive HMM-based text-to-speech synthesis. IEEE Trans. Audio Speech Lang. Process. **17**(6), 1208–1230 (2009)
4. Latorre, J., Iwano, K., Furui, S.: New approach to the polyglot speech generation by means of an HMM-based speaker adaptable synthesizer. Speech Commun. **48**, 1227–1242 (2006)
5. Wu, Y.J., Nankaku, Y., Tokuda, K.: State mapping based method for cross-lingual speaker adaptation in HMM-based speech synthesis. In: Proceedings of Interspeech, pp. 528–531 (2009)
6. Oura, K., Yamagishi, J., Wester, M., King, S., Tokuda, K.: Analysis of unsupervised cross-lingual speaker adaptation for HMM-based speech synthesis using KLD-based transform mapping. Speech Commun. **54**, 703–714 (2012)
7. Dines, J., Liang, H., Saheer, L., Gibson, M., Byrne, W., Oura, K., Tokuda, K., Yamagishi, J., King, S., Wester, M., Hirsimki, T., Karhila, R., Kurimo, M.: Personalising speech-to-speech translation: unsupervised cross-lingual speaker adaptation for HMM-based speech synthesis. Comput. Speech Lang. **27**, 420–437 (2013)

8. Zen, H., Braunschweiler, N., Buchholz, S., Gales, M., Knill, K., Krstulovic, S., Latorre, J.: Statistical parametric speech synthesis based on speaker and language factorization. IEEE Trans. Audio Speech Lang. Process. **20**(6), 1713–1724 (2012)
9. Magariños, C., Erro, D., Banga, E.R.: Language-independent acoustic cloning of HTS voices: a preliminary study. In: Proceedings of ICASSP, pp. 5615–5619 (2016)
10. Zen, H., Nose, T., Yamagishi, J., Sako, S., Masuko, T., Black, A.W., Tokuda, K.: The HMM-based speech synthesis system (HTS) version 2.0. In: Proceedings of 6th ISCA Speech Synthesis Workshop, pp. 294–299. ISCA (2007)
11. Erro, D., Moreno, A., Bonafonte, A.: INCA algorithm for training voice conversion systems from nonparallel corpora. IEEE Trans. Audio Speech Lang. Process. **18**(5), 944–953 (2010)
12. Agiomyrgiannakis, Y.: The matching-minimization algorithm, the INCA algorithm and a mathematical framework for voice conversion with unaligned corpora. In: Proceedings of ICASSP, Shanghai, pp. 5645–5649 (2016)
13. Hansen, J., Hasan, T.: Speaker recognition by machines and humans: a tutorial review. IEEE Signal Process. Mag. **32**, 74–99 (2015)
14. Cumani, S., Brümmer, N., Burget, L., Laface, P.: Fast discriminative speaker verification in the i-vector space. In: Proceedings of ICASSP, pp. 4852–4855 (2011)
15. Dehak, N., Kenny, P.J., Dehak, R., Dumouchel, P., Ouellet, P.: Front end factor analysis for speaker verification. IEEE Trans. Audio Speech Lang. Process. **19**, 788–798 (2011)
16. Moreno, A., Poch, D., Bonafonte, A., Lleida, E., Llisterri, J., Mariño, J.B., Nadeu, C.: Albayzin speech database: design of the phonetic corpus. In: EUROSPEECH (1993)
17. Sainz, I., Erro, D., Navas, E., Hernáez, I., Sánchez, J., Saratxaga, I., Odriozola, I., Luengo, I.: Aholab speech synthesizers for albayzin2010. In: Proceedings of FALA 2010, pp. 343–348 (2010)
18. Bonafonte, A., Aguilar, L., Esquerra, I., Oller, S., Moreno, A.: Recent work on the FESTCAT database for speech synthesis. In: Proceedings of the I Iberian SLTech, pp. 131–132 (2009)
19. Taylor, P., Black, A.W., Caley, R.: The architecture of the festival speech synthesis system. In: Proceedings of the ESCA Workshop in Speech Synthesis, pp. 141–151 (1998)
20. Rodríguez-Banga, E., García-Mateo, C., Méndez-Pazó, F., González-González, M., Magariños, C.: Cotovía: an open source TTS for Galician and Spanish. In: Proceedings of IberSPEECH, pp. 308–315. RTTH and SIG-IL (2012)
21. Erro, D., Sainz, I., Navas, E., Hernáez, I.: Harmonics plus noise model based vocoder for statistical parametric speech synthesis. IEEE J. Scl. Top. Signal Process. **8**(2), 184–194 (2014)
22. Ortega-Garcia, J., Fierrez, J., Alonso-Fernandez, F., Galbally, J., Freire, M.R., Gonzalez-Rodriguez, J., Garcia-Mateo, C., Alba-Castro, J.L., Gonzalez-Agulla, E., Otero-Muras, E., Garcia-Salicetti, S., Allano, L., Ly-Van, B., Dorizzi, B., Kittler, J., Bourlai, T., Poh, N., Deravi, F., Ng, M.W.R., Fairhurst, M., Hennebert, J., Humm, A., Tistarelli, M., Brodo, L., Richiardi, J., Drygajlo, A., Ganster, H., Sukno, F., Pavani, S.K., Frangi, A., Akarun, L., Savran, A.: The multi-scenario multi-environment BioSecure multimodal database (BMDB). IEEE Trans. Pattern Anal. Mach. Intell. **32**(4), 1097–1111 (2009)
23. Povey, D., Ghoshal, A., Boulianne, G., Burget, L., Glembek, O., Goel, N., Hannemann, M., Motlicek, P., Qian, Y., Schwarz, P., Silovsky, J., Stemmer, G., Vesely, K.: The Kaldi speech recognition toolkit. In: IEEE Workshop on Automatic Speech Recognition and Understanding (2011)

# Prosodic Break Prediction with RNNs

Santiago Pascual[✉] and Antonio Bonafonte

Universitat Politècnica de Catalunya, Barcelona, Spain
santiago.pascual@tsc.upc.edu, antonio.bonafonte@upc.edu

**Abstract.** Prosodic breaks prediction from text is a fundamental task to obtain naturalness in text to speech applications. In this work we build a data-driven break predictor out of linguistic features like the Part of Speech (POS) tags and forward-backward word distance to punctuation marks, and to do so we use a basic Recurrent Neural Network (RNN) model to exploit the sequence dependency in decisions. In the experiments we evaluate the performance of a logistic regression model and the recurrent one. The results show that the logistic regression outperforms the baseline (CART) by a 9.5 % in the F-score, and the addition of the recurrent layer in the model further improves the predictions of the baseline by an 11 %.

**Keywords:** Text to speech · Prosodic break · Recurrent Neural Network

## 1 Introduction

Prosodic breaks describe changes in prosody. Speakers group certain words within the utterances they speak [1]. The phrase break or boundary between prosodic phrases is signaled by different acoustic cues as pauses, changes in syllabic duration and intonation discontinuities. The accurate prediction of these is very important for text to speech (TTS) applications, as it enhances the generated voice's naturalness. The most basic approach to predict them is by means of placing a break after every punctuation mark. This is because normally all punctuation marks carry a break, but this does not happen in the other way around, which means we lose many other break events that could be retrieved with a data-driven approach exploiting the patterns that make them happen. Previous work used a wide variety of linguistic features such as Part of Speech (POS) tags [2–6] forward-backward distances in words/syllables to punctuation marks [5], word projections [7], and syntactic features [8] among others. To classify whether there was a break or not, many types of prediction systems were used with the previous mentioned features in different combinations, like Finite State Transducers [3], Artificial Neural Networks [7], Maximum Entropy Classifiers [6] or CART models, either alone [4,5,9] or combined with language models of break sequences [2,4,10], the latter being the most frequently used, and they will serve us as a baseline for our work.

Deep learning techniques have already been applied extensively and successfully to many natural language processing (NLP) and TTS tasks [11],

© Springer International Publishing AG 2016
A. Abad et al. (Eds.): IberSPEECH 2016, LNAI 10077, pp. 64–72, 2016.
DOI: 10.1007/978-3-319-49169-1_7

outperforming existing systems in many cases. Concretely, Recurrent Neural Networks (RNNs) are extensively applied to many sequence processing tasks such as language modeling [12–14], neural machine translation [15] and acoustic mapping for speech synthesis [16,17], among many others. From this it seems natural to foresee that a recurrent neural model can be applied to the prosodic break prediction task to improve previous classification mechanisms that treated the input features as a static window without memory. That windowing approach then makes each decision independent from each other, something that seems unnatural given the dependency of the succeeding set of words happening in a sentence. Moreover previous works showed that modeling the sequential characteristics of the sentence performed better than static modeling [2,4,10].

In this work we propose a RNN model capable of mapping an input sequence of linguistic features into a sequence of break/no-break symbols using a set of features that lets us compare the new methodology with our baseline.

The structure of the paper is the following: Sect. 2 presents a review of RNNs and why are they appropriate to tackle this problem. In Sect. 3 it is described the proposed model and the experiment conditions. Finally, results are depicted in Sect. 4, finishing with Discussion and Conclusions in the remaining sections.

## 2    Recurrent Neural Network Review

Recurrent Neural Networks (RNN) are the specialization of a neural network into the sequences processing problem, where every neuron (or hidden unit) in the recurrent layer has a memory associated that tracks past decisions, in addition to the feed forward decision. A recurrent layer is characterized by the following equation:

$$h_t = g(W \cdot x_t + U \cdot h_{t-1} + b) \tag{1}$$

where $x_t \in \mathbb{R}^n$ is the input vector at time $t$, $b \in \mathbb{R}^m$ is the bias vector, $W \in \mathbb{R}^{m \times n}$ is the feed forward weights matrix and $U \in \mathbb{R}^{m \times m}$ is the recurrent weights matrix, where the temporal patterns are learned. After the linear operators an element-wise non-linear function $g$ is applied to get the output of the recurrent layer, which is in $h_t \in \mathbb{R}^m$, the decision given the input at time $t$ and the previous decision $h_{t-1}$. Sometimes this is called the memory state of the recurrent layer.

Note then that for every $X = \{x_1, x_2, \ldots, x_T\}$ input sequence we obtain an output sequence $H = \{h_1, h_2, \ldots, h_T\}$. This dependency on previous decisions make RNNs suitable to process sequences conditioning each output on its memory, also being able to process different sequence lengths with the same number of static inputs and outputs.

In this work we used Long Short Term Memory (LSTM) units instead of simple RNN units as they cope better with the vanishing gradient problems during training [18], and they also maintain long range dependencies better than conventional RNNs because of their gating mechanisms that control the information flows in and out of the layer without corrupting useful information in the further past [19].

# 3   Model and Experimental Setup

The proposed architecture for the break prediction model is shown in Fig. 1. It is composed of a hidden recurrent layer of LSTM cells connected to a logistic regression layer (LR) that makes the decision at each time step.

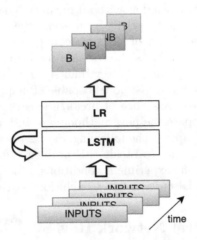

**Fig. 1.** Proposed architecture using a LSTM recurrent layer and a logistic regression layer (LR) to perform the decision of Break/No Break at each time step. Green boxes depict breaks and red boxes depict no breaks. (Color figure online)

The recurrent hidden layer, that is composed of 128 LSTM cells working with tanh non-linearities, processes the sequence whilst keeping in its memory states hidden information about the sequence preceding to the current decision, as stated previously. The output decision is made with a threshold in a sigmoid function. That threshold is set to 0.5 in the results table, although the response in its variation can be seen in the Precision-Recall curves as well (see Sect. 4). The model has been implemented using the Keras [20] Deep Learning library.

## 3.1   Features

The input set of features fed to the model at each time instant are:

– Part of Speech (POS) tags
– Word distance to next punctuation mark
– Word distance to previous punctuation mark

The use of POS tags reduces the sparsity of the vectorized symbols representation from what it could be with words, and they have been proved to perform well regarding the break prediction problem. In addition to the POS, distances to punctuation marks in words have also been included, such that at the current time instant the model knows where was the last punctuation mark and where/how far is the following one. Regarding the word distances, they are normalized by first taking the logarithm to compress the long-tailed distribution of values and then applying a max-min normalization to make every value fall in the range $r \in \{0, 1\}$.

The output of the model is then a binary flag $y \in \{0, 1\}$, where 0 indicates no break and 1 indicates break in the current position.

### 3.2 Database

We used the TCSTAR [21] male baseline TTS database in our experiments, where we had 2984 labeled sentences from the transcriptions of a male spanish speaker (8 h of voice recordings). There are 11057 labeled breaks, and 61.68 % of those come after a punctuation mark. This depicts the importance of exploiting the underlying patterns in the data to extract the remaining amount of breaks.

There is no fixed data split into training and test sets because we perform a 20-fold cross validation per experiment as we have a reduced amount of data available.

### 3.3 Experiments

We compare our model to a set of baseline methods using CART models (see Sect. 3.4). Furthermore, in order to evaluate the effect of the recurrent mechanism in the model, we made two types of tests: a 20-fold cross validation with a static window of features directly inserted to the logistic regression output layer, and a 20-fold cross validation with the RNN delayed model, which can see a small window of information about the future at every time instant.

The static window of the first experiment is composed of the three POS tags previous to the prediction point and the three subsequent POS tags:

$$POS_{t-2}, POS_{t-1}, POS_t, POS_{t+1}, POS_{t+2}, POS_{t+3}$$

In addition to the window, the previously mentioned distances are concatenated, i.e. forward-backward word distances to punctuation marks. Thus the logistic classifier has to predict if there is a break between $POS_t$ and $POS_{t+1}$. The second experiment uses the POS tag previous to the prediction point and the three subsequent ones, in addition to the distances:

$$POS_t, POS_{t+1}, POS_{t+2}, POS_{t+3}$$

The model then predicts whether there is a break or not in the same position as in the first experiment, but without inserting the past information every time as the recurrent hidden layer is supposed to capture that information.

The experiments run for a maximum of 200 epochs, separating a subset of 10 % of the training data in each fold for early stopping by validation. The optimizer used for back-propagation was the Stocastic Gradient Descent with Nesterov momentum, a parameter update momentum term of $\mu = 0.9$ and a learning rate decay applied of $\delta = 10^{-6}$ per iteration [22].

### 3.4    Baseline Methods

In [4], several break prediction methods were analyzed using the male speaker TCSTAR database. Two of these methods will be used as reference:

*CART:* This is one of the most popular and simple methods. A Classification Tree is estimated to predict, for each word, if there is a break. The following features were used: POS window of size 5 (POS of the 3 words before the break and 2 words after the break), punctuation (and its type) associated to the word, and distance (in syllables and words) to last predicted break. Also, forward-backward distance in words and syllables to punctuation marks are given to the CART.

*CART-LM:* This method uses the previous CART model to predict the probability of break in a given context. The final decision combines this probability with the probability of break, given the break/no-break decision of previous words [2]. The probability of the break/no-break sequence is estimated using n-grams. The distance to the previous break is not considered as it is unknown and it is already modeled by the probability of the break sequence. The Viterbi algorithm [23] is used to decide the break/no-break sequence with highest probability.

## 4    Results

The results of all experiments are depicted in Table 1. The evaluation metric used is the F-score as it is a binary classification that can be viewed as a document retrieval problem, thus we consider both the Precision (P) and Recall (R) metrics combined as an harmonic mean:

$$P = \frac{TP}{TP + FP} \tag{2}$$

$$R = \frac{TP}{TP + FN} \tag{3}$$

$$Fscore = \frac{2 \cdot P \cdot R}{P + R} \tag{4}$$

Where $TP$ stands for number of True Positive samples, $FP$ are the number of False Positive samples and $FN$ are the number of False Negative samples. The Recall metric counts how many relevant items are selected in the retrieval, whilst Precision indicates how many items in the selection are truly relevant. F-measure penalizes the worst resulting indicator, so it's a good discriminating measure for the binary retrieval task we are facing here.

**Table 1.** Results of the different experiments: logistic regression (LR) and RNN-LSTM (RNN), compared to the baseline methods CART and CART-LM. LR POS: Logistic Regression with POS window only. LR POS+D: Logistic Regression with POS window and distances. RNN POS: RNN model with POS window only. RNN POS+D: RNN model with POS window and distances.

| Model | Precision | Recall | F-score |
|-------|-----------|--------|---------|
| LR POS | 0.849 | 0.714 | 0.775 |
| LR POS+D | 0.857 | 0.711 | 0.777 |
| RNN POS | 0.862 | 0.73 | 0.79 |
| RNN POS+D | 0.863 | 0.729 | 0.79 |
| CART | 0.783 | 0.651 | 0.71 |
| CART-LM | 0.764 | 0.748 | 0.755 |

As seen in Table 1, the recurrent layer of the complete model yields a better result. Here we analyzed the effect of adding the recurrent layer but also the effect of the distance features for both the logistic regression (LR) and the RNN-LSTM (RNN) models. From this analysis we see how the distances to punctuation marks do not give much improvements in both models, but they do affect the static-window LR model more than the RNN model. The intuition behind this is that, as the RNN recalls what has been given in the past and it also sees a delayed version of the input because of the 3 succeeding *POS* tags available, it has enough data to make proper decisions with fewer input dimensions than LR model, only with the Part of Speech tags. Also, the comparison against the CART baseline model depicts the improvements of 9.5 % and 11 % in the LR and RNN models respectively.

Figure 2 shows the Precision-Recall curve of LR and RNN models with one fold and the complete set of features (i.e. POS window and distances). The RNN curve is a slightly shifted version of the LR one, so the curve improves in a balanced manner from LR to RNN. This means both Precision and Recall metrics improved with the addition of the recurrent layer as the network can now make more robust predictions given the sequence memory it obtained, as expected in the problem statement.

## 5 Discussion

The aim of this work is twofold: improving the baseline results of a prosodic break prediction system and checking the importance of the recurrent characteristics given by the RNN for the break prediction method proposed. As we have seen in the results, the best performing model is indeed the recurrent one, mainly due to its abilities for processing sequences, although the logistic regression with a static window outperforms the baseline predictions already.

Something interesting is the fact that distance features can improve the results slightly in the static window case (LR), where each decision is

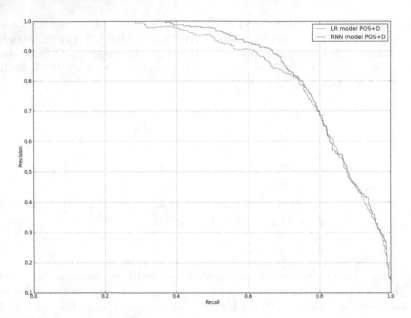

**Fig. 2.** Precision-recall curves for both models, RNN and LR, using all the features in one fold.

independent of any other one, but the recurrent model seems to extract the relevant information regarding the distances with the memory capabilities it has, so distance features make no effect to the RNN.

Up to this point then we have seen the best results with the recurrent model, although the relative difference with the logistic model is not really big. This is something that might be solved with the availability of more data, as the RNN is a deeper model than the LR and it suffers easier from the lack of it.

## 6    Conclusions

In this work we have proposed a RNN architecture for the prosodic break prediction problem out of a sentence by means of using Part of Speech tags and word distances to forward-backward punctuation marks. The results showed how the model outperformed the baseline CART system, even in the case where it is combined with an explicit model of the break sequence. We have also been able to check the effectiveness of adding a recurrent behavior to the model for the required task.

**Acknowledgments.** This work was supported by the Spanish Ministerio de Economía y Competitividad and European Regional Development Fund, contract TEC2015-69266-P (MINECO/FEDER, UE).

# References

1. Taylor, P.: Text-to-Speech Synthesis. Cambridge University Press, Cambridge (2009)
2. Taylor, P., Black, A.W.: Assigning phrase breaks from part-of-speech sequences. Comput. Speech Lang. **12**, 99–117 (1998)
3. Bonafonte, A., Agüero, P.D.: Phrase break prediction using a finite state transducer. In: Proceedings of Advanced Speech Technologies (2004)
4. Agüero, P.D., et al.: Síntesis de voz aplicada a la traducción voz a voz. Ph.D. dissertation, Tesis Doctoral. Universidad Politécnica de Cataluña (2012). http://hdl.handle.net/10803/97035
5. Hirschberg, J., Prieto, P.: Training intonational phrasing rules automatically for English and Spanish text-to-speech. Speech Commun. **18**(3), 281–290 (1996)
6. Li, J., Hu, G., Wang, R.: Prosody phrase break prediction based on maximum entropy model. J. Chin. Inf. Process. **18**, 56–63 (2004)
7. Watts, O., Gangireddy, S., Yamagishi, J., King, S., Renals, S., Stan, A., Giurgiu, M.: Neural net word representations for phrase-break prediction without a part of speech tagger. In: 2014 IEEE International Conference on Acoustics, Speech and Signal Processing (ICASSP), pp. 2599–2603. IEEE (2014)
8. Mishra, T., Kim, Y.-J., Bangalore, S.: Intonational phrase break prediction for text-to-speech synthesis using dependency relations. In: 2015 IEEE International Conference on Acoustics, Speech and Signal Processing (ICASSP), pp. 4919–4923. IEEE (2015)
9. Watts, O., Yamagishi, J., King, S.: Unsupervised continuous-valued word features for phrase-break prediction without a part-of-speech tagger. In: INTERSPEECH, pp. 2157–2160 (2011)
10. Sun, X., Applebaum, T.H.: Intonational phrase break prediction using decision tree and n-gram model. In: INTERSPEECH, pp. 537–540 (2001)
11. Deng, L., Yu, D.: Deep learning: methods and applications. Found. Trends Sig. Process. **7**(3–4), 197–387 (2014)
12. Kim, Y., Jernite, Y., Sontag, D., Rush, A.M.: Character-aware neural language models, arXiv preprint arXiv:1508.06615 (2015)
13. Sutskever, I., Martens, J., Hinton, G.E.: Generating text with recurrent neural networks. In: Proceedings of the 28th International Conference on Machine Learning (ICML-11), pp. 1017–1024 (2011)
14. Mikolov, T., Deoras, A., Kombrink, S., Burget, L., Cernocký, J.: Empirical evaluation and combination of advanced language modeling techniques. In: INTERSPEECH, pp. 605–608 (2011)
15. Cho, K., Van Merriënboer, B., Gulcehre, C., Bahdanau, D., Bougares, F., Schwenk, H., Bengio, Y.: Learning phrase representations using RNN encoder-decoder for statistical machine translation, arXiv preprint arXiv:1406.1078 (2014)
16. Zen, H., Sak, H.: Unidirectional long short-term memory recurrent neural network with recurrent output layer for low-latency speech synthesis. In: Proceedings of the IEEE International Conference on Acoustics, Speech, and Signal Processing (ICASSP), pp. 4470–4474 (2015)
17. Fan, Y., Qian, Y., Xie, F.-L., Soong, F.K.: TTS synthesis with bidirectional LSTM based recurrent neural networks. In: INTERSPEECH, pp. 1964–1968 (2014)
18. Hochreiter, S.: The vanishing gradient problem during learning recurrent neural nets and problem solutions. Int. J. Uncertainty Fuzziness Knowl.-Based Syst. **6**(02), 107–116 (1998)

19. Hochreiter, S., Schmidhuber, J.: Long short-term memory. Neural Comput. **9**(8), 1735–1780 (1997)
20. Chollet, F.: Keras (2015). https://github.com/fchollet/keras
21. Bonafonte, A., Höge, H., Kiss, I., Moreno, A., Ziegenhain, U., van den Heuvel, H., Hain, H.-U., Wang, X.S., Garcia, M.-N.: TC-STAR: specifications of language resources and evaluation for speech synthesis. In: Proceedings of LREC Conference, pp. 311–314 (2006)
22. Sutskever, I., Martens, J., Dahl, G., Hinton, G.: On the importance of initialization and momentum in deep learning. In: Proceedings of the 30th International Conference on Machine Learning (ICML-13), pp. 1139–1147 (2013)
23. Forney Jr., J.D.: The viterbi algorithm. Proc. IEEE **61**(3), 268–278 (1973)

# Surgery of Speech Synthesis Models to Overcome the Scarcity of Training Data

Arnaud Pierard[1], D. Erro[2,3], I. Hernaez[2(✉)], E. Navas[2], and Thierry Dutoit[1]

[1] TCTS, University of Mons, Mons, Belgium
[2] AHOLAB, University of the Basque Country (UPV/EHU), Bilbao, Spain
inma.hernaez@ehu.eus
[3] IKERBASQUE, Basque Foundation for Science, Bilbao, Spain

**Abstract.** In a previous work we developed an HMM-based TTS system for a Basque dialect spoken in southern France. We observed that French words, frequent in daily conversations, were not pronounced properly by the TTS system because the training corpus contained very few instances of some French phones. This paper reports our attempt to improve the pronunciation of these phones without redesigning the corpus or recording the speaker again. Inspired by techniques used to adapt synthetic voices using dysarthric speech, we transplant phones of a different French voice to our Basque voice, and we show the slight improvements found after surgery.

## 1 Introduction

During the last decade, statistical parametric speech synthesis [1] has prevailed over selection + concatenation approaches [2] for several reasons, the most remarkable one being the flexibility of the former to be adapted to new speakers [3], languages [4], speaking styles [5] or emotions [6]. During training, statistical parametric synthesizers learn the correspondence between phonetic, prosodic and linguistic labels extracted from text and acoustic features extracted from audio. This correspondence is typically modeled through hidden Markov models (HMMs) [1]. At synthesis time, voice models are used to derive the most likely sequence of acoustic features given the input text labels. The voice model of an HMM-based speech synthesizer contains a bunch of 5-state left-to-right hidden Semi Markov models (HSMMs ≡ HMMs with explicit state duration modeling [7]). HSMMs are stored as binary-tree structures (see Fig. 1) where intermediate nodes are linked to specific yes/no questions related to the input text labels, while each terminal node contains the multivariate Gaussian emission distribution of the acoustic features (static values + $1^{st}$ and $2^{nd}$-order derivatives) for a given context.

The flexibility of the HMM/HSMM framework enables several assistive applications such as the design of customizable speaking aids. For example, future laryngectomees can record a few samples of their voice before surgery and then get a personalized TTS to overcome their forthcoming communication needs. Similarly, patients who already exhibit severe vocal impairments can select a

© Springer International Publishing AG 2016
A. Abad et al. (Eds.): IberSPEECH 2016, LNAI 10077, pp. 73–83, 2016.
DOI: 10.1007/978-3-319-49169-1_8

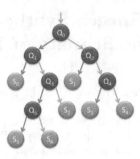

**Fig. 1.** Binary tree that relates input text labels with acoustic feature distributions. $Q_n$: yes/no questions about the content of the current label. $S_n$: states characterized by Gaussian emission distributions. In standard HTS voices there are 5 trees per acoustic stream.

*donor* from a *voice bank* and get a TTS adapted to that voice [8–10]. In case of partial impairments, e.g. several types of dysarthria, the patient's voice can be used for adaptation, and the resulting HSMMs can be "repaired" by an expert to eliminate the traces of abnormal articulation [11,12]. This means replacing some parts of the model (acoustic feature streams, HSMM states, etc.) by those of a donor. Given the parallelism with the medical domain, the terms *model surgery* have been suggested to describe such repair techniques [8].

This paper suggests the use of automatic model surgery techniques when the voice model is not contaminated by the traces of a pathology but by the effect of training data scarcity. In [13] we reported the creation of an HMM-based TTS for one of the Basque dialects spoken in southern France, namely Navarro-Lapurdian Basque. The phoneset used during the design of the corpus was the union of a standard Basque phoneset and a French one. However, the amount of French words in the corpus was limited; consequently, some of the French phones got poorly modeled. This was identified as an important performance limitation, since speakers of this dialect use a lot of French words (mostly proper nouns) in daily-life situations. Given the practical difficulties of re-designing the corpus and recording again, in this work we have investigated the use of model surgery techniques to replace the problematic HSMM states by those of a French voice. After model surgery, the voice has been re-evaluated by native listeners and slight but solid improvements have been found in terms of subjective preference. This can be seen as a confirmation that model surgery is useful when the effects of bad acoustic modeling are localized in a few states, regardless of the cause.

The remainder of this paper is structured as follows. Section 2 gives a brief overview of how the initial Basque synthetic voice was created. Section 3 describes the proposed model surgery. Section 4 presents the evaluation experiments and discusses the results. Finally, conclusions are drawn in Sect. 5.

## 2    Navarro-Lapurdian Basque TTS

A corpus was designed by automatically selecting 4000 short sentences (<15 words) from 90 MB of plain text collected from different books and magazines. The selection criterion was maximizing the diphone coverage after having filtered sentences containing anomalous or foreign words. Under the assumption that French words were far less frequent than Basque ones, only the last 200 sentences of the corpus (2.5 %) were explicitly forced to contain French words so as to ensure a minimal representation of French-specific phones (see Table 1). The final set of sentences was recorded by a semi-professional female speaker in a radio studio. The synthetic voice was trained using HTS v2.2 for modeling, Ahocoder [14] for acoustic feature extraction ($\log f_0$, Mel-cepstral coefficients and maximum voiced frequency), and a Basque/French front-end [13] based on AhoTTS [15,16] for text-to-label conversion.

In practice, it turns out that speakers of this Basque dialect are clearly bilingual and they tend to use a high percentage of French words in daily conversations, mostly proper nouns of people, cities, streets, etc. The same applies to TTS users. Therefore, the phonetic coverage in the initial corpus proved inadequate. In particular, the following French phones were under-represented (see Table 1) and poorly modeled:

- Nasal vowels: /a~/ ("**vent**"), /e~/ ("**vin**"), /o~/ ("**bon**").
- Front-rounded vowels: /y/ ("**dur**"), /2/ ("**deux**").
- Voiced fricatives: /v/ ("**vent**"), /z/ ("**zone**"), /Z/ ("**gens**").

The cost of re-designing the corpus and recording again motivated our research on surgery techniques.

**Table 1.** Number of instances of several phones in the corpus. A high contrast can be observed between phones that are common to French and Basque and those specific from French.

|  |  | Common phones |  | French phones |
|---|---|---|---|---|
| Vowels | /a/ | 37364 | /a~/ | 107 |
|  | /e/ | 29438 | /e~/ | 49 |
|  | /i/ | 17659 | /o~/ | 20 |
|  | /o/ | 12469 | /y/ | 55 |
|  | /u/ | 9863 | /2/ | 43 |
| Voiced fricatives | /B/ | 4342 | /v/ | 36 |
|  | /D/ | 3004 | /z/ | 40 |
|  | /G/ | 4177 | /Z/ | 80 |

## 3   Repairing the Voice via Model Surgery

The goal is to replace the states of the mentioned phones by those of a high-quality French voice. In this study we focused exclusively on the Mel-cepstral part of the models, assuming a correct modeling of both $\log f_0$ and the maximum voiced frequency. The surgery process consisted of three steps: (i) train a new voice model in French using a standard French database; (ii) identify the problematic HSMM states of the Basque voice and their corresponding couterparts in the French voice; (iii) transplant the French states to the Basque voice after compensating for the differences between speakers.

### 3.1   Training of the French Voice

The very first step should have been the selection of a *compatible* donor, i.e. a French speaker that can be acoustically converted into the original Basque speaker with high accuracy and quality. In this case, however, given the quality requirements, we just selected a French voice of the same gender as the original one (female) and with roughly similar acoustic properties. The French database, provided by Acapela Group, contained 1359 phonetically-balanced utterances digitized at 16 kHz sampling frequency (see [17] for details). As shown in Table 2, despite its relatively small size, this database contained a much larger number of instances of the problematic phones than the original one in Basque.

**Table 2.** Number of instances of French-specific phones in the French database in comparison with the Basque database.

| DB | /a~/ | /e~/ | /o~/ | /y/ | /2/ | /v/ | /z/ | /Z/ |
|---|---|---|---|---|---|---|---|---|
| Basque | 107 | 49 | 20 | 55 | 43 | 36 | 40 | 80 |
| French | 1427 | 573 | 905 | 999 | 685 | 965 | 828 | 642 |

In order to train the voice model, text was converted into labels using the eLite-HTS tool [18]. No special care was taken regarding the format of the labels, since the only information needed was the acoustic (Mcel-cepstral) part of the model and the phoneset. As for the acoustic analysis, we used exactly the same vocoder as in the Basque voice, namely Ahocoder [14], to ensure Mel-cepstral compatibility between models.

### 3.2   Identification of the Problematic HSMM States

Since the two voices had been trained using different front-ends, the phonetic symbols were slightly different. Therefore, it was necessary to establish a symbol-to-symbol correspondence between phonesets. Next, we had to locate which states of the two voice models were linked to the problematic phones. We considered two possible ways of doing this:

- By inspecting the phonetic questions applied at intermediate tree nodes of the model.
- By calculating, using the training labels and the voice models, a table of correspondences between phones and states.

By comparing these two approaches, we found that the second one reduces significantly the number of phone-state combinations. In other words, some of the combinations allowed by the model's phonetic questions never happen in practice. One more advantage of the second approach is that it allows obtaining not only the list of states that correspond to a given phone, but also the number of times this combination occurs.

While looking for the phone-state correspondence in the original voice, we found that some states were shared by both problematic and *healthy* phones. To avoid altering the healthy ones during surgery, we split each of these states into two sub-states by inserting an artificial intermediate node with question "Is the current phoneme /X/?", where /X/ denotes the problematic phone under consideration (see Fig. 2). Only the replica on the "yes" side was later considered for surgery.

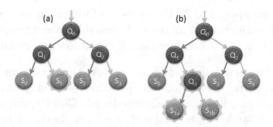

**Fig. 2.** Artificial state splitting to avoid undesired phoneticmodifications. Q: questions with "yes" (red arrow) or "no" (green arrow) answer; S: HSMM states. (a) State $S_1$ cannot be modified directly because it also corresponds to phones other than the problematic one; (b) Two copies of $S_1$ are created, one for healthy phones ($S_{1a}$), which will not be modified, and one for the problematic phone ($S_{1b}$), which will undergo surgery; the phonetic distinction is made by means of $Q_3$. (Color figure online)

## 3.3   Acoustic Conversion and Transplant

Before replacing the original problematic states by those of the donor, it is necessary to transform the voice of the donor to minimize its acoustic distance with respect to the original speaker's voice. Otherwise, listeners may perceive the resulting synthetic speech as uttered by two different speakers. The transformation proposed in this article is a linear projection of the acoustic space conveyed by the Gaussian state emission distributions. Assuming $D$-dimensional Mel-cepstral vectors, this transform can be formulated as

$$\boldsymbol{\mu}' = \bar{\mathbf{A}}\boldsymbol{\mu} + \bar{\mathbf{b}}, \quad \boldsymbol{\Sigma}' = \bar{\mathbf{A}}\boldsymbol{\Sigma}\bar{\mathbf{A}}^\top, \quad \bar{\mathbf{A}} = \begin{bmatrix} \mathbf{A} & 0 & 0 \\ 0 & \mathbf{A} & 0 \\ 0 & 0 & \mathbf{A} \end{bmatrix}, \quad \bar{\mathbf{b}} = \begin{bmatrix} \mathbf{b} \\ 0 \\ 0 \end{bmatrix} \tag{1}$$

where $\mu$ and $\Sigma$ are the original mean vector and covariance matrix of the Gaussian distribution (as 1st and 2nd order derivatives are considered for modeling, their dimensions are $3D \times 1$ and $3D \times 3D$ respectively), $\mu'$ and $\Sigma'$ are their converted counterparts, and $\mathbf{A}$ and $\mathbf{b}$ are the $D \times D$ matrix and $D \times 1$ vector that minimize the error of the transformation.

After studying and comparing different ways of calculating $\mathbf{A}$ and $\mathbf{b}$, we followed the same approach as in [19]. Given the source (French) and target (Basque) sets of Gaussian distributions belonging to the same phone (note each set may contain a different amount of distributions), we considered only the static part (first $D$ elements) of the mean vectors and ignored the covariance matrices. Then, we paired the source and target vectors, allowing repetitions when necessary, by means of the INCA algorithm. This algorithm, originally proposed in [20] and slightly modified in [19], has been shown to provide a good match between acoustic vectors from different speakers, also in a cross-lingual context. Denoting the resulting vector pairs as $\{\mathbf{x}_n, \mathbf{y}_n\}$, $\mathbf{A}$ and $\mathbf{b}$ were calculated as

$$\{\mathbf{A}, \mathbf{b}\} = \arg\min \sum_n \|\mathbf{A}\mathbf{x}_n + \mathbf{b} - \mathbf{y}_n\|^2 \tag{2}$$

If no constraints are imposed to $\mathbf{A}$, the number of unknowns is $D \times (D+1)$, which is large in relation to the typical amount of available paired training vectors. We studied two possible ways of tackling this ill-conditioning problem:

- Limiting the number of diagonal bands of $\mathbf{A}$, thus reducing the number of unknowns. As cepstral coefficients are quite independent from each other, the number of bands can be significantly reduced. Good empirical results were obtained using 9 bands (main diagonal band + 4 above + 4 below).
- Imposing physical constraints to $\mathbf{A}$. By forcing $\mathbf{A}$ to have a physical meaning, namely a warping of the frequency scale [21], it can be robustly estimated from a few data via dynamic frequency warping (DFW) [22]. Thus, the bias term $\mathbf{b}$ can be seen as an amplitude scaling (AS) filter [23]. This transform, referred to as DFWAS, entails almost no quality degradation when trained properly. In this work we used the cepstral-domain DFWAS implementation proposed in [24].

The relative performance of these two approaches is discussed in Sect. 4. The next question is how many transforms we should train and from which specific data. Obviously, it is not adequate to use the problematic states of the Basque voice as target when training a transform; otherwise, the French voice's states would get projected onto the poorly modeled space we try to avoid. Hence, the transforms must be trained from healthy states of both the Basque and the French voice, and we should be able to extrapolate them to states (phones) unseen during training. Even more, it is convenient to train a single global transform which is likely to generalize well. We studied three different training strategies that differ from each other in the training data:

- *All phones*: all the states of the two voice models were considered for training.
- *Common phones*: only the states associated with phones common to both languages were considered.
- *Common vowels*: similar to the previous strategy but restricted to vowels (as reported in [25], this strategy works well when a DFWAS transform is used).

In the three cases, source and target states were translated into vectors, vectors were aligned via INCA, a linear transform $\{A, b\}$ (either unconstrained or DFWAS) was learned through Eq. (2), the transform was applied to the French counterparts of the problematic Basque states through Eq. (1), and finally the acoustically-converted French states were directly transplanted onto the Basque voice model.

## 4    Evaluation and Discussion

Informal listening tests confirmed that direct transplant without acoustic conversion was not convenient at all, as the identity of the French speaker was easily perceived behind the problematic phones of the Basque utterances. By contrast, the fusion was successful when a global linear conversion was applied before state transplant, regardless of the conversion technique. As there was no obvious way to establish an objective measure for validation, we conducted some more informal listening tests to compare the three training strategies proposed in Sect. 3.3. Using only the common phones to train the conversion function resulted in better results than using all of them, whereas the differences between using all the common phones and using only vowels were hardly perceptible. Given the very subtle differences between the last two methods and the lack of an adequate objective criterion, we finally selected the common-vowels approach because it was computationally lighter. As for the type of transform, we observed that the DFWAS transform gave good results for the involved voices while exhibiting more numerical robustness than generic linear transforms with no ad-hoc tuning. We would like to remark that this configuration was found to be adequate for the two specific voices under study; other pairs of voices may require unconstrained linear transforms for a more accurate conversion.

For the selected configuration, we evaluated the *repaired* Basque voice by means of formal subjective listening tests. Two aspects could have been considered for evaluation: the quality and the similarity with respect to the original speaker. However, the evaluation of similarity would have been difficult in the described context as there were very few recordings of the problematic phones from the original speaker to compare with. From a different point of view, the general goal of this work was to obtain a good dialectal Basque voice. Therefore, we decided to carry out a preference test in which the baseline synthetic voice was compared with its post-surgery version. As the modifications are concentrated in a few specific phones (/a~/, /e~/, /o~/, /y/, /2/, /v/, /z/, /Z/), we designed a set of 40 test sentences with only one problematic phone at a time, and we explicitly asked the listeners to focus their attention on that phone (it was easy to identify because it was present exclusively in French words).

A total of 10 volunteer listeners were asked to listen to 24 randomly-selected and randomly-sorted pairs of synthetic utterances {A,B} and rate their preference in a 5-point scale: "Strong preference for A", "Slight preference for A", "No preference", "Slight preference for B", "Strong preference for B". To analyze the results, the listeners' ratings were converted into integer numeric scores between -2 (strong preference for the baseline voice) and +2 (strong preference for the repaired voice), and average scores were calculated for each problematic phone. A global average score was calculated as well. All the listeners were native speakers of the Basque dialect under study and also of French, as we had observed it was really hard for non-native speakers to perceive any difference between the two voices.

Figure 3 shows the resulting mean scores together with their 95 % confidence intervals. Notably, a slight preference towards the repaired voice can be seen for all the problematic phones. Although the preference is not statistically significant in some cases, which was expected because the perceptual effects of surgery are subtle and very localized, the trend is consistent in all of them. The surgery seems to be more effective in voiced fricatives than in vowels. This is possibly not only due to the surgery itself but also to the fact that fricatives were even more poorly modeled than vowels in the baseline voice. A more detailed analysis of the scores indicates that the repaired voice was preferred by the listeners about 31 % of the times, whereas the "No preference" option was selected 58 % of the times. This is a good indicator of how subtle the variations are. Indeed, the global average score is closer to "no preference" (0) than to "slight preference" (1). Nevertheless, the statistical significance of the global average score allows stating that the repaired voice is better than the original one in dealing with French words.

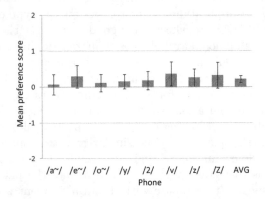

**Fig. 3.** Evaluation results: mean preference scores and 95 % confidence intervals. Scale: $+2/-2 =$ strong preference for repaired/original voice; $+1/-1$: slight preference for repaired/original voice; 0: no preference. AVG: average score.

Beyond the reasons that motivated the present work, i.e. poor statistical modeling due to data scarcity, we have shown that model surgery is feasible and can improve the perceptual quality of the synthetic speech for specific phones. In the authors' opinion, this is relevant in relation to speaking aids and voice banking. In the case of patients suffering dysarthria, for instance, model surgery techniques like those presented in this article can improve the pronunciation of specific phonemes that cannot be well articulated by the speaker. Note that the proposed techniques can be used to replace specific phones, not only specific acoustic feature streams as in [12]. Moreover, the linear transform required to reduce the contrast between the donor and the original speaker can be trained from vowels, which are easier to articulate. A more ambitious goal would be to adapt the whole donor's voice to the identity of the patient just from a few *healthy* sustained vowels (a preliminary work in this direction was presented in [25]). In such a context, a voice bank [9] would play the invaluable role of facilitating the search and selection of an acoustically compatible donor. We think it is also possible to develop automatic methods to get objective speaker compatibility scores, just by checking how similar are the original speaker's spectra and the donor's transformed spectra for well-modeled phones. Before concluding, it is worth remarking that the techniques proposed in this paper are possible thanks to the *phonetically-clustered* structure of the HSMMs, while it would be more difficult to formulate them in modern deep learning frameworks.

## 5  Conclusions

We have shown that it is possible to improve the pronunciation of some phones by an HMM-based speech synthesizer by means of model surgery techniques. The Mel-cepstral feature distribution of the HSMM states that correspond to that phone can be transplanted from a different voice model trained with the same vocoder. To ensure a proper acoustic match, we have used a global linear transform that compensates for the differences between speakers. Perceptual tests reveal a slight preference for the repaired synthetic voice when compared with the original one.

**Acknowledgements.** This work has been partially funded by the Spanish Ministry of Economy and Competitiveness (RESTORE project, TEC2015-67163-C2-1-R MINECO/FEDER, UE) and the Basque Government (ELKAROLA project, KK-2015/00098). The research stay of A. Pierard at UPV/EHU was funded by the Erasmus program. The French database used in this study was generously provided by Acapela Group. We thank B. Picart for his help.

## References

1. Zen, H., Tokuda, K., Black, A.: Statistical parametric speech synthesis. Speech Commun. **51**(11), 1039–1064 (2009)
2. Hunt, A.J., Black, A.W.: Unit selection in a concatenative speech synthesis system using a large speech database. In: Proceedings of ICASSP, pp. 373–376 (1996)

3. Yamagishi, J., Nose, T., Zen, H., Ling, Z.H., Toda, T., Tokuda, K., King, S., Renals, S.: Robust speaker-adaptive HMM-based text-to-speech synthesis. IEEE Trans. Audio Speech Lang. Process. **17**(6), 1208–1230 (2009)
4. Zen, H., Braunschweiler, N., Buchholz, S., Gales, M.J.F., Knill, K., Krstulovic, S., Latorre, J.: Statistical parametric speech synthesis based on speaker and language factorization. IEEE Trans. Audio Speech Lang. Process. **20**(6), 1713–1724 (2012)
5. Obin, N., Lanchantin, P., Lacheret, A., Rodet, X.: Discrete/continuous modelling of speaking style in HMM-based speech synthesis: design and evaluation. In: Proceedings of Interspeech, pp. 2785–2788 (2011)
6. Barra-Chicote, R., Yamagishi, J., King, S., Montero, J.M., Macias-Guarasa, J.: Analysis of statistical parametric and unit selection speech synthesis systems applied to emotional speech. Speech Commun. **52**(5), 394–404 (2010)
7. Zen, H., Tokuda, K., Masuko, T., Kobayashi, T., Kitamura, T.: A hidden semi-Markov model-based speech synthesis system. IEICE Trans. Inf. Syst. **E90–D**(5), 825–834 (2007)
8. Yamagishi, J., Veaux, C., King, S., Renals, S.: Speech synthesis technologies for individuals with vocal disabilities: voice banking and reconstruction. Acoust. Sci. Technol. **33**(1), 1–5 (2012)
9. Erro, D., Hernáez, I., Navas, E., Alonso, A., Arzelus, H., Jauk, I., Hy, N.Q., Magariños, C., Pérez-Ramón, R., Sulír, M., Tian, X., Wang, X., Ye, J.: ZureTTS: online platform for obtaining personalized synthetic voices. In: Proceedings of eNTERFACE 2014 (2014)
10. Erro, D., Hernaez, I., Alonso, A., Garcia-Lorenzo, D., Navas, E., Ye, J., Arzelus, H., Jauk, I., Hy, N., Magariños, C., Perez-Ramon, R., Sulir, M., Tian, X., Wang, X.: Personalized synthetic voices for speaking impaired: website and app. In: Proceedings of Interspeech (2015)
11. Creer, S., Cunningham, S., Green, P., Yamagishi, J.: Building personalised synthetic voices for individuals with severe speech impairment. Comput. Speech Lang. **27**(6), 1178–1193 (2013)
12. Veaux, C., Yamagishi, J., King, S.: Towards personalized synthesized voices for individuals with vocal disabilities: voice banking and reconstruction. In: Proceeding of SLPAT, pp. 107–111 (2013)
13. Navas, E., Hernaez, I., Erro, D., Salaberria, J., Oyharçabal, B., Padilla, M.: Developing a Basque TTS for the Navarro-Lapurdian dialect. In: Navarro Mesa, J.L., Ortega, A., Teixeira, A., Hernández Pérez, E., Quintana Morales, P., Ravelo García, A., Guerra Moreno, I., Toledano, D.T. (eds.) IberSPEECH 2014. LNCS (LNAI), vol. 8854, pp. 11–20. Springer, Heidelberg (2014). doi:10.1007/978-3-319-13623-3_2
14. Erro, D., Sainz, I., Navas, E., Hernáez, I.: Harmonics plus noise model based vocoder for statistical parametric speech synthesis. IEEE J. Sel. Top. Sig. Process. **8**(2), 184–194 (2014)
15. Sainz, I., Erro, D., Navas, E., Hernáez, I., Sánchez, J., Saratxaga, I., Odriozola, I., Luengo, I.: Aholab speech synthesizers for albayzin2010. In: Proceedings of FALA 2010, pp. 343–348 (2010)
16. Erro, D., Sainz, I., Luengo, I., Odriozola, I., Sánchez, J., Saratxaga, I., Navas, E., Hernáez, I.: HMM-based speech synthesis in Basque language using HTS. In: Proceedings of FALA, pp. 67–70 (2010)
17. Picart, B.: Statistical parametric speech synthesis based on the degree of articulation. Ph.D. thesis, Faculté Polytechnique, University of Mons (2013)

18. Roekhaut, S., Brognaux, S., Beaufort, R., Dutoit, T.: eLite-HTS: a NLP tool for French HMM-based speech synthesis. In: Proceedings of Interspeech, pp. 2136–2137 (2014)
19. Magariños, C., Erro, D., Rodriguez-Banga, E.: Language-independent acoustic cloning of HTS voices: a preliminary study. In: Proceedings of ICASSP, pp. 5615–5619 (2016)
20. Erro, D., Moreno, A., Bonafonte, A.: INCA algorithm for training voice conversion systems from nonparallel corpora. IEEE Trans. Audio Speech Lang. Process. 18(5), 944–953 (2010)
21. Pitz, M., Ney, H.: Vocal tract normalization equals linear transformation in cepstral space. IEEE Trans. Speech. Audio Process. 13, 930–944 (2005)
22. Valbret, H., Moulines, E., Tubach, J.: Voice transformation using PSOLA technique. Speech Commun. 11(2–3), 175–187 (1992)
23. Erro, D., Navas, E., Hernaez, I.: Parametric voice conversion based on bilinear frequency warping plus amplitude scaling. IEEE Trans. Audio Speech Lang. Process. 21(3), 556–566 (2013)
24. Zorilă, T.C., Erro, D., Hernaez, I.: Improving the quality of standard GMM-based voice conversion systems by considering physically motivated linear transformations. Commun. Comput. Inf. Sci. 328, 30–39 (2012)
25. Alonso, A., Erro, D., Navas, E., Hernaez, I.: Speaker adaptation using only vocalic segments via frequency warping. In: Proceedings of Interspeech (2015)

# Automatic Speech Recognition

# An Analysis of Deep Neural Networks in Broad Phonetic Classes for Noisy Speech Recognition

F. de-la-Calle-Silos$^{(\boxtimes)}$, A. Gallardo-Antolín, and C. Peláez-Moreno

Department of Signal Theory and Communications,
Universidad Carlos III de Madrid, Leganés (Madrid), Spain
fsilos@tsc.uc3m.es

**Abstract.** The introduction of Deep Neural Network (DNN) based acoustic models has produced dramatic improvements in performance. In particular, we have recently found that Deep Maxout Networks, a modification of DNNs' feed-forward architecture that uses a max-out activation function, provides enhanced robustness to environmental noise. In this paper we further investigate how these improvements are translated into the different broad phonetic classes and how does it compare to classical Hidden Markov Models (HMM) based back-ends. Our experiments demonstrate that performance is still tightly related to the particular phonetic class being *stops* and *affricates* the least resilient but also that relative improvements of both DNN variants are distributed unevenly across those classes having the type of noise a significant influence on the distribution. A combination of the different systems DNN and classical HMM is also proposed to validate our hypothesis that the traditional GMM/HMM systems have a different type of error than the Deep Neural Networks hybrid models.

**Keywords:** Noise robustness · Deep Neural Networks · Dropout · Deep Maxout Networks · Speech recognition · Deep learning

## 1 Introduction

Machine performance in Automatic Speech Recognition (ASR) tasks is still far away from that of humans, and noisy conditions only compound the problem. The last years have witnessed an important leap in performance with the introduction of new acoustic models based on Deep Neural Networks (DNNs) [3,9]. Nevertheless, the performance of these kind of ASR systems in noisy conditions has not yet been fully assessed.

Deep Neural Networks can be applied both in the so-called *tandem* [17] and *hybrid* [16] architectures. In the first case, DNNs can be trained to generate bottleneck features which are fed to a conventional GMM-HMM back-end. In the second, DNNs are employed for acoustic modeling by replacing the GMMs into an HMM system. In this paper we adopt a DNNs hybrid configuration.

DNN-HMM hybrid systems combine several features that make them superior to previous Artificial Neural Network (ANN)-HMM hybrid systems [13]:

© Springer International Publishing AG 2016
A. Abad et al. (Eds.): IberSPEECH 2016, LNAI 10077, pp. 87–96, 2016.
DOI: 10.1007/978-3-319-49169-1_9

(a) DNNs have a larger number of hidden layers leading to systems with many more parameters than the later. As a result, these models are less influenced by the mismatch between training and testing data but can easily suffer from overfitting if the training set is not big enough, (b) the network usually models senones (tied states) directly (although there might be thousands of senones), and (c) long context windows are used. Although conventional ANNs also take into account longer context windows than HMMs or are able to model senones, the key to the success of the DNN-HMM is the combination of these components. DNN-HMM systems with these properties are often named Context-Dependent Deep Neural Network HMM (CD-DNN-HMM).

However, the most remarkable difference with traditional neural networks is that a *pre-training* stage is needed to reduce the chance that the error back-propagation algorithm employed for training falls into a poor local minimum. Besides, some recent methods have been proposed to avoid overfitting and improve the accuracy of the networks, as for example, dropout [10] which randomly omits hidden units in the training stage. Another related technique is the so-called Deep Maxout Networks (DMNs) [7] that split the hidden units at each layer into non-overlapping groups, each of them generating an activation using a max pooling operation. This way, DMNs reduce the size of the parameter space significantly making it very suited for ASR tasks where the training sets and input and output dimensions are normally quite large. For this reason, DMNs have been employed in low-resources speech recognition devices [15] among others [21].

We hypothesized that DMNs could improve recognition rates in noisy conditions given that they were capable to more effectively model speech variability from limited data [2]. Still, the number of research works that evaluate performance of DNNs in noisy conditions is small. Notably, [20] applies DNNs with dropout on the Aurora 4 dataset with encouraging results. Up to our knowledge, [2] is the first attempt of using Deep Maxout Networks in combination with dropout strategies in a noisy speech recognition task showing a substantial increment of the recognition accuracy over DNNs and other traditional HMM-based techniques. In this paper, we improve the results of our previous work and also present an error analysis in broad phonetic classes to try to gain some insight into the behaviour of the different systems.

Thought an analysis of errors in broad phonetic classes for noisy speech recognition has not been performed in depth with DNNs systems, similar studies have been carried out in order to compare the performance of recognizers based on other different techniques. In this context, it is worth mentioning the work in [4] that claims that the error structure produced by traditional HMM, on the one hand and Hidden Trajectory Model (HTM) on the other, is different. The aim of this study is to determine whether the performance improvements achieved by the HTM-based system is restricted to certain classes of phones or is spread over the classes. In particular, the performance comparisons are made considering six broad phonetic classes: *vowels, semivowels, nasals consonants, fricative consonants, affricates consonants, and stop closures and silence segments.*

The main conclusion was that the improvements are more significant in *sonorants (vowels, semivowels, nasals)*, followed by *stops*, whereas no improvement is observed in *fricatives*.

The remainder of this paper is organized as follows: Section 2 introduces deep neural networks and the hybrid automatic speech recognition architecture, and dropout and maxout methods. Our results and the analysis in broad phonetic classes are presented Sects. 3 and 4, respectively. Section 5 contains the experimental results achieved by the combination of different systems, followed by some conclusions and further lines of research in Sect. 6.

## 2   Deep Neural Networks and Hybrid Speech Recognition Systems

A Deep Neural Network (DNN) is a Multi-Layer Perceptron (MLP) with a larger number of hidden layers between its inputs and outputs, whose weights are fully connected and are often initialized using an unsupervised pre-training scheme.

As a traditional MLP, the feed-forward architecture can be computed as follows:

$$\mathbf{h}^{(l+1)} = \sigma \left( \mathbf{W}^{(l)} \mathbf{h}^{(l)} + \mathbf{b}^{(l)} \right), \quad 1 \leq l \leq L \tag{1}$$

where $\mathbf{h}^{(l+1)}$ is the vector of inputs to the $l+1$ layer, $\sigma(x) = (1 + e^{-x})^{-1}$ is the sigmoid activation function, $L$ is the total number of hidden layers, $\mathbf{h}^{(l)}$ is the output vector of the hidden layer $l$ and $\mathbf{W}^{(l)}$ and $\mathbf{b}^{(l)}$ are the weight matrix and bias vector of layer $l$, respectively.

Training a DNN using the well-known error back-propagation (BP) algorithm with a random initialization of its weight matrices may not provide a good performance as it may become stuck in a local minimum. To overcome this problem, DNN parameters are often initialized using an unsupervised technique as Restricted Bolzmann Machines (RBMs) [8] or Stacked Denoising Autoencoders (SDAs) [22].

### 2.1   Hybrid Speech Recognition Systems

In a hybrid DNN/HMM system, just as in classical ANN/HMM hybrids [1], a DNN is trained to classify the input acoustic features into classes corresponding to the states of HMMs, in such a way that the state emission likelihoods usually computed with GMM are replaced by the likelihoods generated by the DNN.

The DNN estimates the posterior probability $p(s|\mathbf{o}_t)$ of each state $s$ given the observation $\mathbf{o}_t$ at time $t$, through a softmax final layer:

$$p(s|\mathbf{o}_t) = \frac{\exp \left( \mathbf{W}^{(L)} \mathbf{h}^{(L)} + \mathbf{b}^{(L)} \right)}{\sum_{\bar{s}} \exp \left( \mathbf{W}^{(L)} \mathbf{h}^{(L)} + \mathbf{b}^{(L)} \right)}. \tag{2}$$

In a hybrid ASR system, the HMM topology is set from a previously trained GMM-HMM, and the DNN training data come from the forced-alignment between the state-level transcripts and the corresponding speech signals obtained by using this initial GMM-HMM system. In the recognition stage, the DNN estimates the emission probability of each HMM state. To obtain the state emission likelihoods $p(\mathbf{o}_t|s)$, the Bayes rule is used, and the $p(s|\mathbf{o}_t)$ estimated by the DNN is scaled by the class prior, $p(s)$, which can be estimated by counting the occurrences of each state on the training data.

## 2.2 Dropout and Maxout Deep Neural Network

The most important problem to overcome in DNN training is overfitting. Normally this problem arises when we try to train a large DNN with a small training set. A training method called *dropout* proposed in [10] tries to reduce overfitting and improves the generalization capability of the network by randomly omitting a certain percentage of the hidden units on each training iteration.

When dropout is employed, the activation function of Eq. (1) can be rewritten as:

$$\mathbf{h}^{(l+1)} = m^{(l+1)} \star \sigma \left( \mathbf{W}^{(l)} \mathbf{h}^{(l)} + \mathbf{b}^{(l)} \right), \quad 1 \leq l \leq L \tag{3}$$

where $\star$ denotes the element-wise product, $m^{(l+1)}$ is a binary vector of the same dimension of $\mathbf{h}^{(l+1)}$ whose elements are sampled from a Bernoulli distribution with probability $p$. This probability is the so called *Hidden Drop Factor (HDF)* and must be determined over a validation set as it will be seen in Sect. 3.

Dropout has already successfully tested on noise robust ASR in [20]. Its benefits come from the improved generalization abilities attained by reducing the DNNs expressivity. Another interpretation of the behaviour of dropout is that in the training stage it adds random noise to the training set resulting in a network that is very robust to variabilities in the inputs (in our particular case, due to the addition of noise).

A Maxout Deep Neural Network (DMN) [7] is a modification of the feed-forward architecture (Eq. (1)) where the maxout activation function is employed. The maxout unit simply takes the maximum over a set of inputs. In a DMN each hidden unit takes the maximum value over the $g$ units of a group. The output of the hidden node $i$ of the layer $l+1$ can be computed as follows:

$$h_i^{(l+1)} = \max_{j \in 1,\dots,g} z_{ij}^{(l+1)}, \quad 1 \leq l \leq L \tag{4}$$

where $z_{ij}^{(l+1)}$ are the linear pre-activation values from the $l$ layer:

$$\mathbf{z}^{(l+1)} = \mathbf{W}^{(l)} \mathbf{h}^{(l)} + \mathbf{b}^{(l)} \tag{5}$$

As can be observed the max-pooling operation is applied over the $\mathbf{z}^{(l+1)}$ vector. Note that DMNs fairly reduce the number of parameters over DNNs, as the weight matrix $\mathbf{W}^{(l)}$ of each layer in the DMN is $1/g$ of the size of its equivalent DNN weight matrix. This makes DMN more convenient for ASR tasks where the training sets and the input and output dimensions are normally very large.

In [7] a demonstration of the capability of maxout units to approximate any convex function by tuning the weights of the previous layers is included. For this matter, the shapes of activation functions are not fixed allowing the DMNs to model the variability of speech more smoothly. DMNs are commonly applied in conjunction with dropout reducing overfitting and improving the model generalization.

## 3 Experiments

Our experiments for evaluating and comparing the performance of conventional GMM-HMM and the different hybrid deep neural networks-based ASR systems on the TIMIT corpus [6] are presented below. In particular, we used the 462 speaker training set, a development set of 50 speakers to tune all the parameters and finally the 24 speakers core test set. Each utterance is recorded at 16 kHz and the corpus includes time-aligned phonetic transcriptions allowing as to give results in terms of Phone Error Rate (PER).

To test the robustness of the different methods we added four different types of noises (white, street, music and speaker) at four different SNRs using the FANT tool [11] (with G.712 filtering) to the clean speech database. These noises are the ones used in [12]. All the noisy tests are evaluated in mismatch conditions (i.e. training with clean conditions and testing on noisy speech).

On the technical side we employed the Kaldi toolkit [19] for implementing the traditional GMM-HMM ASR system and the PDNN toolkit [14] for the hybrid DNN-based ASR systems.

In all the cases, the input features were 12th-order MFCCs plus a log-energy coefficient, and their corresponding first and second order derivatives yielding a 39 component feature vector. Mean and variance normalization on each of the components was applied. A context of 5 frames was chosen for the hybrid models. All the hybrid systems were trained with the labels generated from the best performance GMM-HMM system through forced alignment.

First, we tuned the configuration parameters of the networks (number of hidden layers, HDF, group size and momentum when applicable) under clean conditions on the dev set. The way in which these parameters are tuned, the fine-tuning of the momentum and the correct selection of the batch size are the main differences with respect to the previous results published at [2]. HDF and group size were validated on the development set considering 5 hidden layer networks, yielding an optimal dropout factor of 0.1 for dropout DNNs, 0.2 for DMNs and a group size of $g = 3$. These values of HDR and group size were used throughout the rest of the experiments. DMNs are always employed in conjunction with dropout. The number of hidden nodes in all of the DNNs is 1024. To be fair, we chose 400 hidden maxout units for the DMN since $400 \times 3 = 1200$ yields a number of parameters in the same order as the DNNs. After an exploration of the learning rates, for the networks without dropout the learning rate started at 0.08 for 30 epochs and was subsequently divided in half while the validation error decreased. For the dropout and DMNs networks we started with a higher learning rate of 0.1.

Second, we compared the baseline GMM-HMM-based systems (Monophone, Triphone, Triphone with Lineal Discriminant Analysis (LDA), Maximum Likelihood Lineal Transform (MLLT) and Speaker Adaptive Training (SAT)) with the best configuration of the different hybrid ASR systems under clean conditions. Results for the test set of the TIMIT dataset are shown in Table 1. As can be observed, the hybrid systems outperform the different versions of the baseline systems, in both development and test sets. DNNs with random initialization and pretraining achieve similar results but are outperformed by DNN with dropout and DMN, being DMN the technique that obtains the lowest PER.

**Table 1.** Recognition results in terms of PER(%) for the TIMIT development and core test sets in clean conditions.

| Method | Dev (PER %) | Eval (PER %) |
|---|---|---|
| Mono | 31.90 | 32.57 |
| Triphone | 24.70 | 26.68 |
| Triphone LDA + MLLT + SAT | 20.40 | 21.77 |
| DNN random | 19.80 | 21.25 |
| DNN pretrain | 19.17 | 20.69 |
| DNN pretrain + dropout | 18.49 | 19.46 |
| DMN | 17.73 | 18.54 |

Third, we tested the different systems in noisy conditions. Results achieved by the monophone baseline, the best triphone baseline (LDA + MLLT + SAT), the hybrid DNN with pre-training and dropout and DMN-based ASR systems in the noisy contaminated version of the TIMIT core test set are shown in Fig. 1 for the different types of noises and SNRs. Also Fig. 1 present results of different systems combinations explained in Sect. 5.

As can be seen, DMN performs better in almost every situation for all the noises in comparison to the other systems. It is specially remarkable the performance of DMN in music and speaker noises. For white noise, results obtained with DMN are very similar to those achieved by the DNN, but with a large relative error reduction with respect to Triphone + MLLT.

## 4    Analysis in Broad Phonetic Classes

The most important reason of the high impact of the DNN change of learning paradigm on ASR practitioners is its enhanced overall performance. However, it is worth investigating whether these new systems could be fused with the others to even obtain better robustness. For this to be true, the combined systems should individually present different error behaviors and strengths.

Figure 2 presents the accuracies of the systems of Sect. 3 split into broad phonetic classes as defined in [6] for an SNR of 15 dB. As can be observed, with

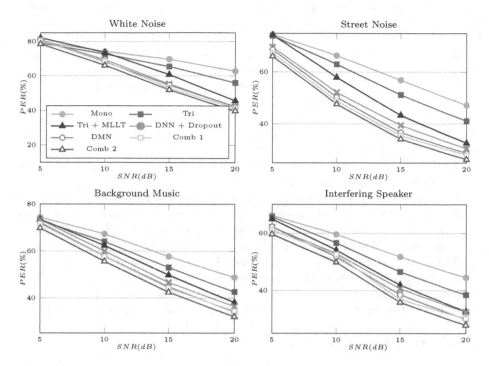

**Fig. 1.** Comparison of the performance of the different systems in terms of PER [%] for TIMIT test set in different noisy conditions.

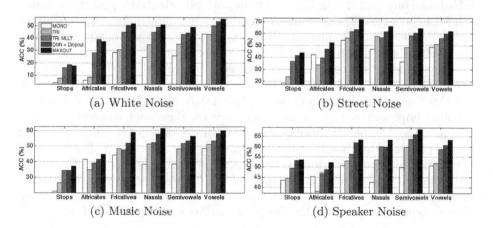

**Fig. 2.** Comparison of the performance in broad phonetic classes of the different systems in terms of PER [%] for TIMIT test set in different noisy conditions at 15 dB SNR.

very few exceptions, sorting the systems according to their performance within these classes leads to the same results than for the overall figures of Table 1 and Fig. 1.

In spite of the improvements of DNN and DMN based systems, performance is still significantly dependent on the phonetic classes, being *stops* and *affricates* the most difficult ones. In fact, it is on *affricates* where most of the aforementioned exceptions to the sorting of the systems according to their accuracies are accumulated. We hypothesize that the reduced number of instances of *affricates* in comparison with the rest causes this, somehow *erratic*, behaviour of the different systems in this class. This is not the case of *stops*, however, that match the performance ordering of the systems with a sole exception on white noise where DNNs are slightly better than DMNs.

For the four remaining phonetic classes, we can conclude that the improvements due to DNN and DMN learning algorithms are translated to all of them but not with the same intensity. The most benefited phonetic class is *fricatives* since the relative loss of the best HMM-based system from the best DNN-based (DMN) is the highest (13 % for white noise, 14 % for street, 19 % for music and 11 % for speaker). However, the type of noise is the most important factor that determines which of the phonetic classes is better in absolute terms (*vowels* in white noise, *fricatives* in street, *nasals* in music and *semivowels* in speaker).

## 5   System Combination

Given the results of the broad phonetic classes performed in Sect. 4, we hypothesize that the combination of the different systems can improve the recognition rates since the types of errors are different for each system.

We propose two combinations: (1) the DNN with dropout system plus the DMN-based one; and (2) the DNN with dropout plus the DMN plus the triphone with MLLT systems. The systems are fused by using the well-known Recognition Output Voting Error Reduction (ROVER) [5] by Average Confidence Scores. The results obtained can be seen in Fig. 1 where "Comb1" and "Comb2" refers to the first and second combinations proposed, respectively.

On the one hand, results show that the combination of DNN with dropout plus DMN provides better accuracies than DMN alone for all of the noises. Although improvements are small in some cases, they are consistent with our analysis where the performance is still significantly dependent on the phonetic classes. On the other hand, results achieved by the second combination show that the inclusion of the triphone-based ASR system improves the recognition rates obtained by the first combination and any of the other systems, supporting our hypothesis that the traditional GMM-HMM-based ASR systems produce different types of errors than the Deep Neural Networks hybrid models.

## 6   Conclusions and Future Work

In this paper Deep Maxout Networks (DMNs) are employed for robust speech recognition using a hybrid architecture showing a better performance over standard DNNs. This is due to the DMNs activation functions ability of modeling speech variability. An analysis of the errors that both HMM and DNN-based systems produce on broad phonetic classes has been presented concluding that differences in behaviours can be observed but that the type of noise is also determinant. There are also important sources of error variability that have not been explored in this paper, notably the feature extraction module. Finally, it has been shown that the combination of GMM-HMM and DNN-based systems improves the results in comparison to the individual ASR systems.

Further lines of research include testing the DMN in bigger datasets and with other novel machine learning techniques like drop-connect [23] on the one hand, and performing more detailed analysis of the confusion matrices using data-driven techniques [18], on the other.

**Acknowledgements.** This contribution has been supported by an Airbus Defense and Space Grant (Open Innovation - SAVIER) and Spanish Government-CICYT project TEC2014-53390-P. We would also like to thank Chanwoo Kim for kindly providing the testing noises.

# References

1. Bourlard, H., Morgan, N.: Connectionist Speech Recognition: A Hybrid Approach. Kluwer International Series in Engineering and Computer Science: VLSI, Computer Architecture, and Digital Signal Processing. Springer, New York (1994)
2. de-la-Calle-Silos, F., Gallardo-Antolín, A., Peláez-Moreno, C.: Deep maxout networks applied to noise-robust speech recognition. In: Navarro Mesa, J.L., Ortega, A., Teixeira, A., Hernández Pérez, E., Quintana Morales, P., Ravelo García, A., Guerra Moreno, I., Toledano, D.T. (eds.) IberSPEECH 2014. LNCS (LNAI), vol. 8854, pp. 109–118. Springer, Heidelberg (2014). doi:10.1007/978-3-319-13623-3_12
3. Dahl, G.E., Yu, D., Deng, L., Acero, A.: Context-dependent pre-trained deep neural networks for large-vocabulary speech recognition. IEEE Trans. Audio Speech Lang. Process. **20**(1), 30–42 (2012)
4. Deng, L., Yu, D., Acero, A.: Structured speech modeling. IEEE Trans. Audio Speech Lang. Process. **14**(5), 1492–1504 (2006)
5. Fiscus, J.G.: A post-processing system to yield reduced word error rates: recognizer output voting error reduction (ROVER). In: Proceedings of 1997 IEEE Workshop on Automatic Speech Recognition and Understanding, pp. 347–354, December 1997
6. Garofolo, J.S., Lamel, L.F., Fisher, W.M., Fiscus, J.G., Pallett, D.S., Dahlgren, N.L.: DARPA TIMIT acoustic phonetic continuous speech corpus CDROM (1993)
7. Goodfellow, I.J., Warde-Farley, D., Mirza, M., Courville, A., Bengio, Y.: Maxout networks. arXiv e-prints, February 2013
8. Hinton, G.E.. A practical guide to training restricted Boltzmann machines. In: Montavon, G., Orr, G.B., Müller, K.-R. (eds.) Neural Networks: Tricks of the Trade. LNCS, vol. 7700, 2nd edn, pp. 599–619. Springer, Heidelberg (2012). doi:10. 1007/978-3-642-35289-8_32
9. Hinton, G.E., Deng, L., Yu, D., Dahl, G.E., Mohamed, A., Jaitly, N., Senior, A., Vanhoucke, V., Nguyen, P., Sainath, T.N., Kingsbury, B.: Deep neural networks for acoustic modeling in speech recognition: the shared views of four research groups. IEEE Sig. Process. Mag. **29**(6), 82–97 (2012)

10. Hinton, G.E., Srivastava, N., Krizhevsky, A., Sutskever, I., Salakhutdinov, R.: Improving neural networks by preventing co-adaptation of feature detectors. CoRR (2012)
11. Hirsch, G.: Fant - filtering and noise adding tool (2005). http://dnt.kr.hsnr.de/download.html
12. Kim, C., Stern, R.M.: Power-normalized cepstral coefficients (PNCC) for robust speech recognition. IEEE/ACM Trans. Audio Speech Lang. Process. **24**(7), 1315–1329 (2016). doi:10.1109/TASLP.2016.2545928
13. Li, J., Deng, L., Gong, Y., Haeb-Umbach, R.: An overview of noise-robust automatic speech recognition. IEEE/ACM Trans. Audio Speech Lang. Process. **22**(4), 745–777 (2014)
14. Miao, Y.: Kaldi+PDNN: building DNN-based ASR systems with Kaldi and PDNN. CoRR (2014)
15. Miao, Y., Metze, F., Rawat, S.: Deep maxout networks for low-resource speech recognition. In: 2013 IEEE Workshop on Automatic Speech Recognition and Understanding, Olomouc, Czech Republic, 8–12 December 2013
16. Mohamed, A., Dahl, G.E., Hinton, G.E.: Acoustic modeling using deep belief networks. IEEE Trans. Audio Speech Lang. Process. **20**(1), 14–22 (2012)
17. Morgan, N.: Deep and wide: multiple layers in automatic speech recognition. IEEE Trans. Audio Speech Lang. Process. **20**(1), 7–13 (2012)
18. Peláez-Moreno, C., García-Moral, A.I., Valverde-Albacete, F.J.: Analyzing phonetic confusions using formal concept analysis. J. Acoust. Soc. Am. **128**(3), 1377–1390 (2010)
19. Povey, D., Ghoshal, A., Boulianne, G., Burget, L., Glembek, O., Goel, N., Hannemann, M., Motlicek, P., Qian, Y., Schwarz, P., Silovsky, J., Stemmer, G., Vesely, K.: The Kaldi speech recognition toolkit. In: IEEE 2011 Workshop on Automatic Speech Recognition and Understanding. IEEE Signal Processing Society, December 2011
20. Seltzer, M.L., Yu, D., Wang, Y.: An investigation of deep neural networks for noise robust speech recognition. In: IEEE International Conference on Acoustics, Speech, and Signal Processing (ICASSP) (2013)
21. Tóth, L.: Convolutional deep maxout networks for phone recognition. In: INTERSPEECH, pp. 1078–1082. ISCA (2014)
22. Vincent, P., Larochelle, H., Lajoie, I., Bengio, Y., Manzagol, P.A.: Stacked denoising autoencoders: learning useful representations in a deep network with a local denoising criterion. J. Mach. Learn. Res. **11**, 3371–3408 (2010)
23. Wan, L., Zeiler, M.D., Zhang, S., LeCun, Y., Fergus, R.: Regularization of neural networks using dropconnect. In: Proceedings of 30th International Conference on Machine Learning, ICML 2013, Atlanta, GA, USA, 16–21 June 2013

# Automatic Speech Recognition with Deep Neural Networks for Impaired Speech

Cristina España-Bonet[1,2]([✉]) and José A.R. Fonollosa[1]

[1] TALP Research Center, Universitat Politècnica de Catalunya, Barcelona, Spain
cristinae@cs.upc.edu, jose.fonollosa@upc.edu
[2] Universität des Saarlandes, Saarbrücken, Germany

**Abstract.** Automatic Speech Recognition has reached almost human performance in some controlled scenarios. However, recognition of impaired speech is a difficult task for two main reasons: data is (*i*) scarce and (*ii*) heterogeneous. In this work we train different architectures on a database of dysarthric speech. A comparison between architectures shows that, even with a small database, hybrid DNN-HMM models outperform classical GMM-HMM according to word error rate measures. A DNN is able to improve the recognition word error rate a 13 % for subjects with dysarthria with respect to the best classical architecture. This improvement is higher than the one given by other deep neural networks such as CNNs, TDNNs and LSTMs. All the experiments have been done with the Kaldi toolkit for speech recognition for which we have adapted several recipes to deal with dysarthric speech and work on the TORGO database. These recipes are publicly available.

**Keywords:** Speech recognition · Speaker adaptation · Deep learning · Neural networks · Dysarthria · Kaldi

## 1 Introduction

Automatic speech recognition (ASR) consists on automatically transcribing voice into text. It is not an easy task: one has do deal with noise, differences among speakers and spontaneous speech phenomena among others. For some controlled scenarios where one can minimise the effect of these phenomena, ASR approaches or exceeds the accuracy of humans on several benchmarks [2,19].

Despite the good performance of the recently proposed end to-end neural speech recognizers [2], Hidden Markov Models (HMM) are still the backbone of competitive speech recognition systems [19]. HMMs model speech signals with a sequence of states with an associated probability distribution for every observed vector. This probability can be represented using different approaches such as Gaussian mixture models (GMM) or artificial neural networks (ANN). In this work, we refer to the former systems as *classical architectures* and to the latter ones as *neural network architectures*.

© Springer International Publishing AG 2016
A. Abad et al. (Eds.): IberSPEECH 2016, LNAI 10077, pp. 97–107, 2016.
DOI: 10.1007/978-3-319-49169-1_10

Although in its infancy ANNs were not able to deal with long time-sequences of speech signal by themselves, hybrid systems ANN-HMM already showed to be state-of-the-art at the beginning of the 90s [24]. ANNs solve at least two problems with respect to GMMs [3]: (*i*) assumptions about the shape of the statistical distribution of input features are not required and (*ii*) all training data is used to train a state (an not only that aligned to that state). On the opposite, they need of larger computing capabilities especially for large vocabularies.

Currently, and due to the existence of huge computing capabilities, hybrid deep neural network architectures DNN-HMM have been able to improve significantly ASR with respect to GMM-HMM systems for large vocabulary tasks [4,8,21]. Increasing the number of neurons and hidden layers in the network improves the word error rate (WER) in the recognition. However, for sparse data—small data sets—such amount of parameters cannot be properly fit and performance diminishes [10].

When dealing with impaired speech, one must face the problems of data sparsity. Since gathering data is even more difficult in this case, few databases exist, and the ones that exist are small. Besides, differences among speakers are larger and databases tend to be more heterogeneous. This poses a problem for ANNs, but also for GMMs which are more sensitive to differences between training and test data.

Here, we study the performance of both classical and neural network architectures when training on a small database of speakers with dysanthria, the TORGO database [9]. We discuss the differences not only between classical and neural systems, but also the suitability of using speaker adaptation techniques in this case. All the systems are trained using the Kaldi Speech Recognition toolkit [15]. We have adapted several recipes in order to prepare the data, extract the features and train the systems[1].

The remaining of the paper is organized as follows. First, Sect. 2 describes the database we use for the experiments. Next, Sect. 3 introduces the main architecture of an ASR and the specific techniques and resources we use. Section 4 makes emphasis in the acoustic model module and presents the different recognition systems that are evaluated in this task. Finally, we discuss the results and draw the conclusions in Sects. 5 and 6 respectively.

## 2   The TORGO Database

Serveral speech disorders can alter the correct uttering of sounds. Speakers with dysarthria show difficulties to articulate phonemes due to a lesion in the nervous system. This may cause changes in voice quality, slow rate of speech or abnormal pitch and rhythm.

The TORGO database [9] contains speeches from 15 subjects, 6 females and 9 males. In total, the database contains about 3 h per speaker of recorded speech, and one third corresponds to impaired speech. Four speakers have severe dysanthria, one is moderately-to-severely dysanthric and one is moderately dysanthric.

---

[1] Recipes are publicly available at https://github.com/cristinae/ASRdys.

**Table 1.** Figures for the 15 speakers in the TORGO database ranked according to their degree of disorder

| Speaker | F01 | M01 | M02 | M04 | M05 | F03 | F04 | M03 |
|---|---|---|---|---|---|---|---|---|
| Degree | severe | severe | severe | severe | sev-mid | mid | mild | mild |
| #audios | 228 | 739 | 772 | 659 | 610 | 1097 | 675 | 806 |

| Speaker | FC01 | FC02 | FC03 | MC01 | MC02 | MC03 | MC04 |
|---|---|---|---|---|---|---|---|
| Degree | none | none | none | none | none | none | none |
| #audios | 296 | 2183 | 1924 | 2141 | 1112 | 1661 | 1614 |

Two other subjects have very mild dysanthria and the remaining 7 subjects are control speakers without any disorder. Table 1 describes the 15 subjects and includes the number of audios available in the database. For most of the utterances we use both, the audio obtained with a head-mounted microphone and the one obtained with a directional microphone.

Using the two microphones, we have 5586 utterances for speakers with dysanthria (a mean of 698 per speaker) and 10931 utterances for control speakers (a mean of 1562). An utterance can be a single word or a sentence, and the mean of words per utterance is of 3.5.

## 3 System's Architecture

All the systems described in the following sections share a common main architecture with four modules: (*i*) feature extraction, (*ii*) acoustic modeling, (*iii*) language modeling and (*iv*) pronunciation lexicon. Only feature extraction and acoustic modeling differ among systems.

### 3.1 Feature Extraction

As basic acoustic features we use 13 Mel-frequency cepstral coefficients (MFCCs). The features are generated in 25 ms windows shifted by 10 ms for the control speakers and 15 ms for dysanthric speech. This configuration for dysanthric speakers was shown to be adequate in Ref. [9]. As explained in Sect. 2, this disorder can make speakers talk slower and widening the shift between consecutive frames helps to homogenise the differences between patients and control speakers. For convolutional neural networks (CNN), we use 40 dimensional filterbank features in order to account for the correlations in the signal, estimated at the same window intervals.

Besides, in order to obtain more evolved speaker independent (SI) features, we apply a Linear Discriminative Analysis transformation (LDA) for projecting sequences of frames into 40 dimensions and, afterwards, a Maximum Likelihood Linear Transformation (MLLT) to diagonalise the matrix and gather the correlations among vectors [6]. For speaker dependent features (SD), we apply a feature-space Maximum Likelihood Linear Regression (fMLLR) [16]. In some cases, we also add 100-dimensional iVectors to gather specific information for every speaker and for the environment [5, 20].

## 3.2   Acoustic Modeling

In this work we use a monophone model and several standard three-state context dependent triphone models that differ on the features used, the training methodology and how the probability associated to each HMM state is calculated. Section 4 describes the main characteristics of the acoustic models used.

## 3.3   Language Modeling and Pronunciation Lexicon

The SRILM Toolkit [22] is used to build a standard 3-gram language model with interpolated Kneser-Ney discounting on the training data transcripts. For the lexicon, we choose the Carnegie Mellon University Pronouncing Dictionary[2] for North American English. It contains over 134,000 words and their pronunciations in the ARPAbet phoneme set with 39 phonemes.

# 4    Acoustic Modeling

Two types of models are distinguished in the following subsections: classical architectures GMM-HMM and hybrid neural network architectures DNN-HMM.

## 4.1   Classical Architectures

We study different variations on the nature of the features and the kind of training used in a standard GMM-HMM architecture. Below, we list the systems analysed in this work with their main characteristics. For an easy comparison, we also show for every system and between parentheses the nomenclature used in Kaldi. We have adapted Kaldi's recipes to fit our data, and trained 7 classical systems with 1800 HMM states and a total of 9000 Gaussians:

**MONO.** Monophone model with MFCC features (*mono*)
**TRI.** Basic triphone model with features MFCC+$\Delta$+$\Delta\Delta$ (*tri2a*)
**TRI-SI.** Triphone model with speaker-independent transformations applied MFCC+LDA+MLLT (*tri2b*)
**TRI-SD.** Triphone model with speaker-dependent transformations added MFCC+LDA+MLLT+fMLLR (*tri3b*)
**TRI-SDdis.** Triphone model TRI-SD with a discriminative Maximum Mutual Information (MMI) and a feature-space MMI training (fMMI), TRI-SD+MMI+fMMI. We use a learning rate of 0.001 (*tri3b_fmmi*)

---

[2] http://www.speech.cs.cmu.edu/cgi-bin/cmudict.

Several discriminative trainings can be done to fit the HMM parameters. We have done experiments with MMI training, boosted MMI, Minimum Phone Error (MPE), and direct and indirect feature-space discriminative MMI training (fMMI) with several learning rates. Model TRI-SDdis is the best performing one for dysarthric speakers and, therefore, it is the one included in the analysis.

Finally, we also consider subspace Gaussian Mixture Models [14] with 8000 states and 19000 substates:

**sGMM.** Subspace GMM on top of SD features MFCC+LDA+MLLT+fMLLR (*sgmm2_4a*)

**sGMM2.** Subspace GMM with additional speaker adapted transformations fM-LLR (*sgmm2_4a_fmllr*)

## 4.2   Neural Network Architectures

In hybrid systems, ANNs are trained to estimate the probabilities of the HMM states. Different networks and configurations can be used for this purpose:

**DNN$_{CE}$.** Deep Neural Network trained on alignments obtained with MFCC+ +LDA+MLLT+fMLLR features using cross-entropy. The DNN has 6 hidden layers, 1024 neurons and 1800 output units. The net is initialised with stacked restricted Boltzmann machines (RBMs) (*dnn4b_pretrain-dbn_dnn*)

**DNN$_{sMBR}$.** We introduce a sequence discriminative training that minimises the error on the state labels in a sentence. Departing from DNN$_{CE}$, 6 iterations of state-level minimum Bayes risk (sMBR) are applied (*dnn4b_pretrain-dbn_dnn_smbr*)

Notice that several kinds of sequence-discriminative training can be used. Reference [25] presents experiments with MMI, MPE, sMBR and boosted MMI. Although their training sets are larger (300 h and 110 h) only small differences were found among objective functions, being slightly better sMBR, the one we use in the following sections.

**CNN$_{ba}$.** CNN with convolution along the frequency axis. It uses 40-dim filter-bank features, two convolutional layers and a learning rate of 0.008 (*cnn4c*)

**CNN$_{sMBR}$.** A DNN$_{sMBR}$ is built on top CNN$_{ba}$. First, the CNN is trained and then we build RBMs on top, train a 6-layer DNN with cross-entropy and afterwards 6 iterations of discriminative training (*cnn4c_pretrain-dbn_dnn_smbr*)

Finally, we select two kinds of neural networks especially devoted to deal with time sequences: time delay neural networks and recurrent neural networks.

**TDNN.** Multi-splice Time Delay Neural Network trained on alignments obtained with MFCC+LDA+MLLT+fMLLR features. It uses high-resolution MFCC features. The network has 3 hidden layers with p-norm input dimension of 2000 and output dimension of 250. The learning rate evolves from 0.01 to 0.007 (*nnet_tdnn_a_noIvec*)

**TDNNiV.** Same characteristics as the previous network but we add 100-dim iVectors to the 40-dim high-resolution MFCC input features for speaker adaptation (*nnet_tdnn_a*)

**LSTM.** Long-Term Short-Term Memory network with 3 hidden layers with 1024 neurons. The network is trained for 10 epochs with a learning rate that evolves from 0.0012 and 0.00036, and with momentum 0.5 (*lstm_noIvec*)

**LSTMiV.** Same characteristics as the previous network but we add 100-dim iVectors to the 40-dim MFCC input (*lstm_ivec*)

## 5    Results and Discussion

We use 14 speakers for training the parameters in the acoustic model and test the systems on the 15th. So, during training, there is no distinction between speakers with and without dysarthria besides the different shift in the frame definition for extracting the features. Since there is few data especially for dysarthric speakers, a training done only with impaired speech does not improve the results. Similarly, the language model used for testing is estimated on the same 14 speakers, and including additional corpora of a different domain to train the language model does not improve the results either. For cross-validation in neural networks training, we always use the data coming from a speaker with mild dysarthria regardless the nature of the test speaker—we use subject F03, or F04 in case the test subject is F03.

**Table 2.** WER scores for the 8 speakers with dysarthria and a set of selected systems.

| | F01 | M01 | M02 | M04 | M05 | F03 | F04 | M03 |
|---|---|---|---|---|---|---|---|---|
| MONO | 70.86 | 80.10 | 76.55 | 88.62 | 77.71 | 57.02 | 29.10 | 43.32 |
| TR1 | 70.68 | 91.18 | 81.09 | 88.62 | 84.59 | 41.80 | 18.62 | 26.01 |
| TRI-SI | 76.80 | 79.12 | 83.67 | 88.68 | 96.71 | 53.08 | 18.97 | 32.59 |
| TRI-SD | 47.30 | 78.91 | 68.49 | 81.16 | 97.16 | 42.88 | 13.29 | 17.06 |
| TRI-SDdis | 45.68 | 74.74 | 66.49 | 79.29 | 70.46 | 39.87 | 12.82 | 11.57 |
| sGMM | 43.71 | 77.83 | 64.01 | 71.46 | 98.43 | 37.26 | 11.42 | 10.19 |
| sGMM2 | 43.53 | 78.37 | 63.33 | 71.34 | 97.31 | 37.22 | 11.24 | **9.74** |
| DNN$_{CE}$ | 39.57 | **62.20** | **42.89** | **69.05** | 62.60 | 39.30 | 13.06 | 17.71 |
| DNN$_{sMBR}$ | **35.61** | 62.30 | 47.95 | 69.30 | **62.53** | 37.01 | **10.95** | 12.76 |
| CNNba | 53.24 | 66.04 | 77.66 | 83.62 | 65.67 | 46.78 | 15.81 | 37.88 |
| CNN$_{sMBR}$ | 53.06 | 66.74 | 50.47 | 81.40 | 65.74 | **33.89** | 11.24 | 10.44 |
| TDNN | 66.19 | 69.50 | 62.28 | 73.51 | 88.18 | 47.46 | 14.34 | 28.04 |
| TDNNiV | 94.96 | 95.62 | 84.14 | 92.59 | 93.94 | 91.98 | 39.29 | 70.97 |
| LSTM | 59.71 | 71.61 | 67.33 | 72.97 | 84.73 | 48.28 | 12.00 | 27.50 |
| LSTMiV | 71.04 | 75.01 | 76.13 | 77.30 | 72.85 | 69.33 | 19.61 | 32.20 |

Table 2 shows the results for speakers with dysarthria. We measure the quality of the systems by means of WER. Notice that for severe dysarthric speakers, triphone models are not able to improve on monophone models. In fact, for these speakers, significant improvements in the WER score only appear when speaker dependent transformations are applied. The same happens for control speakers (Table 3) but in this case a base triphone system is always better than monophone systems. In general, intrinsic differences among the 15 speakers make necessary speaker adaptation techniques.

Subspace Gaussian Mixture Models are the best performing classical models. Only in cases where the recognition is extremely difficult (M01 and M05) the TRI-SDdis system outperforms the sGMM family. It is remarkable the hardness of the task: whereas the mean error rate for control speakers is an 18 %, the mean for the six patients with the most severe disease reaches a 65 %. For patients with a mild pathology WER is lower and equivalent to that of control speakers.

**Table 3.** WER scores for the 7 control speakers.

|            | FC01  | FC02  | FC03  | MC01  | MC02  | MC03  | MC04  |
|------------|-------|-------|-------|-------|-------|-------|-------|
| MONO       | 22.40 | 30.27 | 29.88 | 39.52 | 42.99 | 33.59 | 51.19 |
| TR1        | 13.06 | 24.06 | 23.38 | 36.73 | 30.66 | 30.10 | 42.07 |
| TRI-SI     | 13.20 | 24.73 | 26.30 | 38.30 | 32.98 | 33.28 | 42.48 |
| TRI-SD     | 8.01  | 21.96 | 16.71 | 16.96 | 19.46 | 27.47 | 36.27 |
| TRI-SDdis  | 7.42  | 21.72 | 15.43 | 17.49 | 18.23 | 26.51 | 37.40 |
| sGMM       | 7.86  | 20.87 | 13.57 | 15.12 | 16.16 | 24.89 | 28.82 |
| sGMM2      | 7.57  | 20.93 | 13.55 | 14.90 | 16.12 | 24.96 | 28.38 |
| $DNN_{CE}$ | 6.53  | 19.62 | 11.01 | 15.32 | 14.72 | 22.11 | 27.06 |
| $DNN_{sMBR}$ | **6.38** | 19.24 | **10.41** | **12.03** | **13.38** | **20.37** | 23.76 |
| CNNba      | 15.58 | 22.38 | 14.63 | 25.01 | 38.25 | 33.25 | 44.66 |
| $CNN_{sMBR}$ | 9.64 | **18.28** | 12.35 | 11.65 | 15.91 | 23.79 | 38.16 |
| TDNN       | 10.98 | 18.97 | 12.90 | 35.67 | 58.69 | 32.90 | 31.90 |
| TDNNiV     | 16.32 | 24.51 | 21.48 | 51.31 | 62.00 | 49.92 | 62.99 |
| LSTM       | 8.46  | 19.30 | 13.21 | 24.06 | 41.80 | 25.53 | **21.78** |
| LSTMiV     | **6.38** | 19.93 | 13.91 | 21.47 | 37.20 | 27.25 | 29.92 |

The best performing network resulted to be a DNN trained with GMM-HMM alignments. DNN-HMM systems show the lowest WERs for 11 out of 15 test speakers, 6 out of 8 for the speakers with dysarthria. If we consider all the neural network architectures compared to the classical ones, these figures increase to 14 out of 15 and 7 out of 8 respectively. For subjects with a severe disease, there is no difference between a DNN only trained by minimising cross-entropy ($DNN_{CE}$) and that including a subsequent sequence discriminative training ($DNN_{sMBR}$), the mean error rate varies from 52.6 to 52.5. For the control speakers, WER diminishes from 16.6 to 15.1 when adding the discriminative training.

Several works report improvements using CNNs, TDNNs and LSTMs with respect to DNNs, especially for large vocabularies [1,7,11,13,17,18]. We do not find this behaviour in our task. The reasons are twofold: the TORGO database is small and data are heterogeneous. For comparison with other small databases, the authors in Ref. [13] train a TDNN on the Resource Management database, with about 3 h of recorded speech. In their study, a standard DNN performed slightly better, although for larger amount of data a TDNN got better results. On the other hand, CNNs outperfom DNNs on the 50-hours English Broadcast News task [17] and on the 18-hours Microsoft-internal voice search task [1].

The neural network architectures we present apply speaker adaptation, at least through fMLLR features in the seed classical model and/or in the training of the network itself. For TDNNs and LSTMs, we also study the consequences of including iVectors. Although in other studies with larger databases the inclusion of iVectors improves a baseline without [12,23], in our task it clearly damages the performance. For TDNNs the system with iVectors TDNNiV increments the WER in 24 points for dysarthric speakers and 12 points for control speakers. Results are not so negative for LSTMs but there is still a preference for the base LSTM: for dysarthric speakers the inclusion of iVectors causes an increment of 6 points of WER and for control speakers both systems are even.

This work is not the only one devoted to build an ASR for dysarthric speakers. The creators of the TORGO database trained an ASR in Ref. [9]. In their analysis, as in ours, simple triphone models are not able to improve significantly monophone models. So, instead of experimenting with new architectures built on triphone models, their approach is based on adapting speaker and acoustic models to incorporate a specific lexicon for each speaker. This lexicon includes pronunciations for several words that follow the guidelines of pronunciation detected in patients with dysarthria. When adapting the acoustic models to dysarthric speakers, the authors report a relative improvement in WER of 23 % for the average of the 6 speakers with more severe dysarthria and a 3 % further with the addition of the lexicon.

The creation of lexicons is difficult to generalize automatically since it depends on an analysis of the errors committed by each new speaker. Within our approach, we hope that deep neural networks can learn this behaviour from other speakers with similar problems. Our speaker adaptation models such as TRI-SD and sGMM2 are similar to that in [9]. Still, for the same 6 speakers, we get minor improvements with this adaptation: the sGMM2 model achieves and improvement in WER of a 10 % with respect to the baseline, much smaller than their 23 %. The difference is given mainly by the subject M05, while the best models in [9] reach a 15 % WER, our models do not surpass a 70 % WER for this speaker. The difference can only be explained by different data. Our best architecture with neural networks, $DNN_{sMBR}$, achieves a 23 % of improvement in WER compared to baseline, which is similar to that in Ref. [9] but without building any resource manually.

# 6    Conclusions

Recognising dysarthric speech is a difficult task. We have trained an ASR for speakers with and without dysarthria using the TORGO database, a database of dysarthric articulation. With about three hours of recorded speech per each of the 15 subjects, moderate word error rate scores are obtained even for control speakers. A mean WER of 15 % is obtained in this case, while it rises to 52 % for the six test patients with more severe dysarthria.

Hybrid DNN-HMM systems are those with a best performance. DNNs outperfom the best classical system in 14 out of 15 test speakers: the WER score is improved a 3 % for control speakers and a 13 % for subjects with dysarthria with respect to the best classical architecture, a subspace GMM model with additional speaker adapted transformations fMLLR. Both in classical and neural architectures, speaker adaptation techniques are important for improving the recognition. For classical systems, fMLLR transformations make a qualitative leap with respect to the speaker independent transformations MLLT. Neural networks use TRI-SD models for training. However, in this task, iVector caracterisations of the speaker and the environment have a negative impact on the quality of the final systems.

Current results have been obtained using a database that combines impaired and normal speech. It remains to be seen whether including additional data for normal speech is able to further improve the recognition.

**Acknowledgements.** This work was supported by the Spanish Ministerio de Economía y Competitividad and the European Regional Development Fund, contract INNPACTO IPT-2012-0914-300000 and TEC2015-69266-P (MINECO/FEDER, UE).

# References

1. Abdel-Hamid, O., Deng, L., Yu, D.: Exploring convolutional neural network structures and optimization techniques for speech recognition. In: Interspeech 2013, Lyon, France, 25–29 August 2013, pp. 3366–3370 (2013)
2. Amodei, D., Anubhai, R., Battenberg, E., Case, C., Casper, J., Catanzaro, B.C., Chen, J., Chrzanowski, M., Coates, A., Diamos, G., Elsen, E., Engel, J., Fan, L., Fougner, C., Han, T., Hannun, A.Y., Jun, B., LeGresley, P., Lin, L., Narang, S., Ng, A.Y., Ozair, S., Prenger, R., Raiman, J., Satheesh, S., Seetapun, D., Sengupta, S., Wang, Y., Wang, Z., Wang, C., Xiao, B., Yogatama, D., Zhan, J., Zhu, Z.: Deep Speech 2: End-to-End Speech Recognition in English and Mandarin. CoRR abs/1512.02595 (2015)
3. Bourlard, H.A., Morgan, N.: Connectionist Speech Recognition: A Hybrid Approach. Kluwer Academic Publishers, Norwell (1993)
4. Dahl, G., Yu, D., Deng, L., Acero, A.: Context-dependent pre-trained deep neural networks for large vocabulary speech recognition. IEEE Trans. Audio Speech Lang. Process. **20**(1), 30–42 (2012)
5. Dehak, N., Dehak, R., Kenny, P., Brummer, N., Ouellet, P., Dumouchel, P.: Support vector machines versus fast scoring in the low-dimensional total variability space for speaker verification. In: Interspeech 2009, Brighton, United Kingdom, 6–10 September 2009, pp. 1559–1562 (2009)

6. Gopinath, R.A.: Constrained maximum likelihood modeling with Gaussian distributions. In: Proceedings of ICASSP 1998, Seattle, Washington, USA, 12–15 May 1998, pp. 661–664 (1998)

7. Li, X., Wu, X.: Constructing long short-term memory based deep recurrent neural networks for large vocabulary speech recognition. In: 2015 IEEE International Conference on Acoustics, Speech and Signal Processing, ICASSP 2015, South Brisbane, Queensland, Australia, 19–24 April 2015, pp. 4520–4524 (2015)

8. Maas, A.L., Hannun, A.Y., Lengerich, C.T., Qi, P., Jurafsky, D., Ng, A.Y.: Increasing Deep Neural Network Acoustic Model Size for Large Vocabulary Continuous Speech Recognition. CoRR abs/1406.7806 (2014)

9. Mengistu, K.T., Rudzicz, F.: Adapting acoustic and lexical models to dysarthric speech. In: Proceedings of the IEEE International Conference on Acoustics, Speech, and Signal Processing (ICASSP11), pp. 4924–4927. IEEE (2011)

10. Miao, Y., Metze, F.: Improving low-resource CD-DNN-HMM using dropout and multilingual DNN training. In: Bimbot, F., Cerisara, C., Fougeron, C., Gravier, G., Lamel, L., Pellegrino, F., Perrier, (eds.) Interspeech, pp. 2237–2241. ISCA (2013)

11. Miao, Y., Metze, F.: On speaker adaptation of long short-term memory recurrent neural networks. In: Interspeech 2015, Dresden, Germany, 6–10 September 2015, pp. 1101–1105 (2015)

12. Peddinti, V., Chen, G., Povey, D., Khudanpur, S.: Reverberation robust acoustic modeling using i-vectors with time delay neural networks. In: Interspeech 2015, Dresden, Germany, 6–10 September 2015, pp. 2440–2444 (2015)

13. Peddinti, V., Povey, D., Khudanpur, S.: A time delay neural network architecture for efficient modeling of long temporal contexts. In: Interspeech 2015, Dresden, Germany, 6–10 September 2015, pp. 3214–3218 (2015)

14. Povey, D., Burget, L., Agarwal, M., Akyazi, P., Kai, F., Ghoshal, A., Glembek, O., Goel, N., Karafiát, M., Rastrow, A., Rose, R.C., Schwarz, P., Thomas, S.: The subspace Gaussian mixture model - a structured model for speech recognition. Comput. Speech Lang. 25(2), 404–439 (2011)

15. Povey, D., Ghoshal, A., Boulianne, G., Goel, N., Hannemann, M., Qian, Y., Schwarz, P., Stemmer, G.: The Kaldi speech recognition toolkit. In: IEEE 2011 Workshop on Automatic Speech Recognition and Understanding. IEEE Signal Processing Society (2011)

16. Povey, D., Saon, G.: Feature and model space speaker adaptation with full covariance Gaussians. In: Interspeech 2016 ICSLP, Pittsburgh, PA, USA, 17–21 September (2006)

17. Sainath, T.N., Mohamed, A., Kingsbury, B., Ramabhadran, B.: Deep convolutional neural networks for LVCSR. In: IEEE International Conference on Acoustics, Speech and Signal Processing, ICASSP 2013, Vancouver, BC, Canada, 26–31 May 2013, pp. 8614–8618 (2013)

18. Sak, H., Senior, A.W., Beaufays, F.: Long short-term memory recurrent neural network architectures for large scale acoustic modeling. In: Interspeech 2014, Singapore, 14–18 September 2014, pp. 338–342 (2014)

19. Saon, G., Sercu, T., Rennie, S.J., Kuo, H.J.: The IBM 2016 English Conversational Telephone Speech Recognition System. CoRR abs/1604.08242 (2016)

20. Saon, G., Soltau, H., Nahamoo, D., Picheny, M.: Speaker adaptation of neural network acoustic models using i-vectors. In: ASRU, pp. 55–59. IEEE (2013)

21. Seide, F., Li, G., Yu, D.: Conversational speech transcription using context-dependent deep neural networks. In: Interspeech 2011, Florence, Italy, 27–31 August 2011, pp. 437–440 (2011)

22. Stolcke, A.: SRILM - an extensible language modeling toolkit. In: Proceedings of the Seventh International Conference of Spoken Language Processing (ICSLP2002), Denver, Colorado, USA, pp. 901–904 (2002)
23. Tan, T., Qian, Y., Yu, D., Kundu, S., Lu, L., Sim, K.C., Xiao, X., Zhang, Y.: Speaker-aware training of LSTM-RNNS for acoustic modelling. In: 2016 IEEE International Conference on Acoustics, Speech and Signal Processing, ICASSP 2016, Shanghai, China, 20–25 March 2016, pp. 5280–5284 (2016)
24. Trentin, E., Gori, M.: A survey of hybrid ANN/HMM models for automatic speech recognition. Neurocomputing **37**(14), 91–126 (2001)
25. Veselý, K., Ghoshal, A., Burget, L., Povey, D.: Sequence-discriminative training of deep neural networks. In: Interspeech 2013, Lyon, France, 25–29 August 2013, pp. 2345–2349 (2013)

# Detection of Publicity Mentions in Broadcast Radio: Preliminary Results

María Pilar Fernández-Gallego, Álvaro Mesa-Castellanos,
Alicia Lozano-Díez, and Doroteo T. Toledano[✉]

ATVS Biometric Research Lab. Escuela Politécnica Superior,
Universidad Autónoma de Madrid, Madrid, Spain
{mariapilar.fernandezg,
alvaro.mesa}@estudiante.uam.es,
{alicia.lozano,doroteo.torre}@uam.es

**Abstract.** The advertising mentions are publicity contents that are not prerecorded, usually are said by radio or TV broadcasters to publicize a product or a company. The main difficulty of detecting advertising mentions is that the audio is not exactly repeated every time, as happens with conventional prerecorded advertising where more efficient techniques such as audio fingerprinting can be used. This paper proposes the use of a keyword search system in Spanish for the detection of advertising mentions. For that, it has been necessary to train and evaluate a new speech recognizer in Spanish (LVCSR) using the Kaldi tool and databases Fisher Spanish and Callhome Spanish. The best word error rate we have obtained on conversational telephone speech is 41.10 %. For the evaluation of mentions detection a specific database in Spanish has been created, containing 300 h of audio, 25 of which have been tagged with different types of information, including mentions appearing in the audio. The recognizer has been applied to all advertising mentions in search for mention specific keywords, achieving a detection rate of about 74 %.

**Keywords:** Publicity mention detection · Keyword detection · Speech recognition · Fisher spanish · Callhome spanish

## 1 Introduction

Nowadays, multimedia content has a great relevance and is increasingly abundant. Searching on textual content has achieved a high degree of maturity, accuracy and speed. However, we are still far from achieving similar results for multimedia content (audio and video basically). Of the two components, audio, and in particular speech is a very interesting source of information to start with, in particular given the current development of audio and specially speech processing and speech recognition.

In recent years, large efforts have been made on improving the performance of search on speech contents. In the U.S.A. significant research has been conducted on Spoken Term Detection under the IARPA BABEL program [1], part of which is open to worldwide researchers through the NIST Open KeyWord Search (NIST OpenKWS) Evaluations [2]. These evaluations focus on developing, in a very limited time frame,

A. Abad et al. (Eds.): IberSPEECH 2016, LNAI 10077, pp. 108–116, 2016.
DOI: 10.1007/978-3-319-49169-1_11

technology able to search for keywords in Conversational Telephone Speech (CTS). The DARPA Robust Automatic Transcription of Speech (RATS) program also includes keyword spotting within its research areas. Different to the BABEL program, DARPA RATS program mainly focuses on speech recognition under highly noisy communication channels, where typically speech signals of less than 10 dB are specified. Other efforts for improving this technology include the European MEDIAEVAL evaluation campaigns [3] and in particular the Query-by-Example Search on Speech Task (QUESST) [4] that took place from 2011 to 2015 (under different names). In all these cases Spanish was not considered as a target language. Therefore, our group has organized Spoken Term Detection evaluations in Spanish (ALBAYZIN Search-on-Speech Evaluations) [5] biannually since 2012 and is currently organizing the 2016 edition of this evaluation.

Our goal here is to apply the technology developed in this area to a particular task: the detection of publicity mentions in radio, so that a company can be sure that his product or service is broadcasted as agreed upon. The advertising mentions are publicity contents that are not prerecorded. Instead they are said by radio or TV broadcasters during some of their interventions to publicize a product or a company. The main difficulty of detecting advertising mentions is that the audio is not exactly repeated every time, as happens with conventional pre-recorded advertising where more efficient techniques such as audio fingerprinting can be used. One possibility for finding these publicity mentions is to search for specific keywords (normally the company, product or some product-associated lemma) in the audio.

To achieve this goal, we have captured a database of radio programs in Castilian Spanish (we call it ATVS-Radio database) and have labeled it with several layers of information. One of the layers is the publicity layer, where commercials and publicity mentions are marked separately. We have not transcribed the text of these audios, just labeled the mentions with the company and/or product. We will describe this database in more detail in Sect. 2.

For this preliminary work we have not dealt with one of the most difficult problems of Spoken Term Detection, the out of vocabulary (OOV) words. We assume that our system knows all the products/companies that we are searching for and all their associated keywords.

Spoken Term Detection systems typically make use of one or several of the following approaches [6]: Large vocabulary continuous speech recognizers (LVCSR), keyword spotters modeling the words to detect and using filler models to model the rest of the speech, and systems based on subunits of words (phones/syllables). The former is the most precise, but do not have a direct way to deal with OOVs. The latter does not have a vocabulary; therefore they do not suffer the OOV problem, but are the least precise. Systems based on LVCSR and subunits are often combined to have high precision of in vocabulary words and handle the OOV words with the subunit-based system. Another approach proposed is the use of proxy words (i.e. search for in-vocabulary words that are phonetically similar to the OOV words) [7].

In this work, given that we decided not to handle OOV words at this moment, we will use a LVCSR in Spanish, including in the lexicon of the recognizer the keywords chosen for each publicity mention. We will use Kaldi [8] to build the LVCSR in Spanish. Kaldi can train models based on Hidden Markov Models (HMMs) and Deep

Neural Networks (DNN), but, at the time of writing we only performed experiments with models based on HMMs.

The rest of the paper is organized as follows: Sect. 2 describes the databases used in this work, including the database captured for detection of publicity mentions. Section 3 describes the system and the training of the LVCSR. Section 4 describes the results of the recognizer. Section 5 describes the preliminary results on publicity mention detection, and finally Sect. 6 concludes the work and presents lines for future research.

## 2   Database Description

Several databases have been used in this work (see Table 1). For training the speech recognizer Fisher Spanish [9] and Callhome Spanish [10] have been used. Both are databases from the Linguistic Data Consortium (LDC) [11] and both contain conversational telephone speech in Spanish (recorded in the United States).

For testing the publicity mention detection we have captured and tagged a database which we called ATVS-Radio. The database contains radio programs of different radio broadcast, that have been obtained from the Internet and labeled with different information. This database consists of 300 h of which 25 h were hand labeled. Labeling was performed using the Wavesurfer tool. There were four levels of labeling:

- Voice presence and quality: VOICE/TELEPHONIC VOICE/NON VOICE
- Music presence: MUSIC/NO MUSIC
- Advertising, with three possibilities:
  - Conventional commercials: prerecorded audio segment that is reproduced exactly the same each time it appears.
  - Advertising mentions: audio segment in which the presenter of the program or any other person makes a not-prerecorded intervention (often live) to promote a product or brand.
  - NO ADVERTISING.
- Speaker identities: The speaker identity is tagged. We distinguish between regular and occasional speakers.

From this database we have extracted 62 mentions distributed in different radio programs.

**Table 1.** Summary of the databases used in this work.

| Databases | Hours | Number records | Type of speech | Language |
|---|---|---|---|---|
| Fisher Spanish | 163 | 819 | Conversational telephone speech | Spanish from EEUU |
| Callhome Spanish | 60 | 120 | Conversational telephone speech | Spanish from EEUU |
| ATVS-Radio | 300 | 300 | Broadcast news | Spanish from Spain |

# 3   System Description

The system proposed for detecting the mentions consists of a speech recognizer in Spanish whose lexicon will be augmented to include the keywords designed to find the publicity mentions. Mentions will be detected based on the detection of those keywords in the speech recognizer output.

For the creation of our system we have used the Kaldi tool based on the fisher_callhome_spanish recipe found in the last versions of Kaldi. We did not have all the resources on which this recipe is built (for instance we did not have the Callhome Lexicon, and therefore had to build our own lexicon with our own phonetic transcriptor). Also, we did not have other external resources that the recipe uses (such as Spanish Gigaword corpus), so we had to find a workaround for that too.

We started preparing the audio data (i.e. files linking information obtained from the audio). In parallel, we prepared textual data including the lexicon. This file is essential because it contains the words that speech recognizer knows. It was also one of the more laborious parts, particularly because Fisher Spanish and Callhome Spanish included many words in English and many acronyms.

The next step is generating the language model with the SRILM tool (included in Kaldi). Finally features are extracted from the audio before training of the acoustic models starts. Initial features used by the Kaldi recipe are MFCC features normalized with cepstral mean and variance normalization (CMVN).

**LVCSR Training.** We use different types of training, as proposed in the fisher_callhome_spanish recipe of Kaldi. These have been done incrementally, so the trainings are based on the previous model trained. In particular, the previously trained model is used to perform an alignment between the speech and the transcription.

**Basic Models MFCC.** Firstly we constructed a monophone model that is not dependent on the context, then two triphone models are constructed; these are dependent on the context. All these models work directly with MFCCs features.

**Models LDA + MLLT.** This model applies two techniques, Linear Discriminant Analysis (LDA) and Maximum Likelihood Linear Transform (MLLT). First an expansion of the temporal context of the MFCC features is performed, and then these expanded features are reduced to 40 dimensions using LDA. Later, MLLT is applied on top of LDA to adapt the features more to the model.

**Models fMLLR + SAT.** In this model, speaker adaptive training (SAT) is applied transforming the feature space with feature-space Maximum Likelihood Linear Regression (fMLLR).

**SGMM Models.** At this step the speakers and phonemes are modeled together using subspace techniques over Gaussian Mixture Models (GMMs).

**Models bMMI + SGMM.** Finally, this model tries to maximize the ability of discriminating between different phonemes with boosted Maximum Mutual Information (bMMI).

**Keyword Recognizer.** The detection of publicity mentions is based on the large vocabulary speech recognizer (LVCSR) system previously built.

Only the lexicon has been modified to include the keywords designed manually to detect each of the publicity mentions present in the databases. The language model has been modified to include the new words but these words do not appear in the text used to train it (transcriptions of Fisher Spanish and Callhome Spanish). Therefore, the probabilities assigned to these words are the result of the LM smoothing process. Besides, the text includes only conversational telephone transcriptions in Spanish from the U.S.A., which differs considerably from the target application. These are important potential limitations of our system and should be addressed in future work.

# 4 LVCSR Results

Before evaluating the publicity mention detection results, we have evaluated the speech recognizer on a subset of Fisher Spanish not used during training. We have measured the Word Error Rate (WER) obtained using the different acoustic models built and shown it in Table 2.

**Table 2.** Speech recognizer results on a partition of Fisher Spanish not used in training.

| Training stage | WER (%) |
|----------------|---------|
| MFCC_1 | 57.32 |
| MFCC_2 | 56.76 |
| +LDA + MLLT | 50.63 |
| +fMLLR + SAT | 46.99 |
| SGMM | 45.12 |
| +bMMI + SGMM | 41.10 |

Table 2 shows the improvement achieved by the different stages proposed by the Kaldi recipe. Unfortunately, our results with the recognizer used in this paper still differ by about a 9 % from the best results reported by the Kaldi tool. In particular, the best result [12] (to our current knowledge) reported using Kaldi with Fisher Spanish and Callhome Spanish is a WER of 29.8 %, using DNNs. The best result using Kaldi and bMMI + SGMM is of 32.73 %, which is almost 9 % better than our result. Still, our result is better than the result obtained (using only Fisher Spanish) for the system we developed for the ALBAYZIN 2014 Search-on-Speech evaluation [13], which reached a 49.88 % WER and was 13 % worse at that point than the best result we found [14] although these results are not totally comparable with our system because they did not use the Callhome Spanish database. Table 3 summarizes these comparative results. At the time of writing we are developing a new recognizer which reduces the difference with the Kaldi best results to 6 %, but this new recognizer has not been used for publicity detection yet.

**Table 3.** Comparasion of speech recognizers performance

|  | Our initial system [13] | System developed in this work | Best result by 2014 [14] | Best result by Kaldi with DNNs [12] | Best result by Kaldi with bMMI + SGMM (from Kaldi download) |
|---|---|---|---|---|---|
| % WER | 49.88 | 41.10 | 36.50 | 29.80 | 32.73 |

Although it may seem that a WER of 41.10 % is very high, looking at the recognitions and the manual transcriptions we get a different impression. Table 4 includes examples of manual transcriptions and the recognized text.

**Table 4.** Examples of speech recognizer

| Manual Transcription: porque nadie le entiende lo que esta diciendo | Manual Transcription: y siempre andan la gente peleando lo que es |
|---|---|
| Recognized: porque nadien entiendes lo que esta diciendo | Recognized: y siempre anda en la gente peleando de o lo que el |

As we can see, most errors are in short words, while long words (which provide more meaning) are relatively well recognized. The first example shows that many errors are just morphological variations of the same word (entiende/entiendes) and also that the lexicon built from the text in the Fisher Spanish and Callhome Spanish corpora requires debugging (nadien is not a valid Spanish word). The second example is chosen to show that although it may seem to be a particularly good case, there are 2 substitutions and 3 insertions (and 0 deletions) in a phase of 9 words, which produces a WER of 55.56 %, worse than the speech recognizer average.

## 5 Results of Publicity Mention Detections

For this evaluation we have used the 62 publicity mentions extracted from the ATVS-Radio database (the duration of the mentions range from 3 to 73 s). These 62 occurrences of publicity mentions corresponded to 21 different products/companies. The more frequent mention appeared 10 times, while the least frequent mentions only appeared once (this happened for 21 different products/companies).

For the detection of these mentions we have selected a total of 51 keywords for the different 21 products/companies advertised in the mentions. To select these keywords we listen to the mentions and choose the keywords manually. The mention with more keywords associated included 7 keywords, while the mention with least keywords associated included only 1 keyword. Some of the keywords were multi-words that appeared in the mentions.

For our preliminary results we extracted the audio corresponding to the mentions based on the manual time alignments of the mention start and end, and processed only the audio corresponding to the mentions. This is an important limitation since in this way we do not analyze the probability of having a false positive, which is a crucial performance measure for a practical system. This is something we need to address in the future.

For these preliminary results, we just considered that if any of the keywords associated with a publicity mention is detected, the publicity mention has been detected, and otherwise we considered that it has not been detected.

Table 5 shows the results obtained (as percentage of true positives or hits). The best results were obtained with the LDA + MLLT model, which is not the one with best results on speech recognition. This seems to indicate that more advanced models including speaker adaptation and speaker adaptive training have trouble when trying to adapt to a very short segment of audio or to audio from a database of different characteristics. We will have to investigate this performance drop from LDA + MLLT to fMLLR + SAT in the future.

**Table 5.** Preliminary results or publicity mention detection

| Training stage | Hit (%) |
|----------------|---------|
| MFCC_1 | 42.37 |
| MFCC_2 | 45.76 |
| +LDA + MLLT | 74.57 |
| +fMLLR + SAT | 64.40 |
| SGMM | 69.49 |
| +bMMI + SGMM | 67.79 |

Other limitation of the results is the fact that the statistical language model was not adapted to the task. To see if this was really important in our results we performed some experiments varying the weight of the acoustic score, with the hope that increasing the weight of the acoustic score (i.e. decreasing the weight of the LM score) would increase the detection rate of the publicity mentions. However, results (in Table 6) showed that increasing or decreasing the acoustic weight from its default value worsened results.

**Table 6.** Publicity mention detection results when varying the weight of the acoustic score

| Weight of the acoustic score | 0.07 | 0.075 | 0.083 (default) | 0.09 | 0.12 |
|------------------------------|------|-------|-----------------|------|------|
| % hit | | 71.18 | 74.57 | 74.57 | 72.88 | 72.88 |

## 6 Conclusions and Future Work

Publicity mentions have the difficulty that they are different each time they are produced, both in the text said, how it is said, and even in the speaker that produces it. Therefore we propose the use of spoken term detection systems in order to detect the presence of keywords that help us to detect publicity mentions. In order to evaluate this strategy we have captured and tagged a database (ATVS-Radio) containing 62 mentions in labeled hours of radio programs. An essential part of a spoken term detection system is a large vocabulary continuous speech recognizer. In this work we have trained a new speech recognizer in Spanish (using Fisher Spanish and Callhome Spanish) that has achieved a 41.1 % WER on Fisher Spanish. This is about 9 % better than our previous recognizer but still 9 % worse than the best results provided by Kaldi with a similar system. Once this recognizer has been available, we have manually chosen 51 keywords and have processed the audio corresponding to the 62 mentions in search for these 51 keywords. Our best result has been able to detect 74 % of these mentions by detecting the keywords associated to these mentions.

While this result is encouraging, there are a number of limitations in our preliminary study that need to be addressed. First, the speech recognizer can be improved. At the time of writing we have already reduced the difference in WER with the best results provided by Kaldi from 9 % to 6 %, and we still have not used DNNs. Regarding the detection of mentions itself, we need to test with language model adaptation and investigate why there is a drop in performance for the most advanced acoustic models. In the future we need to extend our experimental framework to process all the audio and not only the audio corresponding to the mentions (something we have not yet done due to time constraints), so that we can also measure the percentage of false positives, which is crucial for the practical applicability of the system.

**Acknowledgements.** This work has been partly funded by the Spanish Ministry of Economy and Competitiveness under project TEC2015-68172-C2-1-P (DSSL) and project TEC2012-37585-C02-01 (CMC-V2).

# References

1. IARPA: Babel Program. Intelligence Advanced Research Projects Activity (IARPA), Washington DC, USA (2011). http://www.iarpa.gov/images/files/programs/babel/Babel-Kickoff-Summary.pdf
2. NIST Open KeyWord Search (OpenKWS). http://www.nist.gov/itl/iad/mig/openkws.cfm. Accessed 19 June 2016
3. MEDIAEVAL Evaluations. http://www.multimediaeval.org/. Accessed 19 June 2016
4. MEDIAEVAL Query by Example Search on Speech Task (QUESST) Evaluation. http://www.multimediaeval.org/mediaeval2015/quesst2015/. Accessed 19 June 2016
5. ALBAYZIN Search-on-Speech Evaluation (2016). https://iberspeech2016.inesc-id.pt/index.php/albayzin-evaluation/#sos-identifier. Accessed 19 June 2016
6. Tejedor, J., et al.: Spoken term detection ALBAYZIN 2014 evaluation: overview, systems, results, and discussion. EURASIP J, Audio Speech Music Process. **2015**(1), 1–27 (2015)
7. Chen, G., Yilmaz, O., Trmal, J., Povey, D., Khudanpur, S.: Using proxies for OOV keywords in the keyword search task. In: 2013 IEEE Workshop on Automatic Speech Recognition and Understanding (ASRU), pp. 416–421. IEEE (2013)
8. Povey, D., Ghoshal, A., Boulianne, G., Burget, L., Glembek, O., Goel, N., Silovsky, J.: The Kaldi speech recognition toolkit. In: IEEE 2011 Workshop on Automatic Speech Recognition and Understanding. IEEE Signal Processing Society (2011)
9. Corpus Switchboard. It is available in Linguistic Data Consortium. Ref. LDC2010S01. https://catalog.ldc.upenn.edu/LDC2010S01. Accessed 16 May 2016)

10. Corpus Switchboard. It is available in Linguistic Data Consortium .Ref. LDC96S35. https://catalog.ldc.upenn.edu/LDC96S35. Accessed 16 May 2016
11. Linguistic Data Consortium. https://ldc.upenn.edu/. Accessed 18 May 2016
12. Kaldi. http://kaldi-asr.org/doc/examples.html. Accessed 20 Sep 2016
13. Post, M., Kumar, G., López, A., Karakos, D., Callison-Burch, C., Khudanpur, Y.S.: Improved speech-to-text translation with the fisher and Callhome Spanish–English speech translation corpus. In: International Workshop on Spoken Language Translation, p. 4, December 2013
14. Xu, J., Toledano, D.T., Tejedor, J.: The ATVS-GEINTRA STD system for ALBAYZIN 2014 search-on-speech evaluation. In: Proceedings of the IberSPEECH 2014, Las Palmas de Gran Canaria, Spain, pp. 290–298. http://iberspeech2014.ulpgc.es/images/Iberspeech2014_OnlineProceedings.pdf. Accessed 20 June 2016

# Deep Neural Network-Based Noise Estimation for Robust ASR in Dual-Microphone Smartphones

Iván López-Espejo$^{(\boxtimes)}$, Antonio M. Peinado,
Angel M. Gomez, and Juan M. Martín-Doñas

Department of Signal Theory, Telematics and Communications,
University of Granada, Granada, Spain
{iloes,amp,amgg}@ugr.es, mdjuamart@correo.ugr.es

**Abstract.** The performance of many noise-robust automatic speech recognition (ASR) methods, such as vector Taylor series (VTS) feature compensation, heavily depends on an estimation of the noise that contaminates speech. Therefore, providing accurate noise estimates for this kind of methods is crucial as well as a challenge. In this paper we investigate the use of deep neural networks (DNNs) to perform noise estimation in dual-microphone smartphones. Thanks to the powerful regression capabilities of DNNs, accurate noise estimates can be obtained by just using simple features as well as exploiting the power level difference (PLD) between the two microphones of the smartphone when employed in close-talk conditions. This is confirmed by our word recognition results on the AURORA2-2C (AURORA2 - 2 Channels - Conversational Position) database by largely outperforming single- and dual-channel noise estimation algorithms from the state-of-the-art when used together with a VTS feature compensation method.

**Keywords:** Noise estimation · Deep neural network · VTS feature compensation · Automatic speech recognition · Dual-microphone · Smartphone

## 1 Introduction

Providing robustness against acoustic noise is still a challenge in automatic speech recognition (ASR) [1]. Many techniques devoted to noise-robust ASR such as vector Taylor series (VTS) feature compensation [2] or Wiener filtering [3] might require an explicit estimation of the noise that contaminates speech. The performance of this kind of techniques heavily depends on the accuracy of the given noise estimation. Therefore, accurate noise estimation algorithms are needed and we can find a great variety of them in the literature [4–7].

---

I. López-Espejo et al. This work has been supported by the Spanish MINECO TEC2013-46690-P project.

A. Abad et al. (Eds.): IberSPEECH 2016, LNAI 10077, pp. 117–127, 2016.
DOI: 10.1007/978-3-319-49169-1_12

Particularly nowadays, providing robustness in ASR is a crucial task because of the wide use of mobile devices such as smartphones or tablets which can be employed for ASR purposes in many different acoustic environments. Mobile devices often integrate small microphone arrays which have been successfully exploited for both speech enhancement [8,9] and noise-robust ASR [10]. In our previous work [11], noise-robust ASR in a dual-microphone smartphone, a particular case of interest of small microphone array, was addressed. In that work, a missing-data mask estimation method was proposed in order to perform spectral reconstruction. The method proposed consists of a deep neural network (DNN) fed with dual-channel noisy observations which provides a missing-data mask. It was proven that this rather simple and straightforward approach supplies quite accurate missing-data masks by exploiting the power level difference (PLD) between the two microphones of the smartphone. When a dual-microphone smartphone is employed in close-talk conditions (i.e. the loudspeaker of the smartphone is placed on the ear of the user) the primary microphone (which is located at the bottom of the device) captures more speech power than the secondary one (located at the rear of the smartphone) since the latter is placed in an acoustic shadow with respect to the speaker's mouth. Additionally, the noise power observed by both microphones is assumed to be very similar because of the typical existence of a homogeneous noise field [8]. Thus, it is clear that a missing-data mask can be easily derived from a comparison between the noisy speech power present in both channels, where the secondary channel is a good noise reference.

Based on the discussion above, in this work we investigate noise estimation for noise-robust ASR in dual-microphone smartphones by exploiting the PLD between the two sensors of the device. Similarly to our previous work [11], a DNN is used to find a mapping function between the dual-channel noisy observation and the noise that contaminates speech at the primary channel. While DNNs have been employed for many different tasks from noise-robust ASR such as missing-data mask estimation [11,12], surprisingly they have not yet been applied to directly estimate noise. DNN-based noise estimates will be used by a VTS feature compensation method to perform noise-robust ASR. The resulting robust ASR system gathers the advantages of two different approaches. Thus, it combines a traditional signal processing technique for feature compensation with a novel DNN-based approach for noise estimation, which undoubtedly is a difficult task with the classical signal processing tools. It is expected that this kind of hybrid architectures will be extensively explored in the near future [13]. Our experimental evaluation on the AURORA2-2C (AURORA2 - 2 Channels - Conversational Position) database [10] shows the effectiveness of our proposal in terms of word accuracy by achieving the best performance among several single- and dual-channel noise estimation algorithms from the state-of-the-art.

The rest of the paper has been organized as follows. In Sect. 2 a system overview is presented along with the proposed DNN-based noise estimation method. Both the experimental framework and results are shown in Sect. 3. Finally, in Sect. 4 our conclusions and future work are drawn.

## 2  Proposed Method

The noise-robust ASR framework considered in this paper is depicted in Fig. 1. The noisy speech signal captured by the primary microphone of the smartphone is denoted as $y_1(m)$, where $m$ is the sampling time index. Similarly, $y_2(m)$ refers to the noisy speech signal recorded by the secondary microphone of the device. As presented in Sect. 1, the noise components in $y_1(m)$ and $y_2(m)$ are assumed to be quite similar while speech is very attenuated at the secondary sensor with respect to the primary one since the former is placed in an acoustic shadow regarding the speaker's mouth. Then, log-Mel spectral features $\mathbf{y}_i$ are extracted from the noisy signals $y_i(m)$, $i = 1, 2$, which are employed by a DNN-based stage in order to provide a noise estimate of the primary channel, $\hat{\mathbf{n}}_1$. To obtain the clean speech log-Mel features at the primary channel, $\hat{\mathbf{x}}_1$, this noise estimate is used along with $\mathbf{y}_1$ by a VTS feature compensation method. Finally, $\hat{\mathbf{x}}_1$ is transformed into the cepstral domain by application of the discrete cosine transform (DCT) prior to be used by the speech recognizer.

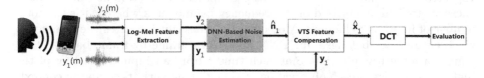

**Fig. 1.** Block diagram of the noise-robust ASR framework considered in this work.

Subsection 2.1 is devoted to show the fundamentals of the DNN-based noise estimation stage marked in gray in Fig. 1, while a noise-aware training (NAT)-based extension to it, intended to increase the awareness of the DNN about the noise that contaminates speech, is presented in Subsect. 2.2.

### 2.1  Dual-Channel Noise Estimation Based on DNN

A DNN (i.e. a feed-forward neural network with multiple hidden layers) is considered in this work to find a non-linear mapping function between dual-channel noisy speech and noise log-Mel features at the primary channel of the smartphone. This DNN-based method exploits the PLD between the two microphones of the device when employed in close-talk conditions to effectively provide accurate noise estimates. An illustration on how the DNN is used to this end can be seen in Fig. 2.

First, let

$$\mathbf{y}_i(t) = (y_i(0, t), y_i(1, t), ..., y_i(\mathcal{M} - 1, t))^{\mathrm{T}}, \quad i = 1, 2, \tag{1}$$

and

$$\mathbf{n}_1(t) = (n_1(0, t), n_1(1, t), ..., n_1(\mathcal{M} - 1, t))^{\mathrm{T}} \tag{2}$$

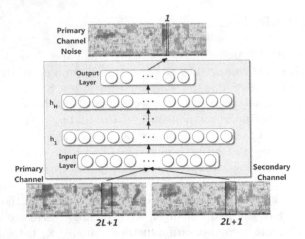

**Fig. 2.** An outline of the DNN as used for noise estimation purposes.

respectively be noisy speech and noise log-Mel feature vectors at time frame $t$. These vectors are comprised of $\mathcal{M}$ frequency components where $\mathcal{M}$ is the total number of filterbank channels. Moreover, the subscript indicates the channel to which each vector belongs. Our DNN works on a frame-by-frame basis so that it gives a noise frame estimate at each time $t$ from an input consisting of the dual-channel noisy speech observation at time $t$ along with its temporal context. In particular, if we define

$$\mathbf{y}(t) = \begin{pmatrix} \mathbf{y}_1(t) \\ \mathbf{y}_2(t) \end{pmatrix}, \tag{3}$$

the DNN input vector becomes

$$\boldsymbol{\mathcal{Y}}(t) = \left(\mathbf{y}^{\mathrm{T}}(t-L), \ \ldots, \ \mathbf{y}^{\mathrm{T}}(t+L)\right)^{\mathrm{T}}, \tag{4}$$

where the variable $L$ determines the size of the temporal context considered (i.e. the size of the temporal window used is $2L + 1$). Therefore, the dimension of the input vector is $\dim(\boldsymbol{\mathcal{Y}}(t)) = 2\mathcal{M}(2L + 1)$. Additionally, as expected, the corresponding $\mathcal{M}$-dimensional target vector is that of Eq. (2).

The DNN training consists of an unsupervised generative pre-training, where it is considered each pair of layers as restricted Boltzmann machines (RBMs) [14], followed by a supervised fine-tuning step. The goal of this pre-training is to avoid getting stuck in plateaus or local minima during the fine-tuning phase because of the complex error surface as a result of the deep architecture [15]. Thus, the input and first hidden layers form a Gaussian-Bernoulli RBM (i.e. a visible layer of Gaussian variables connected to binary units in a hidden layer) since the input vector is real-valued. The successive pairs of layers form Bernoulli-Bernoulli RBMs (i.e. two layers with connections between their binary units). Input data are used to train the Gaussian-Bernoulli RBM and the inferred states of its hidden units are employed to train the following Bernoulli-Bernoulli RBM, and so on. The parameters resulting from this generative model consisting of the stack of RBMs are used to initialize the DNN, which is then fine-tuned by performing a supervised training by means of the backpropagation algorithm. For backpropagation learning the minimum mean square error (MMSE) criterion was chosen. Furthermore, the activation function type considered for the hidden layers is sigmoid while that is linear for the output layer, as could be expected for regression purposes.

The values chosen for the DNN hyperparameters and the rest of details about the DNN setup can be found in Subsect. 3.2.

## 2.2 Noise-Aware Training

DNN noise-aware training (NAT) is a method first appeared in [16] to strengthen the DNN-based acoustic modeling for ASR. It basically consists of appending a noise estimate to the network's input vector containing the noisy speech features to improve word recognition rates when employing multi-style acoustic modeling. Since then, NAT has been successfully applied to different tasks such as, for instance, DNN-based speech enhancement [17]. In this work, we want to explore if the DNN-based noise estimation approach of Subsect. 2.1 can be improved by increasing the awareness of the DNN about the noise that contaminates speech in each case.

A simple noise estimator, which has demonstrated to be quite accurate [18], consists of the linear interpolation between the averages of the first and last $M$ frames of an utterance in the log-Mel domain. It should be pointed out that this method assumes that the first and last $M$ frames in each utterance contain only noise energy. To imitate this method, and assuming that an utterance is $T$ frames long, the initial input vector $\mathcal{Y}(t)$ is augmented by appending the aforementioned averages,

$$\bar{\mathbf{n}}_1^{(0)} = \frac{1}{M} \sum_{t=0}^{M-1} \mathbf{y}_1^{\mathrm{T}}(t); \qquad \bar{\mathbf{n}}_1^{(1)} = \frac{1}{M} \sum_{t=T-M}^{T-1} \mathbf{y}_1^{\mathrm{T}}(t), \qquad (5)$$

as well as a time index to indicate the frame's relative position within the utterance:

$$\tau(t) = t/(T-1). \qquad (6)$$

Additionally, we decided to also use noise variance information by computing and appending the following sample quantities:

$$\boldsymbol{\sigma}_1^{(0)} = \frac{1}{M-1} \sum_{t=0}^{M-1} \left( \mathbf{y}_1^{\mathrm{T}}(t) - \bar{\mathbf{n}}_1^{(0)} \right)^2; \qquad \boldsymbol{\sigma}_1^{(1)} = \frac{1}{M-1} \sum_{t=T-M}^{T-1} \left( \mathbf{y}_1^{\mathrm{T}}(t) - \bar{\mathbf{n}}_1^{(1)} \right)^2, \qquad (7)$$

where $(\cdot)^2$ is applied element-wise. Thus, the final DNN input vector is

$$\mathcal{Y}_{NAT}(t) = \left( \mathcal{Y}^{\mathrm{T}}(t), \; \bar{\mathbf{n}}_1^{(0)}, \; \bar{\mathbf{n}}_1^{(1)}, \; \boldsymbol{\sigma}_1^{(0)}, \; \boldsymbol{\sigma}_1^{(1)}, \; \tau(t) \right)^{\mathrm{T}}, \qquad (8)$$

with dimension $\dim(\mathcal{Y}_{NAT}(t)) = \dim(\mathcal{Y}(t)) + 4\mathcal{M} + 1 = 4\mathcal{M}\left(L + \frac{3}{2}\right) + 1$.

# 3  Experimental Evaluation

The performance of the proposed dual-channel DNN-based noise estimator is evaluated in terms of word accuracy (WAcc) when used together with a VTS feature compensation method as depicted in Fig. 1. Subsects. 3.1 and 3.2 describe the recognition framework considered and how the DNN has been set up for experiments, respectively. Then, our DNN-based noise estimation results and a comparison with other noise estimation algorithms when they are also used together with a VTS feature compensation method are presented in Subsects. 3.3 and 3.4, respectively.

## 3.1  Recognition Framework

The AURORA2-2C (AURORA2 - 2 Channels - Conversational Position) database first reported in [10] is employed for ASR experiments. The AURORA2-2C database is an extension to the well-known Aurora-2 database [19] that comprises the acquisition of noisy speech with a dual-microphone smartphone used in close-talk conditions. Two test sets, $A$ and $B$, are defined in AURORA2-2C with different noise types in each one. The types of noise used in test set $A$ are bus, babble, car and pedestrian street, while test set $B$ considers the noises café, street, bus station and train station.

For VTS feature compensation we employ the first-order implementation reported in [18]. The only difference with respect to [18] consists of the use of different noise estimation algorithms. VTS is performed using a 256-component clean speech Gaussian mixture model (GMM) with diagonal covariance matrices. This GMM was obtained by performing the expectation-maximization (EM) algorithm on the same dataset as that used for clean acoustic model training.

To extract acoustic features from the speech signals, the European Telecommunication Standards Institute front-end (ETSI FE, ES 201 108) is used [20]. Log-Mel feature vectors employed by both the DNN and VTS are composed of $\mathcal{M} = 23$ frequency bins. Twelve Mel-frequency cepstral coefficients (MFCCs) along with the 0th order coefficient are obtained by application of the DCT to the enhanced log-Mel features. Then, their velocity and acceleration coefficients are appended to them to form the 39-dimensional feature vector employed by the recognizer. To strengthen the speech recognizer against channel mismatches cepstral mean normalization (CMN) is also applied.

Regarding the speech recognizer, both clean and multi-style acoustic models are considered for evaluation. The latter models are trained with distorted speech features to strengthen the ASR system against noisy conditions. In AURORA2-2C, the multi-style training dataset is created from the training clean utterances of Aurora-2 and consists of dual-channel utterances contaminated with the types of noise in test set $A$ at the signal-to-noise ratios (SNRs) of 5 dB, 10 dB, 15 dB and 20 dB, along with the clean condition. Noisy utterances are compensated with VTS using the corresponding noise estimation algorithm prior to training the multi-style acoustic models. To model each digit, left to right continuous density hidden Markov models (HMMs) with 16 states and 3 Gaussians per state are used. Silences and short pauses are modeled by HMMs with 3 and 1 states, respectively, and 6 Gaussians per state [19].

## 3.2 DNN Setup

Taking into account the speech recognition task as well as the different noise conditions considered in this paper, for the sake of efficiency and to avoid data redundancy, our DNN was trained using 25600 sample pairs of input-target vectors. Training input data consisted of a mixture of samples contaminated with the noises of test set $A$ at the SNRs of $-5$ dB, 0 dB, 5 dB, 10 dB, 15 dB and 20 dB. Thus, the noise types of test set $B$ are useful to test the generalization capability of the DNN to unseen noise conditions during training. On the one hand, for the unsupervised pre-training stage the number of epochs in each RBM was 40 and the learning rate was set to 0.0005. On the other hand, for the fine-tuning step the number of epochs was 100 and a learning rate of 0.1 was employed. The momentum rate used was 0.9. Following the tips from the Hinton's report in [21], the mini-batch size was 10 sample pairs. To improve the generalization capability of the network, early-stopping was adopted as a regularization strategy to avoid overfitting during training. Moreover, since the task addressed in [11] is similar to that in this paper, and assuming that noise has weak temporal correlations, $L$ was set to 2 as in [11]. Since $\mathcal{M} = 23$, the input layer has $\dim(\mathcal{Y}(t)) = 230$ and $\dim(\mathcal{Y}_{NAT}(t)) = 323$ neurons for the DNN of Subsects. 2.1 (without NAT) and 2.2 (with NAT), respectively. For both DNN configurations the output layer has $\mathcal{M} = 23$ neurons and five hidden layers were set up, according to preliminary recognition experiments, with 512 neurons each. For NAT, $M = 20$ was considered. Finally, the implementation of the DNN was done using Python along with the library Theano [22].

## 3.3 DNN-Based Noise Estimation Results

Tables 1 and 2 present a comparison in terms of WAcc between our DNN without NAT (DNN$_2$) and other techniques when employing clean and multi-style acoustic models, respectively. These reference techniques are a single-channel DNN-based noise estimator (DNN$_1$) as well as our previous approach reported in [11] (TGI+DNN), which shares similarities with this work. It should be noticed that the only difference between DNN$_1$ and DNN$_2$ is that Eq. (3) is redefined as $\mathbf{y}(t) = \mathbf{y}_1(t)$ for the former one. Baseline results are obtained by directly using the noisy speech features from the primary channel with no compensation. For both types of acoustic models, the best results are achieved by DNN$_2$, which makes it a better choice than TGI+DNN to provide robustness for ASR in dual-microphone smartphones. Also by a large margin (11.13 % and 9.06 % on average under clean and multi-style acoustic modeling, respectively) DNN$_2$ is clearly superior to DNN$_1$ as it exploits the information from the secondary channel, which is a good noise reference since speech is very attenuated in it as previously discussed. As expected, better WAcc results are generally obtained by employing multi-style instead of clean acoustic models, since the mismatch

**Table 1.** WAcc results (%) for $DNN_2$ and other comparison techniques when clean acoustic models are employed. Results are averaged across all types of noise in each test set.

| SNR (dB) | Baseline | | | TGI+DNN | | | $DNN_1$ | | | $DNN_2$ | | |
|---|---|---|---|---|---|---|---|---|---|---|---|---|
| | Test $A$ | Test $B$ | Avg. | Test $A$ | Test $B$ | Avg. | Test $A$ | Test $B$ | Avg. | Test $A$ | Test $B$ | Avg. |
| −5 | 21.14 | 15.15 | 18.15 | 54.80 | 32.29 | 43.55 | 41.69 | 20.72 | 31.21 | 63.02 | 40.87 | 51.95 |
| 0 | 38.19 | 25.50 | 31.85 | 79.42 | 60.24 | 69.83 | 67.21 | 45.81 | 56.51 | 85.74 | 71.09 | 78.42 |
| 5 | 64.60 | 47.61 | 56.11 | 92.67 | 84.12 | 88.40 | 85.56 | 73.57 | 79.57 | 94.53 | 90.20 | 92.37 |
| 10 | 87.71 | 77.84 | 82.78 | 97.08 | 94.38 | 95.73 | 93.09 | 88.56 | 90.83 | 97.72 | 96.21 | 96.97 |
| 15 | 95.99 | 93.44 | 94.72 | 98.45 | 97.54 | 98.00 | 96.28 | 94.36 | 95.32 | 98.59 | 98.17 | 98.38 |
| 20 | 98.13 | 97.38 | 97.76 | 98.93 | 98.38 | 98.66 | 96.92 | 96.50 | 96.71 | 98.94 | 98.77 | 98.86 |
| Clean | 99.13 | 99.13 | 99.13 | 99.13 | 99.13 | 99.13 | 97.59 | 97.59 | 97.59 | 99.02 | 99.02 | 99.02 |
| Avg. (−5 to 20) | 67.63 | 59.49 | 63.56 | 86.89 | 77.83 | 82.36 | 80.13 | 69.92 | 75.03 | **89.76** | **82.55** | **86.16** |

**Table 2.** WAcc results (%) for $DNN_2$ and other comparison techniques when multi-style acoustic models are employed. Results are averaged across all types of noise in each test set.

| SNR (dB) | Baseline | | | TGI+DNN | | | $DNN_1$ | | | $DNN_2$ | | |
|---|---|---|---|---|---|---|---|---|---|---|---|---|
| | Test $A$ | Test $B$ | Avg. | Test $A$ | Test $B$ | Avg. | Test $A$ | Test $B$ | Avg. | Test $A$ | Test $B$ | Avg. |
| −5 | 47.64 | 26.22 | 36.93 | 57.89 | 35.75 | 46.82 | 48.14 | 24.10 | 36.12 | 67.05 | 44.37 | 55.71 |
| 0 | 76.99 | 56.39 | 66.69 | 82.18 | 65.88 | 74.03 | 72.91 | 51.93 | 62.42 | 87.95 | 75.02 | 81.49 |
| 5 | 92.36 | 85.33 | 88.85 | 94.12 | 87.15 | 90.64 | 89.29 | 78.73 | 84.01 | 95.39 | 91.57 | 93.48 |
| 10 | 96.94 | 94.52 | 95.73 | 97.50 | 95.02 | 96.26 | 95.19 | 91.96 | 93.58 | 97.93 | 96.84 | 97.39 |
| 15 | 97.98 | 97.14 | 97.56 | 98.46 | 97.41 | 97.94 | 97.59 | 96.04 | 96.82 | 98.60 | 98.34 | 98.47 |
| 20 | 98.49 | 98.12 | 98.31 | 98.85 | 98.02 | 98.44 | 98.16 | 97.68 | 97.92 | 98.79 | 98.65 | 98.72 |
| Clean | 98.77 | 98.77 | 98.77 | 98.61 | 98.61 | 98.61 | 98.49 | 98.49 | 98.49 | 98.99 | 98.99 | 98.99 |
| Avg. (−5 to 20) | 85.07 | 76.29 | 80.68 | 88.17 | 79.87 | 84.02 | 83.55 | 73.41 | 78.48 | **90.95** | **84.13** | **87.54** |

between training and test data is lower. In addition, test set $B$ baseline results are substantially worse than those of test set $A$. Nevertheless, $DNN_2$ exhibits some generalization capabilities to noise conditions not seen during training. Finally, it is worth mentioning that word recognition results for both TGI+DNN and baseline are slightly different from those reported in [11]. This is because in this work the AURORA2-2C database was generated considering an anechoic chamber instead of a semi-anechoic environment for the acoustic path estimation, as in [11].

Table 3 shows the WAcc results achieved by both $DNN_1$ and $DNN_2$ when integrating the NAT approach of Subsect. 2.2, $DNN_1^{NAT}$ and $DNN_2^{NAT}$. On the one hand, $DNN_1$ has experienced an average relative improvement of 3.74 % and 2.27 % in terms of WAcc when employing clean and multi-style acoustic models, respectively, by incorporating a noise reference by means of NAT. On the other hand, NAT degrades the performance of $DNN_2$. This could be explained because the secondary channel is a better noise reference itself than the information considered in our NAT-based approach, which introduces a greater uncertainty.

**Table 3.** WAcc results (%) for NAT when both clean and multi-style acoustic models are employed. Results are averaged across all types of noise in each test set.

| | Clean models | | | | | | | | | Multi-style models | | | | | | | | |
| | $\text{DNN}_1^{NAT}$ | | | $\text{DNN}_2^{NAT}$ | | | $\text{DNN}_1^{NAT}$ | | | $\text{DNN}_2^{NAT}$ | | |
| SNR (dB) | Test $A$ | Test $B$ | Avg. | Test $A$ | Test $B$ | Avg. | Test $A$ | Test $B$ | Avg. | Test $A$ | Test $B$ | Avg. |
|---|---|---|---|---|---|---|---|---|---|---|---|---|
| −5 | 41.93 | 22.70 | 32.32 | 52.85 | 33.04 | 42.95 | 46.73 | 26.40 | 36.57 | 58.21 | 38.17 | 48.19 |
| 0 | 71.02 | 54.18 | 62.60 | 78.76 | 63.17 | 70.97 | 75.01 | 60.24 | 67.63 | 82.77 | 69.69 | 76.23 |
| 5 | 90.03 | 82.11 | 86.07 | 92.06 | 86.74 | 89.40 | 91.91 | 85.33 | 88.62 | 93.80 | 88.99 | 91.40 |
| 10 | 96.62 | 93.61 | 95.12 | 96.70 | 94.51 | 95.61 | 96.73 | 94.32 | 95.53 | 97.44 | 95.36 | 96.40 |
| 15 | 98.32 | 97.37 | 97.85 | 98.23 | 97.34 | 97.79 | 98.24 | 97.15 | 97.70 | 98.30 | 97.56 | 97.93 |
| 20 | 98.82 | 98.49 | 98.66 | 98.84 | 98.40 | 98.62 | 98.63 | 98.29 | 98.46 | 98.72 | 98.31 | 98.52 |
| Clean | 98.83 | 98.83 | 98.83 | 98.60 | 98.60 | 98.60 | 98.89 | 98.89 | 98.89 | 98.74 | 98.74 | 98.74 |
| Avg. (−5 to 20) | 82.79 | 74.74 | 78.77 | 86.24 | 78.87 | 82.56 | 84.54 | 76.96 | 80.75 | **88.21** | **81.35** | **84.78** |

## 3.4   A Comparison with Other Noise Estimation Algorithms

To conclude our experimental evaluation, $\text{DNN}_2$, which has exhibited the best performance so far, is compared with different single-channel noise estimation algorithms when applied on the primary channel: Rangachari's algorithm (RANG) [4], improved minima controlled recursive averaging (IMCRA) [5], minimum statistics (MS) [6], MMSE-based noise estimation (MMSE) [7] and linear interpolation (INT) as described in Subsect. 2.2 with $M = 20$. Furthermore, power level difference noise estimation (PLDNE) [8], which is a dual-channel noise estimation algorithm based on recursive averaging, is also tested. PLDNE is especially interesting since it is intended for dual-microphone smartphones employed in close-talk conditions by assuming both a homogeneous diffuse noise field and that clean speech at the secondary channel is very attenuated with respect to the primary one. The corresponding WAcc results obtained when clean and multi-style acoustic models are used can be seen in Tables 4 and 5, respectively. As can be observed, on average and for all the SNRs considered but the clean case, $\text{DNN}_2$ shows the best performance among the noise estimation

**Table 4.** Comparison between several noise estimation algorithms in terms of WAcc (%) when clean acoustic models are employed. Results are averaged across all types of noise in test sets $A$ and $B$.

| Method/SNR (dB) | −5 | 0 | 5 | 10 | 15 | 20 | Clean | Avg. (−5 to 20) |
|---|---|---|---|---|---|---|---|---|
| Baseline | 18.15 | 31.85 | 56.11 | 82.78 | 94.72 | 97.76 | **99.13** | 63.56 |
| RANG | 38.15 | 64.35 | 83.30 | 92.22 | 95.42 | 96.40 | 96.48 | 78.31 |
| IMCRA | 35.07 | 63.38 | 83.60 | 93.04 | 96.99 | 98.21 | 99.01 | 78.38 |
| MS | 35.51 | 63.79 | 83.81 | 92.98 | 96.86 | 98.27 | 98.90 | 78.54 |
| MMSE | 38.87 | 66.27 | 85.57 | 93.65 | 97.14 | 98.33 | 99.08 | 79.97 |
| INT | 44.25 | 72.75 | 89.69 | 95.44 | 97.71 | 98.49 | 99.09 | 83.06 |
| PLDNE | 40.57 | 69.32 | 87.05 | 94.22 | 97.07 | 98.08 | 98.95 | 81.05 |
| $\text{DNN}_2$ | **51.95** | **78.42** | **92.37** | **96.97** | **98.38** | **98.86** | 99.02 | **86.16** |

**Table 5.** Comparison between several noise estimation algorithms in terms of WAcc (%) when multi-style acoustic models are employed. Results are averaged across all types of noise in test sets $A$ and $B$.

| Method/SNR (dB) | −5 | 0 | 5 | 10 | 15 | 20 | Clean | Avg. (−5 to 20) |
|---|---|---|---|---|---|---|---|---|
| Baseline | 36.93 | 66.69 | 88.85 | 95.73 | 97.56 | 98.31 | 98.77 | 80.68 |
| RANG | 45.76 | 73.26 | 89.72 | 95.62 | 97.44 | 98.22 | 98.40 | 83.34 |
| IMCRA | 41.78 | 71.49 | 88.80 | 95.32 | 97.69 | 98.47 | 98.88 | 82.26 |
| MS | 49.65 | 71.71 | 88.96 | 95.49 | 97.75 | 98.53 | 98.89 | 83.68 |
| MMSE | 44.99 | 72.85 | 89.22 | 95.38 | 97.58 | 98.49 | **99.01** | 83.09 |
| INT | 47.98 | 76.07 | 91.22 | 96.00 | 97.91 | 98.49 | 98.79 | 84.61 |
| PLDNE | 48.11 | 77.70 | 92.68 | 96.65 | 98.05 | 98.53 | 98.71 | 85.29 |
| $DNN_2$ | **55.71** | **81.49** | **93.48** | **97.39** | **98.47** | **98.72** | 98.99 | **87.54** |

algorithms evaluated. In particular, thanks to the powerful regression capabilities of DNNs, $DNN_2$ is able to achieve a greater performance than PLDNE with no other assumptions than just exploiting the PLD between the two channels of the device.

## 4    Conclusions

In this paper we have presented a novel noise estimation method for noise-robust ASR in dual-microphone smartphones. In particular, a DNN has successfully been used to find a non-linear mapping function between dual-channel noisy speech and noise log-Mel features at the primary channel of the smartphone. Thanks to the powerful regression capabilities of DNNs, very high word recognition results have been obtained by just using simple features as well as exploiting the PLD between the two channels of the device when employed in close-talk conditions. As future work, we would like to explore the performance of this approach under different mobile devices with different small array configurations (e.g. with more than two microphones) as well as employed in arbitrary positions and not only in close-talk conditions.

## References

1. Li, J., Deng, L., Gong, Y., Haeb-Umbach, R.: An overview of noise-robust automatic speech recognition. IEEE Trans. Audio Speech Lang. Process. **22**(4), 745–777 (2014)
2. Moreno, P.J., et al.: A vector Taylor series approach for environment-independent speech recognition. In: ICASSP, Atlanta, USA, pp. 733–736 (1996)
3. Wu, J., Droppo, J., Deng, L., Acero, A.: A noise-robust ASR front-end using Wiener filter constructed from MMSE estimation of clean speech and noise. In: ASRU, Virgin Islands, pp. 321–326 (2003)
4. Rangachari, S., Loizou, P.C.: A noise-estimation algorithm for highly non-stationary environments. Speech Commun. **48**, 220–231 (2006)

5. Cohen, I.: Noise spectrum estimation in adverse environments: IMCRA. IEEE Trans. Speech Audio Process. **11**, 466–475 (2003)
6. Martin, R.: Noise power spectral density estimation based on optimal smoothing and minimum statistics. IEEE Trans. Speech Audio Process. **9**, 504–512 (2001)
7. Hendriks, R.C., Heusdens, R., Jensen, J.: MMSE based noise PSD tracking with low complexity. In: ICASSP, Dallas, USA (2010)
8. Jeub, M., et al.: Noise reduction for dual-microphone mobile phones exploiting power level differences. In: ICASSP, Kyoto, Japan, pp. 1693–1696 (2012)
9. Zhang, J., et al.: A fast two-microphone noise reduction algorithm based on power level ratio for mobile phone. In: ISCSLP, Hong-Kong, pp. 206–209 (2012)
10. López-Espejo, I., et al.: Feature enhancement for robust speech recognition on smartphones with dual-microphone. In: EUSIPCO, Lisbon, Portugal (2014)
11. López-Espejo, I., González, J.A., Gómez, Á.M., Peinado, A.M.: A deep neural network approach for missing-data mask estimation on dual-microphone smartphones: application to noise-robust speech recognition. In: Navarro Mesa, J.L., Ortega, A., Teixeira, A., Hernández Pérez, E., Quintana Morales, P., Ravelo García, A., Guerra Moreno, I., Toledano, D.T. (eds.) IberSPEECH 2014. LNCS (LNAI), vol. 8854, pp. 119–128. Springer, Heidelberg (2014). doi:10.1007/978-3-319-13623-3_13
12. Wang, Y., Wang, D.L.: Towards scaling up classication-based speech separation. IEEE Trans. Audio Speech Lang. Process. **21**(7), 1381–1390 (2013)
13. Vincent, E.: Is audio signal processing still useful in the era of machine learning? In: WASPAA, New York, USA (2015)
14. Hinton, G.E., Osindero, S., Teh, Y.W.: A fast learning algorithm for deep belief nets. Neural Comput. **18**, 1527–1554 (2006)
15. Hinton, G.E., Salakhutdinov, R.: Reducing the dimensionality of data with neural networks. Science **313**(5786), 504–507 (2006)
16. Seltzer, M.L., et al.: An investigation of deep neural networks for noise robust speech recognition. In: ICASSP, Vancouver, Canada, pp. 7398–7402 (2013)
17. Xu, Y., Du, J., Dai, L.R.: A regression approach to speech enhancement based on deep neural networks. IEEE Trans. Audio Speech Lang. Process. **23**(1), 7–19 (2015)
18. Segura, J.C., et al.: Model-based compensation of the additive noise for continuous speech recognition. Experiments using the AURORA II database and tasks. In: EUROSPEECH, Aalborg, Denmark (2001)
19. Pearce, D., Hirsch, H.G.: The Aurora experimental framework for the performance evaluation of speech recognition systems under noisy conditions. In: ICSLP, Beijing, China (2000)
20. ETSI ES 201 108 - Distributed speech recognition; Front-end feature extraction algorithm; Compression algorithms
21. Hinton, G.E.: A practical guide to training restricted Boltzmann machines. UTML TR 2010–003 (2010)
22. Theano Library. http://deeplearning.net/software/theano/

# Better Phoneme Recognisers Lead to Better Phoneme Posteriorgrams for Search on Speech? An Experimental Analysis

Paula Lopez-Otero$^{(\boxtimes)}$, Laura Docio-Fernandez, and Carmen Garcia-Mateo

Multimedia Technologies Group (GTM), AtlantTIC Research Center,
University of Vigo, E.E. Telecomunicación, Campus Universitario de Vigo S/N,
36310 Vigo, Spain
{plopez,ldocio,carmen}@gts.uvigo.es

**Abstract.** Phoneme posteriorgrams are widely used for speech representation when performing query-by-example search on speech. These posteriorgrams are computed by obtaining the per-frame a posteriori probability of each unit in a phoneme recogniser, regardless the architecture of this phoneme recogniser. It is straightforward to believe that the higher the quality of the phone transcriptions generated by a phoneme recogniser, the higher the quality of its resulting phoneme posteriorgrams; however, to the best of our knowledge, no analysis exist proving this statement. This paper aims at investigating whether there is a correlation between the phone error rate of a recogniser and the maximum term weighted value obtained when performing query-by-example search on speech. Experiments on the Albayzin corpus in Spanish language showed a slight correlation between these two metrics, which suggests that the goodness of phoneme posteriorgram representation is somehow related to phone error rate, but there are other factors that affect their performance in search on speech tasks.

**Keywords:** Query-by-example search on speech · Phoneme recognition · Phoneme posteriorgram

## 1  Introduction

The growing amount of audio documents that are available nowadays has created the need for tools to perform automatic search in this type of contents, either using a textual or a spoken query. The most typical approach for search on speech consists in producing a transcription of the audio documents by means of an automatic speech recognition (ASR) approach and then performing a textual search [8]. However, the performance of this type of approaches is highly conditioned by the quality of the ASR system, since its output contains errors that lead to incorrect detections when performing the search. Hence, instead of performing textual search on the 1-best hypothesis produced by the recogniser, it is common to represent speech by means of lattices [5,6], which allows to find terms that were not the most likely option when producing the 1-best hypothesis [23].

© Springer International Publishing AG 2016
A. Abad et al. (Eds.): IberSPEECH 2016, LNAI 10077, pp. 128–137, 2016.
DOI: 10.1007/978-3-319-49169-1_13

The use of ASR-based approaches is also common when dealing with search on speech using spoken queries (query-by-example spoken term detection, QbESTD) [12]. Nevertheless, due to the growing interest in speech research devoted to low-resource languages, partly encouraged by the organization of different evaluations on this topic [2,3,13,14,25], QbESTD is commonly approached by means of pattern matching techniques: first features representing the documents and the queries are obtained, and then a search strategy usually based on dynamic time warping (DTW) is applied [11]. One of the most common speech representation approaches in QbESTD consists in using phoneme posteriorgrams: each frame is represented by means of the a posteriori probabilities of each phonetic class in a given time instant [9]. These a posteriori probabilities are obtained using a phoneme recogniser that does not have to be specifically trained for the language of the documents to be represented, which increases the usability of this approach.

Different phone recognition architectures have been used in the QbESTD literature to obtain phoneme posteriorgrams. In general, two different groups of architectures can be differentiated: one of them consists in using Gaussian-mixture models (GMMs) as state probability density functions (PDF) of hidden Markov models (HMMs), namely GMM-HMM [4]; while the other consists in hybrid approaches using deep neural networks (DNNs) for PDF modelling combined with HMMs (DNN-HMM architectures). In the latter type of architecture, the DNN can be a multi-layer perceptron (MLP) as in [1,20,22,26] or any other type of DNN [28]. Nevertheless, which is the best strategy to obtain phoneme posteriorgrams and what makes phoneme posteriorgrams extracted with a given architecture better than others is a topic that has not been addressed yet.

This paper aims at analysing the performance of different phone recognition architectures in two different tasks: phoneme recognition and QbESTD using phoneme posteriorgram representation of the audio contents. The different architectures were evaluated when performing these tasks in terms of phone error rate (PER) and maximum term weighted value (MTWV), respectively, in order to try to find a relation between these two performance measures. The experiments required for this analysis were performed on the Albayzin corpus [15]. This database in Spanish language is manually transcribed, allowing to assess the phone transcriptions generated by the different phoneme recognisers. In addition, a QbESTD experiment was designed using this data, which implied the manual extraction of a set of spoken queries. The experimental results indicated that there is a relation between the PER and the MTWV; nevertheless, this relation was not observed in all the evaluated architectures, which suggests that the quality of the phoneme recogniser is not the only relevant factor when it comes to producing phoneme posteriorgram representations.

This paper is organized as follows: the different phoneme recognition architectures and the QbESTD approach are described in Sects. 2 and 3, respectively; in Sect. 4, the metrics used to evaluate these systems are presented; the experimental framework used in these experiments is described in Sect. 5; the experimental results are commented in Sect. 6; to finish, conclusions and future work are summarized in Sect. 7.

## 2    Phoneme Recognition Approaches

In this work, several phoneme recognisers employing different acoustic models were developed. These acoustic models consist in either three-state GMM-HMM or DNN-HMM architectures that were trained using Kaldi toolkit [19]. Acoustic model training was done using the standard incremental methodology, in which more complex models are initialised using phone alignments obtained using more simple models that were previously trained. The procedure followed for acoustic model training is described below:

– First, monophoneme models (**mono**) were trained starting from an initial alignment of the training data, in which all the phonemes are assumed equiprobable and with the same mean and variance (*flat-start*). These models use a parametrization of the input audio consisting of 13 Mel-frequency cepstral coefficients (MFCCs) plus their corresponding delta ($\Delta$) and acceleration ($\Delta\Delta$) coefficients.

– A forced alignment is performed using the **mono** acoustic models, which is employed to train triphoneme models (**tri1**) using the same parametrization (13 MFCCs+$\Delta$+$\Delta\Delta$).

– A new forced alignment is done using the **tri1** models, and a linear discriminant analysis + maximum likelihood linear transformation (LDA+MLLT) is trained using a window of 7 frames that includes the current frame and a left and right context of three frames. A new set of triphoneme models (**tri2**) is trained using this new parametrization and the aforementioned forced alignment.

– Starting from the alignment obtained using the **tri2** models, new triphoneme models are obtained (**tri3**) by performing a speaker adaptation step (speaker adaptive training, SAT) using the constrained maximum likelihood linear regression (fMLLR) approach [7]. A set of models that do not apply this adaptation step is also obtained (**tri3.si**).

– Triphoneme models using the subspace Gaussian mixture models (**sgmm**) are trained using the forced alignment obtained employing **tri3** models. To do so, a fMLLR transformation and a new speaker adaptation step based on subspaces are performed.

– Starting from the **sgmm** models and their corresponding alignment, four iterations of discriminative training using boosted maximum mutual information [17] were performed, resulting in the set of models **sgmm_bmmi_it**.

– A hybrid approach combining DNNs and HMMs was used to obtain a set of models (**dnn_smbr**), which was trained using a method based on the minimization of the Bayes error at the state level (SMBR) [27].

– To finish, a different DNN-based architecture using activation functions of type *tanh* [18] was employed to train another set of acoustic models (**nnet2**).

These acoustic models were used in a phoneme recogniser that uses either a language model based on phoneme bigrams or a phone loop. The bigram LM was trained using the transcriptions of the training data.

# 3    Query-by-Example Search on Speech Strategy

The QbESTD strategy used in this paper encompasses two different stages: feature extraction, where phoneme posteriorgrams are used; and the search stage, which is performed using a dynamic time warping (DTW) approach.

## 3.1    Speech Representation by Means of Phoneme Posteriorgrams

As mentioned in Sect. 1, one of the most widely used techniques for representing documents and queries in QbESTD consists in using phoneme posteriorgrams [9]: given a speech document and a phoneme recogniser with U phonetic units, the a posteriori probability of each phonetic unit is computed for each time frame, leading to a set of vectors of dimension U that represent the probability of each phonetic unit at every time instant.

In this paper, phoneme posteriorgrams were obtained by collecting posterior probabilities from the lattices generated using the phoneme recognisers described in Sect. 2.

## 3.2    Search Algorithm: Subsequence-DTW

The search stage of QbESTD systems is usually carried out using the DTW algorithm [21]: given a document $D = \{d_1, \ldots, d_m\}$ and a query $Q = \{q_1, \ldots, q_n\}$ of m and n frames respectively, with $n \ll m$, DTW finds the best alignment path between these two sequences. In search on speech, the use of modifications of this algorithm such as subsequence DTW (S-DTW) [16] or non-segmental DTW [11] is very common. In this system, S-DTW is employed.

To perform S-DTW, first a cost matrix $M \in \Re^{n \times m}$ must be defined, in which the rows and columns correspond to the query and document frames, respectively:

$$M_{i,j} = \begin{cases} c(q_i, d_j) & \text{if } i = 0 \\ c(q_i, d_j) + M_{i-1,0} & \text{if } i > 0, \ j = 0 \\ c(q_i, d_j) + M^*(i, j) & \text{else} \end{cases} \tag{1}$$

where $c(q_i, d_j)$ is a function that defines the cost between the query vector $q_i$ and the document vector $d_j$, and

$$M^*(i, j) = min\left(M_{i-1,j}, M_{i-1,j-1}, M_{i,j-1}\right) \tag{2}$$

Different metrics can be used to define the cost function, such as the Euclidean distance or the cosine similarity. In this system, Pearson's correlation coefficient $r$ was used [26] due to its superior performance in previous experiments [10]:

$$r(q_i, d_j) = \frac{U(q_i \cdot d_j) - \|q_i\| \|d_j\|}{\sqrt{(U\|q_i^2\| - \|q_i\|^2)(U\|d_j^2\| - \|d_j\|^2)}} \tag{3}$$

where $q_i \cdot d_j$ denotes the dot product of $q_i$ and $d_j$.

High values of $r$ correspond to low costs and vice versa; hence, in order to be able to use this correlation as a cost function defined in the interval $[0,1]$, the following transformation is applied:

$$c(q_i, d_j) = \frac{1 - r(q_i, d_j)}{2} \tag{4}$$

Once matrix M is computed, the end of the best warping path between Q and D is obtained as

$$b^* = \underset{b \in 1,...,m}{\arg\min}\ M(n, b) \tag{5}$$

The starting point of the path ending at $b^*$, namely $a^*$, is computed by backtracking, hence obtaining the best warping path $P(Q, D) = \{p_1, \ldots, p_k, \ldots, p_K\}$, where $p_k = (i_k, j_k)$, i.e. the $k$-th element of the path is formed by $q_{i_k}$ and $d_{j_k}$, and K is the length of the warping path.

It is possible that a query Q appears several times in a document D, especially if D is a long recording. Hence, not only the best warping path must be detected but also others that are less likely. One approach to overcome this issue consists in detecting a given number of candidate matches $n_c$: every time a warping path, that ends at frame $b^*$, is detected, $M(n, b^*)$ is set to $\infty$ in order to ignore this element in the future.

A score must be assigned to every detection of a query Q in a document D. One of the most common methods consists in normalising the cumulative cost of the path $P(Q, D)$ by the length in frames of the document and the query [1]. After that, z-norm can be applied in order to equalise the score distributions of the different queries [24].

## 4   Performance Measures

The most common manner to assess the performance of a phoneme recogniser is by means of the phone error rate (PER). The PER is the average number of phoneme errors that are produced in a phonetic transcription, taking into account three different types of error: phoneme substitutions (S), phoneme deletions (D) and phoneme insertions (I). This metric, which is equivalent to the word error rate in continuous speech recognition, is defined as the sum of these three types of error normalised by the number of reference phonemes P:

$$PER = \frac{S + D + I}{P} \tag{6}$$

One of the most widely used metrics to assess QbESTD approaches is the maximum term weighted value (MTWV). To define the MTWV, first the average term weighted value (ATWV)[1] must be defined:

---

[1] The Spoken Term Detection (STD) 2006 Evaluation Plan, National Institute of Standards and Technology (NIST): http://www.itl.nist.gov/iad/mig/tests/std/2006/docs/std06-evalplan-v10.pdf.

$$\text{ATWV}(\Theta) = 1 - \underset{\text{term}}{\text{average}}\{P_{\text{Miss}}(\text{term}, \Theta) + \beta \cdot P_{\text{FA}}(\text{term}, \Theta)\} \qquad (7)$$

where $P_{\text{Miss}}(\text{term}, \Theta)$ is the probability of not detecting *term* with a decision threshold $\Theta$, $P_{\text{FA}}(\text{term}, \Theta)$ is the probability of producing false alarms of *term* given $\Theta$, and $\beta$ is a weighting factor that gives more or less relevance to false alarms or to mis-detections.

The MTWV is defined as the ATWV at the optimal decision threshold $\Theta_{\text{opt}}$, i.e. $\text{ATWV}(\Theta_{\text{opt}})$. MTWV is equal to ATWV when the system is appropriately calibrated. Hence, in this paper, the quality of the QbESTD is assessed in terms of MTWV in order to avoid the influence of calibration.

## 5   Experimental Framework

In these experiments, the Albayzin corpus of non-spontaneous speech in Spanish language [15] was used. This corpus has two partitions: training (FA) and test (FP). FA encompasses recordings of 164 speakers, while FP includes 40 speakers.

The manual transcriptions included in Albayzin corpus were used to assess phoneme recognition by means of the PER. For the QbESTD experiments, a set of acoustic queries to be searched in the FP partition were extracted from the FA partition, in order to avoid biasing the experiments. Hence, a set of terms that were present in FA and FP partitions were detected; these terms were cut from sentences in the FA corpus, leading to a set of 58 queries. All the examples were extracted from recordings of different speakers in order to enrich the variability of this set. The selected queries are enumerated in Table 1.

**Table 1.** List of terms used as queries in the QbESTD experiments.

| | | | | | | |
|---|---|---|---|---|---|---|
| agua | ambiente | amigo | apartamento | blanco | cabeza | cabeza |
| café | capacidad | cariño | Carmen | carne | carretera | Cataluña |
| causa | cenar | clase | comunista | derecho | dinero | disgustos |
| distinguida | estudios | falda | final | franceses | gafas | gente |
| globo | grupo | habitación | hierro | historia | hombre | iglesia |
| imposible | inglés | lengua | llorar | matrimonio | mercado | miedo |
| minutos | mujer | mundo | niño | padre | partido | primero |
| pueblo | quince | recuerdos | sangre | semana | siglo | suerte |
| verano | viaje | viento | | | | |

## 6   Results

Table 2 shows the results obtained on the phoneme recognition and QbESTD experiments when using the bigram LM and the phone loop. In terms of PER, the worst performance was obtained when using the **mono** system, while the best one was achieved with the **nnet_smbr** approach. These results were as expected, since simpler approaches were expected to obtain worse results than more complex strategies. In addition, using the bigram LM improved the phoneme recognition performance with respect to using a phone loop, since the former strategy eases the task of looking for the most probable sequence of phonemes, while the latter allows for any phoneme combination, even those that are not possible in Spanish language.

In terms of MTWV, results in Table 2 suggest that there is not a clear relation between the PER and the QbESTD performance: the highest MTWV was achieved with the **tri2** and **tri1** systems when using the bigram LM and the phone loop, respectively. It is also noticeable that, in the case of the **nnet_smbr** approach, good search on speech results were achieved when using the phone loop but this did not happen when using the bigram LM. This suggests that language modelling is not a value-added when performing QbESTD since, in general, better QbESTD results were achieved when using the phone loop. However, in the case of the **tri2** system, results were better when using the bigram LM, but the opposite happened when using any other approach. Lastly, it can be noted that using speaker adaptation in the **tri3** system reduced QbESTD performance, contrarily to what happened in the phoneme recognition task.

**Table 2.** Results of the phoneme recognition experiment, in terms of PER; and the QbESTD experiment, in terms of MTWV.

|  | System | Bigram LM | | Phone loop | |
|---|---|---|---|---|---|
|  |  | PER (%) | MTWV | PER (%) | MTWV |
| GMM-HMM | mono | 23.7 | 0.0585 | 30.7 | 0.0771 |
|  | tri1 | 20.8 | 0.2307 | 27.9 | **0.2698** |
|  | tri2 | 17.4 | **0.2607** | 22.4 | 0.1808 |
|  | tri3.si | 18.0 | 0.2377 | 22.9 | 0.2430 |
|  | tri3 | 14.7 | 0.1804 | 19.6 | 0.2069 |
|  | sgmm | 13.3 | 0.1580 | 17.8 | 0.2322 |
|  | sgmm_bmmi_it1 | 13.5 | 0.1928 | 18.4 | 0.2342 |
|  | sgmm_bmmi_it2 | 13.3 | 0.1946 | 18.2 | 0.2325 |
|  | sgmm_bmmi_it3 | 13.2 | 0.1946 | 17.9 | 0.2325 |
|  | sgmm_bmmi_it4 | 13.1 | 0.1928 | 17.8 | 0.2434 |
| DNN-HMM | nnet2 | 15.3 | 0.1834 | 17.7 | 0.1249 |
|  | nnet_smbr | **12.5** | 0.1766 | **14.1** | 0.2427 |

Figure 1 presents a graphic representation of the results in Table 2, with the aim of visualising the presumed existence of a correlation between PER and MTWV. For this purpose, the systems were sorted in increasing order according to their MTWV, and the complementary of the PER was represented for each system (i.e. 100-PER) in order to have a direct relation between the two variables. As observed in the figure, the premise 'better phoneme recognisers lead to better phoneme posteriorgrams for QbESTD' is not fulfilled in most of the systems: this fact is especially noticeable in the case of the systems **tri1**, **tri2** and **tri3.si** when using the bigram LM, since they show the worst results in terms of PER but, nevertheless, their QbESTD results are the best of all the assessed approaches. In the case of the phone loop, unexpected results can also be observed in the case of systems **nnet2**, **tri1** and **tri3.si**.

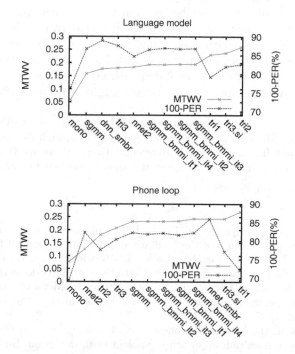

**Fig. 1.** Graphic representation of the phoneme recognition results, in terms of the complementary of PER; and the QbESTD results, in terms of MTWV.

The results in Table 2 were used to compute the correlation between MTWV and PER: this value was equal to $-0.2645$ when using the bigram LM and equal to $-0.3977$ when using the phone loop. These numerical results suggest that there is a slight correlation between QbESTD and phoneme recognition performance, as shown in Fig. 1.

## 7  Conclusions and Future Work

This paper presented a series of phoneme recognition and QbESTD experiments, aiming at finding out whether there is a relation between the phone error rate and QbESTD performance, measured in terms of the MTWV. The present study, which was carried out using the Albayzin corpus of non-spontaneous speech in Spanish language, suggests that there is a slight relation between phoneme recognition and QbESTD performances. This relation was more evident when using a phone loop instead of a language model, but still some inconsistencies appeared, such as systems with a poor performance in QbESTD but a good one in phoneme recognition and vice versa.

Future experiments in this research line will focus in finding out which are the factors that influence the quality of phoneme posteriorgrams by means of an in-deep analysis of the obtained results: the confusion between different phonemes and the approach used to extract the phoneme posteriorgrams will be analysed in depth. With respect to the latter issue, it must be mentioned that the phoneme posteriorgrams used in this paper were obtained from phoneme lattices, but there are other possibilities that can be explored such as directly using the likelihoods of the acoustic model distribution functions computed frame by frame.

**Acknowledgements.** This research was funded by the Spanish Government under the project TEC2015-65345-P, the Galician Government through the research contract GRC2014/024 (Modalidade: Grupos de Referencia Competitiva 2014) and AtlantTIC Project CN2012/160, and by the European Regional Development Fund (ERDF).

# References

1. Abad, A., Astudillo, R., Trancoso, I.: The L2F spoken web search system for Medi-aeval 2013. In: Proceedings of the MediaEval 2013 Workshop (2013)
2. Anguera, X., Metze, F., Buzo, A., Szöke, I., Rodriguez-Fuentes, L.: The spoken web search task. In: Proceedings of the MediaEval 2013 Workshop (2013)
3. Anguera, X., Rodriguez-Fuentes, L., Szöke, I., Buzo, A., Metze, F.: Query by example search on speech at MediaEval 2014. In: Proceedings of the MediaEval 2014 Workshop (2014)
4. Buzo, A., Cucu, H., Molnar, I., Ionescu, B., Burileanu, C.: SpeeD @ MediaEval 2013: a phone recognition approach to spoken term detection. In: Proceedings of the MediaEval 2013 Workshop (2013)
5. Can, D., Saraclar, M.: Lattice indexing for spoken term detection. IEEE Trans. Audio Speech Lang. Process. **19**(8), 2338–2347 (2011)
6. Chelba, C., Hazen, T.J., Saraclar, M.: Retrieval and browsing of spoken content. IEEE Sig. Process. Mag. **25**(3), 39–49 (2008)
7. Gales, M.: Maximum likelihood linear transformations for hmm-based speech recognition. Comput. Speech Lang. **12**(2), 75–98 (1998)
8. Garofolo, J., Auzanne, G., Voorhees, E.: The TREC spoken document retrieval task: a success story. In: Proceedings of the 4th International Workshop on Spoken Language Technologies for Under-Resourced Languages (SLTU) (2014)
9. Hazen, T., Shen, W., White, C.: Query-by-example spoken term detection using phonetic posteriorgram templates. In: IEEE Workshop on Automatic Speech Recognition & Understanding, ASRU, pp. 421–426 (2009)
10. Lopez-Otero, P., Docio-Fernandez, L., Garcia-Mateo, C.: Phonetic unit selection for cross-lingual query-by-example spoken term detection. In: IEEE Workshop on Automatic Speech Recognition and Understanding (ASRU), pp. 223–229 (2015)
11. Mantena, G., Achanta, S., Prahallad, K.: Query-by-example spoken term detection using frequency domain linear prediction and non-segmental dynamic time warping. IEEE/ACM Trans. Audio Speech Lang. Process. **22**(5), 944–953 (2014)

12. Martinez, M., Lopez-Otero, P., Varela, R., Cardenal-Lopez, A., Docio-Fernandez, L., Garcia-Mateo, C.: GTM-UVigo systems for Albayzin 2014 search on speech evaluation. In: Iberspeech 2014: VIII Jornadas en Tecnologa del Habla and IV SLTech Workshop (2014)
13. Metze, F., Barnard, E., Davel, M., Heerden, C.V., Anguera, X., Gravier, G., Rajput, N.: The spoken web search task. In: Proceedings of the MediaEval 2012 Workshop (2012)
14. Metze, F., Rajput, N., Anguera, X., Davel, M., Gravier, G., Heerden, C.V., Mantena, G., Muscariello, A., Pradhallad, K., Szöke, I., Tejedor, J.: The spoken web search task at MediaEval 2011. In: Proceedings of ICASSP (2012)
15. Moreno, A., Poch, D., Bonafonte, A., Lleida, E., Llisterri, J., Mariño, J., Nadeu, C.: Albayzin speech database: design of the phonetic corpus. In: Proceedings of Eurospeech (1993)
16. Müller, M.: Information Retrieval for Music and Motion. Springer, Heidelberg (2007)
17. Povey, D., Kanevsky, D., Kingsbury, B., Ramabhadran, B., Saon, G., Visweswariah, K.: Boosted MMI for model and feature-space discriminative training. In: Proceedings of ICASSP, pp. 4057–4060 (2008)
18. Povey, D., Zhang, X., Khudanpur, S.: Parallel training of deep neural networks with natural gradient and parameter averaging. CoRR abs/1410.7455 (2014). http://arxiv.org/abs/1410.7455
19. Povey, D., Ghoshal, A., Boulianne, G., Burget, L., Glembek, O., Goel, N., Hannemann, M., Motlicek, P., Qian, Y., Schwarz, P., Silovsky, J., Stemmer, G., Vesely, K.: The Kaldi speech recognition toolkit. In: IEEE 2011 Workshop on Automatic Speech Recognition and Understanding. IEEE Signal Processing Society (2011)
20. Rodriguez-Fuentes, L., Varona, A., Penagarikano, M.: GTTS-EHU systems for QUESST at MediaEval 2014. In: Proceedings of the MediaEval 2014 Workshop (2014)
21. Sakoe, H., Chiba, S.: Dynamic programming algorithm optimization for spoken word recognition. IEEE Trans. Acoustics Speech Sig. Process. **26**(1), 43–49 (1978)
22. Schwarz, P.: Phoneme recognition based on long temporal context. Ph.D. thesis, Brno University of Technology (2009)
23. Siohan, O., Bacchiani, M.: Fast vocabulary independent audio search using path based graph indexing. In: Proceedings of Interspeech/Eurospeech, pp. 53–56 (2005)
24. Szöke, I., Burget, L., Grézl, F., Černocký, J., Ondel, L.: Calibration and fusion of query-by-example systems - BUT SWS 2013. In: Proceedings of ICASSP, pp. 7899–7903 (2014)
25. Szöke, I., Rodriguez-Fuentes, L., Buzo, A., Anguera, X., Metze, F., Proenca, J., Lojka, M., Xiong, X.: Query by example search on speech at Mediaeval 2015. In: Proceedings of the MediaEval 2015 Workshop (2015)
26. Szöke, I., Skácel, M., Burget, L.: BUT QUESST2014 system description. In: Proceedings of the MediaEval 2014 Workshop (2014)
27. Veselý, K., Ghoshal, A., Burget, L., Povey, D.: Sequence discriminative training of deep neural networks. In: Proceedings of Interspeech, pp. 2345–2349, no. 8 (2013)
28. Yang, P., Xu, H., Xiao, X., Xie, L., Leung, C.C., Chen, H., Yu, J., Lv, H., Wang, L., Leow, S., Ma, B., Chng, E., Li, H.: The NNI query-by-example system for MediaEval 2014. In: Proceedings of the MediaEval 2014 Workshop (2014)

# Crowdsourced Video Subtitling with Adaptation Based on User-Corrected Lattices

João Miranda[1,2], Ramón F. Astudillo[2,3(✉)], Ângela Costa[2], André Silva[3],
Hugo Silva[3], João Graça[3], and Bhiksha Raj[4]

[1] VoiceInteraction, São Paulo, Brazil
[2] INESC-ID/Instituto Superior Técnico, Lisboa, Portugal
ramon@astudillo.com
[3] Unbabel Inc., San Francisco, USA
[4] School of Computer Science, Carnegie Mellon University, Pittsburgh, PA, USA

**Abstract.** This paper investigates an approach for fast hybrid human and machine video subtitling based on lattice disambiguation and posterior model adaptation. The approach aims at correcting Automatic Speech Recognition (ASR) transcriptions requiring minimal effort from the user and facilitating user corrections from smart-phone devices. Our approach is based on three key concepts. Firstly, only a portion of the data is sent to the user for correction. Secondly, user action is limited to selecting from a fixed set of options extracted from the ASR word lattice. Thirdly, user feedback is used to update the ASR parameters and further enhance performance. To investigate the potential and limitations of this approach, we carry out experiments employing simulated and real user corrections of TED talks videos. Simulated corrections include both the true reference and the best combination of the options shown to the user. Real corrections are obtained from 30 editors through a special purpose web-interface displaying the options for small video segments. We analyze the fixed option approach and the trade-off between model adaptation and increasing the amount of corrected data.

## 1 Introduction

The widespread use of the internet has had a profound impact in many aspects of human life. One good example of this is crowdsourcing, which can be defined as solving a task by joining the forces of many non-experts through an open call [6]. Unsurprisingly, for data-hungry fields like automatic speech processing, crowdsourcing is a growing trend in the last years. One particular brand of crowdsourcing approaches are those based on post-editing of automaticaly processed tasks. In this type of approach, machine learning techniques are applied to obtain an initial solution of the task at hand, which is then crowdsourced to a number of post-editors, who improve upon it.

Post-editing of automatically processed tasks considerably lowers the effort of task completion for humans and outperforms fully automatic approaches. Therefore, its use in a number of different tasks has been investigated including

© Springer International Publishing AG 2016
A. Abad et al. (Eds.): IberSPEECH 2016, LNAI 10077, pp. 138–147, 2016.
DOI: 10.1007/978-3-319-49169-1_14

Machine Translation (MT) [4,9,12] Automatic Speech Recognition (ASR) [17, 18] as well as Optical Character Recognition (OCR) [14], among other tasks.

Unbabel[1] is a start-up specializing on crowd-sourced MT post-editing. At Unbabel, each translation job is divided into a number of smaller tasks that can be directed to different users for post-edition. Unbabel also provides editors with a mobile application for easy access to small chunks of post-editing work. This approach facilitates the use of editor spare time and allows a number of strategies for quality control or optimization of the available manpower.

Following this model, in this paper we investigate an approach for crowd-sourced ASR post-editing that minimizes editor effort. The approach is based on three main concepts:

1. Only a portion of the data is presented to the users for correction. Data is also chunked into small tasks.
2. User action is limited to selecting from a fixed set of options determined by simplifying the recognition lattice provided by the ASR system.
3. User feedback is used to update the ASR system parameters and further enhance performance with a second recognition pass.

Fixing the options lowers the difficulty of the task and is particularly useful in the case of mobile applications, where text input requires additional effort. It can be thus expected that fast transcriptions can be attained on small chunks of a transcription job. These can be used in turn to fine tune models for a specific task or attain initial reference statitics, which could be useful for task partition.

In order to explore the potentials and limitations of this approach, various experiments were carried out. The experiments analyzed the effect of varying the quantity of data to be corrected, the effect of limiting the corrections to a fixed set of options and the parameter adaptation using the initial corrections. For this purpose, both oracle and real user corrections were employed. Real user experiments were carried out with the help of Unbabel's infrastructure.

This work can be related to others dealing with hypothesis fusion and acoustic model adaptation from crowdsourced data. In [2], both supervised and unsupervised methods to determine the reliability of the crowdsourced transcription are investigated. In [3] a similar approach is utilized to deal with noisy speech transcriptions. Both papers employ ROVER [8] to combine input from multiple transcriptions and well known general purpose crowdsourcing platforms such as Mechanical Turk [5], and Crowd Flower to obtain these transcriptions. Compared to these works, the work presented here focuses on limiting the effort of the user and employs a custom crowdsorcing platform with a small set of high quality editors. For these reason only a single transcription for each utterance is, at best, available which does not allow the use of ROVER. For the same reason, both acoustic and language model adaptation are investigated, rather than the fusion of multiple hypotheses.

The paper is organized as follows: Sect. 2 provides an overview of the system utilized in the experiments. Section 3 focuses in user corrections and its

---

[1] http://unbabel.com/.

integration in the posterior adaptation process. Section 4 details the experiments carried out to assess our system. Finally, in Sect. 5, we conclude and lay out future research.

## 2   System Overview

The system utilized for the proposed experiments is depicted in Fig. 1. It is composed of three main modules: an ASR-based transcription service, provided by INESC-ID, a task correction service, provided by Unbabel and a pool of registered editors who interact with the services through a web interface. The components communicate through the internet by exchanging JSON format files through the HTTP protocol. During operation the following steps are executed:

1. A video URL is input into the Task Correction service, which forwards this to the ASR service
2. The ASR service answers with the initial transcription of a small portion of the data
3. The Task Correction service distributes this through the pool of editors, collects the corrections and sends them back to the ASR service
4. The ASR service updates its parameters based on the provided transcriptions and carries out a second ASR run over the whole data.

Each service is now described in detail.

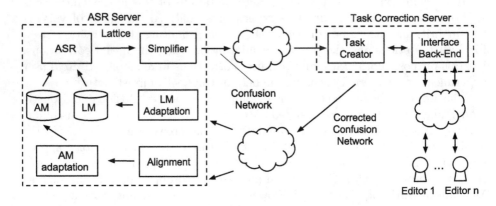

**Fig. 1.** Block Diagram of the system architecture developed for the presented experiments. Clouds indicate communication through the internet via HTTP and JSON format files.

### 2.1   ASR Service

**Lattice Simplification into Confusion Network.** The process at the ASR Server starts upon reception of the URL of a video to be transcribed. The server then retrieves the audio and performs ASR to obtain a recognition lattice. This lattice can be seen as a distribution over all possible word sequences given the audio and the information given by the recognizer's knowledge sources. In order to present the users with a set of options that is manageable and in an appealing format, the ASR lattice undergoes various simplifications.

The first step of this process consists in using a pivot-based algorithm [10] to obtain confusion networks from the word lattices. This is done by topologically sorting the lattices, computing posterior probabilities for each word, grouping together words that occur at the same time into the same slot, merging consecutive slots into single slots and the words in these slots into phrases.

The final confusion network is divided into tasks of 50 words each. Each slot in the task contains a maximum of 8 options to choose from, depending on the uncertainty present in the original lattice.

**Model Adaptation and Second Recognition Pass.** A second functionality of the ASR Service is the adaptation of models given the user corrected confusion matrix. This is triggered upon reception of a JSON file containing the corrections collected by the correction service. The corrected text is used to perform language model adaptation. The ASR system then executes a forced alignment to obtain frame level phoneme transcriptions. These are used to perform acoustic model adaptation. Since this adaptation stage plays a vital role in the experiments carried out, it is detailed in a separate section.

### 2.2   Task Correction Service

The correction service is hosted at Unbabel. It receives the ASR transcription of a video, in the form of a confusion network encoded in the JSON format. Each individual video is termed a transcription job, and divided into tasks of 50 words as computed in the ASR server. The number of tasks per job depends on the video length and ranges from 30 to 60 tasks.

The interface back-end creates one individual web page for each task as depicted in Fig. 2. This web page can then be sent to one or more editors to start the correction process. Each editor has access to a web interface displaying the video and the options in the confusion network. Each task is displayed to the editor as 10 consecutive segments. The video corresponding to each segment can be played by clicking on the link adjacent to the displayed text. In addition to this, the editors have full control over the video player, which provides all basic functionalities including pause and fine grained selection of particular time segments. Upon clicking on a word, a drop-down menu appears displaying the options on the confusion network. A user can select the correct option by clicking on the correct word. Note that the option to "delete" a word ($\epsilon$) is also available in those cases this option was probable enough.

Once all tasks have been completed, the correction service collects and rebuilds the original confusion network for a given video, providing only the options selected by the users. These are then sent back to the ASR server for the adaptation phase.

**Fig. 2.** Unbabel task correction interface. On the left hand pane is the talk being transcribed. At the right are the automatically transcribed segments, including their start and end times, together with the alternatives that the system generated for the word 'work'.

## 2.3  Pool of Editors

In the context of this work, the editor pool was sensibly different from the one employed at Unbabel for Machine Translation correction. Unbabel maintains a large pool of editors with different categorizations based on a reputation system. Editors apply online and are identified by their Unbabel account. Various mechanisms are also in place to prevent system abuse, including peer rating of tasks to detect lower quality work.

In the context of this experiment, a number of volunteer editors were directly contacted. Editors lacked, therefore, an economical incentive to perform. This editors, however, were not anonymous. We believe that this partially compensated the lack of incentives. Manual revision of the results seem also to corroborate this fact.

## 3   Task Correction and Adaptation

As indicated in the previous section, after all tasks coresponding to a video have been completed, the result is sent back to the ASR server for adaptation. For ASR we employ our own in-house AUDIMUS ASR, which is an hybrid HMM-MLP system using the Weighted Finite State Transducer (WFST) approach to integrate knowledge sources. AUDIMUS combines three feature streams (RASTA, PLP and MSG) for improved robustness to different acoustic conditions [13].

### 3.1   Acoustic Model Adaptation

Adapting the models with the user feedback obtained from the web front-end presents various difficulties. As indicated in Sect. 2, the ASR lattice is simplified into a small confusion network to be presented to the user. User-disambiguated confusion networks have to be therefore re-aligned with the speech. This can introduce errors, since users may not select the best options and the generated alternatives may not contain the correct phrases. Thus, we select for adaptation only those words of the force aligned transcript that have a confidence measure value, computed by Audimus, above an empirically set threshold.

For adaptation, feature Discriminative Linear Regression (fDLR) [15,19] and conventional Stochastic Gradient Descent (SGD) [16] were used. SGD showed to be consistently better than fDLR for this task and was employed in the final system. To avoid overfitting, 10 % of the available data was held out for validation. The best model on the validation set after 50 iterations was selected.

### 3.2  Language Model Adaptation

User corrections were also employed to adapt the language model of the ASR system. The amount of data is available for language adaptation was small, ranging from a few utterances to several tens of utterances, depending on the size of the sample used to perform adaptation, see Sect. 4. Therefore, only the probabilities of a small number of n-grams were modified. The n-grams selected were those corrected by human annotators with low background LM probability. This proved to be useful as it boosted the probability of topic-related vocabulary occuring several times throughout the talk.

The conditional probability of a word is given by Eq. 1:

$$P(w_i|w_{i-n+1}..w_{i-1}) = \alpha P_{ng}(w_i|w_{i-n+1}..w_{i-1}) + (1-\alpha)P_c(w_i|w_{i-n+1}..w_{i-1}) \quad (1)$$

$$P_c(w_i|w_{i-n+1}..w_{i-1}) = \frac{\sum_{j \in occur(w_{i-n+1}..w_i)} d(j,i)}{\sum_{k \in occur(w_{i-n+1}..w_{i-1})} d(k,i)} \quad (2)$$

In Eq. 1, $P_{ng}$ represents the background n-gram probability and $\alpha$ is the mixing weight, used to combine it with the cache language model probability, and determined empirically on the development set. In Eq. 2, $d(i,j) = a^{-|i-j|}$ represents the distance function between two word positions $i$ and $j$, and $occur(n)$ is the set of positions where n-gram $n$ occurred. The term $d$ gives an emphasis to occurrences of an n-gram close to the current word position, which decreases exponentially with distance. This is similar to a cache LM [11].

We approximate the LM $P$ with an n-gram model for each sentence, for efficient decoding. In order to do this, each n-gram probability is kept fixed within each sentence. This is achieved by setting the position $i$, of each n-gram, in Eq. 2 to the beginning of that sentence. The resulting approximation to LM $P$ is then used when re-scoring the lattices corresponding to uncorrected human sentences, in place of the n-gram $P_{ng}$.

## 4    Experimental Results

### 4.1    Dataset and Model Training

The acoustic model was trained using 140 h of audio from a set of publicly available TED talks [1]. All of the talks are in English, containing a mix of native and non-native speakers. The TED talks subtitles were used as reference during the alignment to obtain the targets for acoustic model training. Since these subtitles have a number of errors, a confidence threshold was used to exclude regions that are likely to be incorrectly aligned. The language model used by the ASR system was trained using the TED Talk subtitles.

A set of 11 TED talks amounting to around 4 h 30 m was used for development (2 talks) and testing (9 talks). Our baseline ASR system has a WER of 25.78 % on the test set, measured on the existing English subtitles. It should be noted that, compared to other TED ASR test sets such as the one of IWSLT [7], the set here used is much smaller, since the experiments involving user corrections imposed strong limitations on the amount of data that could be processed.

The experiments were carried out following the procedure described in Sect. 2. Once the user corrections had been collected, three data-sets were created:

- *Ref. Oracle* contained the correct transcriptions (talk subtitles).
- *CN Oracle* contained the best paths through the confusion networks presented to the users. This can be regarded as an idealized user correction, in which the selected slots minimize WER with reference to the *Ref. Oracle* transcriptions. The oracle corrections of the test set have a WER of 12.1 %.
- *User* data-set contained the transcriptions corrected by the editors, but restricted to select from fixed options of the confusion network.

As mentioned in Sect. 2.3, editors were directly contacted to allow better control of the experimental conditions. The editor pool comprised 30 editors, who were non-native English speakers with a high level of proficiency. Although non-nativeness may affect the system performance, it is expected that they are representative of the target editor pool. Given the experimental results attained, non-nativeness of the editors had likely a low impact in performance.

### 4.2    Results of the Limited Quantity Plus Adaptation Approach

The first set of experiments evaluated the improvements that it is possible to obtain when limiting the amount of data sent for correction but compensating this with adaptation of the ASR system on the corrected data. For this, the Ref. Oracle and User datasets were sampled randomly to obtain sub-sets of different sizes. The adaptation approach detailed in Sect. 3 was then applied. To allow for a more fine-grained analysis, Acoustic Model (AM) adaptation and Language Model (LM) adaptation were applied separately and jointly.

Figure 3(a) shows the effect of selecting an increasing amount of data to be corrected. However, the correction is idealized by using the reference transcripts, previously described. It should be noted that the *adapted* versions also include

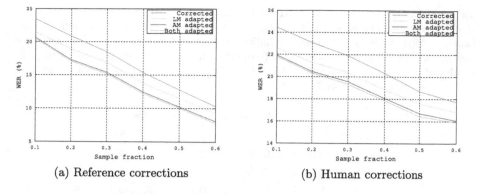

(a) Reference corrections                     (b) Human corrections

**Fig. 3.** Results (% WER) for the adaptation of the acoustic and language models using transcription samples of increasing sizes, as a fraction of the total talk size. In (a) reference sentences are used whereas in (b) human corrections are used. The *corrected* line represents the WER when replacing the sentences in the sample with the human corrections, without performing any adaptation.

the corrections employed in the *corrected* versions. Figure 3(b) shows the same effect but using the real user editions, which correspond to selecting fixed options of the confusion network.

As it can be observed, the absolute improvement provided by each of the three methods is approximately constant regardless of the sample size used for adaptation, which means that for larger sample fractions there is an improvement of larger relative magnitude. An interesting observation is that the WER when using just reference corrections and a sample fraction of 0.30 is approximately the same as the WER when using both adaptation methods and a sample fraction of 0.20. Figure 3(b) reveals similar trends in the case of human corrected data, but here the sample size that is necessary to correct in order to match a sample size of 0.20 is approximately 0.40. This is probably a consequence of the fact that not all of the errors are corrected in the human data, due to the fixed set of options approach. The limited experiments with free text corrections seem to corroborate this hypothesis, since the differences in WER with respect to the *reference* were around 1 % in these experiments.

### 4.3   Results on the Fixed Choice Interface Approach

The second set of experiments aims at measuring how far the human corrections are from the best possible solution, given the hypotheses they had to choose from. We compare these with a confusion network oracle which returns the lowest WER paths for each of the sentences to be corrected, for the same set of options. Here, we also compare the effectiveness of using human corrections with that of using reference transcriptions, which enables us to establish the performance of our adaptation methods under optimal conditions.

We see in Table 1 that the results are best when we use the reference transcriptions for adaptation. Also, using CN oracle sentences outperforms the

**Table 1.** Results (% WER) for system adaptation when using the reference transcription, the user selections and the confusion network oracle. The first row indicates the baseline ASR WER. The second row indicates the WER after replacing the corrected sentences with the appropriate type of feedback. On the last three rows, we display the results of additionally performing AM adaptation, LM adaptation or both, and then recognizing with the adapted models.

| Type | Ref. oracle | CN oracle | User |
|---|---|---|---|
| ASR | 25.78 | 25.78 | 25.78 |
| 20 % corrected | 20.85 | 22.85 | 23.18 |
| +AM adapted | 17.26 | 20.16 | 20.46 |
| +LM adapted | 18.91 | 21.06 | 21.40 |
| +Both adapted | 17.06 | 20.05 | 20.33 |

human corrections, but by a smaller margin, which suggests that humans are performing very well on this task. We also observe that combining AM adaptation and LM adaptation outperforms either technique used in isolation, although AM adaptation tends to be more effective than LM adaptation.

## 5    Conclusions

In this paper, we presented a system for fast hybrid human/machine video subtitling based on lattice disambiguation and posterior model adaptation. Our system corrects ASR transcriptions with minimal user intervention in the process, provided in the form of option selections. When receiving human corrections of only part of the tasks, we also improved the automatic transcription of the remaining sentences, thus reducing the remaining necessary user effort. We experimented with the use of language and acoustic model adaptation, finding that both these techniques improve ASR accuracy in manually uncorrected sentences.

In the future, we would like to explore different ways to select which segments are to be corrected by the users, rather than selecting them randomly. The order of presentation may interact with adaptation techniques, reducing the total effort required: segments that contain a higher density of vocabulary related to the talk's topic are likely to improve the effectiveness of language model adaptation.

**Acknowledgements.** This work has been partially supported by national funds through Fundação para a Ciência e a Tecnologia (FCT) with reference UID/CEC/50021/2013, the grant number SFRH/BPD/68428/2010 and by the TRATAHI Portugal-CMU Project CMUP-EPB/TIC/0065/2013. Ângela Costa was supported by a Ph.D. fellowship from Fundação para a Ciência e Tecnologia (SFRH/BD/85737/2012).

# References

1. TED Talks. http://www.ted.com/talks
2. Audhkhasi, K., Georgiou, P.G., Narayanan, S.S.: Reliability-weighted acoustic model adaptation using crowd sourced transcriptions. In: INTERSPEECH, pp. 3045–3048 (2011)
3. Audhkhasi, K., Georgiou, P.G., Narayanan, S.S.: Analyzing quality of crowd-sourced speech transcriptions of noisy audio for acoustic model adaptation. In: IEEE International Conference on Acoustics, Speech and Signal Processing (ICASSP), pp. 4137–4140. IEEE (2012)
4. Bertoldi, N., Simianer, P., Cettolo, M., Wäschle, K., Federico, M., Riezler, S.: Online adaptation to post-edits for phrase-based statistical machine translation. Mach. Translation **28**(3–4), 309–339 (2014)
5. Buhrmester, M., Kwang, T., Gosling, S.D.: Amazon's mechanical turk: a new source of inexpensive, yet high-quality, data? Perspect. Psychol. Sci. **6**(1), 3–5 (2011)
6. Eskenazi, M., Levow, G.A., Meng, H., Parent, G., Suendermann, D.: Crowdsourcing for Speech Processing: Applications to Data Collection Transcription and Assessment. Wiley, Hoboken (2013)
7. Federico, M., Bentivogli, L., Paul, M., Stüker, S.: Overview of the IWSLT 2012 evaluation campaign. In: IWSLT, pp. 11–27 (2011)
8. Fiscus, J.: A post-processing system to yield reduced word error rates: recognizer output voting error reduction (ROVER). In: Proceedings of the ASRU, Santa Barbara, USA (1997)
9. Green, S., Heer, J., Manning, C.D.: The efficacy of human post-editing for language translation. In: Proceedings of the SIGCHI Conference On Human Factors In Computing Systems, pp. 439–448. ACM (2013)
10. Hakkani-Tür, D.Z., Béchet, F., Riccardi, G., Tür, G.: Beyond ASR 1-best: using word confusion networks in spoken language understanding. Comput. Speech Lang. **20**(4), 495–514 (2006)
11. Kuhn, R., De Mori, R.: A cache-based natural language model for speech recognition. IEEE Trans. Pattern Anal. Mach. Intell. **12**(6), 570–583 (1990)
12. Lavie, A., Denkowski, M., Dyer, C.: Learning from post-editing: online model adaptation for statistical machine translation. In: EACL 2014 (2014)
13. Meinedo, H., Abad, A., Pellegrini, T., Trancoso, I., Neto, J.A.: The L2F broadcast news speech recognition system. In: Proceedings of Fala, pp. 93–96 (2010)
14. Mühlberger, G., Zelger, J., Sagmeister, D.: User-driven correction of OCR errors: combing crowdsourcing and information retrieval technology. In: Digital Access to Textual Cultural Heritage (DATeCH 2014), pp. 53–56, Madrid, Spain (2014)
15. Neto, J.a., Almeida, L., Hochberg, M., Martins, C., Nunes, L., Renals, S., Robinson, T.: Speaker-adaptation for hybrid HMM-ANN continuous speech recognition system (1995)
16. Rumelhart, D.E., Hinton, G.E., Williams, R.J.: Learning internal representations by error propagation. Technical report, DTIC Document (1985)
17. Vertanen, K., MacKay, D.J.: Speech dasher: fast writing using speech and gaze. In: Proceedings of the SIGCHI Conference on Human Factors in Computing Systems, pp. 595–598. ACM (2010)
18. Wald, M.: Crowdsourcing correction of speech recognition captioning errors. In: W4A. ACM (2011)
19. Yao, K., Yu, D., Seide, F., Su, H., Deng, L., Gong, Y.: Adaptation of context-dependent deep neural networks for automatic speech recognition. In: 2012 IEEE Spoken Language Technology Workshop (SLT), pp. 366–369. IEEE (2012)

# Paralinguistic Speaker Trait Characterization

# Acoustic Analysis of Anomalous Use of Prosodic Features in a Corpus of People with Intellectual Disability

Mario Corrales-Astorgano[(⊠)], David Escudero-Mancebo,
and César González-Ferreras

Department of Computer Science, University of Valladolid, Valladolid, Spain
{mario.corrales,descuder,cesargf}@infor.uva.es

**Abstract.** An analysis of the prosodic characteristics of the voice of people with intellectual disability is presented in this paper. A serious game has been developed for training the communicative competences of people with intellectual disability, including those related with prosody. An evaluation of the video game was carried out and, as a result, a corpus with the recordings of the spoken turns of the game has been collected. This corpus is composed of a set of utterances produced by the target group of people with intellectual disability. The same set of sentences is pronounced by a control group of people without intellectual disability. This allows us to compare the prosodic profiles between the target and control groups. Prosodic features (F0, energy and duration) are automatically extracted and analyzed, revealing significant differences between the two groups. We trained an automatic classifier using exclusively prosodic features and 80 % of the sentences were correctly discriminated.

**Keywords:** Prosody · Speech · Intellectual disabilities · Down syndrome · Serious games

## 1  Introduction

Some intellectually disabled (ID) people have problems in their social relationships because of their communication difficulties [3,4,12].

Speech in general [11] and prosody in particular [16] can be affected, resulting in a limited control of many communicative functions. The work presented in this paper is framed in a project[1] whose goal is to develop a serious game for young

---

[1] This work has been partially funded by Recercaixa, ACUP, Obra Social La Caixa (project "¡Juguemos a comunicar mejor! La mejora de la competencia prosódica como vía de integración educativa e inclusión social del alumnado con Necesidades Específicas de Apoyo Educativo" http://prado.uab.es/recercaixa/es/index.html) and by Ministerio de Economía y Competitividad (project TIN2014-59852-R "Videojuegos Sociales para la Asistencia y Mejora de la Pronunciación de la Lengua Española").

© Springer International Publishing AG 2016
A. Abad et al. (Eds.): IberSPEECH 2016, LNAI 10077, pp. 151–161, 2016.
DOI: 10.1007/978-3-319-49169-1_15

ID people (mainly but not exclusively people with Down syndrome (DS)) to train and improve their pronunciation. The users of the video game are invited to perform a set of perception and oral production activities that have been designed to practise a number of communicative functions of speech, mainly those related with prosody. In this paper, we show that the use of the video game permits us to collect a corpus that is used to detect ID people's anomalous use of prosody when their utterances are compared with those produced by people without ID.

There are few works in the literature that have analyzed the speech of ID people using a corpus-based approach. Most of the studies in the state of the art have followed an approach based on tests of perception, not on measuring and comparing the values of acoustic variables across corpora [11]. Among the reasons for this sparsity of works, we can point out the lack of specific corpora and the difficulties for analysing ID-affected speech. Concerning the lack of corpora, the recording of ID people's voices in controlled contexts is not an easy task due to the short term memory problems, attention deficit and language development problems of these people [3]. Our video game incorporates a number of game elements in the interface [5] to increase the motivation of the users, resulting in a corpus that contains the utterances produced by the players during the interaction.

Concerning the difficulties of analyzing ID people's altered speech, it must be taken into account that this type of voice usually contains disfluencies and abnormal productions that can originate in physiological and/or perception problems. As a result, the quality of the phonetic production is low, which limits the use of automatic speech recognition systems so that automatic segmentation is, in many cases, unaffordable [8]. Prosody operates at a supra-segmental level (for example word, phrase or sentence levels), so that capturing the prosodic features is a more robust process. In this work, we show that computing a set of acoustic variables related with fundamental frequency, energy and pauses allows us to detect unusual prosodic patterns in the utterances of the corpus.

The possibility of analyzing the prosodic productions of users in real time and the training of automatic systems for identifying prosodic problems is allowing the game to be enriched by providing useful information for the therapists to assist the players and for the players to improve their interaction experience. In this work we have used the prosodic features to train automatic classifiers that allowed the utterances of the corpus to be classified in terms of the type of speaker with about 80 % success rates.

In Sect. 2, we present the serious game activities. In Sect. 3, the experimental procedure is described, which includes the procedure for collecting data, the processing of the speech material and the classification of the samples. The results section shows the effectiveness of the procedure. We end the paper with a discussion about the relevance of the results and the conclusions and future work section.

**Fig. 1.** The user is represented in this game screen by a personalized avatar (backwards position in this case). The parrot acts as the virtual assistant. User and game characters (the bus driver in this case) interact with voice.

## 2  Game Description

The video game has the structure of a graphic adventure game, including conversations with characters, getting and using items and navigating through scenarios. A number of activities are included in the general context of the graphic adventure and players need to solve them in order to progress in the game. Three activity types are defined to practice speech, communication and prosodic skills:

- **Comprehension activities** that are focused on lexical-semantic comprehension and on improving prosodic perception in specific contexts, such as making a question or asking something politely.
- **Production activities** that are focused on oral production, so the players are encouraged by the game to train their speech, keeping in mind prosodic aspects like intonation, expression of emotions or syllabic emphasis.
- **Visual activities** focused on improving specific aspects of prosody, with the corresponding visual response to the user voice input and other activities designed to add variety to the game and to reduce the feeling of monotony while playing.

Two users interact with the system: the player and the trainer. The player is normally an adolescent or a child with language deficits, specifically in prosodic comprehension and production. The trainer (typically the teacher, a speech therapist or a relative) assists the player during the game sessions. When trainer and player work together on a game activity, the trainer helps the player in the correct use of voice and also to configure the system. Production and prosodic activities allow the trainer to evaluate the players, making them repeat the exercise when the result is not correct. The role of the trainer is essential to maximize the educational potential of the game. The trainer supports and guides players during the game, adapts the difficulty level, encourages players to continue when they have difficulties; helps them to solve difficulties such as understanding the story and the activities and gives clues for helping to improve their performance.

During the game session, information about user interaction is stored, as well as the audio recordings of the production activities. This information can be used by the speech therapist to analyze the evolution of the user in successive game sessions and the audio recordings increase the speech corpus. This user interaction log has information about game time, the attempts to complete a task, number of mouse clicks or the audio helps showed to the user.

A set of usability tests have been performed showing that the degree of satisfaction of players and trainers is high. The game elements engage the users, motivating them to use the software. It has been analyzed in perception tests and confirmed by the teachers that the oral productions of the players improve with use.

## 3   Experimental Procedure

### 3.1   Data Collection

The game sessions consisted in completing all the game and were done in the facilities of the centers where the players attended their regular classes to assure their comfort. In addition, a staff member of the centers was always with the players. The game sessions were held at the Niu School (Barcelona), Aura Foundation (Barcelona), and the College of Special Education "El Pino de Obregón" (Valladolid). In total, 4 game sessions were held. During the first of them, a usability test was carried out to see how the users interacted with the game and to detect deficiencies in the user interface. The other 3 sessions were carried out by staff members of the center of Valladolid, with the aim of getting more recordings to be analyzed later. During game sessions, the role of the trainer (a teacher or speech therapist) is twofold: first, he/she evaluates the player's recordings and second, he/she helps players if necessary. The trainer has to sit next to the player. To evaluate the player's recordings, the trainer uses the keyboard of the same computer that the player is using. Besides, to reduce the ambient noise in the recording process, the players use a headset with microphone incorporated.

25 users participated in the game sessions. All of them have a moderate or mild intellectual disability, so they can follow the game in a reliable way. In addition, the number of male and female users was the same and the age range was between 13 and 30 years. Of these 25 users, 18 have Down syndrome and 7 have intellectual disability without diagnosis of a specific syndrome. As the four game sessions were carried out over different periods of time, not all the users

participated in all the game sessions. Some users were not available during the development of some game sessions, so we do not have their recordings.

One of the purposes of the tool is to collect examples of sentences with different modalities (i.e. declarative, interrogative and exclamatory) produced by people with intellectual disabilities in order to analyze the most common difficulties. The recorded sentences can be seen in Table 1.

**Table 1.** Sentences recorded during game sessions

| Sentence in Spanish | Sentence in English |
| --- | --- |
| ¡Hasta luego, tío Pau! | See you later, uncle Pau! |
| ¡Muchas gracias, Juan! | Thank you very much, Juan! |
| ¡Hola! ¿Tienen lupas? Quería comprar una. | Hello, do you have magnifiers? I wanted to buy one. |
| Sí, la necesito, ¿Cuánto vale? | Yes, I need it. How much is it? |
| ¡Hola tío Pau! Ya vuelvo a casa. | Hello uncle Pau! I'll be back home. |
| Sí, esa es. ¡Hasta luego! | Yes, it is. Bye! |
| ¡Hola, tío Pau! ¿Sabes dónde vive la señora Luna? | Hello uncle Pau! Do you know where Mrs Luna lives? |
| ¡Nos vemos luego, tío Pau! | See you later, uncle Pau! |
| Has sido muy amable, Juan. Muchas gracias! | You have been very kind, Juan. Thank you very much! |
| ¡Hola! ¿Tienen lupas? Me gustaría comprar una. | Hello, do you have magnifiers? I'd like to buy one. |
| Sí, necesito una sea como sea. ¿Cuánto vale? | Yes, I really need one. How much is it? |
| Sí, lo es. Vivo allí desde pequeño. ¡Hasta luego! | Yes, it is. I have lived there since I was a child. Bye! |
| ¡Hola, tío Pau! Tengo que encontrar a la señora Luna ¿Sabes dónde vive? | Hello uncle Pau! I have to find Mrs Luna. Do you know where she lives? |

## 3.2 Processing

The information about the corpus generated during the game sessions can be seen in Table 2. This table shows the number of recordings that each user has made, as well as the duration of these recordings in seconds. To obtain control samples, a series of recordings of 20 adult people, 11 men and 9 women were made.

The prosodic features extracted from recordings were fundamental frequency, energy and silent pauses. To extract fundamental frequency from the recordings, an algorithm for pitch analysis based on an autocorrelation method implemented by Praat [2] was used. Energy was calculated using the root mean square (rms) with a window size of 1024 samples (recordings are performed at 44100 Hz). Both rms and F0 were computed every 0.01 s. Finally, silence and speech were also detected automatically using the Praat tools.

**Table 2.** Number of recordings (first number) and duration (second number) in seconds of each session of user recording

| User | Session 1 | Session 2 | Session 3 | Session 4 | Total |
|------|-----------|-----------|-----------|-----------|-------|
| U1   | 8/50      |           |           |           | 8/50     |
| U2   | 14/46     | 16/42     | 10/20     |           | 40/109   |
| U3   | 12/34     |           |           |           | 12/34    |
| U4   |           | 3/10      | 7/23      | 10/59     | 20/93    |
| U5   |           | 12/56     |           |           | 12/56    |
| U6   | 7/34      |           |           |           | 7/34     |
| U7   | 11/93     |           |           |           | 11/93    |
| U8   |           | 13/43     | 8/29      | 12/57     | 33/130   |
| U9   |           | 3/14      | 9/48      | 11/40     | 23/103   |
| U10  | 10/34     |           |           |           | 10/34    |
| U11  | 8/24      |           |           |           | 8/24     |
| U12  |           | 9/31      | 12/49     | 11/28     | 32/109   |
| U13  | 11/44     |           |           |           | 11/44    |
| U14  | 9/31      | 10/28     | 10/28     | 12/39     | 41/127   |
| U15  | 10/40     |           |           |           | 10/40    |
| U16  | 14/55     | 4/22      | 10/34     | 11/48     | 39/161   |
| U17  | 13/39     | 10/30     | 9/19      |           | 32/90    |
| U18  | 10/38     |           |           |           | 10/38    |
| U19  | 7/23      | 11/29     |           | 13/46     | 31/98    |
| U20  |           | 3/9       | 8/20      |           | 11/29    |
| U21  | 9/46      |           |           |           | 9/46     |
| U22  |           | 11/41     | 10/40     |           | 21/82    |
| U23  | 13/46     | 10/38     | 10/42     |           | 33/127   |
| U24  | 7/37      |           |           |           | 7/37     |
| U25  | 8/33      |           |           |           | 8/33     |
| Total | 181/757  | 115/398   | 103/357   | 80/320    | 479/1,832 |

To analyze the prosody of the recordings and to compare them to the recordings of people without ID, a set of features was computed. The features concern frequency: within word F0 range (`f0_range`), difference between maximum and average within word F0 (`f0_maxavg_diff`), difference between average and minimum within word F0 (`f0_minavg_diff`); energy: within word energy range (`e_range`), difference between maximum and average within word energy (`e_maxavg_diff`), difference between average and minimum within word energy (`e_minavg_diff`); and duration: number of silences (`num_silences`), silence duration in percent with respect to total duration (`silence_percent`). These sets of features have shown to be effective in previous experiments on analyzing prosody for the automatic prosodic labeling of spoken utterances [1,9]. Besides, we use semitones and decibels to give a perceptual interpretation to these ranges and differences.

In order to make an automatic classification of the recordings, the Weka machine learning toolkit [10] was used. We made use of the implementations of the classifiers C4.5 decision trees (DT), Multilayer perceptron (MLP) and Support Vector Machine (SVM). We were interested in contrasting the behavior of these three types of classifiers, as we observed in [7] that they behave differently in prosodic labeling tasks.

# 4    Results

Table 3 shows the variables of the different groups. In general, all the variables in Table 3 present high mean and sd values due to the type of sentences to be uttered, which include many questions, exclamations and orthographically marked pauses. As for time variables (*num_silences* and *silence_percent*), Down syndrome users needed more pauses to complete their turns (0.88 vs 2.02), which is also projected in the percent of silences that they used (21 % vs 13 %). The impact of the use of pauses seems to be lower in the case of $\overline{DS}$ users: 0.88 vs 1.59 for *num_silences*.

Concerning the variables that refer to $F0$, both Target and Control users modulate the pitch with similar ranges (9.23 vs 9.15 st). *f0_maxavg_diff* is higher in the Control groups (4.74 vs 3.66 st), indicating higher F0 excursions. When energy is analyzed, the range is significantly different (50.11 vs 40.44 dB) and the excursions are shorter both from the mean value to the maximum (9.53 vs 8.63 dB) and to the minimum (40.58 vs 31.81 dB). No relevant differences are observed between $DS$ and $\overline{DS}$ users.

**Table 3.** Average and standard deviation of recording features of people without intellectual disabilities (control group) and people with intellectual disabilities (target group). $DS$ refers to users with Down syndrome, $\overline{DS}$ refers to users with an intellectual disability that is different to Down syndrome and $ID = DS \cup \overline{DS}$. The boldfaced cells indicate significant differences with $p - value < 0.01$ applying the Mann-Whitney U test.

|  | Control | Target | | |
|---|---|---|---|---|
|  |  | $DS$ | $\overline{DS}$ | $ID$ |
| f0_maxavg_diff (st) | 4.74 ± 1.7 | **3.71 ± 1.6** | **3.54 ± 1.3** | **3.66 ± 1.5** |
| f0_minavg_diff (st) | 4.49 ± 2.1 | **5.42 ± 2.7** | **5.64 ± 3.3** | **5.49 ± 2.9** |
| f0_range (st) | 9.23 ± 3.2 | 9.13 ± 3.6 | 9.18 ± 4.0 | 9.15 ± 3.7 |
| e_maxavg_diff (dB) | 9.53 ± 1.9 | **8.52 ± 2.5** | 8.86 ± 2.4 | **8.63 ± 2.4** |
| e_minavg_diff (dB) | 40.58 ± 16.0 | **32.14 ± 6.9** | **31.16 ± 5.9** | **31.82 ± 6.6** |
| e_range (dB) | 50.11 ± 16.2 | **40.65 ± 7.3** | **40.02 ± 6.3** | **40.44 ± 7.0** |
| num_silences (#) | 0.88 ± 0.8 | **2.02 ± 2.0** | **1.59 ± 1.6** | **1.88 ± 1.9** |
| silence_percent [0,1] | 0.13 ± 0.1 | **0.21 ± 0.2** | 0.13 ± 0.1 | **0.18 ± 0.2** |

**Table 4.** Ranking of the acoustic features based on information gain. $DS$ refers to users with down syndrome, $\overline{DS}$ refers to users with an intellectual disability that is different to Down syndrome and Control refers to user without intellectual disability

| Attribute | $DS$ vs Control | | $\overline{DS}$ vs Control | |
|---|---|---|---|---|
| | InfoGain | GainRatio | InfoGain | GainRatio |
| e_range | 0.1311 | 0.1119 | 0.1523 | 0.1105 |
| num_silences | 0.1291 | 0.1743 | 0.113 | 0.205 |
| e_minavg_diff | 0.0987 | 0.2812 | 0.151 | 0.1105 |
| f0_maxavg_diff | 0.0737 | 0.0739 | 0.1076 | 0.1229 |
| e_maxavg_diff | 0.0707 | 0.1538 | 0.087 | 0.1476 |
| silence_percent | 0.0463 | 0.0628 | 0 | 0 |
| f0_minavg_diff | 0.0365 | 0.0483 | 0.0565 | 0.0875 |
| f0_range | 0 | 0 | 0 | 0 |

Table 4 presents a ranking of the acoustic features. $InfoGain$ and $GainRatio$ are entropy-based metrics that indicate how relevant the acoustic features are for classifying the analyzed utterances in terms of the type of user that produced them. The ranking has been computed with the Weka tools [10]. $e\_range$ and $num\_silence$ are the most relevant features, both for classifying the $DS$ and the $\overline{DS}$ users. Energy related variables are more discriminant than the F0 ones. Thus, for example, $f0\_range$ is not discriminant at all. The duration of the silences ($silence\_percent$ variable) again seems to be similar for Control and $\overline{DS}$ users.

Table 5 shows that the classification of the users through the prosodic features permits us to correctly identify about 80 % of the utterances. The SVM classifier permits us to obtain the best classification results in all the cases, with an accuracy of 81 % and with the lowest (on average) false positive rates in the Control vs $DS$ case. The worst results are obtained with the $MLP$ classifiers with false positive rates of the target group close to or over 50 %.

**Table 5.** Classification results of the three classifiers. In every cell, Ac; FPC; FPT are the accuracy, the false positive classification rates of Control samples and the false positive classification rates of the Target samples.

| | Control vs $DS$ | Control vs $\overline{DS}$ | Control vs $ID$ |
|---|---|---|---|
| DT | 78.1 %; 25.8 %; 19.6 % | 76.4 %; 22.2 %; 25.3 % | 80.5 %; 41.8 %; 10.4 % |
| MLP | 78.1 %; 44.8 %; 8.1 % | 79.3 %; 19.1 %; 22.8 % | 80.2 %; 61.3 %; 2.9 % |
| SVM | 80.6 %; 26.8 %; 15.0 % | 79.8 %; 14.9 %; 26.6 % | 81.0 %; 40.2 %; 10.4 % |

# 5    Discussion

The results presented in Tables 3 and 4 show that $ID$ players have problems with the use of the pauses. This is an expected result as many authors have reported fluency disorders, including stuttering and cluttering, that mainly affects $DS$ speakers [11].

Additionally, we have observed a different use of the prosodic variables of F0 and energy, which could indicate an anomalous production of intonation and emphatic stress by $ID$ speakers. Limitations in the production of prosodic features have already been reported in works such as the one presented in [13] and others [11]. The difference between our proposal and the previous works is that we use acoustic features instead of perceptual tests for evidencing the abnormal use of prosody.

Of particular interest is the fact that the control of energy seems to be more problematic than the control of F0 for intellectually disabled speakers. This fact was also observed in [15] when analyzing the Alborada corpus [14].

To discuss about the practical implications of these results, let us go back to the video game. Our goal is that the interface [5,6] permits the user to operate either autonomously or with the supervision of the trainer. In the assisted mode, the trainer decides whether the user should change the activity or continue practicing it. In the autonomous mode, the program must take the decision automatically, so users are invited to keep trying until their pronunciation is estimated to be good enough (or until a given number of repetitions is exceeded to avoid user frustration and abandonment). In the assisted mode, the trainer can receive real time information about the deviation of the prosodic features of the user with respect to the expectations. This information could be used by the trainer to decide whether the user should repeat the sentence production or continue the game. In the autonomous mode, the automatic classification results could be used to judge the quality of the production: the higher the probability of being a sample of the Control group, the better the pronunciation is. This practical concern will determine the type of classifier to be used, because a wrong classification of a user of the Control group can decrease dramatically the overall perception of the quality of the system.

# 6    Conclusions and Future Work

As a conclusion, prosodic features are able to discriminate speakers with intellectual disabilities with a high success rate. The most discriminant features are the number of pauses and the duration of the silences, because of their less fluent speech. Moreover, we have observed that these speakers make an anomalous use of F0 and energy features.

We have used global statistical metrics of F0 and intensity that do not allow a study of details about their local temporal evolution. We are currently working on obtaining information about the dynamics of those acoustic correlates, in order to learn more about the particular acoustic deviations of speakers with ID.

A deeper knowledge of the type of prosodic deviations will allow us to design specific exercises to correct the anomalies.

The approach used in this work to identify anomalous utterances contrasts with the alternative approach of using a reference speaker or golden speaker, which is used to compare each utterance. We are currently undertaking a comparative study of both techniques in order to analyze the advantages and disadvantages of each alternative.

# References

1. Ananthakrishnan, S., Narayanan, S.S.: Automatic prosodic event detection using acoustic, lexical, and syntactic evidence. IEEE Trans. Audio Speech Lang. Process. **16**(1), 216–228 (2008)
2. Boersma, P., et al.: Praat, a system for doing phonetics by computer. Glot Int. **5**(9/10), 341–345 (2002)
3. Chapman, R.S.: Language development in children and adolescents with down syndrome. Ment. Retard. Dev. Disabil. Res. Rev. **3**(4), 307–312 (1997)
4. Cleland, J., Wood, S., Hardcastle, W., Wishart, J., Timmins, C.: Relationship between speech, oromotor, language and cognitive abilities in children with down's syndrome. Int. J. Lang. Commun. Disord. **45**(1), 83–95 (2010)
5. Corrales, M., Escudero, D., Flores, V., González, C., Gutiérrez, Y.: Arquitectura para la interacción en un videojuego para el entrenamiento de la voz de personas con discapacidad intelectual. In: Actas del XXI Congreso Internacional de Interación Persona-Ordenador, pp. 445–448, September 2015
6. Corrales-Astorgano, M., Escudero-Mancebo, D., González-Ferreras, C.: The magic stone: a video game to improve communication skills of people with intellectual disabilities. In: Show and tell demostrations, Interspeech 2016, September 2016
7. Escudero-Mancebo, D., González-Ferreras, C., Vivaracho-Pascual, C., Cardenoso-Payo, V.: A fuzzy classifier to deal with similarity between labels on automatic prosodic labeling. Comput. Speech Lang. **28**(1), 326–341 (2014)
8. Feng, J., Lazar, J., Kumin, L., Ozok, A.: Computer usage by children with down syndrome: challenges and future research. ACM Trans. Accessible Comput. **2**(3), 13 (2010)
9. Gonzalez-Ferreras, C., Escudero-Mancebo, D., Vivaracho-Pascual, C., Cardeñoso Payo, V.: Improving automatic classification of prosodic events by pairwise coupling. IEEE Trans. Audio Speech Lang. Process. **20**(7), 2045–2058 (2012)
10. Hall, M., Frank, E., Holmes, G., Pfahringer, B., Reutemann, P., Witten, I.H.: The WEKA data mining software: an update. ACM SIGKDD Explor. Newsl. **11**(1), 10–18 (2009)
11. Kent, R.D., Vorperian, H.K.: Speech impairment in down syndrome: a review. J. Speech Lang. Hear. Res. **56**(1), 178–210 (2013)
12. Martin, G.E., Klusek, J., Estigarribia, B., Roberts, J.E.: Language characteristics of individuals with down syndrome. Topics Lang. Disord. **29**(2), 112 (2009)
13. Pettinato, M., Verhoeven, J.: Production and perception of word stress in children and adolescents with down syndrome. Down Syndr. Res. Practice **13**, 48–61 (2008)
14. Saz, O., Lleida, E., Vaquero, C., Rodríguez, W.R.: The Alborada-I3A corpus of disordered speech. In: LREC (2010)

15. Saz, O., Simón, J., Rodríguez, W., Lleida, E., Vaquero, C., et al.: Analysis of acoustic features in speakers with cognitive disorders and speech impairments. EURASIP J. Adv. Sig. Process. **2009**, 1 (2009)
16. Stojanovik, V.: Prosodic deficits in children with down syndrome. J. Neurolinguistics **24**(2), 145–155 (2011)

# Detecting Psychological Distress in Adults Through Transcriptions of Clinical Interviews

Joana Correia[1,2,3](✉), Isabel Trancoso[2,3], and Bhiksha Raj[1]

[1] Language Technologies Institute, Carnegie Mellon University, Pittsburgh, USA
Joana@cmu.edu
[2] Instituto Superior Técnico, Universidade de Lisboa, Lisbon, Portugal
[3] Spoken Language Systems Laboratory, INESC-ID, Lisbon, Portugal

**Abstract.** Automatic detection of psychological distress, namely post-traumatic stress disorder (PTSD), depression, and anxiety, is a valuable tool to decrease time, and budget constraints of medical diagnosis. In this work, we propose two supervised approaches, using global vectors (GloVe) for word representation, to detect the presence of psychological distress in adults, based on the analysis of transcriptions of psychological interviews conducted by a health care specialist. Each approach is meant to be used in a specific scenario: online, in which the analysis is performed on a per-turn basis and the feedback from the system can be provided nearly live; and offline, in which the whole interview is analysed at once and the feedback from the system is provided after the end of the interview. The online system achieves a performance of 66.7 % accuracy in the best case, while the offline system achieves a performance of 100 % accuracy in detecting the three types of distress. Furthermore, we re-evaluate the performance of the offline system using corrupted transcriptions, and confirm its robustness by observing a minimal degradation of the performance.

## 1 Introduction

Affective disorders such as post-traumatic stress disorder (PTSD), depression, and anxiety are common disorders that require specialized health care professionals to diagnose and assess them. However, the availability of such professionals might not always exist or even be affordable. An alternative is to use computerized system that perform automatic detection of psychological distress. Though these systems could not fully replace a health care specialist, they could be used as a valuable screening tool or to aid in diagnosis, thus reducing the time and budget requirements to perform a diagnosis.

Over the last few decades there has been significant interest in studying the descriptors of psychological distress. Some verbal descriptors of psychological distress include aggregate dialogue-level features, and features that represent subject behavior during specific moments in the dialogues show significant differences in subjects with depression and PTSD, compared to non-distressed subjects [1]. Furthermore, it has been showed that the prevalence of certain words

© Springer International Publishing AG 2016
A. Abad et al. (Eds.): IberSPEECH 2016, LNAI 10077, pp. 162–171, 2016.
DOI: 10.1007/978-3-319-49169-1_16

such a "I" is correlated with the presence of depression, as well as the prevalence of some function words [2]. Even in social media platforms, some forms of psychological distress, such as depression, can be detected through rule-based data mining approaches and analysis of the use of emotions, interaction with others and other behaviours [3,4]. However, the descriptors of psychological distress can vary across cultures and languages [5].

In this work, we focus on the analysing the word content and verbal descriptors of psychological distress. We hypothesis that such cues are different for subjects suffering from psychological distressed (PTSD, depression and anxiety), compared to non-distressed subjects. To test this hypothesis, we propose two new methods that analyse a corpus of transcriptions of clinical interviews to adults that might suffer from psychological distress.

Our main contribution is the introduction of two new systems that take advantage of global vectors (GloVes) [6] for word representation to perform a diagnosis regarding the presence of psychological distress in a subject. The first proposed system performs a per-turn analysis of the interview, which allows its use in an online setting, providing near live feedback to the health care specialist. The second system analyses the interview as a whole, and attributes a "healthy" or "distressed" connotation to the interview. Since GloVe models are capable of mapping words into a space where the distance between words reflects their semantic similarity (closer words are more similar), we can take advantage of this property to deal with new words in the test data, by looking to its neighbours in the model, and inferring its meaning. Furthermore, simple arithmetic operations with GloVes, such as summing, averaging, etc. yield a meaningful result in the same space.

The rest of the document is organized as follows: in Sect. 2 we introduce the corpus we used in this work; in Sect. 3 we introduce the proposed systems; in Sect. 4 we present our experiments and results, and finally, in Sect. 5, we draw the main conclusions and propose possible future work.

## 2    Corpus

The Distress Analysis Interview Corpus (DAIC) [7] consists of video recordings of semi-structured clinical interviews. In this work, we use a subset of DAIC, consisting of interviews conducted by a health care specialist, face-to-face with the subject. The study sample is a group of adults and is biased towards participants who have been diagnosed with PTSD, depression, or anxiety at some point in their lives.

The subset of the corpus being used contains recordings of interviews from 65 subjects, with each interview spanning from 30 to 60 min. In total, this translates to roughly 25 h of recordings and 300 000 words uttered by the patients. Each subject turn can range from a single word to several sentences, and on average, a turn has 22 words. We discard the contributions of the interviewer and focus only on the patient side of the conversation.

The presence, and severity of psychological distress, in this case, PTSD, depression or anxiety, in the subjects was accessed using standard clinical screening measures:

- Post-traumatic stress disorder checklist-civilian (PCL-C): a widely used 5-point scale self-report measure that evaluates 17 PTSD criteria [8]
- State/Trait Anxiety Inventory (STAI): a self-report questionnaire used to help differentiate anxiety from depression [9]
- Patient Health Questionnaire-Depression 9 (PHQ-9): a ten-item self-report measure based directly on the diagnostic criteria for major depressive disorder in the DSM-IV [10]

The incidence of each form of distress in the subjects being studied is reported in Table 1. We note that each form of distress is not exclusive in a subject, for example, a subject can suffer from depression and PTSD simultaneously.

**Table 1.** Incidence of each form of distress in the subjects of the DAIC subset

|  | Form of distress | | |
| --- | --- | --- | --- |
|  | PTSD | Depression | Anxiety |
| Healthy | 43 | 38 | 27 |
| Distressed | 22 | 27 | 38 |
| Total | 65 | 65 | 65 |

Our subset of the DAIC includes high quality audio, video and depth sensor recordings of all the interactions, as well as manual transcriptions and annotations.

## 3 Detection of Psychological Distress with GloVe

There are two settings in which automatic detection of psychological distress might be useful: the first one is online, for example, during an interview with health specialist. It should be useful to have a system providing live feedback to the health care specialist of the analysis of the subject in terms of the presence of psychological distress. It would be an additional tool to help the health care specialist steer the interview. However, given the online nature of the system, it would be limited to analysing short segments of the interview at a time, for instance, the most recent turn from the subject. The second one is offline, for example, after the clinical interview is finished. In this scenario, the health care specialist could refer back to the system and obtain feedback from the analysis of the whole interview. In this scenario, the system would have access to the whole interview, which would allow a more in depth analysis, at the sacrifice of live feedback.

In this work, we introduce two systems, which take advantage of the GloVe for word representation framework, that implement an online system and an offline system that detect psychological distress from the analysis of psychological interviews. In the case of the online system, it analyses one patient turn at a time to provide a diagnosis regarding the presence of cues related to psychological distress in that turn. The offline system analyses the whole interview at once to provide a diagnosis regarding the presence of psychological distress in the subject that was interviewed.

The GloVe framework is described in more detail in 3.1 two systems are described in further detail in Sects. 3.2 and 3.3.

## 3.1    GloVe for Word Representation

GloVe is a word representation model know for its ability to map words into a meaningful space where the distance between words is related to their semantic similarity [6].

It is a global log-bilinear regression model used to learn vector space representations of words [6]. The model can be estimated as follows: Given a very large corpus, collect word co-occurrence statistics in a form of word co-occurrence matrix $X$. Each element $X_{ij}$ of such matrix represents measure of how often word $i$ appears in context of word $j$. The context of a word is defined as a predefined number of words before and after it. For each word pair, the following soft constraint is defined:

$$w_i' w_j + b_i + b_j = log(X_{i,j}) \tag{1}$$

where $w_i$ is the vector of the main word, $w_j$ is the vector of the next word, $b_i$ and $b_j$ are scalar biases for the main and context words, respectively. The model is obtained by minimizing the cost function:

$$J = \sum_{i=1}^{V} \sum_{j=1}^{V} f(X_{i,j})(w_i' w_j + b_i + b_j - log(X_{i,j})) \tag{2}$$

where $f(.)$ is a weighting function used to prevent learning only the most common pairs:

$$f(X_{ij}) = \begin{cases} (\frac{X_{ij}}{x_{max}})^a & if X_{ij} < x_{max} \\ 1 & otherwise \end{cases}$$

## 3.2    Online Detection of Psychological Distress with GloVe

To achieve a system that performs a per-turn analysis of the interview, we use the GloVe framework to compute a vector for each turn. The resulting vectors are used as the feature vector to train a binary classifier that detects the presence of a given form of psychological distress.

In more detail, assuming we have a GloVe model already trained according to Sect. 3.1, given a turn from an interview, consisting of $n$ words, we retrieve the GloVes for each word to obtain $\mathbf{w} = w_1, w_2, \ldots, w_n$, where each $w_i \in \mathbb{R}^D$, where $D$ is the dimensionality of the GloVe model. Since the distance between GloVes is a measure of the semantic similarity of their corresponding words, we can compute a meaningful turn vector, $t$, as the average of the GloVes for the words of the turn:

$$\mathbf{t} = \frac{\sum_{i=1}^{n} w_i}{n} \tag{3}$$

The set of turn vectors from the train corpus are used to train a support vector machine (SVM) with with radial basis function (RBF) kernel.

## 3.3   Offline Detection of Psychological Distress with GloVe

This work proposes a second system that uses GloVe for word representation, that takes in account the transcription of the whole interview at once to perform the diagnosis. The proposed system relies on determining the tendency of word being more correlated with healthy or distressed people, which we call "connotation" of a word.

Given a word in the test corpus, its connotation is computed by finding the words in the training corpus that are most semantically similar to the test word, and then computing whether these neighbour words are more correlated with healthy or distressed people. This approach is particularly useful when dealing with new words in the test data that were not present in the train data, since we can infer their connotation from their neighbours regardless if they were seen during previously.

Given a train corpus of $N$ words and a vocabulary size of $V$, we compute the connotation for each word, $i = 1, \ldots, V$, in the vocabulary as follows:

$$f_H(i) = \frac{\#w_H(i)}{N_H} \tag{4}$$

$$f_D(i) = \frac{\#w_D(i)}{N_D} \tag{5}$$

$$\Delta f(i) = f_H(i) - f_D(i) \tag{6}$$

$$c_{train}(i) = sign(\Delta f(i)) \tag{7}$$

where $f_H(i)$ and $f_D(i)$ are the relative frequencies of the word $i$ in the healthy and distressed sub-corpora, respectively; $\#w_H(i)$ and $\#w_D(i)$ are the counts of the word $i$ in the healthy and distressed sub-corpora, respectively; $N_H$ and $N_D$ are the total counts of words in the healthy and distressed sub-corpora, respectively; $\Delta f(i)$ is the relative frequency for word $i$; and $c_{train}(i)$ is the binary label that corresponds the "healthy" or "distressed" connotation to the word $i$ in the training corpus.

At test time, the connotation of a test word $t$ is computed assuming a GloVe model, as described in Sect. 3.1, is available. For a test word $t$, present in the GloVe model, we retrieve its GloVe, $\mathbf{w}_t \in \mathbb{R}^D$ and compute the similarity to all the GloVes for the words in the train vocabulary $\mathbf{w}_v$, for $v = 1, \ldots, V$:

$$s(\mathbf{w}_t, \mathbf{w}_v) = |\mathbf{w}_t.\mathbf{w}'_v|     \tag{8}$$

Computing the similarity allows us to find the top $K$ most similar train words, which can include the test word itself, in case it was present in the training data. Each of the top $K$ words has a connotation associated to is, as computed in Eq. 7.

To find the connotation of a test word $t$, $c_{test}(t)$, we compute the average connotation of its $K$ closest neighbours:

$$c_{test}(t) = \frac{\sum_{k=1}^{K} c_{train}(k)}{K}     \tag{9}$$

For $K = 1$, the model corresponds to a Naive Bayes model with flat distribution, and as $K$ increases the distributed smooths out.

The connotation for a whole interview is obtained by averaging the connotation of each word in it. Finally, the interview connotation scores are used to train an SVM with linear kernel, which in a 1D problem translates to finding the optimal scalar decision threshold.

## 4   Experiments and Results

In all the experiments performed in this work we used the DAIC subset described in Sect. 2 to train and validate the performance of the models proposed in Sects. 3.2 and 3.3. The corpus was split into training and validation, by randomly assigning 55 interviews for training and the remaining 10 for validation. There is no overlap between speakers in training and validation sets. All the experiments are performed three times, to evaluate the presence of each form of distress: PTSD, depression and anxiety.

We also used a pre-trained GloVe for word representation model of dimensionality 50, trained from a twitter corpus of 2 billion tweets, 27 billion tokens, and a vocabulary of 1.2 million words.

First, we evaluate the online system described in Sect. 3.2. The pre-trained GloVe model was used to obtain the turn representation vectors of all the turns in the corpus, computed as the mean of the word representation vectors for each turn. The vectors from the training set of the corpus were used to train an SVM with RBF kernel. The model was validated with the remaining turn representation vectors.

The performance of the online system using GloVe, for each form of distress are summarized in Table 2. The performance is reported in accuracy.

The performances obtained by this approach was generally poor across all forms of psychological distress. To some extent, a parallel can be drawn between the performance of the systems and of a human: it is hard to assess whether

**Table 2.** Performance in accuracy of the online system used to detect PTSD, depression, and anxiety

| Approach | Form of distress [acc.] | | |
|---|---|---|---|
| | PTSD | Depression | Anxiety |
| Online GloVe | 0.567 | 0.533 | 0.667 |

someone sounds depressed or suffering from PTSD from just a few words, without any temporal dependency in the model. Nevertheless, the results show that the easiest form of distress to capture is anxiety.

In the case of the offline system proposed in Sect. 3.3, the training interviews were used to build the relative frequency difference table. Each word from the validation interviews was used to find the 20 most similar words to compute the connotation of each test word. Using the 20 neighbours allows for a smother model, compared to a smaller number. Should the number of neighbours used to compute the connotation of a test word be 1, and the model would correspond to a Naive Bayes with flat distribution.

The classifier was trained in a leave on out fashion. Since there were only 10 interviews left for testing only 9 interview scores were used to train the classifier at a time. Due to time constraints and the heavy nature of the approach, it was impossible perform cross validation of the model. The main consequence of this compromise is the increase of variance in the results (Table 3).

The performance for the offline approach was measured in accuracy and is presented in Table 4.

**Table 3.** Performance in accuracy of the online systems for detecting PTSD, depression, and anxiety

| Approach | Form of distress [acc.] | | |
|---|---|---|---|
| | PTSD | Depression | Anxiety |
| Offline GloVe | 1.000 | 1.000 | 1.000 |

We can see that the proposed model achieves a perfect classification score for all labels. However, it is important to note that since there were only 10 validation interviews there is a significant variance in the reported results. Nevertheless, the system performs remarkably well, showing the added value of taking in account longer periods of information at a time. Given the exceptional performance of this method, we refrained from benchmarking it against other state-of-the-art methods, since their performance would always be comparable or worse. Establishing a parallel with humans, this would resemble how a health care specialist pays attention to the interview as a whole to perform a diagnosis.

The conditions present in this dataset - handmade transcriptions - are not always available, for time and budget constraints. To replace those, we can use a sub-par alternative, such as an automatic speech recognition (ASR) system. In an attempt to simulate these conditions, we corrupt our handmade transcriptions with some noise, corresponding to mistakes from the ASR. In our approach that can be achieved by replacing a given percentage of GloVes for the words of the validation interviews by random vectors of the same dimensionality.

We experimented with simulations of increasingly worse ASRs, introducing a word corruption rate of 20 %, 40 % and 60 %. The performance of the offline approach using the corrupted corpora is reported in accuracy in Table 4. From it, we can see that even in extremely noisy scenarios, this system is robust to noise, being able to maintain the perfect performance in almost all settings.

**Table 4.** Performance in accuracy of the offline system with different levels of corruption of the transcription for PTSD, depression, and anxiety

| GloVe corruption rate | Form of distress [acc.] | | |
|---|---|---|---|
| | PTSD | Depression | Anxiety |
| 20 % | 1.000 | 1.000 | 1.000 |
| 40 % | 1.000 | 1.000 | 1.000 |
| 60 % | 0.800 | 1.000 | 1.000 |

Finally, we provide some interesting examples of words with healthy and distressed connotation, by analysing a subset of the sorted relative frequency table. In Fig. 1 we can see that healthy people tend to talk more about casual subjects like school, prom; about relationships and feelings, and to laugh more than distressed people. Conversely, distressed people talk tend to talk more about traumatic events or topics, such as alcoholism, prison, and drugs, as well as to be generally more uninterested and bored by the conversations, saying "blah" and

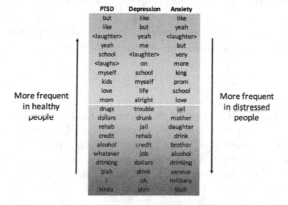

**Fig. 1.** Examples of words with large relative frequency difference for each label

"uh" much more than healthy people. All these findings correlate well with the general perception from a human, of what is the content of distressed discourse.

## 5    Conclusions and Future Work

In this work, we performed a study on the detection of three forms of psychological distress: PTSD, depression and anxiety in adults, though the analysis of transcriptions of clinical interviews. We considered two approaches to analyse the transcriptions, both using GloVe for word representation models.

In the first approach, we propose a system that can be used online, and that performs a per-turn analysis of the interview. This approach was not successful in assessing the presence of psychological distress, which meant that the systems was incapable of learning to detect meaningful cues that describe psychological distress in the short-term. Nevertheless, it showed that the easiest form of distress to capture with little information was anxiety, which might be an indicator that there are short-term descriptors of anxiety.

For the second approach, we propose a system meant to be used offline, that analyses the whole interview at once. Naturally, this approach used more information from the subject in order to perform a diagnosis, than the first one. Taking in account more information provided a significant improvement in performance. This approach was able to capture perfectly the presence of all forms of distress, obtaining an accuracy of 100 % for the detection of the three forms of distress, which is a very significant result: the proposed method cannot be outperformed by any other in the conditions of this experiment. Even after corrupting the transcriptions to simulate machine made transcriptions with a variable rate of errors, the performance of the system remained the same in most of the scenarios, thus confirming the robustness of the approach. The performance of this model can be attributed to the proposed "connotation" system introduced in this work.

Finally, there are still a number of issues were left to be addressed to fully solve this research problem. As an examples, it would be useful to use a model with temporal dependencies at a turn-level analysis of the interview, to better capture the short-term cues that describe PTSD, and depression, thus maybe overcoming the poor performance our system achieved.

## References

1. DeVault, D., Georgila, K., Artstein, R., Morbini, F., Traum, D., Scherer, S., Rizzo, A., Morency, L.-P.: Verbal indicators of psychological distress in interactive dialogue with a virtual human. In: Proceedings of SIGDIAL (2013)
2. Watson, D., Pennebaker, J.W.: Health complaints, stress, and distress: exploring the central role of negative affectivity. Psychol. Rev. **96**(2), 234 (1989)
3. Wang, X., Zhang, C., Ji, Y., Sun, L., Wu, L., Bao, Z.: A depression detection model based on sentiment analysis in micro-blog social network. In: Li, J., Cao, L., Wang, C., Tan, K.C., Liu, B., Pei, J., Tseng, V.S. (eds.) PAKDD 2013. LNCS (LNAI), vol. 7867, pp. 201–213. Springer, Heidelberg (2013). doi:10.1007/978-3-642-40319-4_18

4. Hutto, C.J., Gilbert, E.: Vader: a parsimonious rule-based model for sentiment analysis of social media text. In: 8th International AAAI Conference on Weblogs and Social Media (2014)
5. Ramirez-Esparza, N., Chung, C.K., Kacewicz, E., Pennebaker, J.W.: The psychology of word use in depression forums in English and in Spanish: texting two text analytic approaches. In: ICWSM (2008)
6. Pennington, J., Socher, R., Manning, C.D.: GloVe: global vectors for word representation. In: EMNLP, vol. 14, pp. 1532–1543 (2014)
7. Scherer, S., Lucas, G., Gratch, J., Rizzo, A., Morency, L.-P.: Self-reported symptoms of depression and PTSD are associated with reduced vowel space in screening interviews
8. Blanchard, E.B., Jones-Alexander, J., Buckley, T.C., Forneris, C.A.: Psychometric properties of the PTSD checklist (PCL). Behav. Res. Therapy **34**(8), 669–673 (1996)
9. Spielberger, C.D.: STAI manual for the state-trait anxiety inventory. In: Self-Evaluation Questionnaire, pp. 1–24 (1970)
10. Kroenke, K., Spitzer, R.L.: The PHQ-9: a new depression diagnostic and severity measure. Psychiatr. Ann. **32**(9), 509–515 (2002)

# Automatic Annotation of Disfluent Speech in Children's Reading Tasks

Jorge Proença[1,2(✉)], Dirce Celorico[1], Carla Lopes[1,3], Sara Candeias[4], and Fernando Perdigão[1,2]

[1] Instituto de Telecomunicações, Coimbra, Portugal
{jproenca, direcelorico, calopes, fp}@co.it.pt
[2] Department of Electrical and Computer Engineering,
University of Coimbra, Coimbra, Portugal
[3] Polytechnic Institute of Leiria, Leiria, Portugal
[4] Microsoft Language Development Centre, Lisbon, Portugal
t-sacand@microsoft.com

**Abstract.** The automatic evaluation of reading performance of children is an important alternative to any manual or 1-on-1 evaluation by teachers or tutors. To do this, it is necessary to detect several types of reading miscues. This work presents an approach to annotate reading speech while detecting false-starts, repetitions and mispronunciations, three of the most common disfluencies. Using speech data of 6–10 year old children reading sentences and pseudowords, we apply a two-step process: first, an automatic alignment is performed to get the best possible word-level segmentation and detect syllable based false-starts and word repetitions by using a strict FST (Finite State Transducer); then, words are classified as being mispronounced or not through a likelihood measure of pronunciation by using phone posterior probabilities estimated by a neural network. This work advances towards getting the amount and severity of disfluencies to provide a reading ability score computed from several sentence reading tasks.

**Keywords:** Children's speech · Disfluency detection · Reading performance

## 1 Introduction

For young children that are learning how to read, their oral reading fluency depends on how quickly, accurately and properly expressive they read text aloud [1]. The use of automatic speech recognition technologies to analyse reading performance gains prominence as an alternative to any kind of 1-on-1 evaluation, as teachers usually have to spend a considerable amount of time on the task of manually assessing a child's reading ability. The automatic evaluation of literacy or reading aloud ability is always related to detecting correctly read words, or optionally detecting what kind of mistakes are made. Computer Assisted Language Learning (CALL) is the area closely related to this task, were applications allow a self-practice or an oriented training of the language. These systems are most often created for foreign language learning [2, 3], and are therefore targeted at adults or young adults for whom speech technologies are significantly mature. Nevertheless, for children, there are also applications that deal with the

© Springer International Publishing AG 2016
A. Abad et al. (Eds.): IberSPEECH 2016, LNAI 10077, pp. 172–181, 2016.
DOI: 10.1007/978-3-319-49169-1_17

improvement of reading aloud performance, such as reading tutors. Some projects aim at creating an automatic reading tutor that follows and analyses a child's reading, such as LISTEN [4], Tball [5], SPACE [6] and FLORA [7].

The main objective of the LetsRead project [8], in which this work is inserted, is to create an application that can automatically evaluate the reading aloud performance of European Portuguese (EP) children from 6 to 10 years old ($1^{st}$–$4^{th}$ grades), and not necessarily provide feedback to them, but to their teachers and tutors. For that goal, it is necessary to detect several types of reading miscues and deviations to the correct reading for different reading tasks. These are all the linguistic and extra-linguistic events which affect the smooth flow of the speech such as repetitions, mispronunciations, and corrected false starts [9]. There are several known methods to detect disfluencies, such as based on Hidden Markov Models, Maximum Entropy, Conditional Random Fields [10] and Classification and Regression Trees [11], though most efforts focus on spontaneous speech, and different speaking styles vary the production of disfluencies [12]. Disfluencies in reading have different nuances, and certain works have targeted their automatic detection in children's reading, using complex lattice search modules or specialized grammar structures at the phonetic level [5, 13, 14] or word level context free grammars [15]. However, most works focus on individual word reading tasks (apart from [15] and part of [14]), whereas the present work, an extension of [16], will be focused in sentence reading. Some studies go further and attempt to provide an overall reading ability index that should be well correlated with the opinion of expert evaluators [13, 17], which is one of the final objectives of the LetsRead project [8]. These studies always focus on individual word reading tasks, and use reading speed and number of correctly read words to estimate the overall score. It is expected that, by working with sentence tasks, a better understanding of a child's reading ability can be achieved.

This paper will first describe the LetsRead dataset used to train acoustic models and evaluate the system. In Sect. 3, the automatic segmentation and alignment method that detects syllable-based false-starts and repetitions is presented. Section 4 will describe the classification of words/segments as correctly pronounced or not, thus detecting mispronunciations.

## 2 Dataset

The LetsRead corpus [18] includes 20 h of audio of European Portuguese (EP) read speech by 6–10 year old children from public and private primary/elementary schools, from the first to fourth grades. 284 children completed tasks by reading 20 sentences and 10 pseudowords from a computer screen running prompt recording software. The material of the tasks is of varying difficulty and a large number of disfluencies and reading miscues are identified. A subset of the data was manually annotated as a training set (104 children amounting to 5h30m of audio – 46 male and 58 female with 26 from each grade), where 5601 disfluency events were tagged. Excluding phone extensions and intra-word pauses that can occur simultaneously with other events, 91 % of these are either false-starts, mispronunciations or repetitions. Insertions and deletions are the remaining ones. Further details can be consulted in [18]. An additional 1h31m of utterances were manually transcribed and used as a test set.

# 3 Detection of False Starts and Repetitions

To annotate the data, false-starts and repetitions represent most of the occurring extra segments. As such, for the automatic annotation, it is decided to apply this first stage to try to align the data as best as possible into word-relevant segments. One problem is not considering mispronunciations, but it is still hoped that by forcing the original word to be aligned on top of the mispronounced segment, correct time stamps are obtained. For this stage, Kaldi [19] is used to train acoustic models using only the manually anno-tated train set and to perform the decoding. From previous work [16], it was found that using a small amount of child speech data to train acoustic models was better than using models trained with a large amount of adult speech adapted to child speech. We used standard Kaldi triphone models with 12000 Gaussians.

The proposed method follows these steps:

1. Voice activity detection is applied to the audio to deal with intra-word pauses.
2. A specific word-level lattice for each given sentence or task is built.
3. Decoding is performed using the specific lattices, obtaining the best label/segment sequence.
4. A reconstruction of the alignment is done, taking into account the silences previ-ously removed.

Intra-word pauses occur when words are pronounced syllable by syllable, with silences in between, most often for first grade children. Although still not perfectly representing phone transitions between syllables, the inexistence of silence when a full word is expected is crucial for decoding. Thus, we apply a voice activity detection method to cut silent segments. Even if silence between words is cut, which would help to clearly separate them, results improve due to the amount of intra-word pause cases solved. We detect the silence segments by analyzing the smoothed logarithmic energy of the signal, and selecting low energy segments longer than 150 ms, using a moving threshold depending on the high and low energy levels of the signal.

For the decoding stage, we build task specific lattices to allow some of the common patterns found in the data about false-starts and repetitions. Finite State Transducers (FST) are used and, comparing to previous work [16], there are less freedoms of word sequence repetition, avoiding any back transitions that complicate the FST and increase decoding times, undesirable for a live application. As an example, Fig. 1 describes the FST grammar for the three word sentence "ele sonhava muito" [elə suɲavɐ mũjtu] ("he dreamed a lot" in English). There is a basic unit employed for every word allowing false-starts and repetitions of the word, represented, e.g., for the word "ele" by the nodes 0, 1 and 2, and the transitions arriving to nodes 1 or 2. The same applies for the word "sonhava" with nodes 2, 3 and 4, and for the word "muito" with nodes 6, 7 and 8.

The word units with the suffix "PRE" represent syllable-based false-starts (pre-corrections). Although many false-starts are mispronounced, they often corre-spond to interrupting the pronunciation attempt at a word's syllables. Therefore, these cases are considered with multi-pronunciations for PRE up to (and excluding) the last syllable, e.g., for a four syllable word: the first syllable; the first followed by the second; or the first, second and third consecutively. Specifically, "elePRE" can only be [e]; "sonhavaPRE" can be [su] or [suɲa]; "muitoPRE" can only be [mũj].

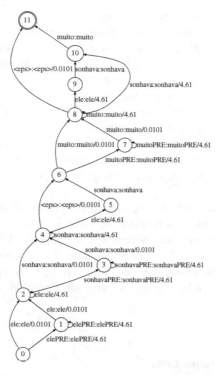

**Fig. 1.** Sentence FST for the three word sentence "ele sonhava muito" [elə suɲavɐ mũĩtu].

We also included an additional possibility of repeating the previous sequence of two or three words maximum. This kind of occurrence, e.g., "ele sonhava ele sonhava muito" is very common in the data, and often represents an attempt to correct a mistake by starting the sentence or clause from the beginning. In the example FST, paths that go through nodes 5, 9 and 10, represent these possibilities. Furthermore, following the left-most arcs, one gets the original sentence without any false-starts or repetitions (<eps> is an epsilon arc, consuming no input or output).

Other than not accounting for mispronunciations, a limitation of the described method is not taking into account any deletions or insertions. In fact, these are not too common in the data as children practically always try to finish reading the sentence. For a more general application, it may be preferable to allow deletions/skips, accounting for cases where a sentence is only partially pronounced. After this segmentation, we need to classify each segment as correctly pronounced or not.

## 4    Detection of Mispronunciations

In order to detect mispronunciations we trained a neural network for phoneme recognition, using the Brno University of Technology neural network system [20], which is based on long temporal context. The manually annotated set was used for training and testing the neural network, achieving about 70 % of phoneme recognition accuracy. With this neural network we obtained the posterior probabilities of the phoneme model states for all sentences of the database, the so called posteriorgrams. These posteriorgrams can be used as as input for the FST decoder, however, doing so did not improve the results of the previous method.

Using the posteriorgrams, we can use a spotter system to try to detect correctly pronounced words. The spotting system is based on the log likelihood ratio (LLR) between the spotting model (the sequence of phonemes of the spotting word) and a filler model that consists of a loop of all phoneme models [21]. The token-passing paradigm is used to compute the likelihoods and track the starting time of the tokens at the output of the spotter model. A match is assigned if a peak value of the LLR is above a given threshold.

We apply the spotter system to each word hypothesis given by the previous alignment, and find the peak LLR on the close vicinity of the given alignment. Several intervals to define this close vicinity were tested. If the peak LLR of a word is below a certain threshold, it is classified as mispronounced. The trade-off of false alarm rate versus miss rate on mispronunciation detection can be represented with a Detection Error Tradeoff (DET) curve by varying the decision threshold, as described below.

## 5    Results

### 5.1    False-Starts and Repetitions

The WER of the forced alignment using only the text of the original prompts is only 9 %. This means that repetitions, false-starts, insertions and deletions, occurring in the manual transcription, account for these 9 %. By using the described method to allow repetitions and false-starts, the best WER achieved in the training set was 3.75 %. To evaluate the system's performance on detecting events (PRE or REP) in terms of misses (false negatives) and false alarms (false positives), we consider that:

- Extra detected events are false alarms;
- Any undetected event is a miss;
- An event erroneously detected as an event of an adjacent word (a substitution) is also a miss.

These assumptions are similar to the NIST evaluations [22], although to calculate the false alarm rate we divide the number of false alarms by the number of original words. By using a wide search beam during decoding along with different word insertion penalties and lattice rescoring weights, a Detection Error Tradeoff (DET) curve can be obtained, as presented in Fig. 2, for the training set.

The best WER obtained (3.75 %), corresponds to a very low false alarm rate of 0.89 % and a 23.53 % miss rate. Comparing to a previous method [16], where 30.62 % miss rate is obtained for the same false alarm rate, this represents a 23 % relative improvement in miss rate for this operational point. Using the word insertion penalty and rescoring weight from the best WER, the results on the test set are: 4.47 % WER, 1.94 % false alarm rate and 20.60 % miss rate. The best possible WER would be

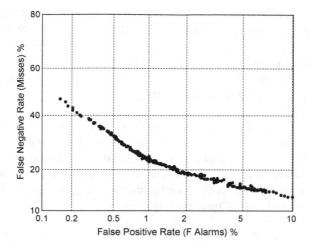

**Fig. 2.** Detection Error Tradeoff (DET) curve for the detection of false-starts and repetition events on the training set.

4.01 % by varying word insertion penalty. Certain aspects of our system can account for errors in specific event labeling: for small words with one syllable only repetitions are marked; and since some PRE tags of larger words are mispronunciations of the whole word, they can be decoded as the word followed by repetitions. Furthermore, there are insertions that are never accounted for, always leading to false alarms or segment mismatches, lowering overall accuracy.

This stage outputs a time-stamp alignment of the data according to word relevant segments, which is used for the next classification stage.

## 5.2   Mispronunciations

During manual annotation, two classes of mispronunciations of different severity were considered: PHO – variations of only one phoneme; and SUB – severe mispronunciation or substitution of the word. For the mispronunciation decision task, we present results using two ground truths: SUB or PHO segments as a mispronounced class (SUB + PHO) versus correctly pronounced words; and only SUB versus correct words (since PHO is usually too difficult to detect). We consider both the manual and the automatic segmentation to take segments for a decision on mispronunciation. In the case of automatic segmentation, we allow some misalignments with the ground truth, however, segments must overlap in order to be considered as matches to a particular ground truth segment.

The discriminant to decide mispronunciation is the maximum LLR of a word spotting in a segment and we considered several intervals to search maximum LLR around the final time of an aligned segment. An optimization revealed that the best interval for using manually annotated segments was −100 ms to +50 ms and for the automatic segments −250 ms to +50 ms. We also experimented several LLR score normalizations: dividing by number of phones of the searched word; dividing by the number of frames occupied by the best spot; and dividing by the LLR area of the spot as described in [21]. All of these normalized scores benefited from adding an extra value: the original LLR score scaled with a small constant factor (the optimal factor varying per normalization approach). By doing this, the results are very similar, with the number of phones normalization gaining a slight advantage, and it is the one considered for the presented results.

Figure 3 presents the DET curve for the SUB + PHO vs. correct words classification, using manual or automatic segmentation. Figure 4 presents the results for the SUB vs. correct words classification. Table 1 summarizes the results for the considered cases when a false alarm rate of 5 % is obtained. We target a low false alarm rate that still provides miss rates under 50 % as we should be indulgent with the child, allowing some non-detections instead of frequent false alarms.

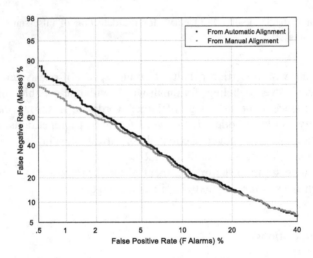

**Fig. 3.** Detection Error Tradeoff (DET) curves for mispronunciation classification of SUB + PHO class on the test set.

As expected, miss rates for using the automatic alignment are slightly worse, although still very close to manual alignment as observed in the DET curves. Nevertheless, we believe that these results can be improved by using the fusion of different scores or different normalizations.

After applying the proposed methods, we obtain both an automatic detection of the number of disfluencies per utterance and an automatic annotation with the suggestion of phone sequence for mispronounced segments. The impact of the results on an overall reading performance computation based on the analysis of several reading tasks should also be investigated.

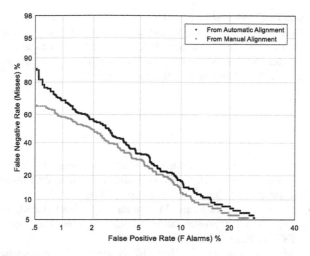

**Fig. 4.** Detection Error Tradeoff (DET) curve for mispronunciation classification of SUB class on the test set.

**Table 1.** Mispronunciation classification/detection miss rates for a 5 % false alarm rate on the test set.

| Classes | Manual alignment | Automatic alignment |
| --- | --- | --- |
| SUB + PHO | 40.99 % | 44.94 % |
| SUB | 28.88 % | 32.62 % |

# 6   Conclusions

A method was proposed to automatically detect false-starts, repetitions and mispronunciations on child reading aloud tasks, the three most commons miscues observed in the LetsRead database. The first stage is focused on segmentation while detecting extra segments and this approach shows promising results. The second stage takes the alignment and classifies words as correctly pronounced or not, further specializing the automatic annotation. As the first iteration of mispronunciation detection, it is foreseeable to develop improvements to the proposed method, such as applying a phone confusability matrix while computing the log-likelihood ratio of a given phone sequence.

The developed methods were applied to the unannotated set of the LetsRead database and an automatic annotation is provided. The next step involves a manual validation of the automatic annotation to enlarge the dataset, needing severally less effort than the initial manual annotation and allowing the training of more robust acoustic models. The final objective of this work is to automatically detect all reading miscues and compute a reading performance score that is well correlated with the opinion of teachers and experts.

**Acknowledgements.** This work was supported in part by Fundação para a Ciência e Tecnologia under the project UID/EEA/50008/2013 (pluriannual funding in the scope of the LETSREAD project). Jorge Proença is supported by the SFRH/BD/97204/2013 FCT Grant. We would like to thank *João de Deus*, *Bissaya Barreto* and *EBI de Pereira* school associations and CASPAE parent's association for collaborating in the database collection.

# References

1. National Reading Panel: Teaching children to read: an evidence-based assessment of the scientific research literature on reading and its implications for reading instruction. National Institute of Child Health and Human Development (2000)
2. Abdou, S.M., Hamid, S.E., Rashwan, M., Samir, A., Abdel-Hamid, O., Shahin, M., Nazih, W.: Computer aided pronunciation learning system using speech recognition techniques. In: INTERSPEECH (2006)
3. Cincarek, T., Gruhn, R., Hacker, C., Nöth, E., Nakamura, S.: Automatic pronunciation scoring of words and sentences independent from the non-native's first language. Comput. Speech Lang. **23**(1), 65–88 (2009)
4. Mostow, J., Roth, S.F., Hauptmann, A.G., Kane, M.: A prototype reading coach that listens. In: Proceedings of 12th National Conference on Artificial Intelligence, vol. 1, Menlo Park, pp. 785–792 (1994)
5. Black, M., Tepperman, J., Lee, S., Price, P., Narayanan, S.: Automatic detection and classification of disfluent reading miscues in young children's speech for the purpose of assessment. Presented at the Proceedings of Interspeech, pp. 206–209 (2007)
6. Duchateau, J., Kong, Y.O., Cleuren, L., Latacz, L., Roelens, J., Samir, A., Demuynck, K., Ghesquière, P., Verhelst, W., Hamme, H.V.: Developing a reading tutor: design and evaluation of dedicated speech recognition and synthesis modules. Speech Commun. **51**(10), 985–994 (2009)
7. Bolaños, D., Cole, R.A., Ward, W., Borts, E., Svirsky, E.: FLORA: fluent oral reading assessment of children's speech. ACM Trans. Speech Lang. Process. **7**(4), 16:1–16:19 (2011)
8. The LetsRead Project - Automatic assessment of reading ability of children. http://lsi.co.it.pt/spl/projects_letsread.html. Accessed 25 Mar 2016
9. Candeias, S., Celorico, D., Proença, J., Veiga, A., Perdigão, F.: HESITA(tions) in Portuguese: a database. In: ISCA, Interspeech Satellite Workshop on Disfluency in Spontaneous Speech - DiSS, pp. 13–16. KTH Royal Institute of Technology, Stockholm (2013)
10. Liu, Y., Shriberg, E., Stolcke, A., Harper, M.P.: Comparing HMM, maximum entropy, and conditional random fields for disfluency detection. In: Proceedings of Interspeech, pp. 3313–3316 (2005)
11. Medeiros, H., Moniz, H., Batista, F., Trancoso, I., Nunes, L., et al.: Disfluency detection based on prosodic features for university lectures. In: Proceedings of Interspeech, Lyon, France, pp. 2629–2633 (2013)
12. Moniz, H., Batista, F., Mata, A.I., Trancoso, I.: Speaking style effects in the production of disfluencies. Speech Commun. **65**, 20–35 (2014)
13. Duchateau, J., Cleuren, L., Hamme, H.V., Ghesquière, P.: Automatic assessment of children's reading level. In: Proceedings of Interspeech, Antwerp, Belgium, pp. 1210–1213 (2007)

14. Yilmaz, E., Pelemans, J., Hamme, H.V.: Automatic assessment of children's reading with the FLaVoR decoding using a phone confusion model. In: Proceedings of Interspeech, Singapore, pp. 969–972 (2014)
15. Li, X., Ju, Y.-C., Deng, L., Acero, A.: Efficient and robust language modeling in an automatic children's reading tutor system. In: Proceedings of IEEE International Conference on Acoustics, Speech and Signal Processing (ICASSP), vol. 4, pp. 193–196 (2007)
16. Proença, J., Celorico, D., Candeias, S., Lopes, C., Perdigão, F., Children's reading aloud performance: a database and automatic detection of disfluencies. In: ISCA - Conference of the International Speech Communication Association - INTERSPEECH, Dresden, Germany, pp. 1655–1659 (2015)
17. Black, M.P., Tepperman, J., Narayanan, S.S.: Automatic prediction of children's reading ability for high-level literacy assessment. Trans. Audio Speech and Lang. Process. **19**(4), 1015–1028 (2011)
18. Proenca, J., Celorico, D., Candeias, S., Lopes, C., Perdigão, F.: The LetsRead corpus of portuguese children reading aloud for performance evaluation. In: Proceedings of 10th Edition of the Language Resources and Evaluation Conference (LREC 2016), Portorož, Slovenia (2016)
19. Povey, D., Ghoshal, A., Boulianne, G., Burget, L., Glembek, O., Goel, N., Hannemann, M., Motlicek, P., Qian, Y., Schwarz, P., Silovsky, J., Stemmer, G., Vesely, K.: The Kaldi speech recognition toolkit. In: IEEE 2011 Workshop on Automatic Speech Recognition and Understanding, Hilton Waikoloa Village, Big Island, Hawaii, US (2011)
20. Phoneme recognizer based on long temporal context. Brno University of Technology, FIT. http://speech.fit.vutbr.cz/software/phoneme-recognizer-based-long-temporal-context. Accessed 06 May 2015
21. Veiga, A., Lopes, C., Sá, L., Perdigão, F.: Acoustic similarity scores for keyword spotting. In: Baptista, J., Mamede, N., Candeias, S., Paraboni, I., Pardo, Thiago, A.,S., Volpe Nunes, M.d.G (eds.) PROPOR 2014. LNCS (LNAI), vol. 8775, pp. 48–58. Springer, Heidelberg (2014). doi:10.1007/978-3-319-09761-9_5
22. Fiscus, J.G., Ajot, J., Garofolo, J.S., Doddingtion, G.: Results of the 2006 spoken term detection evaluation. In: Proceedings of SIGIR, vol. 7, pp. 51–57 (2007)

# Automatic Detection of Hyperarticulated Speech

Eugénio Ribeiro[1,2](✉), Fernando Batista[1,3], Isabel Trancoso[1,2],
Ricardo Ribeiro[1,3], and David Martins de Matos[1,2]

[1] L²F – Spoken Language Systems Laboratory, INESC-ID Lisboa, Lisbon, Portugal
[2] Instituto Superior Técnico, Universidade de Lisboa, Lisbon, Portugal
eugenio.ribeiro@l2f.inesc-id.pt
[3] ISCTE-IUL – Instituto Universitário de Lisboa, Lisbon, Portugal

**Abstract.** Hyperarticulation is a speech adaptation that consists of adopting a clearer form of speech in an attempt to improve recognition levels. However, it has the opposite effect when talking to ASR systems, as they are not trained with such kind of speech. We present approaches for automatic detection of hyperarticulation, which can be used to improve the performance of spoken dialog systems. We performed experiments on Let's Go data, using multiple feature sets and two classification approaches. Many relevant features are speaker dependent. Thus, we used the first turn in each dialog as the reference for the speaker, since it is typically not hyperarticulated. Our best results were above 80 % accuracy, which represents an improvement of at least 11.6 % points over previously obtained results on similar data. We also assessed the classifiers' performance in scenarios where hyperarticulation is rare, achieving around 98 % accuracy using different confidence thresholds.

**Keywords:** Hyperarticulation · Speech · Let's Go

## 1   Introduction

When people face recognition problems by their conversational partners, they tend to adopt a clearer form of speech in an attempt to improve recognition levels. This speech adaptation is called hyperarticulation. However, although it may work in child-directed speech or when talking to people with hearing impairment, it typically has the opposite result when talking to an Automatic Speech Recognition (ASR) system, decreasing its performance [7,17]. This happens because ASR systems are not trained with hyperarticulated speech. Furthermore, these situations typically occur in attempts to recover from previous recognition errors. This means that the supposed correction will also be misrecognized, leading to further hyperarticulation and recognition errors, completely disrupting the dialog flow [11].

Automatic detection of hyperarticulated speech is important because if a dialog system is able to do so, it can try to recognize the utterance using ASR models trained with hyperarticulated speech, or at least try to guide the user towards the use of unmarked speech. Furthermore, automatic hyperarticulation

© Springer International Publishing AG 2016
A. Abad et al. (Eds.): IberSPEECH 2016, LNAI 10077, pp. 182–191, 2016.
DOI: 10.1007/978-3-319-49169-1_18

detection can be used to find possible causes of hot spots in a dialog, reducing the need for manual annotations.

Our experiments on automatic detection of hyperarticulation were performed on data from real user interactions with an Interactive Voice Response (IVR) system along multiple years. In this paper we present several approaches to the task, using multiple feature sets and classification algorithms.

The remaining sections are structured as follows: Sect. 2 presents the related work. Section 3 describes the datasets, features and approaches used. Results are presented and discussed in Sect. 4, and, finally, Sect. 5 states the conclusions and suggests paths for future work.

## 2   Related Work

Hyperarticulation is widely accepted as an important factor that should be dealt with by speech applications. However, not much effort has been put into its automatic detection. Research involving hyperarticulation is usually directed towards the evaluation of its impact in ASR and how systems can adapt to it or redirect the users towards the use of unmarked speech. Nonetheless, there are multiple studies that explore the characteristics of hyperarticulated speech. This is important for the automatic detection of hyperarticulation as those characteristics help selecting relevant features for the task.

The work by Fandrianto and Eskenazi [5] on prosodic entrainment of shouting and hyperarticulation is, to our knowledge, the only one that provides concrete results for automatic hyperarticulation detection. The automatic detection approach consists of a Support Vector Machine (SVM) classifier trained using Let's Go [14] data from the years of 2009 and 2010 that had been used in previous experiments [12]. In terms of features, the authors used a small set of six acoustic features – fundamental frequency range and average, intensity, harmonic-noise ratio, and pause duration and frequency –, extracted using openSMILE [4], and two dialog-level features – ASR confidence and explicit confirm repetition. Using this approach, the authors achieved 70 % accuracy on a balanced test set.

Oviatt et al. [11] studied hyperarticulated speech and analyzed how a set of features changed when people started to hyperarticulate. The analyzed features involved durations of both speech and pauses, speech rate, amplitude, fundamental frequency, intonation contour, phonological alternations, and disfluencies. The authors reported a significant increase in both the number and duration of pauses during hyperarticulated speech. On the contrary, the number of disfluencies reduced significantly. Also, the final fall in intonation, speech elongation, and the use of hyper-clear phonology moderately increased. Finally, minimum and average pitch slightly decreased.

Soltau and Waibel [18] analyzed hyperarticulated speech at the phone level in order to develop acoustic models able to deal with that kind of speech. By analyzing vowel formants, the authors only found significant differences for the vowel/uw/. In terms of duration, all phones lasted longer during hyperarticulated speech. However, the difference for consonants was two times the one for vowels.

Also, the duration of voiced plosives increased over 40 %. Finally, in terms of the place of articulation, retroflex and labiodental sounds revealed no dependence of hyperarticulated speech, while velar, alveolar, and bilabial sounds revealed at least some level of dependence.

Stent et al. [19] also studied hyperarticulation at the phone level. The authors paid special attention to the /t/ phone, specially when it comes before an unstressed vowel, at the end of the word, or after an $n$, as its pronunciation differs during clear speech. The presence of a full vowel in the definite article $a$ and of the /d/ phone in $and$ was also analyzed. However, in these cases, the studies showed no clear differences, which, according to the authors, may be explained by the tendency to use clearer speech on content words rather than on function words when repairing, as content words are more critical to understand a message. Furthermore, the authors analyzed the vowel formants and concluded that front vowels become even more fronted during hyperarticulated speech.

Overall, we can conclude that hyperarticulated speech is characterized by changes in multiple acoustic-prosodic features, as well as articulatory changes in specific phones.

# 3    Experimental Setup

This section describes our experimental setup, starting with the adopted datasets, followed by the used feature sets, classification approaches, and evaluation methodology.

## 3.1    Datasets

In our experiments we used data from three years of The Let's Go corpus. The corpus features data from the CMU Let's Go Bus Information System, which provides information about bus schedules in the city of Pittsburg, through spoken telephonic interaction with a dialog system. Subsets of the data from the three years were annotated for hyperarticulation in a joint effort by $L^2F$ and KTH [8]. 834 turns from 2009, 1110 from 2012, and 1449 from 2014 were annotated, out of which 113, 90, and 77, respectively, were labeled as hyperarticulated. It is important to notice that the system evolved over the years, both in terms of ASR performance and dialog management. Thus, the characteristics of the data change according to the year. Since the datasets are highly unbalanced, we balanced them using the Spread Subsample filter provided by the Weka Toolkit [6] to obtain datasets with the same number of examples of each class. We performed experiments using each of the balanced yearly datasets individually, as well as together in an aggregated dataset. Furthermore, we used the unbalanced datasets for precision evaluation.

## 3.2    Features

Taking the characteristics of hyperarticulated speech mentioned in Sect. 2 into account, we extracted sets of acoustic, segmental, and disfluency-based features that intend to capture some of those characteristics. Furthermore, we used the ComParE 2013 feature set, since it is widely used in speech-related tasks.

**ComParE 2013.** The ComParE 2013 feature set [16], extracted using openS-MILE, provides a large amount of acoustic-prosodic features and is widely used in speech analytics tasks. Hyperarticulation is inherently related to acoustic and prosodic factors, thus, this set may be suitable for this task.

**Segmental.** Hyperarticulation is highly related to rhythmic and durational features. The extraction of such features requires segmentation of the original audio file into smaller, informative segments. We obtained a phone tokenization of the audio using the neural networks that are part of our in-house ASR system [9].

From the segmentation directly, we extracted features related to phones – count, total speech duration, average phone duration, speech ratio, and phone-based speech rate – and pauses – count, total silence duration, average pause duration, silence ratio, and silence-to-speech ratio. In terms of Inter-Pausal Units (IPUs), i.e., sequences of phones between two pauses, we extracted the count, rate, and 9 statistics – maximum, minimum, mean, standard deviation, median, mode, slope, concavity, and range – of their duration, in seconds, and length, in number of phones. The IPUs were also important for the extraction of acoustic features, as described below.

**Acoustic.** In terms of base acoustic features, we extracted energy, pitch, and Harmonic-Noise Ratio (HNR) using openSMILE, with overlapping windows of 50ms, and a 10ms step. We also extracted normalized amplitude using SoX[1]. We computed the same 9 statistics listed in the previous section for each of the features, using the whole audio file. Furthermore, we computed the same statistics for the data corresponding to each IPU in the audio file, and repeated the same procedure to obtain IPU-based statistics for the whole file. Finally, we also computed the same 9 statistics for pitch, discarding null values, that is, those corresponding to unvoiced speech or non-speech.

**Disfluencies.** As stated in related work [11], the number of disfluencies tends to decrease during hyperarticulated speech. Thus, we counted the number and calculated the ratio of IPUs that contained disfluencies. We took advantage of the speech disfluency detection module [10] provided by the SPA[2] speech analytics platform. However, it is important to notice that this module was trained using data from the CORAL [20] corpus, which contains non-English data.

---

[1] http://sox.sourceforge.net.
[2] https://www.l2f.inesc-id.pt/spa/.

**First Turn Differences.** Most of the characteristics of hyperarticulated speech are speaker dependent. For instance, when hyperarticulated speech is character- ized as slower, it is slower in relation to the normal speech rate of the person. Since our dataset consists of turns extracted from human-machine dialogs, we are able to extract all the previously described features from the first human turn of each dialog. That turn is highly unlikely to contain hyperarticulated speech, as the person has not faced recognition problems by the machine. Thus, it can be used as a reference for the remaining turns in the dialog. Taking advantage of this, we computed the difference between the value for each of the previously described features and the corresponding value for the first turn in the same dialog.

### 3.3   Classification

In our experiments, we considered the detection of hyperarticulated speech a binary classification task. From the multiple classification approaches that could be used, we opted for SVMs [3], which are widely used and typically produce acceptable results, and Random Forests (RFs) [2], an approach based on decision trees, which has been proved successful in experiments using similar data [15].

To train our SVMs, we took advantage of the Sequential Minimal Optimiza- tion (SMO) algorithm [13] implementation provided by the Weka Toolkit. We used the linear kernel and kept the C parameter with its default 1.0 value, as it led to the best results in our experiments. We also took advantage of the Weka Toolkit to train our RFs. Since the number of instances is small, it is affordable to generate a large amount of trees. Thus, we used 1000 as the value of that parameter.

### 3.4   Evaluation

In order to evaluate our approaches, we used two different procedures. One that evaluated the importance of different feature sets for the task and the performance of the different classification approaches, and one that evaluated the capabilities of the approaches to adapt to real situations, with unbalanced datasets.

For the first, we used 10-fold cross-validation on both each yearly balanced dataset, as well as on the aggregated dataset. In this case, given the use of balanced datasets, the binary nature of the task, and the objective of evaluating the overall performance of the different feature sets and classification approaches, we relied solely on accuracy as evaluation measure.

For the second procedure, we used all data from each year, in order to sim- ulate a real situation, with rare occurrences of hyperarticulated speech. In this case, in addition to accuracy, we also looked into precision, recall, and F-measure, to identify the best confidence threshold that reduced the number of false posi- tives without highly increasing the number of false negatives.

# 4    Results

In this section we present the results obtained by the SVM and RF approaches using the different feature set combinations.

## 4.1    Balanced Datasets

Table 1 presents the accuracy results obtained by the SVM and RF approaches on the four datasets, using different feature sets. The table is split into three subtables, which contain the results obtained using the ComParE 2013 feature set, our acoustic-prosodic features, and the combination of the two. The rows labeled as **All** refer to the results obtained using all features of each subtable's category. The sets labeled as **Selected** were obtained by applying the Best First feature selection algorithm, with five consecutive nodes without improvement as the stop criterion, to the corresponding **All** set.

**Table 1.** Accuracy results obtained using the SVM and Random Forest approaches and the different feature sets.

| Feature Set | Let's Go 2009 | | Let's Go 2012 | | Let's Go 2014 | | All | |
|---|---|---|---|---|---|---|---|---|
|  | SVM | RF | SVM | RF | SVM | RF | SVM | RF |
| **ComPaRe 2013** | | | | | | | | |
| Current Turn | 0.668 | 0.717 | 0.761 | 0.750 | 0.727 | 0.773 | 0.689 | 0.748 |
| 1st Turn Difference | 0.721 | 0.730 | 0.761 | 0.778 | 0.721 | 0.760 | 0.704 | 0.723 |
| All | 0.695 | 0.730 | 0.800 | 0.794 | 0.792 | 0.825 | 0.723 | 0.771 |
| Selected | **0.805** | **0.841** | **0.839** | **0.872** | **0.818** | **0.935** | **0.766** | **0.805** |
| **Acoustic-Prosodic** | | | | | | | | |
| Amplitude | 0.664 | 0.695 | 0.572 | 0.678 | 0.623 | 0.721 | 0.613 | 0.723 |
| Energy | 0.708 | 0.712 | 0.633 | 0.683 | 0.662 | 0.747 | 0.673 | 0.713 |
| Pitch | 0.655 | 0.655 | 0.656 | 0.661 | 0.649 | 0.675 | 0.639 | 0.679 |
| HNR | 0.606 | 0.686 | 0.611 | 0.672 | 0.682 | 0.682 | 0.613 | 0.675 |
| Pitch + Energy | **0.730** | 0.730 | **0.683** | 0.672 | 0.649 | 0.766 | 0.671 | 0.723 |
| Acoustic | 0.690 | 0.735 | 0.622 | 0.711 | 0.662 | **0.812** | 0.684 | 0.730 |
| Segmental | 0.664 | 0.646 | 0.661 | 0.667 | 0.675 | 0.721 | 0.666 | 0.673 |
| Disfluencies | 0.566 | 0.571 | 0.600 | 0.617 | 0.468 | 0.552 | 0.555 | 0.559 |
| P + E + H + Sil [5] | 0.655 | 0.677 | 0.611 | 0.711 | 0.636 | 0.695 | 0.655 | 0.718 |
| All | 0.637 | 0.708 | 0.622 | 0.689 | 0.591 | 0.721 | 0.670 | 0.725 |
| Selected | 0.695 | **0.739** | 0.622 | **0.712** | **0.766** | **0.812** | **0.718** | **0.738** |
| **Combination** | | | | | | | | |
| All | 0.699 | 0.735 | 0.772 | 0.783 | 0.773 | 0.792 | 0.720 | 0.764 |
| Selected | **0.827** | **0.836** | **0.844** | **0.861** | **0.812** | **0.922** | **0.761** | **0.816** |

The first important point to notice is that the RF approach systematically obtained better results than the SVM approach. This suggests that at least some of the features follow a distribution that is highly discriminative for the hierarchical structure of decision trees. Thus, the following remarks will be based on RF results.

Starting with ComPare 2013 features, we can see that this feature set on its own obtained accuracy results over 70 % on every dataset, which defines a relatively high baseline, already above the one defined by Fandrianto and Eskenazi [5]. The use of feature value differences between the current turn and the first turn in the dialog improved the baseline results on every dataset except the one from 2014. Furthermore, the combination of the two sets, **All**, improved the results on every dataset. This proves the importance of the relation between the current turn and the first in the dialog, reducing the effects of speaker dependence. Performing feature selection on such a large set of features is very important, as many features provide no information. This can be proved by the results obtained by the **Selected** feature set, which are above 80 % on every dataset.

In terms of our acoustic-prosodic features, the results presented for each set already contain the features related to the value differences in relation to the first turn, since those features were always able to improve the results. Starting with acoustic features, energy features were typically the most informative. The combination of pitch and energy, a typical combination when acoustic features are used, was able to achieve at least the same result as the best individual acoustic feature class. Furthermore, by appending the remaining two classes, the results improved for every dataset, surpassing the baseline for the 2009 and 2014 datasets. Segmental features were less informative, with accuracy results below each single acoustic class. However, this can be explained by the disappointing results obtained by some of the features in that set. For instance, speech rate only achieved results below 60 %. However, there were also positive results, obtained by features based on durations, length, silence and speech. Still, in this sense, durational features were more informative than the ones related to length and the same happened with speech-based features in relation to silence-based features. Disfluency-based features also obtained disappointing results, below 60 % accuracy. However, in this case, the results can be explained by the fact that the disfluency detector was trained using data in a different language. The combination of pitch, energy, HNR, and silence, which approaches the set of acoustic features used by Fandrianto and Eskenazi [5], achieved results similar to the ones reported in their article, in spite of not including dialog-level features. Furthermore, the combination of all acoustic-prosodic features was only able to outperform the acoustic feature set when feature selection was applied, leading to the best results in the subtable, but only with slight improvements.

Finally, by combining the ComParE 2013 set with our acoustic-prosodic features, the result differences in relation to the case when only the first was used were practically negligible, with an improvement of 0.5 % points on the Let's Go 2009 dataset and decreases up to 3 % points on the remaining datasets. The results obtained by the **Selected** feature set have a similar relation with the

**Table 2.** Accuracy, Precision, Recall, and F-measure results obtained on the unbalanced datasets using different Thresholds.

| T | Let's Go 2009 | | | | Let's Go 2012 | | | | Let's Go 2014 | | | |
|---|---|---|---|---|---|---|---|---|---|---|---|---|
| | A | P | R | F | A | P | R | F | A | P | R | F |
| **50 %** | 0.807 | 0.412 | **1.000** | 0.584 | 0.770 | 0.261 | **1.000** | 0.414 | 0.669 | 0.138 | **1.000** | 0.242 |
| **80 %** | **0.982** | 0.971 | 0.894 | **0.931** | **0.986** | 0.920 | 0.900 | **0.910** | 0.970 | 0.649 | 0.935 | 0.766 |
| **85 %** | 0.965 | 0.988 | 0.752 | 0.854 | 0.968 | 0.966 | 0.633 | 0.765 | **0.985** | 0.877 | 0.831 | **0.853** |
| **90 %** | 0.912 | **1.000** | 0.354 | 0.523 | 0.950 | **1.000** | 0.389 | 0.560 | 0.972 | **1.000** | 0.468 | 0.638 |

ones obtained with the **Selected** set for the ComPaRe 2013 set. However, in this case, the results were only improved on the aggregated dataset, leading to our best result when using all data, with 81.6 % accuracy.

Overall, the obtained results show that this task benefits from the use of large feature sets, out of which the most important features can be selected using automatic methods. Furthermore, differential features are important to reduce the effects of speaker dependence. Finally, the information provided by the ComPaRe 2013 feature set seems to be similar to the one provided by our acoustic-prosodic features, since, in general, the combination of both sets did not lead to improved results.

## 4.2   Unbalanced Datasets

Although we used balanced datasets to train our classifiers, we want them to be able to deal with real situations, where hyperarticulated speech is rare and the focus is on identifying such situations with precision. To assess that capability, we classified all instances of each yearly unbalanced dataset using an RF classifier trained on the aggregated balanced dataset with the **Selected** set of ComPaRe 2013. The first row of Table 2 shows the results obtained by the classifier on each dataset. We can see that, although recall values are high, which means that hyperarticulated speech is identified when it really exists, precision values are low, which means that there are many misclassified examples of non-hyperarticulated speech. This was expected given the lack of balance of the datasets, and we can see that precision decreases as the level of balance decreases. However, these results go against the objective of identifying hyperarticulation with precision. Thus, we looked into the levels of confidence reported by the classifier and performed experiments using different confidence thresholds.

By analyzing the confidence levels, we noticed that the highest confidence value for an example mistakenly classified as hyperarticulated was 89.6 %. In Table 2 we can see that using a fixed threshold of 90 % effectively increased precision levels. However, as a trade-off, recall was drastically reduced, which means that many hyperarticulated examples were not identified. We defined two more fixed thresholds – 80 % and 85 % –. We can see that the threshold leading to the higher F-value tends to increase as the level of balance of the dataset decreases. This hardens the process of selecting a generic threshold. However, we suggest values between 80 % and 85 %.

Finally, it is important to notice that by performing threshold changes we were able to obtain accuracy results around 98 % for every dataset. These values are always above the ones obtained by a chance classifier – 86.5 %, 91.9 %, and 94.7 % for the 2009, 2012, and 2014 datasets, respectively.

## 5   Conclusions

In this article we presented our approaches on automatic detection of hyper-articulation. We used multiple feature sets and two classification algorithms – SVMs and RFs –, with the latter systematically outperforming the widely used SVMs.

In terms of features, we discovered that this task benefits from large sets of features, out of which the most important can be selected using automatic approaches. This was proved by the results obtained using the ComPaRe 2013 feature set and the combination of all the features we extracted. Furthermore, the feature value differences between the turn being classified and the first in the dialog revealed to be very important features, due to the speaker dependence of many of the extracted features. On the other hand, speech rate and disfluency-based features produced disappointing results, in spite of being classified as relevant features for hyperarticulation detection in the literature.

We achieved accuracy results over 80 % on each balanced yearly dataset, as well as on the aggregated dataset. These results surpass the ones obtained by Fandrianto and Eskenazi [5] on similar data by at least 11.6 % points.

By modifying the confidence thresholds, we were able to obtain accuracy results around 98 % on every unbalanced dataset, while maintaining high precision values.

As future work, we intend to explore features extracted at the phone level, such as the ones described by Soltau and Waibel [18] and Stent et al. [19].

**Acknowledgements.** This work was supported by national funds through Fundação para a Ciência e a Tecnologia (FCT) with reference UID/CEC/50021/2013, by Universidade de Lisboa, and by the EC H2020 project RAGE under grant agreement No 644187.

## References

1. Batista, F., Curto, P., Trancoso, I., Abad, A., Ferreira, J., Ribeiro, E., Moniz, H., de Matos, D.M., Ribeiro, R.: SPA: web-based platform for easy access to speech processing modules. In: Proceedings of the 10th International Conference on Language Resources and Evaluation (LREC) (2016)
2. Breiman, L.: Random Forests. Mach. Learn. **45**(1), 5–32 (2001)
3. Cortes, C., Vapnik, V.: Support-Vector Networks. Mach. Learn. **20**(3), 273–297 (1995)
4. Eyben, F., Weninger, F., Gross, F., Schuller, B.: Recent developments in openS-MILE, the Munich open-source multimedia feature extractor. In: Proceedings of the 21st ACM International Conference on Multimedia, pp. 835–838 (2013)

5. Fandrianto, A., Eskenazi, M.: Prosodic entrainment in an information-driven dialog system. In: Proceedings of INTERSPEECH 2012, pp. 342–345 (2012)
6. Hall, M., Frank, E., Holmes, G., Pfahringer, B., Reutemann, P., Witten, I.H.: The WEKA data mining software: an update. SIGKDD Explor. Newsl. 11(1), 10–18 (2009)
7. Litman, D.J., Hirschberg, J., Swerts, M.: Predicting automatic speech recognition performance using prosodic cues. In: Proceedings of NAACL, pp. 218–225 (2000)
8. Lopes, J., Chorianopoulou, A., Palogiannidi, E., Moniz, H., Abad, A., Louka, K., Iosif, E., Potamianos, A.: The SpeDial datasets: datasets for spoken dialogue system analytics. In: Proceedings of the 10th International Conference on Language Resources and Evaluation (LREC) (2016)
9. Meinedo, H., Viveiros, M., Neto, J.A.: Evaluation of a live broadcast news subtitling system for Portuguese. In: Proceedings of INTERSPEECH 2008, pp. 508–511 (2008)
10. Moniz, H., Ferreira, J., Batista, F., Trancoso, I.: Disfluency in spontaneous speech. In: Proceedings of DISS 2015 (2015)
11. Oviatt, S., MacEachern, M., Levow, G.A.: Predicting hyperarticulate speech during human-computer error resolution. Speech Commun. 24(2), 87–110 (1998)
12. Parent, G., Eskenazi, M.: Lexical entrainment of real users in the Let's Go spoken dialog system. In: Proceedings of INTERSPEECH 2010, pp. 3018–3021 (2010)
13. Platt, J.: Fast Training of support vector machines using sequential minimal optimization. In: Schoelkopf, B., Burges, C., Smola, A. (eds.) Advances in Kernel Methods - Support Vector Learning. MIT Press (1998)
14. Raux, A., Bohus, D., Langner, B., Black, A.W., Eskenazi, M.: Doing research on a deployed spoken dialogue system: one year of Lets Go! experience. In: Proceedings of INTERSPEECH 2006, pp. 65–68 (2006)
15. Ribeiro, E., Batista, F., Trancoso, I., Lopes, J., Ribeiro, R., de Matos, D.M.: Assessing user expertise in spoken dialog system interactions. In: IberSPEECH 2016 (2016)
16. Schuller, B., Steidl, S., Batliner, A., Vinciarelli, A., Scherer, K.R., Ringeval, F., Chetouani, M., Weninger, F., Eyben, F., Marchi, E., Mortillaro, M., Salamin, H., Polychroniou, A., Valente, F., Kim, S.: The INTERSPEECH 2013 computational paralinguistics challenge: social signals, conflict, emotion, autism. In: Proceedings of INTERSPEECH 2013, pp. 148–152 (2013)
17. Soltau, H., Waibel, A.: On the influence of hyperarticulated speech on recognition performance. In: Proceedings of ICSLP (1998)
18. Soltau, H., Waibel, A.: Acoustic models for hyperarticulated speech. In: Proceedings of IEEE International Conference on Acoustics, Speech, and Signal Processing ICASSP, pp. 1779–1782 (2000)
19. Stent, A.J., Huffman, M.K., Brennan, S.E.: Adapting speaking after evidence of misrecognition: local and global hyperarticulation. Speech Commun. 50(3), 163–178 (2008)
20. Trancoso, I., do Céu Viana, M., I., Matos, G.: Corpus de Diálogo CORAL. In: PROPOR 1998 (1998)

# Acoustic-Prosodic Automatic Personality Trait Assessment for Adults and Children

Rubén Solera-Ureña[1(✉)], Helena Moniz[1,2], Fernando Batista[1,3],
Ramón F. Astudillo[1,4], Joana Campos[5,6], Ana Paiva[5,6], and Isabel Trancoso[1,6]

[1] Spoken Language Systems Laboratory, INESC-ID Lisboa, Lisboa, Portugal
{rsolera,helenam,fmmb,ramon.astudillo,imt}@l2f.inesc-id.pt
[2] FLUL/CLUL, Universidade de Lisboa, Lisboa, Portugal
[3] ISCTE-IUL – Instituto Universitário de Lisboa, Lisboa, Portugal
[4] Unbabel Inc., Lisboa, Portugal
[5] Intelligent Agents and Synthetic Characters Group,
INESC-ID Lisboa, Lisboa, Portugal
joana.campos@gaips.inesc-id.pt, ana.paiva@inesc-id.pt
[6] Instituto Superior Técnico, Universidade de Lisboa, Lisboa, Portugal

**Abstract.** This paper investigates the use of heterogeneous speech corpora for automatic assessment of personality traits in terms of the *Big-Five* OCEAN dimensions. The motivation for this work is twofold: the need to develop methods to overcome the lack of children's speech corpora, particularly severe when targeting personality traits, and the interest on cross-age comparisons of acoustic-prosodic features to build robust paralinguistic detectors. For this purpose, we devise an experimental setup with age mismatch utilizing the Interspeech 2012 Personality Sub-challenge, containing adult speech, as training data. As test data, we use a corpus of children's European Portuguese speech. We investigate various features sets such as the Sub-challenge baseline features, the recently introduced eGeMAPS features and our own knowledge-based features. The preliminary results bring insights into cross-age and -language detection of personality traits in spontaneous speech, pointing out to a stable set of acoustic-prosodic features for Extraversion and Agreeableness in both adult and child speech.

**Keywords:** Computational paralinguistics · Automatic personality assessment · OCEAN · Cross-lingual · Cross-age

## 1 Introduction

The intents, emotions, and even personality traits of a speaker are coded in paralinguistic information, beyond the linguistic structures of a language. The **OCEAN** (*Big-Five*) dimensions of personality traits are a psychological construct summarized as follows: Openness (artistic, imaginative, original), Conscientiousness (organized, efficient, thorough), Extraversion (energetic, outgoing, talkative), Agreeableness (kind, generous, sympathetic), and Neuroticism (anxious, self-pitying, worrying).

© Springer International Publishing AG 2016
A. Abad et al. (Eds.): IberSPEECH 2016, LNAI 10077, pp. 192–201, 2016.
DOI: 10.1007/978-3-319-49169-1_19

The analysis of personality traits has a plethora of applications, e.g., discriminating natural from disordered behaviors or automatically assessing personality traits, either in human-human communications or in human-computer interactions. Much of the literature on automatic processing of personality traits is still mostly focused on assessing and detecting the traits based on several sets of distinct features. Artificial intelligence applications are, however, giving steps towards displaying robots and virtual agents with certain traits to better interact with humans, making the communication more idiosyncratic and tuned to the paralinguistic fingerprints of an interlocutor.

The automatic assessment/detection of personality traits is still a very challenging task, either due to the individual spectrum of a speaker, or to the spectrum of the trait itself: whenever the richness of a person is defined in 5 classes, it may not cover all the sub-specifications or the boundaries between such classes, as psychological studies have been pointing out [4]. It is clear in the literature that some traits can be more easily recognized by means of automatic procedures than others, but this fact may vary according to the data and the methodologies applied (see [21] for a survey). Moreover, it has been timidly pointed out that different personality dimensions/traits are revealed in spontaneous speech by means of different sets of representative acoustic/prosodic features [11,14–16,21], but exhaustive categorizations of such features and studies on their impact across ages, cultures, etc. are still missing.

Psychological studies have shown a strong debate between change and continuity of personality traits from childhood to adult age or even elderly in longitudinal studies [3,7,9,18]. The studies in [3] show that children's personality traits are linked to that ones displayed in adult age; for instance: *"When observed at age 3, children classified as Inhibited were shy, fearful, and socially ill at ease. At age 26, they were characterized by an overcontrolled and nonassertive personality style; they expressed little desire to exert influence over others and reported taking little pleasure in life"*.

Reasoning about these findings from an automatic processing point of view, we could expect to find similar sets of acoustic/prosodic features for a given trait in adult and children speech, which could lead to reasonable performance rates for the classification of personality traits across languages and ages. This is the main motivation for our work here that targets the experimental evaluation of personality models trained on French adults' speech on a completely different corpus consisting of Portuguese children's speech.

## 2   Cross-Age and Cross-Language Datasets

Two very different speech corpora have been used in this work, namely the Speaker Personality Corpus (SPC) [13,19,20] and the Game-of-Nines (GoN) corpus [2]. The markedly different characteristics of the speakers in these two corpora (adults vs. children, French vs. Portuguese speakers, respectively) constitute a good basis to investigate whether we can leverage the presence of common, language- and age-independent acoustic and prosodic cues to detect/assess basic personality traits across heterogeneous groups of target speakers. The more populated SPC database was used in this work to learn (and evaluate) statistical models for the binary classification tasks corresponding to each personality trait in the *Big-Five* model (**OCEAN**). These models were then used to automatically assess the perceived personality traits of the children present in the GoN corpus. Below, we present a description of these two speech data sets.

## 2.1   Speaker Personality Corpus

The Speaker Personality Corpus consists of 640 speech files from 322 different adult individuals, collected from the French news bulletin of Radio Suisse Romande, Switzerland. Each file contains 10 s of speech from just one speaker (around 1 h and 40 min in total). All the files were independently assessed by 11 judges (non-French speakers) using the BFI-10 personality questionnaire [17]. For each file, final labels for the *Big-Five* dimensions are calculated by a majority vote procedure: for each trait, a high/low level (O/NO, C/NC, E/NE, A/NA, N/NN) is assigned if at least 6 judges scored it above/below their personal averages for that trait.

The SPC corpus was used in the Interspeech 2012 Speaker Trait Challenge-Personality Sub-challenge [19,20]. On that occasion, the corpus was split into 3 speaker-independent train, development and test subsets consisting of 256, 183 and 201 files, respectively. In this work, the same experimental setup has been adopted.

## 2.2   Game-of-Nines Corpus

The Game-of-Nines corpus was originally designed to study how conflict unfolds in social interactions by looking at behavioral cues (e.g. gaze) in a mixed-motive social interaction (i.e. a scenario with competitive and cooperative incentives) with children. It comprises synchronized video- and audio-recordings of 11 dyadic sessions with 22 Portuguese children (13 girls and 9 boys) aged 10 to 12 years-old playing a competitive-cooperative bargaining card game (a modified version of the *Game of Nines* [8]). The duration of the recordings vary between 9 and 18.6 min, with an average duration of 12.8 min and a total of 2 h and 20 min. Personality annotations for the children that participated in the experiments were provided with the database; the self-administered PBPS-C v2 personality questionnaire for children [10] was employed in that case. However, the original annotations were discarded in this work and an alternative annotation process was conducted. The reason behind this is that the original personality scores, directly derived from children's self-reports, might be biased towards the ideal personal image that the children would like to project. Finally, manual transcriptions of the conversations are also provided with this database.

The original Game-of-Nines database was pre-processed in order to adapt it for our purposes. Firstly, all the video information was discarded for this work and just the audio tracks were used. Secondly, the speech transcriptions were used to identify and extract all the speech segments corresponding to each child.

Those parts with overlapped conversations (both playmates speaking at the same time) were removed in order to avoid processing mixed speech segments. After this pre-processing procedure, two different speech subsets were generated:

1. *GoN-complete*: for each child, all their speech segments in the game session were concatenated together in one single speech file. As a results, the *GoN-complete* subset consists of 22 files ranging from 49 s to 8.1 min of speech (average duration of 4.2 min).
2. *GoN-20seconds*: for each child, 4 different files with around 20 s of speech each were generated by concatenating their longer speech segments in the game. Very short segments (below 2 s) were discarded in order to avoid an excessive variability in the speech characteristics. Also, a speaker-balanced subset was considered advisable. With these restrictions, just 4 files could be generated for the majority of the children, while just 2 files could be generated for one of the participants. As a result, the *GoN-20seconds* subset consists of 86 files with an approximate duration of 20 s.

Finally, both speech subsets were independently annotated in terms of the *Big-Five* personality dimensions by a professional psychologist using the BFI-10 personality questionnaire. These annotations have been used as the ground-truth labels in this work. The psychologist that participated in this work has substantial experience in annotating data and has already participated in several research projects in this field.

These two GoN subsets have been used in this work to study how personality models built up from French adults' speech can be used to assess the *Big-Five* dimensions of personality of Portuguese children. Additionally, differences in the average length of the files in these two subsets allow a comparison of the effect of short versus long acoustic cues on the personality assessment systems.

## 3 Classification System for Paralinguistics

This section presents a description of the speech representations and statistical models used in this work.

### 3.1 Recent Progress in Parameterizations for Paralinguistics

In our experiments, we used two sets of features extracted with openSMILE [6], and a set of knowledge-oriented features known in the literature to have impact on the personality classification tasks tackled here, henceforth referred to as knowledge-based features. The Interspeech 2012 Speaker Trait Challenge-Personality Sub-challenge feature set consists of 6125 features, and has been used in the present work to provide a set of baseline results (IS2012). We have also used the eGeMAPS feature set [5] (an extended version of GeMAPS - Geneva Minimalistic set of Acoustic Parameters for Voice Research and Affective Computing) that consists of 88 features, well-known for their usefulness in a wide range of paralinguistic tasks.

Our knowledge-based features (KB-features) are based on a phone tokenization of the speech files using the neural network-based acoustic models of the AUDIMUS speech recognizer [12]. The phonetic tokenizations provide phone alignments for each speech file, which can be used to extract duration-related features and to generate more advanced features. In this way, for instance, it is possible to extract the silence ratio, speech duration ratio, and speech rate features in terms of phones per second. The phone tokenizations also provide us with means to characterize each speech segment using n-grams of phones. Based on these tokenizations, we then derive *Inter Pausal Units* (IPUs), that consist of sequences of phones delimited by silences.

The experiments presented in this work use a set of 40 knowledge-based features, including duration of speech with and without internal silences, and tempo measurements such as speech and articulation rates (number of phones or syllables divided by the duration of speech with and without internal silences, respectively) and phonation ratio (duration of speech without internal silences divided by the duration of speech including internal silences). Other features involve pitch (f0), energy, jitter and shimmer, including pitch and energy average, median, standard deviation, dynamics, range, and slopes, both within and between IPUs [1]. Pitch related features were calculated based on semitones rather than frequency. On top of such features, we extracted elaborated prosodic features for the whole sentence involving the sequence of derived IPUs, that were expressed in terms of standard deviation and slope. The Snack Sound Toolkit[1] was used to extract the pitch and energy from the speech signal. Jitter and shimmer were extracted from openSMILE low-level descriptors. For the time being KB-features are still not extensive and must be used in combination with other features in order to achieve improved performances.

## 3.2    Models for Personality Assessment

Speech corpora annotated in terms of personality traits are scarce and generally small. Therefore, the application of too elaborated machine learning methodologies to learn complex models is neither advisable nor viable in many cases. In general, complex models are described by a high number of parameters that require larger training data sets; otherwise, overfitting may easily occur.

In this work, the same experimental setup as that employed in the Interspeech 2012 Speaker Trait Challenge-Personality Sub-challenge [19,20] has been adopted. The models used in this work are linear support vector machines (SVM) trained by means of the well-known SMO algorithm. Logistic functions have been fitted to the SVM soft outputs in order to transform them into pseudo-posterior probabilities. Two different types of feature normalization ([0, 1] range, and zero-mean and unit-variance) have been used.

Each trait in the *Big-Five* personality model has been considered as an independent binary classification problem, where the goal is to assign (classify) a high/low level on that trait (O/NO, C/NC, E/NE, A/NA, N/NN) to every

---

[1] http://www.speech.kth.se/snack/.

speech file. Thus, five different models were trained in this work corresponding to Openness, Conscientiousness, Extraversion, Agreeableness, and Neuroticism. The SVM models were trained using data from the SPC corpus. Firstly, a grid-search process was applied to find the optimal value for the complexity parameter $C$ of the SVMs. For this purpose, different SVMs were trained on the training subset (values for $C$ in the range $10^{-5}$ to 10 were used) and the associated unweighted average recall (UAR) on the development subset were calculated. The value for $C$ providing the higher UAR on the development subset was then selected as the optimal value. Then, the training and development subsets were merged together and the definitive SVM models were trained on this data set, using the selected values for $C$. Finally, the UAR on three different test sets (SPC test set, *GoN-complete* and *GoN-20seconds* sets) is calculated to evaluate the models on both same- and cross-language conditions.

## 4    Experiments and Results

This section is devoted to the presentation and discussion of the experimental results obtained by the systems described previously. Three key aspects have been studied in this work: (1) the performance of three different parameterizations; (2) the consequences of using cross-lingual and cross-age speech corpora for the automatic assessment of personality traits; and (3) the effects of the use of short versus long acoustic-prosodic cues on this task. The results are presented in terms of unweighted average recall (UAR) and accuracy (Acc). The UAR is a fairer measure (and thus preferred) when the data present a substantial imbalance, which is the case of the data sets employed here. The number of examples in each class (high or low level for a trait) for the SPC corpus and for the two GoN subsets are shown in Tables 1 and 2, respectively.

**Table 1.** Number of examples in each class (high/low level for a trait) for the SPC corpus.

| Trait | SPC Train | | | | | SPC Devel. | | | | | SPC Test | | | | |
|-------|---|---|---|---|---|---|---|---|---|---|---|---|---|---|---|
| | O | C | E | A | N | O | C | E | A | N | O | C | E | A | N |
| #High | 97 | 110 | 121 | 139 | 140 | 70 | 81 | 92 | 79 | 88 | 80 | 99 | 107 | 105 | 90 |
| #Low | 159 | 146 | 135 | 117 | 116 | 113 | 102 | 91 | 104 | 95 | 121 | 102 | 94 | 96 | 111 |

Table 3 shows the results obtained on the SPC corpus used in the Interspeech 2012 Speaker Trait Challenge-Personality Sub-challenge. We present here development and test results for the IS2012 baseline features (6125), eGeMAPS features (88), and the combined eGeMAPS+KB-based features (128). Also, the optimal values for the complexity parameter $C$ of the SVMs, selected from the results on the development set, are presented.

We can see that the baseline IS2012 feature set achieves the best test results (in terms of UAR) for Conscientiousness and Agreeableness, while the eGeMAPS

**Table 2.** Number of examples in each class (high/low level for a trait) for the *GoN-20seconds* and *Gon-complete* subsets.

| Trait | GoN-20seconds | | | | | GoN-complete | | | | |
|-------|---|---|---|---|---|---|---|---|---|---|
|       | O | C | E | A | N | O | C | E | A | N |
| #High | 9 | 52 | 53 | 51 | 33 | 6 | 14 | 18 | 13 | 13 |
| #Low  | 77 | 34 | 33 | 35 | 53 | 16 | 8 | 4 | 9 | 9 |

**Table 3.** Results achieved on the SPC data set.

| Trait | IS2012 | | | | | eGeMAPS | | | | | eGeMAPS+KB-features | | | | |
|---|---|---|---|---|---|---|---|---|---|---|---|---|---|---|---|
| | C | Devel. | | Test | | C | Devel. | | Test | | C | Devel. | | Test | |
| | | UAR | Acc | UAR | Acc | | UAR | Acc | UAR | Acc | | UAR | Acc | UAR | Acc |
| O | 1E-05 | 63.5 | 66.7 | 58.6 | 60.2 | 3E-04 | 66.4 | 68.9 | 59.3 | 62.2 | 1E-03 | 62.1 | 63.9 | 53.9 | 55.7 |
| C | 1E-02 | 74.5 | 74.9 | 80.1 | 80.1 | 1E+00 | 74.8 | 74.9 | 76.1 | 76.1 | 1E-01 | 73.9 | 73.8 | 79.1 | 79.1 |
| E | 1E-04 | 82.0 | 82.0 | 75.4 | 75.6 | 3E-03 | 83.0 | 83.1 | 72.0 | 72.1 | 1E-03 | 83.0 | 83.1 | 77.2 | 77.6 |
| A | 3E-05 | 68.1 | 66.1 | 62.5 | 62.7 | 3E-02 | 65.8 | 63.4 | 59.4 | 59.7 | 1E-04 | 67.4 | 65.0 | 57.8 | 58.2 |
| N | 1E-04 | 69.1 | 69.4 | 63.4 | 63.7 | 1E-05 | 69.9 | 69.9 | 63.7 | 64.2 | 1E-01 | 70.9 | 71.0 | 63.4 | 63.7 |

features achieve best results for Openness and Neuroticism, and the combined eGeMAPS+KB-based feature set provides the best result for Extraversion. It is worth mentioning the poor results of the eGeMAPS features for Conscientiousness, Extraversion and Agreeableness, which suggest that such a small feature set is not able to fully capture the essence of those personality traits. For Conscientiousness and Extraversion, the addition of the KB-based features leads to a considerable improvement in the UAR. This shows that the particular nature of the KB-based features, based on an initial phone tokenization of the speech files, endows them with the capability to complement the eGeMAPS feature set in certain cases. However, the addition of the knowledge-based features has the opposite effect for Openness and, to a lesser extent, Agreeableness.

From these results, we must emphasize that the task of automatic personality assessment based on speech information requires a careful selection of acoustic and prosodic feature sets specific for each personality trait. Furthermore, it is shown that a wise selection of a modest number of adequate features based on task-specific knowledge can lead to similar or even better results that those obtained with huge, generic feature sets.

Tables 4 and 5 show the results obtained on the *GoN-20seconds* (86 speech files) and *GoN-complete* (22 files) subsets, respectively. The personality models employed in these experiments are those previously trained on the SPC corpus. To the best of our knowledge, our approach is quite novel and it does not exist any previous work with a similar cross-age and cross-language setup that could be used as a proper baseline for the results presented here. It is also worth mentioning that the results for the Openness trait should be analyzed with certain reservations, since it was very difficult for the psychologist involved in this work to assess the items in the BFI-10 personality questionnaire related to the Openness trait (namely, "The speaker has few artistic interests" and "The speaker has an

**Table 4.** Results achieved on the *GoN-20seconds* data set.

| Trait | IS2012 | | | eGeMAPS | | | eGeMAPS+KB-features | | |
|-------|--------|------|-----|---------|------|-----|---------------------|------|-----|
| | C | Test | | C | Test | | C | Test | |
| | | UAR | Acc | | UAR | Acc | | UAR | Acc |
| O | 1E-05 | 50.0 | 89.5 | 3E-04 | 49.4 | 88.4 | 1E-03 | 50.0 | 89.5 |
| C | 1E-02 | 50.8 | 43.0 | 1E+00 | 50.0 | 50.0 | 1E-01 | 44.9 | 40.7 |
| E | 1E-04 | 64.5 | 60.5 | 3E-03 | 57.9 | 55.8 | 1E-03 | 61.1 | 57.0 |
| A | 3E-05 | 65.0 | 68.6 | 3E-02 | 61.5 | 64.0 | 1E-04 | 61.7 | 66.3 |
| N | 1E-04 | 50.0 | 38.4 | 1E-05 | 48.6 | 50.0 | 1E-01 | 50.3 | 46.5 |

**Table 5.** Results achieved on the *GoN-complete* data set.

| Trait | IS2012 | | | eGeMAPS | | | eGeMAPS+KB-features | | |
|-------|--------|------|-----|---------|------|-----|---------------------|------|-----|
| | C | Test | | C | Test | | C | Test | |
| | | UAR | Acc | | UAR | Acc | | UAR | Acc |
| O | 1E-05 | 80.2 | 86.4 | 3E-04 | 60.4 | 72.7 | 1E-03 | 50.0 | 72.7 |
| C | 1E-02 | 50.0 | 63.6 | 1E+00 | 64.3 | 54.5 | 1E-01 | 48.2 | 40.9 |
| E | 1E-04 | 66.7 | 45.5 | 3E-03 | 59.7 | 50.0 | 1E-03 | 69.4 | 50.0 |
| A | 3E-05 | 51.3 | 54.5 | 3E-02 | 73.5 | 72.7 | 1E-04 | 67.9 | 68.2 |
| N | 1E-04 | 50.0 | 59.1 | 1E-05 | 33.8 | 31.8 | 1E-01 | 46.2 | 54.5 |

active imagination"). In most of the cases, the psychologist assigned default values to these items, which harms the statistical relevance of the results for Openness.

The most relevant outcome from these experiments is that reasonable and consistent results across different setups (three different feature sets and short vs. long acoustic-prosodic cues) are obtained for Extraversion and Agreeableness. The UAR values for these personality traits are consistently above 60 % in most of the cases, with a maximum value of 73.5 % for Agreeableness on the *GoN-complete* subset, using the eGeMAPS features. These results point out to the existence of a stable set of acoustic-prosodic features for these traits in both adult and children speech, which supports our aim of using cross-language and cross-age speech corpora for the assessment of personality traits in those situations where data are specially scarce. On the other hand, the results do not show relevant performances for Conscientiousness and Neuroticism. In our opinion, the reasonable and promising results obtained for Extraversion and Agreeableness are strongly linked to the specific design and characteristics of the Game-of-Nines study, where different classmate dyads play a competitive cooperative bargaining card game for a final reward. This particular situation might favor more noticeable expressions of those traits more closely related to this specific dyadic interaction setup, such as Extraversion and Agreeableness.

Tables 4 and 5 do not show clearly better results for any of the three parameterizations. If we focus on Extraversion and Agreeableness, the IS2012 feature set achieves better results on the *GoN-20seconds* subset, while the eGeMAPS and combined eGeMAPS+KB-based feature sets perform better on the *GoN-complete* subset. Finally, the experimental results show that, in general, better results are achieved on the *GoN-complete* subset for those traits. This result points out the limitations of our 20 s-long speech segments constructed by concatenating several smaller segments.

## 5    Conclusions and Future Work

This work investigates the use of heterogeneous speech corpora for automatic personality assessment tasks. The main motivation for this work is the need to develop methods to overcome the lack of children's speech corpora in this field. With this purpose, we evaluated the use of personality models trained on French adults' speech to classify a completely different corpus of Portuguese children's speech. Our preliminary results bring insights into cross-age and cross-language detection of personality traits in spontaneous speech. The reasonable performance rates obtained for Extraversion and Agreeableness point out to a stable set of acoustic-prosodic features in both adult and children speech. Also, the importance of a sensible selection of specific feature sets for each personality trait is shown in this paper.

Further work will be carried out in this research line. In particular, the acquisition of more speech data, together with the inclusion of more assessors to improve the statistical significance of our personality annotations, is of paramount importance to perform more exhaustive and relevant experimentation. This will allow the study of more elaborated feature selection procedures and learning methodologies with the aim of developing robust personality assessment systems.

**Acknowledgments.** Work supported by national funds through Fundação para a Ciência e a Tecnologia (FCT) with reference UID/CEC/50021/2013, under Postdoc grant SFRH/PBD/95849/2013, by project CMUP-ERI/HCI/0051/2013 (INSIDE), and by project H2020-EU.3.7 contract 653587 (LAW-TRAIN).

## References

1. Batista, F., Moniz, H., Trancoso, I., Mamede, N.J.: Bilingual experiments on automatic recovery of capitalization and punctuation of automatic speech transcripts. IEEE Trans. Audio Speech Lang. Proces. **20**(2), 474–485 (2012). Special Issue on New Frontiers in Rich Transcription
2. Campos, J., Oliveira, P., Paiva, A.: Looking for conflict: gaze dynamics in a dyadic mixed-motive game. Auton. Agents Multi-Agent Syst. **30**(1), 112–135 (2016)
3. Caspi, A., Harrington, H., Milne, B., Amell, J., Theodore, R., Moffitt, T.: Children's behavioral styles at age 3 are linked to their adult personality traits at age 26. J. Pers. **71**(4), 495–514 (2003)
4. Cloninger, S.: Conceptual issues in personality theory. In: Corr, P., Matthews, G. (eds.) The Cambridge Handbook of Personality Psychology, vol. 4, pp. 3–26. Cambridge University Press, Cambridge (2009). Chap. 8

5. Eyben, F., Scherer, K.R., Schuller, B.W., Sundberg, J., André, E., Busso, C., Devillers, L.Y., Epps, J., Laukka, P., Narayanan, S.S., Truong, K.P.: The geneva minimalistic acoustic parameter set (gemaps) for voice research and affective computing. IEEE Trans. Affect. Comput. **7**(2), 190–202 (2016)
6. Eyben, F., Weninger, F., Gross, F., Schuller, B.: Recent developments in openS-MILE, the Munich open-source multimedia feature extractor. In: Proceedings of the 21st ACM International Conference on Multimedia, New York, NY, USA, pp. 835–838, October 2013
7. Kagan, J.: Three pleasing ideas. Am. Psychol. **51**, 901–908 (1996)
8. Kelley, H., Beckman, L., Fischer, C.: Negotiating the division of a reward under incomplete information. J. Exp. Soc. Psychol. **3**(4), 361–398 (1967)
9. Lewis, M.: Altering Fate: Why the Past does not Predict the Future. Guilford Press, New York (1997)
10. Maćkiewicz, M., Cieciuch, J.: The picture based personality survey for children - a new instrument to measure the big five in childhood. In: Proceedings of the 11th Conference on Psychological Assessment, Riga, Latvia, September 2011
11. Mairesse, F., Walker, M., Mehl, M., Moore, R.: Using linguistic cues for the automatic recognition of personality in conversation and text. J. Artif. Intell. Res. **30**(1), 457–500 (2007)
12. Meinedo, H., Viveiros, M., Neto, J.: Evaluation of a live broadcast news subtitling system for Portuguese. In: Proceedigs of Interspeech 2008, Brisbane, Australia, pp. 508–511, September 2008
13. Mohammadi, G., Vinciarelli, A.: Automatic personality perception: prediction of trait attribution based on prosodic features. IEEE Trans. Affect. Comput. **3**(3), 273–284 (2012)
14. Polzehl, T., Moeller, S., Metze, F.: Automatically assessing acoustic manifestations of personality in speech. In: Spoken Language Technology Workshop, Berkeley, CA, USA, pp. 7–12, December 2010
15. Polzehl, T., Moeller, S., Metze, F.: Automatically assessing personality from speech. In: International Conference on Semantic Computing, Pittsburgh, PA, USA, pp. 134–140, September 2010
16. Polzehl, T., Moeller, S., Metze, F.: Modeling speaker personality using voice. In: Proceedings of Interspeech 2011, Florence, Italy, pp. 2369–2372, August 2011
17. Rammstedt, B., John, O.: Measuring personality in one minute or less: a 10-item short version of the big five inventory in English and German. J. Res. Pers. **41**, 203–212 (2007)
18. Roberts, B., Walton, K., Viechtbauer, W.: Patterns of mean-level change in personality traits across the life course: a meta-analysis of longitudinal studies. Psychol. Bull. **132**(1), 1–25 (2006)
19. Schuller, B., Steidl, S., Batliner, A., Nöth, E., Vinciarelli, A., Burkhardt, F.: The INTERSPEECH 2012 speaker trait challenge. In: Proceedings of Interspeech 2012, Portland, OR, USA, September 2012
20. Schuller, B., Steidl, S., Batliner, A., Nöth, E., Vinciarelli, A., Burkhardt, F., van Son, R., Weninger, F., Eyben, F., Bocklet, T., Mohammadi, G., Weiss, B.: A survey on perceived speaker traits: personality, likability, pathology, and the first challenge. Comput. Speech Lang. **29**(1), 100–131 (2015)
21. Vinciarelli, A., Mohammadi, G.: A survey of personality computing. IEEE Trans. Affect. Comput. **5**(3), 273–291 (2014)

# Speech and Language Technologies
# in Different Application Fields

# Evaluating Different Non-native Pronunciation Scoring Metrics with the Japanese Speakers of the SAMPLE Corpus

Vandria Álvarez Álvarez, David Escudero Mancebo[(✉)],
César González Ferreras, and Valentín Cardeñoso Payo

Department of Computer Science, Universidad de Valladolid, Valladolid, Spain
descuder@infor.uva.es

**Abstract.** This work presents an analysis over the set of results derived from the goodness of pronunciation (GOP) algorithm for the evaluation of pronunciation at phoneme level over the SAMPLE corpus of non native speech. This corpus includes several recordings of uttered sentences by distinct speakers that have been rated in terms of quality by a group of linguists. The utterances have been automatically rated with the GOP algorithm. The phoneme dependence is discussed to suggest the normalization of intermediate results that could enhance the metrics performance. As result, new scoring proposals are presented which are based on computing the log-likelihood values obtained from the GOP algorithm and the application of a set of rules. These new scores show to correlate with the human rates better than the original GOP metric.

**Keywords:** Computer Assisted Pronunciation Training (CAPT) · Goodness of Pronunciation (GOP) · Hidden Markov Models (HMM) · Automatic Speech Recognition (ASR) · L2 pronunciation

## 1 Introduction

The Computer-Assisted Pronunciation Training (CAPT) has grown in the last years due to the necessity of L2 learners at improving their pronunciation using an automatic system. By using CAPT, students can benefit from continuous feedback without a teacher by their side all the time, providing a self-service way to practice [1].

The CAPT field growth has been almost parallel to the evolution of technologies, since computers and mobile devices computing capacity and portability has greatly increased. As pointed out in [2] the CAPT commercialization and

We would like to thank Ministerio de Economía y Competitividad y Fondos FEDER project key: TIN2014-59852-R Videojuegos Sociales para la Asistencia y Mejora de la Pronunciación de la Lengua Española, and Junta de Castilla y Leon project key: VA145U14 Evaluación Automática de la Pronunciación del Español Como Lengua Extranjera para Hablantes Japoneses.

© Springer International Publishing AG 2016
A. Abad et al. (Eds.): IberSPEECH 2016, LNAI 10077, pp. 205–214, 2016.
DOI: 10.1007/978-3-319-49169-1_20

work started in the earliest 2000's but it was not until 2007 when its relevance showed up again. With this, the SLATE (Speech and Language Technology for Education) group was created. This group of research is dedicated to the development of education applications by means of automatic speech processing, natural language processing and in some cases spoken dialogue processing. These systems (SLATE/CAPT) make necessary multidisciplinary groups of researchers, from spoken language technologists, language teachers and experts, statisticians, among others [3].

According to several authors the error detection and teaching of pronunciation is a very hard job for CAPT systems, researchers major concern is to derive systems that are capable of identifying errors accurately and reliably to provide correct feedback [1–4].

The Automatic Speech Recognition (ASR) often refers to technologies used in the detection and assessment of pronunciation errors, perception training, etc. [3]. The use of ASR started in the 1980s, but it was not useful for all speakers due to the acoustic differences among them and other related aspects. Then, ASR emerged in actual systems at the beginning of 2000s parallel to the advancements in computing technologies.

The evolution of ASR technologies during the last years has left encountered opinions among researchers about whether or not they are suitable for CAPT systems. In [5] is pointed out that probably the problems found in research are not due to mere ASR but also to the lack of familiarity with the ASR-based CAPT.

Another fact, is that ASR needs to be adapted for non-native speakers, ASRs developed specifically with native speech have demonstrated worst performance when tested with non-native [5]. To overcome this issue, usually the ASR engine is trained with both native and non-native speech. Knowing users language (L1) is a must, since problems that arise when learning a second language (L2) are different in every case and for that matter the ASR needs to understand these before providing feedback [3].

The recognition task also depends on the types of learning activities. Results will not have the same accuracy if there is a huge set of possible answers than when is limited to a small number. Also evaluating an ASR system scoring phase can be done by comparing the scores provided by human judges for a given speech sample.

In this paper we present an experiment for scoring the quality of non-native speech with automatic methods. In Sect. 2.1 we present the corpus of Japanese students of L2 Spanish that has been used in this study. Section 2.2 revises the literature of the state of the art measures for scoring L2 speakers. The application of these metrics to our corpus encouraged us to test other alternative metrics that are described in Sect. 2.3. Results presented in Sect. 3 show that the new metrics correlate better than the previous ones with the scores assigned by human evaluators to L2 students. We end with discussion and conclusions.

## 2    Experimental Procedure

### 2.1    The SAMPLE Corpus

In the framework of the SAMPLE research project, a corpus of spoken Spanish by non-native speakers was developed as a means to support future CAPT studies. The central part of the corpus includes a set of sentences and paragraphs selected from news database of a popular Spanish radio news broadcasting station. The texts cover various information domains related to everyday's life. They were obtained from the Glissando corpus, which was developed in connection to another project related to automatic prosodic labelling. The materials used in this study belong to the subset of prosodically balanced sentences in Glissando, which statistically resemble the prosodic variability found in Spanish [6].

The whole corpus is described in [7]. It contains different materials: read sentences, the Aesop's Fable 'The North Wind' and news paragraphs. In this study, fifteen read sentences from the news paragraphs of the Glissando corpus [6] were selected to be read by a group of non-native Spanish speakers. The list of sentences is described in [7] (see Table 1 of that paper). All sentences followed a phonetic coverage criterion. In this study we only focus on the Japanese speakers for the sake of simplicity. These speakers are referred as *f11*, *m03*, *f12*, *f14* and *f13* in the database where *f* means female and *m* means male. The orthographic transcriptions used to identify the uttered phones in every sentence were realized by a group of linguists that collaborated with our research group.

The training of the phonetic models is based on a standard parameterization by using cepstral coefficients over mel frequencies (MFCC) and a 39 dimensions feature vector. More precisely, 12 MFCCs and the normalized power logarithm along with the first and second order derived. The features vectors are obtained with a time slot of 25 ms and time offset of 10 ms. The Albayzin corpus was used to train the acoustic mono-phoneme models since this contains recordings of phonetically balanced phrases [8]. Finally, all the sentences uttered by the 22 speakers of the SAMPLE corpus were computed by the forced alignement algorithm using HTK. The results present the logarithmic scores (likelihoods) of all existent phonemes for every expected phoneme in the utterances of the speakers.

### 2.2    Confidence Measures

The confidence measures help determine the certainty of the recognizer when it identifies if an utterance (a part or all) was pronounced properly. Confidence measures can be computed with low difficulty by ASR engines and does not vary greatly among different sounds [9].

A confidence measure can be considered as a statistic that quantifies the fitting of a model with the corresponding data. For speech recognition acoustic and language models are typically used (together or separately) to extract these confidence measures [10].

Likelihood ratios convert to a useful statistic the outcome of HMM-based ASRs. The HMMs help finding the value of H, that maximizes the joint probability $P(X, H)$ , where H is the acoustic model and X is the acoustic observation [10].

$$P(H|X) = \frac{P(X, H)}{P(X)} = \frac{P(X|H)P(H)}{P(X)} \tag{1}$$

The Bayes theorem is applied usually to calculate the relation between the joint probability with the posterior probability of the model H given the acoustics $X$, $P(H|X)$ and also the likelihood given the model $H$, $P(X|H)$.

There are different proposals that have showed good and well accepted results for auto matic scoring, next some of them extracted from the different previous work are listed, considering their results and continuous application.

The use of likelihood based phoneme level error detection started back in the 1990s [2]. The **log-likelihood** logarithm of the speech data is computed by Viterbi algorithm using the HMMs from native speakers. According to [10,11] this is a good way for measuring similarity or matching between native speech and users speech.

The log likelihood score $\hat{l}$ for each phone segment is [12]:

$$\hat{l}_i = \frac{1}{d} \sum_{t=t_0}^{t_0+d-1} \log p(y_t|q_i) \tag{2}$$

where $p(y_t|q_i)$ is the likelihood of the current frame, $y_t$ is the vector of observations, $d$ is the duration in frames of the phone segment and $t_0$ is the starting frame index of the phone segment. Dividing over $d$ eliminates the time duration of the phone, with this, the score is normalized. Also according to [11] the likelihood-based score for a whole sentence $L$ is the average of the individual scores $L = \frac{1}{N} \sum_{i=1}^{N} \hat{l}_i$ with $N$, the number of phones in the sentence.

The **log-posterior probability** has showed better correlation results with the human judgments [12].

$$P(q_i|y_t) = \frac{p(y_t|q_i)P(q_i)}{\sum_{j=1}^{J} p(y_t|q_j)P(q_j)} \tag{3}$$

where $P(q_i|y_t)$ is the frame based posterior of the i-th phone given the observation vector $y_t$. $P(q_i)$ represents the prior probability of the phone class $q_i$. The sum over $j$ operates on a set of context-independent models for all phone classes. The posterior score $\hat{\rho}$ for the i-th segment is the average of the logarithm over the frame-based phone posterior probability over all the frames of the segment, see equation.

$$\hat{\rho}_i = \frac{1}{d} \sum_{t=t_0}^{t_0+d-1} \log P(q_i|y_t) \tag{4}$$

The complete sentence posterior-based score can be obtained with the average of all individual scores over the $N$ phone segments in the sentence: $\rho = \frac{1}{N} \sum_{i=1}^{N} \hat{\rho}_i$

Compared to the likelihood metric in Eq. 2 the log-posterior probability score could be less affected since the acoustic matching to the models is in both numerator and denominator [11].

The **GOP** was first introduced by Witt with the purpose of providing an algorithm capable of scoring each phone of an utterance, therefore to accomplish this, the GOP must have previously the following data [13]: (1) The orthographic transcriptions previously annotated by human judges that describes exactly which is the phone sequence uttered. (2) The Hidden Markov models to calculate the likelihood, $p(O^{(q)}|q_j)$, where $O^{(q)}$ is the acoustic segment corresponding to each phone $q^j$.

Based on the latter the GOP for a phone $q_i$ is computed by:

$$GOP(q_i) = |\log(P(q_i|O))|/NF(O^{q_i}) \tag{5}$$

Based on Eq. 5, the quality of pronunciation of any phone $q_i$ can be obtained by normalizing the logarithm $P(q_i|O)$, which is the posterior probability that the speaker uttered the phone $q_i$ over the acoustic segment $O^{q_i}$. The normalization takes place when is divided by the number of frames $NF(O^{q_i})$ in the acoustic segment.

As showed in Eq. 3 the log-posterior probability can be computed by knowing the likelihood of the acoustic observations given the phone $q_i$ and the likelihood of the acoustic observations given the phone models. By applying this we get:

$$GOP(q_i) = \frac{1}{NF(O^{q_i})}\left|\log\left(\frac{p(O^{q_i}|q_i)P(q_i)}{\sum_{j=1}^{J}p(O^{q_i}|q_j)P(q_j)}\right)\right| \tag{6}$$

For Eq. 6 $J$ is the total number of phone models for the $j$ possible phones existent in the annotated database. If we assume that all phones are equally likely, meaning $P(q_i) = P(q_j)$ for all $j$ and $i$, and that the sum of the denominator can be approximated by its maximum, then the GOP is equal to:

$$GOP(q_i) = \frac{1}{NF(O^{q_i})}\left|\log\left(\frac{p(O^{q_i}|q_i)}{\max_{j=1}^{J}p(O^{q_i}|q_j)}\right)\right| \tag{7}$$

The numerator of Eq. 7 is computed by using the forced alignment block where the sequence of phone models is fixed by the known transcription. On the other hand, the denominator is obtained by the phoneme loop, which realizes an unconstrained loop comparing the acoustic observations of the i-th phone with all the possible phonemes transcription [14].

A variant of the GOP utilizes the forced alignment block as in Witt allowing to set the phoneme boundaries. Once these boundaries are known the computation of the $p(O^{q_i}|q_j)$ (logarithmic scores) for all the $j$ existent phonemes is realized. Thus, to obtain the GOP, is necessary to determine: (1) The annotated(orthographic transcription) utterances that will allow to determine which is the expected phoneme $q_i$; (2) All the log likelihoods for every phoneme $p(O^{q_i}|q_j)$.

Afterwards, the computation of the GOP is realized by subtracting the expected phoneme $q_i$ logarithmic score with the maximum logarithmic score among all phonemes, as in formula 7. This is the implementation that has been used in this work.

The implementation of the GOP metric has been widely used by several groups of researchers with different native and non-native languages. Nevertheless it exists also controversial due to the difficulties on adapting this score to different corpora. In the thesis of Witt [14], some thresholds calculations formulas are proposed to improve results. In order to distinguish between individual and systematic mispronunciations, Witt [1] used a recognition network that comprehended both correct pronunciation and common pronunciation errors ans sublattices for each phone. Another GOP variant proposed for the PRASER system [15] normalizes the GOP score by a sigmoid function. Similarly, the proposal from [9] modified the GOP metric focusing on the establishment of thresholds that best suited the data. In this work we also propose to adapt the metric to face up the dependences of the scores on the expected phoneme.

The GOP metric has also been used in assistive technologies for evaluating the degree of comprehensibility of disordered speech [16].

### 2.3 Alternative Scoring Proposals

Figure 1 shows that the logarithmic scores depict the same trend over the whole phonemes. Thus, for example, the values for the phoneme $f$, are in average higher than the values for the surrounding phonemes in the figures (phonemes $e$ and $g$). This high dependency on the expected phoneme, which seems to be speaker independent, inspired us to normalize these scores before using them to rate the quality of the non-native pronunciation. Based on the latter we decided

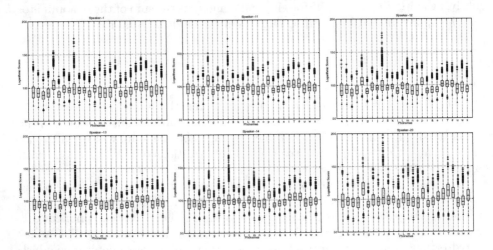

**Fig. 1.** From left to right and from top to bottom, the figures refer to the speakers m03, f11, f12, f13, f14 and to the tranning corpus Albayzin. Each of the boxplots corresponds with one single phoneme.

to create a set of new scorings by computing a new parameter obtained from the logarithmic scores and a set of rules explained next.

**Case 1:** The computation of a new score $\rho$ for every expected phoneme $q_i$ (that is evaluated in the corpus) is done by using the logarithmic score $\hat{\rho}_i$ associated to it and the average $\mu_i$ and standard deviation $\sigma_i$ previously computed.

$$\hat{\underline{\rho}}_i = \frac{|\hat{\rho}_i - \mu_i|}{\sigma_i} \tag{8}$$

The values $\mu_i$ and $\sigma_i$ are obtained by computing all the logarithmic scores of the expected phoneme when uttered by the same speaker and that also comply with some rules for choosing or not the logarithmic score of $q_i$. These are explained later for every sub-case.

Thus, there is a value of $\mu_i$ and $\sigma_i$ for every phoneme and a given speaker on every sub-case studied, although as we will discuss later depending on the sub-case there are or not $\mu_i$ and $\sigma_i$ values for all phonemes, and therefore some conditions are applied.

**Case 1.a:** it computes the $\mu_i$ and $\sigma_i$ values over all the $\hat{\rho}_i$ that correspond to the expected phoneme $q_i$ when its GOP value was equal to zero. As explained before the logarithmic score is only selected if we are analyzing the i-th phoneme.

For most of the speakers there are no values that can be used for every phoneme, because the speaker didn't uttered correctly the expected phoneme. To overcome this issue, we use the Albayzin values, since they are the reference and has $\mu_i$ and $\sigma_i$ values for every phoneme. If only, one utterance is made for a phoneme then $\sigma_i$ is changed to one to avoid division over zero.

**Case 1.b:** it is based on choosing the logarithmic scores that correspond to the expected phoneme $q_i$ when this was uttered by the same speaker, there is no dependency on the GOP value.

**Case 1.c:** it is based on only choosing the logarithmic scores that correspond to the expected phoneme $q_i$ when its GOP value is different from zero to compute $\mu_i$ and $\sigma_i$ , in opposite to case 1.a.

Although, for this case there is at least more than one case in which a phoneme was uttered incorrectly then $\mu_i$ and $\sigma_i$ can be obtained. In the worst scenario if only one utterance is made for a phoneme then $\sigma_i$ is changed to one to avoid division over zero. Or if no $\mu_i$ and $\sigma_i$ were obtained for a phoneme then the Albayzin values are used.

**Case 2** The case 1 made use of the logarithmic score of the phoneme $q_i$. The case 2 on the other hand chooses the maximum logarithmic score among all the logarithmic scores calculated for all the phonemes in that specific utterance. With these values it is possible to calculate the average $\mu'_i$ and standard deviation $\sigma'_i$ of all the maximum logarithmic scores for every expected phoneme.

$$\hat{\underline{\rho}}_i = \frac{|\hat{\rho}_i - \mu'_i|}{\sigma'_i} \tag{9}$$

This Case 2 is sub-divided into two, whose difference is basically using or removing the absolute value from the numerator in Eq. 9.

**Case 2.a** use the formula 9 as it is and **Case 2.b** does not use absolute values in the numerator.

Once all these new scores have been obtained for every expected phoneme in the corpus, a global new pronunciation score is obtained for every speaker: $\underline{\rho} = \frac{1}{N} \sum_{n=1}^{N} \underline{\rho}_n$; where $N$ is the total of all phonemes uttered by the given speaker.

# 3    Results

Table 1 shows the quality measures of the Japanese speakers of the Sample corpus. All the figures represent the mean values of the metrics computed by sentence. The row entitled Albayzin presents the metrics computed with the sentences of the training corpus so that it is a baseline that indicates the degree of quality of the non-native pronunciation.

**Table 1.** Comparison of all the different scores analyzed.

| SPK | PHO | DELE | GOP | CASE 1.a | CASE 1.b | CASE 1.c | CASE 2.a | CASE 2.b |
|---|---|---|---|---|---|---|---|---|
| f11 | 2.92 | 2.86 | 3.81 | 1.85 | 0.78 | 0.75 | 1.11 | −0.70 |
| f12 | 3.01 | 3.28 | 3.00 | 2.04 | 0.78 | 0.76 | 1.01 | −0.58 |
| m03 | 3.08 | 3.09 | 5.14 | 2.69 | 0.77 | 0.78 | 1.31 | −1.15 |
| f14 | 3.12 | 3.18 | 3.17 | 2.60 | 0.78 | 0.77 | 1.06 | −0.65 |
| f13 | 3.77 | 3.92 | 2.96 | 1.76 | 0.79 | 0.82 | 0.98 | −0.58 |
| Albaycin | - | - | 0.87 | 1.00 | 0.75 | 1.61 | 0.84 | −0.14 |

The columns PHO and DELE are subjective metrics given by a team of human evaluators [7]. PHO indicate the phonetic quality and DELE is the overall quality. The index PHO has been used to sort the speakers in terms of his proficiency: the better the pronunciation of the speaker, the lower he or she is in the table.

The GOP results do not correlate with the subjective metrics so that the speaker m03 has GOP value (5.14) that is greater than the one obtained by apparently worse speakers like f11 and f12. The metric CASE 1.b and specially the metric CASE 1.c seem to correct this fact, with values that highly correlate with the subjective metrics: best and worst speaker (f13 and f11 respectively) are match with the ranking obtained by using the columns PHO and DELE.

Table 2 confirms this correlation when it is computed with all the non-native speakers of the corpus (American and Japanese ones). Case 2 metrics reproduce the behavior of the GOP metric getting to very high correlations of 0.88 and 0.99. Case 1.c seems to reproduce the best the subjective evaluation with a correlation of 0.81 with the PHO metric and 0.74 with the DELE metric.

**Table 2.** Correlation coefficients among pronunciation scores at speaker level for non-native speakers of the SAMPLE corpus.

|          | PHO   | DELE  | GOP   | Case 1.a | Case 1.b | Case 1.c | Case 2.a | Case 2.b |
|----------|-------|-------|-------|----------|----------|----------|----------|----------|
| HJ PHO   | 1     |       |       |          |          |          |          |          |
| HJ DELE  | 0.87  | 1     |       |          |          |          |          |          |
| GOP      | −0.35 | −0.31 | 1     |          |          |          |          |          |
| Case 1.a | −0.26 | −0.45 | 0.22  | 1        |          |          |          |          |
| Case 1.b | 0.50  | 0.49  | −0.34 | −0.13    | 1        |          |          |          |
| Case 1.c | **0.81** | **0.74** | −0.03 | −0.23 | 0.49 | 1 |          |          |
| Case 2.a | −0.41 | −0.46 | **0.88** | 0.42 | −0.38 | −0.09 | 1       |          |
| Case 2.b | 0.30  | 0.38  | **−0.90** | −0.36 | 0.37 | −0.01 | −0.96 | 1        |

## 4  Discussion and Conclusions

The results presented in this paper are aligned with others cited in Sect. 2.2 that have also observed the difficulties of the GOP index for correlating with subjective evaluations. In this case we have contrasted this fact with Japanese speakers of L2 Spanish language. The modification introduced by Case 1.3 for taking into account the dependencies of the likelihood ratio with the predicted phoneme, has permitted to improve results so that the correlation between this metric and the subjective one increase up to 0.83.

In this paper we have shown that the computation of a metric permits to assign a score to non-native speakers that correlates with the marks assigned by human evaluators. Nevertheless, scoring non-native speakers is only one of the tasks that concerns CAPT techniques. A straight forward extension of our results is the detection of errors which be identified by prominent values of the scores over phonemes. It is current work of our research team the implementation of a diagnosis module that permits to specify the speaker the type of error and consequently advise him or her. A last phase of feedback comprehends the design issues related on how to present results for the speakers to improve their pronunciation.

## References

1. Witt, S.M., Young, S.J.: Phone-level pronunciation scoring and assessment for interactive language learning. Speech Commun. **30**, 95–108 (2000)
2. Witt, S.M.: Automatic error detection in pronunciation training: where we are and where we need to go. In: Proceedings of IS ADEPT, vol. 6 (2012)
3. Eskenazi, M.: An overview of spoken language technology for education. Speech Commun. **51**, 832–844 (2009)
4. van Doremalen, J., Cucchiarini, C., Strik, H.: Automatic pronunciation error detection in non-native speech: the case of vowel errors in dutch. J. Acoust. Soc. Am. **134**, 1336–1347 (2013)

5. Neri, A., Cucchiarini, C., Strik, W.: Automatic speech recognition for second language learning: how and why it actually works. In: Proceedings of ICPhS, pp. 1157–1160 (2003)

6. Garrido, J.M., Escudero, D., Aguilar, L., Cardeñoso, V., Rodero, E., de-la Mota, C., González, C., Vivaracho, C., Rustullet, S., Larrea, O., Laplaza, Y., Vizcaíno, F., Estebas, E., Cabrera, M., Bonafonte, A.: Glissando: a corpus for multidisciplinary prosodic studies in Spanish and Catalan. Lang. Resour. Eval. **47**, 945–971 (2013)

7. Escudero-Mancebo, D., González-Ferreras, C., Cardeñoso Payo, V.: Assessment of non-native spoken Spanish using quantitative scores and perceptual evaluation. In: Chair, N.C.C., Choukri, K., Declerck, T., Loftsson, H., Maegaard, B., Mariani, J., Moreno, A., Odijk, J., Piperidis S. (eds.) Proceedings of the Ninth International Conference on Language Resources and Evaluation (LREC 2014), Reykjavik, Iceland, European Language Resources Association (ELRA), pp. 3967–3972 (2014)

8. Moreno, A., Poch, D., Bonafonte, A., Lleida, E., Llisterri, J., Marino, J.B., Nadeu, C.: Albayzin speech database: design of the phonetic corpus. In: Third European Conference on Speech Communication and Technology (1993)

9. Strik, H., Truong, K., De Wet, F., Cucchiarini, C.: Comparing different approaches for automatic pronunciation error detection. Speech Commun. **51**, 845–852 (2009)

10. Neumeyer, L., Franco, H., Digalakis, V., Weintraub, M.: Automatic scoring of pronunciation quality. Speech Commun. **30**, 83–93 (2000)

11. Franco, H., Neumeyer, L., Kim, Y., Ronen, O.: Automatic pronunciation scoring for language instruction. In: 1997 IEEE International Conference on Acoustics, Speech, and Signal Processing, ICASSP-97, vol. 2, pp. 1471–1474. IEEE (1997)

12. Kim, Y., Franco, H., Neumeyer, L.: Automatic pronunciation scoring of specific phone segments for language instruction. In: Eurospeech (1997)

13. Witt, S.M., Young, S.J., et al.: Language learning based on non-native speech recognition. In: Eurospeech (1997)

14. Witt, S.M.: Use of Speech Recognition in Computer-Assisted Language Learning. University of Cambridge, Cambridge (1999)

15. Mak, B., Siu, M., Ng, M., Tam, Y.C., Chan, Y.C., Chan, K.W., Leung, K.Y., Ho, S., Chong, F.H., Wong, J., et al.: Plaser: pronunciation learning via automatic speech recognition. In: Proceedings of the HLT-NAACL 03 Workshop on Building Educational Applications Using Natural Language Processing, vol. 2, pp. 23–29. Association for Computational Linguistics (2003)

16. Fontan, L., Pellegrini, T., Olcoz, J., Abad, A.: Predicting disordered speech comprehensibility from goodness of pronunciation scores. In: Workshop on Speech and Language Processing for Assistive Technologies (2015)

# Global Analysis of Entrainment in Dialogues

Vera Cabarrão[1,2(✉)], Isabel Trancoso[1,3], Ana Isabel Mata[2],
Helena Moniz[1,2], and Fernando Batista[1,4]

[1] L2F, INESC-ID, Lisbon, Portugal
veracabarrao@gmail.com, {isabel.trancoso,
Helena.Moniz,Fernando.Batista}@inesc-id.pt
[2] Faculdade de Letras da Universidade de Lisboa (FLUL)/Centro de Linguística
da Universidade de Lisboa (CLUL), Lisbon, Portugal
aim@letras.ulisboa.pt
[3] Instituto Superior Técnico, Universidade de Lisboa, Lisbon, Portugal
[4] ISCTE-IUL – Instituto Universitário de Lisboa, Lisbon, Portugal

**Abstract.** This paper performs a global analysis of entrainment between dyads in map-task dialogues in European Portuguese (EP), including 48 dialogues, between 24 speakers. Our main goals focus on the acoustic-prosodic similarities between speakers, namely if there are global entrainment cues displayed in the dialogues, if there are degrees of entrainment manifested in distinct sets of features shared amongst the speakers, if entrainment depends on the role of the speaker as either giver or follower, and also if speakers tend to entrain more with specific pairs regardless of the role. Results show global entrainment in almost all the dyads, but the degrees of entrainment (stronger within the same gender), and the role effects tend to be less striking than the interlocutors' effect. Globally, speakers tend to be more similar to their own speech in other dialogues than to their partners. However, speakers are also more similar to their interlocutors than to speakers with whom they never spoke.

**Keywords:** Entrainment · Acoustic-prosodic features · Map-task dialogues

## 1 Introduction

In human-human interactions, interlocutors naturally converge or diverge in their opinions and thoughts. For the dialogue to succeed, it is crucial to understand what is being said and how that content is being expressed. Humans have the ability to do immediate adjustments to their behavior and speech, acting accordingly to the situation [2, 6]. Moreover, several studies have shown that people who adapt to the partner's speech are considered to be more socially attractive and likeable [1], the interactions being much more successful.

The study of speech entrainment, whether between humans or human-computer systems, implies the evaluation of the degree of adaptation one has towards the other. In Spoken Dialogue Systems, understanding and predicting how to adjust to a human may be more challenging than recognizing the speech signal content.

A. Abad et al. (Eds.): IberSPEECH 2016, LNAI 10077, pp. 215–223, 2016.
DOI: 10.1007/978-3-319-49169-1_21

Entrainment can occur at different levels: acoustic-prosodic [8, 10, 11], phonetic-phonological [15], lexical-syntactic [12, 14, 15], multimodal, via facial expressions and gestures [4], and social [1].

Entrainment has been studied in languages such as English or Mandarin, but in European Portuguese this topic is just starting to be explored. In our study, we adopt an acoustic-prosodic approach to globally identify entrainment in human-human spontaneous speech. We focus on a wide set of features that have already proven to be effective in studying entrainment in American English, namely pitch, energy, speaking rate, and voice quality, and we also analyze duration.

Following the work of Levitan and Hirschberg [10] and Levitan [11], we applied the metrics of session-level proximity, meaning we analyze the similarities between speakers per dialogue. Our main goal is to perform a global analysis of entrainment in map-task dialogues, where speakers interact with different partners and also play different roles, giver or follower. This will allow us to understand if speakers entrain differently according to the role they're playing and/or according to the interlocutor.

This paper is organized as follows: Section 2 overviews the work previously reported on this subject. Section 3 describes the data and adopted methodology. Section 4 presents the achieved results, both in terms of global and dyad entrainment. Section 5 presents our conclusions and the future work.

## 2 Related Work

Several studies of people interacting in different communicative situations have emerged, mainly to understand how they adapt to each other to solve problems or specific tasks (e.g., map-task dialogues, card games [8, 10], marital therapy [9], romantic relationships [20]). There is a large amount of literature covering not only linguistic aspects of entrainment, but also task success, social implications of speech adaptation, and its automatic applications.

The seminal work by [11], studying acoustic-prosodic entrainment in multiple dimensions in American English, measured the adaptation of speakers at a global level, the entire session, and at a local level, turn-by-turn, in the Columbia Games Corpus [7]. The authors describe that speakers were globally more similar to their partners than to their non-partners, meaning speakers with whom they were never paired with, in mean and max intensity, max pitch, shimmer, and speaking rate. The authors also found that speakers were more similar to their own speech in different sessions than to their partners in mean pitch, jitter, shimmer, Noise-to-Harmonics-Rate (NHR), and speaking rate.

Building upon the previous study, [10] also found that speakers of Mandarin Chinese were more similar to their partners than to their non-partners in intensity mean, max, pitch max, and speaking rate, differing from American English speakers only in pitch max. The author also describes that speakers paired in different gender groups (male-male, female-female, and mixed-gender), both in American English and Mandarin Chinese, entrain on intensity mean and max, but differ in all of the other features: mixed-gender pairs present the highest degree of entrainment, being more similar to each other than female-female and male-male pairs.

Pardo [15] describes evidences of phonetic proximity between speakers at the beginning and later in the conversation. In a more recent perceptual study [16], the author found that the gender pairs and the role of the speaker influenced the degree of phonetic convergence during the dialogue. Moreover, the judgments of phonetic convergence were not related to individual acoustic–phonetic attributes, and the situational factors, such as pair gender, speaker role, and imitator role, were the ones with more influence. .

While studying affirmative answers in European Portuguese, [3], in the same corpus used in this study, found evidences of pitch concord effects in context-answer pairs with different pragmatic functions. The authors found correlations regarding pitch height between the pairs instruct-agreement and propositional question (yes-no question) - confirm, although expressed in different degrees.

# 3 Methodology

The corpus used in this paper is the CORAL corpus [18, 19] (ISLRN 499-311-025-331-2), which comprises 64 dialogues between 32 speakers, amounting to 7 h orthographically transcribed. The dialogues are produced in map-task format between two speakers, the giver and the follower. The first one has a map with a route drawn and some landmarks and the latter has an incomplete map with different landmarks. The giver's task is to provide the correct directions so that the follower can reconstruct the same route in his/her map.

This work uses a subset of 48 dialogues[1] between 24 speakers (12 male and 12 female divided into 16 male-male pairs, 16 female-female pairs and 16 mixed-gender pairs). The degree of familiarity between interlocutors varied, going from people who never talked with each other to a pair of identical twin sisters (s21 and s24). All speakers play the role of giver and follower twice with different interlocutors. The subset is divided into sentence-like units (SUs), with a total of about 42 k words.

In order to measure entrainment, a set of acoustic-prosodic features was extracted for each SU, and their mean values were calculated per speaker in each dialogue. Since our goal is to perform a global analysis of entrainment, this work focuses on the similarities between speakers at the session level and not locally, i.e., between turns.

Two sets of features were used, namely knowledge-based features, i.e., features known in the literature to have impact on the task, and GeMAPS (Geneva Minimalistic Acoustic Parameters for Voice Research and Affective Computing), typically adopted in paralinguistic tasks. The first ones, extracted in the context of [13], are the following: duration of speech with and without internal silences, pitch (f0), and energy normalized maximum, minimum, average, mean, and standard deviation, as well as pitch and energy slopes. Tempo measures encompass: articulation rate (number of phones or syllables per duration of speech without internal silences); speech rate (number of phones or syllables divided by the duration of speech with internal silences), and

---

[1] For the adopted subset, the two recording channels have been post-processed to reduce the interference from the other channel. Using unprocessed data could bias pitch measures.

phonation ratio (100 % times the duration of speech without internal silences divided by the duration of speech including the internal silences). As for GeMAPS [5], this is a set of functionals based on a set of low-level descriptors, totaling 62 acoustic parameters.

$$ENT(s,f) = -\left| s_f - s_f^i \right| \tag{1}$$

$$ENTX(s,f) = -\frac{\sum_{x=0}^{n-1} \left| s_f - s_f^x \right|}{n} \tag{2}$$

$$ENT_{self}(s,f) = -\left| s_f - s_f' \right| \tag{3}$$

Following the work of [10, 11], we have used Eqs. 1, 2 and 3 to calculate the partner similarity, the non-partner similarity, and the self-similarity, respectively. In the equations, s is a speaker in a session, $s_f$ corresponds to the speaker's mean feature value for that session, $s_f^i$ refers to the interlocutor's mean feature for that session, n is the number of non-partners, $s_f^x$ is the mean feature for one of those speakers, and $s_f'$ is the mean value for feature f of speaker s in another session. Thus, we have used Eq. 1 to measure the level of proximity between interlocutors in the same dialogue by calculating the difference between a speakers' mean for a feature with the same value for his/her partner. Equation 2 measures the difference between a speakers' mean value for each feature and the ones of the speakers with whom he/she is never paired with. According to [10], such metric establishes a baseline measure of the degree of similarity that one expects to see if there is no entrainment. A final measure of similarity is the comparison between the same speakers' mean values in different dialogues. Given the fact that in CORAL corpus speakers participate in 4 dialogues, 2 as a giver and 2 as a follower, the self similarity or self-entrainment measure was done according to the roles they play, meaning that a speaker was compared to him/herself only when playing the same role. This allows us to verify if speakers are consistent regardless of the role they're playing or if that happens only with a specific role.

Again, in line with the work of [10], all of these measures were compared with a paired t-test to obtain statistically significant differences between them. Moreover, when comparing the means for each feature of the partner, non-partner, and self-similarities, it was possible to see which one has a greater degree of entrainment. For example, if the similarity between partners in a certain feature is greater than between the same speaker in other session, there is entrainment between interlocutors.

## 4   Results

### 4.1   Global Entrainment

At the session level, there are statistical significant differences ($p < 0.05$ represented with **, and $p < 0.01$ represented with *) between partners and non-partners in almost all of the features analyzed (Table 1). The comparison of each feature means shows that pitch maxima, minima, average, median, and standard deviation are more similar between interlocutors than between non-partners (see positive t-values in Table 1), clearly showing entrainment between dyads. The same pattern occurs with energy features, except for energy range, standard deviation, and slope. As for speaking rate, even though the differences between partner and non-partner are not significant, partner similarities are greater than non-partner ones expressed in a positive t-value (Table 1). As for voice quality features, namely shimmer and HNR, again speakers are more similar to their interlocutors than to their non-partners. The same happens with jitter, even though this feature does not show statistically significant differences.

When comparing the similarities of a speaker between him/herself in another session and between his/her partner, results show that speakers are more similar with their own speech in all the features, except in energy minima, average, and median. These three features are more similar between partners than between the same speaker

**Table 1.** T-tests: partner vs. non-partner differences (left columns), and partner vs. self-differences (right columns)

| Features | t | Df | Sig. | Features | t | Df | Sig. |
|---|---|---|---|---|---|---|---|
| duration speech (with internal silences) | -8.195 | 95 | * | duration speech (with internal silences) | -15.001 | 95 | * |
| duration speech (without internal silences) | -8.645 | 95 | * | duration speech (without internal silences) | -15.204 | 95 | * |
| pitch max | 5.329 | 95 | * | pitch max | -7.415 | 95 | * |
| pitch min | 3.585 | 95 | * | pitch min | -8.686 | 95 | * |
| pitch range | -2.259 | 95 | ** | pitch range | -7.384 | 95 | * |
| pitch avg | 5.592 | 95 | * | pitch avg | -7.705 | 95 | * |
| pitch med | 5.474 | 95 | * | pitch med | -7.788 | 95 | * |
| pitch stdev | 2.627 | 95 | ** | pitch stdev | -7.611 | 95 | * |
| pitch slope | 0.213 | 95 | | pitch slope | -3.825 | 95 | * |
| energy max | 3.186 | 95 | ** | energy max | -3.561 | 95 | * |
| energy min | 6.41 | 95 | * | energy min | 0.911 | 95 | |
| energy range | -0.672 | 95 | | energy range | -5.568 | 95 | * |
| energy avg | 10.234 | 95 | * | energy avg | 1.013 | 95 | |
| energy med | 9.482 | 95 | * | energy med | 0.978 | 95 | |
| energy stdev | -2.176 | 95 | ** | energy stdev | -5.851 | 95 | * |
| energy slope | -0.676 | 95 | | energy slope | -2.99 | 95 | ** |
| articulation rate phone | -1.497 | 95 | | articulation rate phone | -6.736 | 95 | * |
| rate of speech phone | -0.415 | 95 | | rate of speech phone | -5.754 | 95 | * |
| phonation ratio | -2.019 | 95 | ** | phonation ratio | -6.75 | 95 | * |
| articulation rate syl | -0.058 | 95 | | articulation rate syl | -4.703 | 95 | * |
| rate of speech syl | 0.12 | 95 | | rate of speech syl | -4.808 | 95 | * |
| jitter amean | 1.684 | 95 | | jitter amean | -2.675 | 95 | |
| shimmer amean | 2.907 | 95 | ** | shimmer amean | -5.474 | 95 | * |
| HNR amean | 3.059 | 95 | ** | HNR amean | -7.886 | 95 | * |

in different sessions, an evidence more for entrainment. [10, 11] also found more similarities between conversational partners in intensity features, namely intensity mean and maxima.

As for the comparison of similarities within roles, results show that speakers have a more consistent style as a giver mainly in tempo measures (positive t-values for articulation rate phone and syllable, 0.785 and 1.200; rate of speech phone and syllable, 1.011 and 1.916; and phonation ratio, 0.089), voice quality features (positive t-values for jitter, 0.572; shimmer, 0.966, and HNR, 1.355), pitch median and slope (t-value of 0.009 and 0.899, respectively), and also energy min, range, and slope (t-values of 0.613, 0.493, and 0.508, respectively). Looking at each speaker individually, results show that almost half of the speakers are more consistent as a giver (N = 13) and the other half (N = 11) as a follower. These results show trends of more plasticity in speakers adjusting to their partners as followers than as givers.

Given these results, it is possible to conclude that there is global entrainment, but expressed in different degrees: speakers are more similar to their own productions than they are to their interlocutors, but they are also more similar to their interlocutors than they are to speakers with whom they never spoke to.

## 4.2   Dyad Entrainment

Considering the fact that the same speaker interacts with 2 different partners, 2 times as a giver and 2 as a follower, we aim at verifying with whom they entrain more, specifically if they entrain with the same speaker regardless of the role they are playing and in which features.

In order to measure the degree of entrainment between all the pairs, we considered the percentage of similar features each pair shares. If one pair is more similar in a greater number of features, they entrain more than the other pair.

Results show that 14 speakers entrain with the same interlocutor whether they are playing the role of giver or follower (Table 2). Nonetheless, the amount of features is different. Speakers like s1, s2, s3, s5, s9, s19, and s17 entrain in a greater number of features when they are followers and their partner is the giver. The pair s6 (giver)-s1 (follower) entrains in 92 % of the features, the highest entrainment found in this data. The remaining 10 speakers entrain only with one partner. In these dyads, speakers are similar in a smaller number of features (from 50 % to 75 %), as those who entrain twice with the same partner reveal stronger similarities. Only two speakers entrain equally (50 %) in two different dyads, namely the s7–s4/s5 and s11–s21/s9. All of the followers in these pairs (s4, s5, s11, and s9) display more similarities with different partners.

Looking at the type of features where speakers entrain more, results reflect the analysis presented previously (Table 1): partners entrain more on energy (18 dyads), pitch (9 dyads), tempo measures (8 dyads), and voice quality features (12 dyads).

Results also show that pairs within the same gender tend to entrain much more than mixed-gender pairs. There are 10 female speakers that entrain with the same partner in both dialogues they participate, and regardless of the role they're playing. The same only occurs with 4 male speakers. The remaining tends to entrain with speakers of the same gender, but only in one dialogue. Mixed-gender entrainment only occurs with the

**Table 2.** Partner entrainment per speaker per role

| Entrain both as a giver and as a follower (↔) | | | | | The giver entrains with the follower (→) | | | | |
|---|---|---|---|---|---|---|---|---|---|
| Speakers/ Gender | | % of similar features | | Speakers/ Gender | | % of similar features | | Speakers/ Gender | |
| | | | | | | | | | |
| s1 | F | 71% | ↔ | s6 | F | 92% | | | |
| s2 | F | 54% | ↔ | s14 | F | 67% | | | |
| s3 | F | 63% | ↔ | s23 | F | 75% | | | |
| s5 | F | 75% | ↔ | s8 | F | 83% | | | |
| s9 | F | 54% | ↔ | s24 | F | 88% | | | |
| s19 | M | 71% | ↔ | s22 | M | 88% | | | |
| s17 | M | 71% | ↔ | s18 | M | 80% | | | |

| Speakers/ Gender | | % of similar features | | Speakers/ Gender | |
|---|---|---|---|---|---|
| s4 | M | 54% | → | s7 | M |
| s7 | M | 50% | → | s4/s5 | M/F |
| s10 | M | 71% | → | s16 | M |
| s16 | M | 63% | → | s15 | M |
| s15 | M | 67% | → | s20 | M |
| s20 | M | 63% | → | s10 | M |
| s11 | F | 50% | → | s21/s9 | F/F |
| s21 | F | 54% | → | s24 | F |
| s11 | M | 58% | → | s13 | M |
| s13 | M | 75% | → | s23 | F |

pairs s7–s5 and s13–s23, the latter being the strongest one (they present similarities in 75 % of the features). In the first pair, speaker s7 entrains 50 % of the times with both speakers with whom he is paired with. This preliminary gender analysis allows only for an overview of what we can expect from the data. A more fine-grained analysis is needed, specifically a global (session level) and local (turn level) comparison with non-partners playing the same role and with the same gender as the real partners [11].

Taking into account that 2 speakers are identical sisters (s21 and s24), we were expecting to find a clear entrainment between them in almost all of the features. In Table 2, we can see that s21, as a giver, has similarities with s24, as a follower, in 54 % of the features, as s24 entrains more with s9 twice, as a giver (88 %) and as a follower (54 %). These results may be due to the small amount of interactions produced by the sisters. The dialogues where they both interact are the briefest when compared to all the other partners. In the dyad s24–s21, a successful task is achieved with only 36 SUs from the giver and 11 from the follower. In the other dyad, where their roles are reversed, there are 30 and 38 SUs, respectively. These speakers, who already know each other so well, do not need to talk much to complete the task and succeed. This fact points out to a strong entrainment between them. However, due to the almost minimal dialogue we will also perform a turn-by-turn analysis to better understand how they interact and adapt to each other.

As for the dyad entrainment, we can conclude that, despite the role the speakers are playing, they tend to display more sensitivity to some partners. Thus, we can hypothesize that in this data there is a stronger partner effect than a role effect.

In order to verify in detail which speaker adapts the most and which maintains a more consistent personal style, a turn-by-turn analysis (local entrainment) is required, and will be applied in future work, not only to the twin sisters dialogues but to the remaining dyads.

## 5  Conclusions

This study is our first attempt to describe acoustic-prosodic entrainment in European Portuguese map-task dialogues. Using statistical tests based on proximity metrics at the session level [11], we found evidences of entrainment between partners in pitch, energy, tempo measures, and voice quality features, even though expressed in different degrees. Speakers do not entrain with the same partners and in the same features. We also found that female-female dyads tend to entrain more regardless of the role they are playing, followed by male-male dyads, and, finally, by mixed-gender pairs. These results are not in line with the findings of [11] for American English and Mandarin Chinese, since the author found more entrainment in mixed-gender pairs. Our results also show that speakers are more similar to their interlocutors than to their non-partners, but speakers are also more similar with their own productions in different dialogues than they are to their partners. Despite that, while playing the role of giver, speakers are more consistent, being similar in a greater amount of features to themselves than as a follower, which allows for more adjustment while playing this role.

In a future work, we will explore other metrics at a local level, namely acoustic-prosodic convergence turn-by-turn, and also the progression of entrainment throughout the dialogue (beginning, middle and end). This local entrainment analysis may be also relevant to extend this study to different domains, namely police interrogations, in the scope of the European Project LAW-TRAIN (REF.: H2020-EU.3.7. – 653587).

**Acknowledgments.** This work was supported by national funds through Fundação para a Ciência e a Tecnologia (FCT) with references UID/CEC/50021/2013, and UID/LIN/00214/2013, through the European Project LAW-TRAIN with reference H2020-EU.3.7. – 653587, and under PhD grant SFRH/BD/96492/2013, and Post-doc grant SFRH/PBD/95849/2013.

## References

1. Beňuš, Š.: Social aspects of entrainment in spoken interaction. Cogn. Comput. **6**(4), 802–813 (2014)
2. Brennan, S.E., Clark, H.H.: Conceptual pacts and lexical choice in conversation. J. Exp. Psychol.: Learn. Memory Cogn. **22**(6), 1482 (1996)
3. Cabarrão, V., Mata, A.I., Trancoso, I.: Affirmative constituents in European Portuguese dialogues: prosodic and pragmatic properties. In Proceedings of Speech Prosody 2016, Boston (2016)
4. Chartrand, T.L., Bargh, J.A.: The chameleon effect: the perception–behavior link and social interaction. J. Personal. Soc. Psychol. **76**(6), 893 (1999)
5. Eyben, F., Scherer, K.R., Schuller, B.W., Sundberg, J., André, E., Busso, C., Devillers, L.Y., Epps, J., Laukka, P., Narayanan, S., Truong, K.P.: The Geneva minimalistic acoustic parameter set (GeMAPS) for voice research and affective computing. IEEE Trans. Affect. Comput. **7**(2), 190–202 (2016)
6. Giles, H., Mulac, A., Bradac, J.J., Johnson, P.: Speech accommodation theory: the first decade and beyond. Ann. Int. Commun. Assoc. **10**(1), 13–48 (1987)

7. Gravano, A.: Turn-taking and affirmative cue words in task-oriented Dialogue. Ph.D. thesis, Columbia University (2009)
8. Gravano, A., Beňuš, Š., Levitan, R., Hirschberg, J.: Three ToBI-based measures of prosodic entrainment and their correlations with speaker engagement. In: 2014 IEEE Spoken Language Technology Workshop (SLT), pp. 578–583. IEEE, December 2014
9. Lee, C.C., Black, M., Katsamanis, A., Lammert, A.C., Baucom, B.R., Christensen, A., Narayanan, S.S.: Quantification of prosodic entrainment in affective spontaneous spoken interactions of married couples. In: INTERSPEECH, pp. 793–796, September 2010
10. Levitan, R., Hirschberg, J.: Measuring acoustic-prosodic entrainment with respect to multiple levels and dimensions. In: INTERSPEECH 2011 (2011)
11. Levitan, R.: Acoustic-prosodic entrainment in human-human and human-computer dialogue. Doctoral dissertation, Columbia University (2014)
12. Lopes, J., Eskenazi, M., Trancoso, I.: Automated two-way entrainment to improve spoken dialog system performance. In: 2013 IEEE International Conference on Acoustics, Speech and Signal Processing, pp. 8372–8376. IEEE, May 2013
13. Moniz, H., Batista, F., Mata, A.I., Trancoso, I.: Speaking style effects in the production of disfluencies. Speech Commun. **65**, 20–35 (2014)
14. Nenkova, A., Gravano, A., Hirschberg, J.: High frequency word entrainment in spoken dialogue. In: Proceedings of 46th Annual Meeting of the Association for Computational Linguistics on Human Language Technologies: Short Papers, pp. 169–172. Association for Computational Linguistics, June 2008
15. Pardo, J.S.: On phonetic convergence during conversational interaction. J. Acoust. Soc. Am. **119**(4), 2382–2393 (2006)
16. Pardo, J.S., Jay, I.C., Krauss, R.M.: Conversational role influences speech imitation. Atten. Percept. Psychophys. **72**(8), 2254–2264 (2010)
17. Reitter, D., Moore, J.D.: Predicting success in dialogue. In: Proceedings of 45th Annual Meeting of the Association of Computational (2007)
18. Trancoso, I., do Céu Viana, M., Duarte, I., Matos, G.: Corpus de diálogo CORAL. In: PROPOR 1998 - III Encontro para o Processamento Computacional da Língua Portuguesa Escrita e Falada, Porto Alegre, Brasil (1998)
19. Viana, M.C., Trancoso, I., Duarte, I., Matos, G., Oliveira, L.C., Campos, H., Correia, C.: Apresentação do Projecto CORAL-Corpus de Diálogo Etiquetado. In: Marrafa, P., Mota, M. A. (orgs) Linguística Computacional: Investigação Fundamental e Aplicações, pp. 337–345. Edições Colibri/APL, Lisboa (1998)
20. Weidman, S., Breen, M., Haydon, K.C.: Prosodic speech entrainment in romantic relationships. In: Proceedings of Speech Prosody 2016, Boston (2016)

# A Train-on-Target Strategy for Multilingual Spoken Language Understanding

Fernando García-Granada[✉], Encarna Segarra, Carlos Millán,
Emilio Sanchis, and Lluís-F. Hurtado

Departament de Sistemes Informàtics i Computació,
Universitat Politècnica de València, Valencia, Spain
{fgarcia,esegarra,esanchis,lhurtado}@dsic.upv.es

**Abstract.** There are two main strategies to adapt a Spoken Language Understanding system to deal with languages different from the original (source) language: test-on-source and train-on-target. In the train-on-target approach, a new understanding model is trained in the target language, which is the language in which the test utterances are pronounced. To do this, a segmented and semantically labeled training set for each new language is needed. In this work, we use several general-purpose translators to obtain the translation of the training set and we apply an alignment process to automatically segment the training sentences. We have applied this train-on-target approach to estimate the understanding module of a Spoken Dialog System for the DIHANA task, which consists of an information system about train timetables and fares in Spanish. We present an evaluation of our train-on-target multilingual approach for two target languages, French and English.

**Keywords:** Spoken Language Understanding · Language portability · Corpora alignment · Train-on-target

## 1 Introduction

Spoken Language Understanding (SLU) is an important challenge in human-machine interaction systems either oral or written [7,17]. Although the semantic interpretation of a text in a semantically unrestricted universe is still far from being solved, there are SLU systems developed for tasks semantically restricted that provide reasonable results. One of the areas of application of SLU systems is Spoken Dialogue Systems for limited domains. In a large number of those systems it is necessary to obtain a template with the information to make a query to an information system. This is done over several dialog turns, so that for each turn it is necessary to obtain the semantic information provided by the user, i.e., the specific data that have been provided as well as the information on the intention behind the turn.

This work has been partially funded by the project ASLP-MULAN: Audio, Speech and Language Processing for Multimedia Analytics (MEC TIN2014-54288-C4-3-R).

A. Abad et al. (Eds.): IberSPEECH 2016, LNAI 10077, pp. 224–233, 2016.
DOI: 10.1007/978-3-319-49169-1_22

Generally, the aim of a SLU system is to provide a semantic interpretation of the input sentence in terms of some semantic units (or concepts), and to identify the relevant information (or values) that are attached to each of them. The semantic units are defined beforehand according to the nature of the task and represent both the user intention and the types of pieces of information that are expected to be provided to the system.

For the construction of SLU systems different statistical approaches can be found. Some of these approaches are based on Markov Models or Stochastic Grammars [5,8,9,14–16]. They are also approaches based on discriminative models such as Support Vector Machines (SVM) or Conditional Random Fields (CRF) [4,12,13]. In all these approaches one of the main problems that must be addressed is the segmentation of the input sentence, since the goal is not only to obtain one or more classes associated to a sentence but also the text segment that corresponds to each semantic meaning found, considering the context of the whole sentence. This is the main reason why the CRF are the best solution among the discriminative models, since in its decision the whole sentence participates jointly and associates each word/segment with a meaning.

The process of segmenting and labeling the training corpus, in most cases manually done, is a very time-consuming task which makes the adaptation of SLU systems to different tasks or languages difficult and expensive. When the problem is to adapt a SLU system that was developed for one language to another language, it would be desirable to take advantage of the effort made for the original language and not have to replicate the work for the other language.

The multilingual approaches to SLU can be grouped in two classes, so-called test-on-source and train-on-target. In the test-on-source approach, there is a SLU system developed for a source language and the test are utterances in another language. The process consists of translating the test sentence into a sentence in the source language and performing the SLU of this translated sentence by using the SLU system in the source language. In the train-on-target approach, a new SLU model is trained in the target language, which is the language in which the test utterances are pronounced. To do this, it is necessary to translate the training corpus from the original language to this new language and to learn the corresponding SLU models. It must be noted that the translation of the training corpus not only consists of the translation of the sentences but also in the segmentation and semantic labeling of the training sentences into this new language. Once we have a model in this target language, the understanding process can be solved as in the monolingual SLU because the input utterance and the models are in the same language.

Some works that focus on the adaptation of SLU systems to other languages have been presented in the last years [2,3,6,10,16] in both test-on-source and train-on-target approaches. An essential aspect to ensure the viability of this kind of SLU systems is the performance of the translation process. If we use Statistical Machine Translation (SMT) systems, such as MOSES [11], it is necessary to have a parallel corpus in both languages that must be specifically designed for the domain, and this corpus is not always easy to obtain. On the other hand, we could use general-purpose translators that can be found on the web. The problem is that these translators often generate many errors; however, by using different translators and combining these translations, we may be able to correct the errors as well as improve the coverage.

The work presented in this paper addresses the problem of developing a multilingual SLU system that translates the training corpus to learn models in the target language, that is, the work presents a train-on-target strategy. Applying this strategy involves the estimation of SLU models in the target language, and to do this, a training set in each new language is needed. In this work we have used several general-purpose translators. Due to the good performance of the CRF-based SLU systems, we estimate CRF SLU models from the translated training set.

We have applied this train-on-target approach to the SLU module of a Spoken Dialog System for the DIHANA task [1], which consists of an information system about train timetables and fares in Spanish. To evaluate the multilingual approach, we have acquired a French and an English corpus for testing, which consists of written and spoken sentences. In a previous work [3], we applied a test-on-source approach to the same task.

## 2    The DIHANA Corpus

The Spanish DIHANA corpus is a set of 900 dialogs in Spanish in a telephone-based information service for trains. The corpus was acquired using the Wizard of Oz technique, it contains therefore many phenomena of spontaneous speech. Three scenarios were defined and posed to the speakers: in the first scenario the aim of the user is to obtain the timetables for a one-way trip, in the second scenario the users were told to obtain the price of the tickets, and optionally the timetables, of one-way trains, and the third scenario was analogous to the second one, but considering a round trip. The corpus has a total of 10.8 h of speech recordings and 225 speakers.

In order to use this corpus for SLU tasks, a semantic labeling was performed. A total amount of 30 semantic labels were defined, and all the user turns were manually and completely segmented and labeled in terms of these labels. The labeling process, as well as the definition of the set of semantic labels itself, were developed in such a way that each sentence is associated to a sequence of semantic labels and a segmentation of it in terms of these labels (one segment per semantic label). For example, the sentence in Spanish "Me podría decir los horarios para Barcelona este jueves?" (Could you tell me the timetables to go to Barcelona next Thursday?) would be segmented this way (the special symbols <> denote a question about the concept that is between the symbols):

```
me podría decir : courtesy
los horarios de trenes: <time>
para Barcelona : destination_city
este jueves: date
```

Some characteristics of the semantically labeled corpus are shown in Table 1.

**Table 1.** Characteristics of the semantically labeled corpus.

| | |
|---|---|
| Number of user turns: | 6,229 |
| Total number of words: | 47,222 |
| Vocabulary size: | 811 |
| Average number of words per user turn: | 7.6 |
| Total number of semantic segments: | 18,588 |
| Average number of words per semantic segment: | 2.5 |
| Average number of segments per user turn: | 3.0 |
| Average number of samples per semantic unit: | 599.6 |

# 3 Spoken Language Understanding

The Spoken Language Understanding problem can be approached as the search of the concept sequence that represents the meaning of the sentence. Each concept represents the meaning of a sequence of words (a segment) of the sentence, as it is shown in the example of Sect. 2. The output of the understanding system is a sequence of (*segment, concept*) pairs.

In Fig. 1 a scheme of the understanding process is presented, including both training and test processes. For the training process the input sentences should be segmented and labeled in terms of concepts. In the test process, given an input sentence $w = w_1, w_2, \ldots w_N$, the understanding process provide a sequence of (*segment, concept*) pairs $(w_1 \ldots w_j, c_1), (w_{j+1} \ldots w_t, c_2), \ldots, (w_{k+1} \ldots w_N, c_n)$.

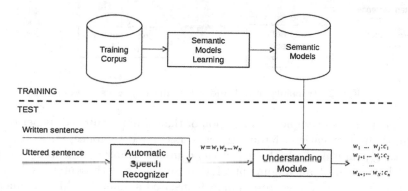

**Fig. 1.** Understanding process scheme

Given a training set of segmented and labeled sentences, the understanding models should be learned. As mentioned in Sect. 1, there are different ways to model the lexical, syntactic and semantic constraints. In this work we present a CRF-based approach.

# 4   Segmentation and Labeling of the Translated Training Corpus

For a train-on-target approach to the SLU problem it is necessary to translate the training corpus, as well as to provide it with a semantic labeling and a segmentation. The most straightforward technique consists on translating separately each one of the segments associated to the semantic labels. This way the sequence of semantic labels is directly translated to the new language. To obtain the complete sentence in the new language it is necessary to concatenate the segments in the order provided by the sequence of semantic labels. This technique presents some drawbacks, the segment concatenation can generates non correct sentences, especially when short segments are translated, because they are translated without considering the context.

Since the translation of very short segments can generate many errors, because the automatic translations take into account the context of the words in the sentence, we have explored another approach that is based on a complete translation of the sentences and a posterior segmentation. Figure 2 shows the scheme of the proposed translation approach for the training corpus.

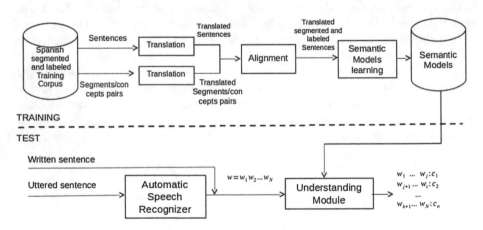

**Fig. 2.** Translation and understanding processes scheme

In a first phase a complete translation of the training sentences is performed, as well as the translation of the segments associated to concepts. In a second phase a segmentation and labeling of the complete translated sentences is performed by means of an alignment of that sentences with sentences built by the concatenation of the corresponding translated segments. This alignment is performed by minimizing the Levenshtein distance. This way a segmentation is induced in the complete translated sentence, and the semantic labels can be associated to the obtained segments. In this approach we assumed that the sequence of semantic units is the same in both languages. Figure 3 shows the translation and alignment of the Spanish sentence *"Quiero conocer el precio de los trenes hacia Ávila"*.

| Spanish: | Quiero conocer \| el precio de los trenes \| hacia Ávila |
|---|---|
| English: | I want to know \| the price of the train \| to Ávila |
| French: | Je veux savoir \| le prix du train \| à Ávila |
| Semantic labels: | query          \|       <price>       \|      destination_city |

**Fig. 3.** Example of translation and alignment

## 5   Experimental Work

In order to study the correctness of our train-on-target proposal for Multilingual Spoken Language Understanding, some experimental work was carried out. The source language was Spanish and the target languages were English and French.

The DIHANA corpus was used both to learn the models and to do the testing of the system. Particularly, 4,887 turns were used as training set and 1,000 turns were used as test set.

DIHANA corpus contains only sentences in Spanish. To get test sentences in English and French a manual translation process was performed. The test set was translated into English by six native speakers. In addition, they also uttered the 1,000 turns. In a similar way for French, the test turns were translated into French by four native speakers. But, for various reasons, only 500 of the 1,000 sentences were uttered. The test sentences uttered by the native speakers were recognized using the Automatic Speech Recognizer (ASR) of Google. The Word Error Rate obtained was 20.0 for English and 19.5 for French.

Four types of experiments were performed: English and French as target language and text input (correct transliteration) or speech input (ASR by Google). In all cases, except for French-Audio, 1,000 samples were used for test.

It is necessary to translate the training corpus into the target language to apply the train-on-target approach. Five free general-purpose on-line translators (T1:Apertium, T2:Bing, T3:Google, T4:Lucy, T5:Systranet) were selected to do this translation. The technique used to segment the translated training sentences was based on minimizing Levenshtein distance, as discussed in the Sect. 4. In regard to the formalism used to learn the understanding models, it should be noted that, in all the experiments, Conditional Random Fields formalism has been used. Two previous and two subsequent words were considered as context.

The first series of experiments consisted of a comparison of the performance of the understanding system depending on the translator used to translate the training set.

As comparison measure, the Concept Error Rate (CER) was selected. CER is a well known and used measure to evaluate understanding systems. It can be seen as the equivalent to WER when, instead of words, semantic labels are considered. Furthermore, to perform a better comparison, the confidence intervals at 95 % of all experiments were also computed. The values for the confidence intervals were around ±1.5 for text.

Table 2 shows the results obtained for English as target language, both for text input (Text column) and speech input (Speech column). Each row shows the performance of the system when the training corpus is translated using each one of the considered translators. For reference purposes, the CER results for monolingual Spanish SLU were 9.6 for text and 16.8 for speech.

**Table 2.** Results for English and the five considered translators in terms of CER

| Translator | Text | Speech |
|------------|------|--------|
| T1 | 30.5 | 37.6 |
| T2 | 24.8 | 30.4 |
| T3 | **23.0** | **28.1** |
| T4 | 34.8 | 40.4 |
| T5 | 31.1 | 38.6 |

Significant differences can be observed depending on the translator considered. The best results are obtained when the T3 is used for both input text and audio. It should be noted that, although the system obtains worse results when speech input is used, this deterioration is not as one could expect (from 23.0 to 28.1) considering that the WER of the recognition process was 20.0. This may be because many of the misrecognized words did not have important semantic information.

The same experimentation was repeated for French as target language. Table 3 shows the results obtained. It must be remembered that, in the case of French and speech input, only 500 turns were used for testing.

**Table 3.** Results for French and the five considered translators in terms of CER

| Translator | Text | Speech |
|------------|------|--------|
| T1 | 35.9 | 38.8 |
| T2 | 24.5 | 25.9 |
| T3 | **21.7** | **25.1** |
| T4 | 27.4 | 32.4 |
| T5 | 26.9 | 31.7 |

Comparing the two tables (Tables 2 and 3) it can be seen that better results are obtained for French, but the overall behavior is quite similar: there are significant differences among translators and speech input produces worse results than text input, but not as bad as it could be expected.

To study the complementarity of the translators, a second series of experiments was carried out. Instead of learning the understanding model with the training sentences translated by a single translator, in these experiments, we learned the models with the union of the sentences translated by two, three, four, and even five (all) translators.

To simplify the display of the combinations in the tables they have been coded in a binary form. As there are five translators, we used a sequence of 5 bits where each bit indicates whether or not the corresponding translator has been used in a combination.

Although all combinations have been tested, because of space problems, only the best performing combinations are shown below. Table 4 shows the results of the best combinations of translations for English as target language for both text and speech input. Each block of rows shows the best results for a specific number of translators, from a single translator (first block) to all translators together (last block).

Analyzing the results, some conclusions can be drawn: not always to use more translators produces better results; in all the best combinations the best single (00100) is used, this is not true for the second best (01000); translators with individually bad results appear in combinations with good results, probably this

**Table 4.** Results for English and the best combinations of the five considered translators in terms of CER

| Combination | Text | Speech |
|---|---|---|
| 00100 | 23.0 | 28.1 |
| 01100 | 22.5 | 27.6 |
| 10100 | 21.9 | 27.6 |
| 10101 | **21.5** | 27.1 |
| 10110 | 21.6 | **27.0** |
| 01111 | 22.2 | 27.2 |
| 10111 | **21.5** | 27.1 |
| 11111 (all) | 21.9 | **27.0** |

**Table 5.** Results for French and the best combinations of the five considered translators in terms of CER

| Combination | Text | Speech |
|---|---|---|
| 00100 | 21.7 | 25.1 |
| 00101 | 20.1 | 22.0 |
| 00110 | 20.3 | 23.1 |
| 00111 | 20.0 | **21.7** |
| 10101 | 19.9 | 22.1 |
| 11100 | 19.9 | 23.4 |
| 01111 | **19.8** | 22.3 |
| 10111 | 20.1 | 22.0 |
| 11101 | **19.8** | 22.7 |
| 11111 (all) | **19.8** | 22.2 |

is due to their complementarity with the best translators. Unfortunately, differences in the results are not statistically significant at 95 % and the conclusions could not be entirely correct.

The same experimentation was repeated for French as target language. Table 5 shows the results of the best combinations.

As happened in the case of individual translators, the results for French are slightly better than the results for English (perhaps because Spanish and French are closer languages). But still, the conclusions are similar in both languages.

## 6    Conclusions and Future Works

In this paper, we have applied a train-on-target approach to the SLU module of a Spoken Dialog System for the DIHANA task. Significant differences can be observed depending on the general-purpose translator used to translate the training set. It can be observed that, in general, the French results are lightly better than the English ones, as we expected due to the fact that French and Spanish are closer than English and Spanish. We can also observe that not always the use of more translators provided better results, in fact, the use of all the translators is not the best combination of them, but is very close to the best. Anyway, it can be concluded that the use of multiple translators improves the results of each one separately.

Although the results slightly improved those obtained with the approach test-on-source [3], the complete process in a train-on-target approach for multilingual SLU is more complex because we have not only to translate a larger set, the training set is usually at least 5 times the test set, but also we have to obtain the segmentation and labeling of the training translated sentences. In counterpart, the use of a train-on-target approach is more efficient because an on-line translation is not necessary during the real use.

As future works, we proposed to explore other alignments strategies allowing, for example, a reordering in the sequence of semantic segments.

## References

1. Benedí, J.M., Lleida, E., Varona, A., Castro, M.J., Galiano, I., Justo, R., López de Letona, I., Miguel, A.: Design and acquisition of a telephone spontaneous speech dialogue corpus in Spanish: DIHANA. In: LREC 2006, pp. 1636–1639 (2006)
2. Calvo, M., Hurtado, L.-F., García, F., Sanchís, E.: A Multilingual SLU system based on semantic decoding of graphs of words. In: Torre Toledano, D., Ortega Giménez, A., Teixeira, A., González Rodríguez, J., Hernández Gómez, L., San Segundo Hernández, R., Ramos Castro, D. (eds.) IberSPEECH 2012. CCIS, vol. 328, pp. 158–167. Springer, Heidelberg (2012). doi:10.1007/978-3-642-35292-8_17
3. Calvo, M., Hurtado, L.F., Garca, F., Sanchis, E., Segarra, E.: Multilingual spoken language understanding using graphs and multiple translations. Comput. Speech Lang. **38**, 86–103 (2016)
4. Dinarelli, M., Moschitti, A., Riccardi, G.: Concept segmentation and labeling for conversational speech. In: Interspeech, Brighton, UK (2009)

5. Esteve, Y., Raymond, C., Bechet, F., Mori, R.D.: Conceptual decoding for spoken dialog systems. In: Proceedings of EuroSpeech 2003, pp. 617–620 (2003)
6. García, F., Hurtado, L., Segarra, E., Sanchis, E., Riccardi, G.: Combining multiple translation systems for spoken language understanding portability. In: Proceedings of IEEE Workshop on Spoken Language Technology (SLT), pp. 282–289 (2012)
7. Hahn, S., Dinarelli, M., Raymond, C., Lefèvre, F., Lehnen, P., De Mori, R., Moschitti, A., Ney, H., Riccardi, G.: Comparing stochastic approaches to spoken language understanding in multiple languages. IEEE Trans. Audio Speech Lang. Process. **6**(99), 1569–1583 (2010)
8. He, Y., Young, S.: A data-driven spoken language understanding system. In: Proceedings of ASRU 2003, pp. 583–588 (2003)
9. Hurtado, L., Segarra, E., García, F., Sanchis, E.: Language understanding using n-multigram models. In: Vicedo, J.L., Martínez-Barco, P., Muñoz, R., Saiz Noeda, M. (eds.) EsTAL 2004. LNCS (LNAI), vol. 3230, pp. 207–219. Springer, Heidelberg (2004). doi:10.1007/978-3-540-30228-5_19
10. Jabaian, B., Besacier, L., Lefèvre, F.: Comparison and combination of lightly supervised approaches for language portability of a spoken language understanding system. IEEE Trans. Audio Speech Lang. Process. **21**(3), 636–648 (2013)
11. Koehn, P., et al.: Moses: open source toolkit for statistical machine translation. In: Proceedings of ACL Demonstration Session, pp. 177–180 (2007)
12. Lafferty, J., McCallum, A., Pereira, F.: Conditional random fields: probabilistic models for segmenting and labeling sequence data. In: International Conference on Machine Learning, pp. 282–289. Citeseer (2001)
13. Lefèvre, F.: Dynamic Bayesian networks and discriminative classifiers for multistage semantic interpretation. In: IEEE International Conference on Acoustics, Speech and Signal Processing, ICASSP 2007, vol. 4, pp. 13–16. IEEE (2007)
14. Ortega, L., Galiano, I., Hurtado, L.F., Sanchis, E., Segarra, E.: A statistical segment-based approach for spoken language understanding. In: Proceedings of InterSpeech 2010, Makuhari, Chiba, Japan, pp. 1836–1839 (2010)
15. Segarra, E., Sanchis, E., Galiano, M., García, F., Hurtado, L.: Extracting semantic information through automatic learning techniques. IJPRAI **16**(3), 301–307 (2002)
16. Servan, C., Camelin, N., Raymond, C., Bchet, F., Mori, R.D.: On the use of machine translation for spoken language understanding portability. In: Proceedings of ICASSP 2010, pp. 5330–5333 (2010)
17. Tür, G., Mori, R.D.: Spoken Language Understanding: Systems for Extracting Semantic Information from Speech, 1st edn. Wiley, Hoboken (2011)

# Collaborator Effort Optimisation in Multimodal Crowdsourcing for Transcribing Historical Manuscripts

Emilio Granell$^{(\boxtimes)}$ and Carlos-D. Martínez-Hinarejos

Pattern Recognition and Human Language Technology Research Center,
Universitat Politècnica de València, Camino Vera s/n, 46022 Valencia, Spain
{egranell,cmartine}@dsic.upv.es

**Abstract.** Crowdsourcing is a powerful tool for massive transcription at a relatively low cost, since the transcription effort is distributed into a set of collaborators, and therefore, supervision effort of professional transcribers may be dramatically reduced. Nevertheless, collaborators are a scarce resource, which makes optimisation very important in order to get the maximum benefit from their efforts. In this work, the optimisation of the work load in the side of collaborators is studied in a multimodal crowdsourcing platform where speech dictation of handwritten text lines is used as transcription source. The experiments explore how this optimisation allows to obtain similar results reducing the number of collaborators and the number of text lines that they have to read.

**Keywords:** Crowdsourcing framework · Collaborator effort · Speech recognition · Document transcription

## 1 Introduction

Automatic transcription of handwritten documents is an important research topic in the field of natural language processing. Transcription is specially interesting for preserving and providing access to cultural heritage that is kept in historical handwritten documents [1], since simple image digitalisation only provides, in most cases, search by image and not by linguistic contents (keywords, expressions, syntactic or semantic categories, . . . ).

Usually, the transcription of historical manuscripts is done by paleographers, who are expert people on ancient script and vocabulary. In the last decade, the development of handwritten text recognition (HTR) [2] tools provided transcribers with an initial transcription that they can properly amend, obtaining a higher productivity in the transcription task.

Moreover, the rise of crowdsourcing transcription platforms [3], where many volunteers could contribute to a given task at a very small or even null cost, reduced the required expert supervision effort. Nevertheless, final expert supervision is still required most times in order to obtain accurate enough transcriptions.

© Springer International Publishing AG 2016
A. Abad et al. (Eds.): IberSPEECH 2016, LNAI 10077, pp. 234–244, 2016.
DOI: 10.1007/978-3-319-49169-1_23

Current crowdsourcing platforms (such as Mechanical Turk[1]) provide a web interface where users provide the labelling or transcription of the considered object. In the case of transcription, where a complex input has to be introduced, these platforms limit the task to desktop or laptop computers, where using keyboard is comfortable enough for most users, whereas the use of mobile devices is disregarded because of the low ergonomy of virtual keyboards. A possible alternative that would allow the use of mobile devices is the employment of voice as the transcription input. Since voice acquisition is available in nearly all mobile platforms, this alternative would provide a dramatically higher number of collaborators. The voice acquisitions can be processed by using Automatic Speech Recognition (ASR) techniques [4] and the corresponding decoding used as the object transcription. However, since ASR systems are far from perfect (although their performance incremented substantially over recent years [5]), voice presents an ambiguity that typed input lacks of, which makes necessary to assess the transcription quality when using this approach.

Anyway, since expert transcribers must finally supervise the transcription, it is not necessary that voice input provides a perfect transcription, since only providing a new more accurate transcription may reduce substantially the supervision effort of final transcribers. Moreover, it can be supposed that the accuracy of the transcription would improve with the number of volunteers that provide their voice transcription [6]. Nevertheless, volunteers are a scarce resource in transcription crowdsourcing platforms, which makes the optimisation of their work load a very important issue in order to get the maximum benefit from their efforts. Anyway, it is universally assumed that is less difficult to obtain the collaboration of volunteer people with low level of expertise than to obtain a well-trained paleographer.

This work studies how to optimise the work load in the side of the collaborators in a multimodal crowdsourcing platform where volunteer speakers dictate the transcription of historical handwritten text images [6]. This framework is based on the combination of language model interpolation techniques [7] and combination techniques [8], that allow the fusion of multimodal outputs in a single transcription hypothesis. The novelty presented in this paper is that the volunteer work load is limited to the dictation of the text images whose transcriptions at the system output need more refinement when the volunteer offers to collaborate.

The rest of the paper is structured as follows: Sect. 2 presents the multimodal crowdsourcing framework including the new line selection module; Sect. 3 describes the experimental conditions; Sect. 4 explains the performed experiments and the obtained results; Sect. 5 summarises the conclusions and future work lines.

## 2    Crowdsourcing Framework

The HTR and ASR problems can be formulated in a very similar way that allows its integration into a multimodal system. The unimodal formulation is:

given a handwritten text image or a speech signal encoded into the feature vector sequence $x = (x_1, x_2, \ldots, x_{|x|})$, finding the most likely word sequence $\hat{w} = (w_1, w_2, \ldots, w_{|w|})$, that is:

$$\hat{w} = \arg \max_{w \in W} \Pr(w \mid x) = \arg \max_{w \in W} \frac{\Pr(x \mid w) \Pr(w)}{\Pr(x)} = \arg \max_{w \in W} \Pr(x \mid w) \Pr(w) \quad (1)$$

where $W$ denotes the set of all permissible sentences, $\Pr(x)$ is the probability of observing $x$, $\Pr(w)$ is the probability of $w$ (approximated by the language model, LM), and $\Pr(x \mid w)$ is the probability of observing $x$ by assuming that $w$ is the underlying word sequence for $x$ (evaluated by the optical or acoustic model, for HTR and ASR respectively).

The main objective of this crowdsourcing framework is to reduce the transcription errors in $\hat{w}$ before giving it to a paleographer for obtaining the actual transcription. This framework is based on two ideas: using the current system output to improve the language model for the next decoding process [9], and combining decoding outputs in order to obtain an output with lower error rate. [10].

Most previous works assumed that the source of speech was a single speaker (usually the same paleographer); in contrast, in this framework [6] the speech is given by a set of collaborators. Given the nature of the historical manuscripts, the collaborators may hesitate on the pronunciation of some old words, have mispronunciations, or even avoid parts of the sentence. Since the appearance of these events could worsen the final output, a speech reliability verification module is included in the framework to exclude those utterances with low reliability. Following the same idea, the reliability of a recognition process can be used to select those lines with poorer recognition results and provide them to the collaborators. Therefore, a line selection module is included in the framework, and its influence is assessed in this work.

Figure 1 presents the working diagram of this multimodal crowdsourcing system. The operation is as follows:

1. The initial system output is given by the HTR decoding module.
2. The crowdsourcing loop starts in the LM interpolation module, where the previous system output is interpolated with the original LM for obtaining an improved LM for the next ASR decoding.
3. The reliability of the system output is evaluated, the lines are sorted by its reliability, and the collaborator is asked to read only a subset of those lines which lower reliability.
4. The collaborator speech is decoded in the ASR module using the improved LM, and the reliability of the obtained ASR output is verified and filtered, i.e., only the decoding output of those utterances which reach a determined reliability threshold are accessible at the output of the reliability verification module.
5. The system output is updated by combining the previous system output with the current and verified ASR output in the multimodal combination module.
6. If the speech of a new collaborator is available, the steps of the crowdsourcing loop (steps from 2 to 5) are repeated with these new audio samples.

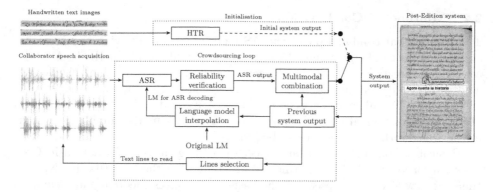

**Fig. 1.** Multimodal crowdsourcing transcription framework.

The following subsections describe in detail the different modules of the framework.

## 2.1 Language Model Interpolation

The language interpolation module builds a statistical LM conditioned on a given input $x$ that can be used to calculate the posterior probabilities of Eq. (1). This adapted LM can be obtained as described in [9].

Basically, the decoding outputs obtained from handwriting and speech recognisers can be formatted as Word Graph (WG) lattices, and as Confusion Networks (CN), which reduce the complexity of WG without losing important information [8]. In Fig. 2 an example of WG and its corresponding CN is presented.

For the language interpolation, first, the decoding outputs are obtained from the decoding process as WG; then the posterior probabilities for each node and link are computed, which allow to calculate counts for a word sequence; from these counts, the word posterior probabilities can be calculated (after applying a suitable discount method, a smoothing method to avoid Out Of Vocabulary words, and a normalisation). Finally, the new conditioned LM is linearly interpolated with the original LM using a weight factor $\lambda$ that balances the relative reliability in the LM interpolation between the LM estimated from the previous system output and the original LM.

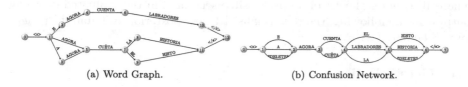

(a) Word Graph.                              (b) Confusion Network.

**Fig. 2.** Word graph and confusion network.

## 2.2  Multimodal Combination

The multimodal combination of the ASR decoding output with the previous system output can be performed by means of CN combination methods. A CN is a weighted directed graph, in which each hypothesis goes through all the nodes. The words and their probabilities are also stored in the edges. A subnetwork (SN) is the set of all edges between two consecutive nodes. The total probability of the words contained in a SN sum up to 1. The multimodal combination used in the framework works as is described in [10].

Basically, from the system and speech decoding outputs formatted in CN, a search for anchor SN is performed in order to align the SN of both CN, and then the new CN is composed (on the basis of the Bayes theorem and assuming a strong independence between both CN) by using the combination, insertion, and deletion editing actions.

The combination of two subnetworks $SN_A$ and $SN_B$ into the combined subnetwork $SN_C$ is obtained by applying a normalisation on the logarithmic interpolation (using an $\alpha$ factor) of the smoothed word posterior probabilities of both SN ($SN_A$ and $SN_B$). For insertion and deletion, the same process is performed: the SN to insert or to delete is combined with a SN with an only *DELETE* arc with probability 1.0. The weight factor $\alpha$ permits balancing the relative reliability in the multimodal combination between the verified ASR decoding output and the previous system output.

## 2.3  Reliability Verification

Given the conventional formulation of the HTR and ASR problems, the posterior probability $\Pr(w \mid x)$ is a good confidence measure for the recognition reliability. However, recognition scores are inadequate to assess the recognition confidence because most recognition systems ignore the term $\Pr(x)$, as seeing in Eq. (1). Nevertheless, when the recognition scores of a fairly large n-best list are re-normalised to sum up to 1, the obtained posterior probability $\Pr_n(w \mid x)$ can serve as a good confidence measure since it represents a quantitative measure of the match between $x$ and $w$ [11,12].

Therefore, the re-normalised 1-best posterior probability $\Pr_n(w_1 \mid x)$ is used in the reliability verification module as the confidence measure:

$$\Pr{}_n(w_1 \mid x) = \frac{\Pr(w_1 \mid x)}{\sum\limits_{w \in W} \Pr(w \mid x)} \tag{2}$$

where $W$ denotes the set of all permissible sentences in the evaluated decoding output. In the following, the re-normalised 1-best posterior probability $\Pr_n(w_1 \mid x)$ will be noted as $R$.

## 2.4  Lines Selection

Since collaborators are a scarce resource, optimisation is very important to get the maximum benefit from their efforts. One way to optimise their effort is to reduce the set of lines that they have to read to the subset of lines that need more refinement. When a collaborator offers to help, the system selects the lines to read as follows:

1. The current system output is evaluated by using the re-normalised 1-best posterior probability -Eq. (2)- in order to estimate the current confidence value of each one of the lines to transcribe.
2. The lines are ranked according to their estimated confidence value.
3. The system selects a subset of the $N$ lines with the lowest confidence value.
4. The collaborator is asked to read only the selected lines.

# 3    Experimental Conditions

## 3.1    Data Sets

The *Rodrigo* corpus [13] was the data set employed in the experiments. It was obtained from the digitalisation of the book "Historia de España del arçobispo Don Rodrigo", written in ancient Spanish in 1545. It is a single writer book where most pages consist of a single block of well separated lines of calligraphical text. It is composed of 853 pages that were automatically divided into lines (see example in Fig. 3), giving a total number of 20,356 lines. The vocabulary size is of about 11,000 words.

This corpus presents several difficulties, such as, text images containing abbreviations (e.g., *nrō* in the second line of Fig. 3) that must be pronounced as the whole word (*nuestro* [ 'nwes tro]), words written in multiple forms (e.g., *xpiãnos* -in the third line of Fig. 3- and *christianos*, or numbers as 5 and *V*) but that are pronounced in the same way ([kris 'tja nos], ['θiŋ ko]), and hyphenated words (e.g., *Toledo* in the fourth and fifth lines of Fig. 3, where a part of the word -*Tole*- is at the end of a line and the second part -*do*- is at the beginning of the following line).

For training the optical models, a standard partition with a total number of 5000 lines (about 205 pages) was used. Test data for HTR was composed of two pages that were not included in the training part (pages 515 and 579) and that were representative of the average error of the standard test set (of about 5000 lines). These two pages contain 50 lines and 514 words.

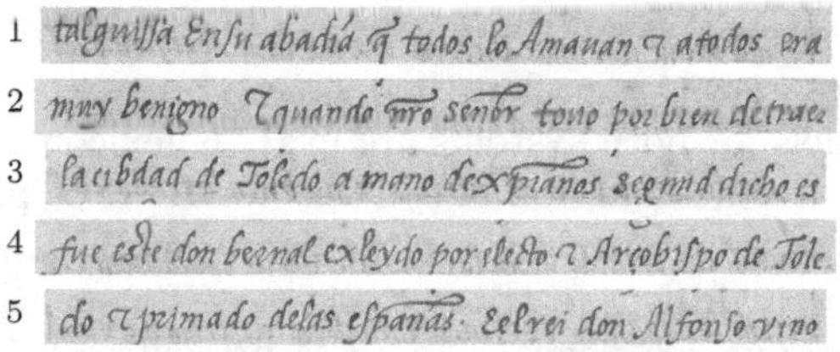

**Fig. 3.** The 5 first lines of the page 515 of *Rodrigo*.

For the training of the ASR acoustic models we used a partition of the Spanish phonetic corpus Albayzin [14]. For the multimodal crowdsourcing test we obtained the collaboration of 7 different native Spanish speakers who read the 50 handwritten test lines (those of pages 515 and 579), giving a total set of 350 utterances (about 15 min) acquired at 16 KHz and 16 bits.

## 3.2   Features

**HTR Features.** Handwritten text features are computed in several steps. First, a bright normalisation is performed. After that, a median filter of size $3 \times 3$ pixels is applied to the whole image. Next, slant correction is performed by using the maximum variance method and a threshold of 92 %. Then, a size normalisation is performed and the final image is scaled to a height of 40 pixels. Finally, features are extracted by using the method described in [15]. Final feature vectors are of 60 dimensions. In Fig. 4 we can see an example of the feature vectors sequence obtained from the image of the third line of the page 515 (Fig. 3).

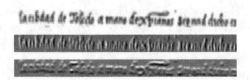

**Fig. 4.** Example of HTR feature vectors sequence.

**ASR Features.** Mel-Frequency Cepstral Coefficients (MFCC) are extracted from the audio files. The Fourier transform is calculated every 10 ms over a window of 25 ms of a pre-emphasised signal. Next, 23 equidistant Mel scale triangular filters are applied and the filters outputs are logarithmised. Finally, to obtain the MFCC, a discrete cosine transformation is applied. We used the first 12 MFCC and log frame energy with first and second order derivatives as ASR features, resulting in a 39 dimensional vector.

## 3.3   Models

Optical and acoustic models were trained by using HTK [16]. On the one hand, symbols on the optical model are modelled by a continuous density gaussian mixture left-to-right of 106 HMM with 6 states and 32 gaussians per state, while on the other hand, phonemes on the acoustic model are modelled as a left-to-right gaussian mixture of 25 HMM (23 monophones, short silence, and long silence) with 3 states and 64 gaussians per state.

The lexicon models for both systems are in HTK lexicon format, where each word is modelled as a concatenation of symbols for HTR or phonemes for ASR.

The baseline LM was estimated as a 2-gram with Kneser-Ney back-off smoothing [17] directly from the transcriptions of the pages included on the HTR training set (about 205 pages). This LM presents a 6.2 % of OOV words and a perplexity of 298.4 with respect to the test set.

## 3.4   Evaluation Metrics

The quality of the transcription is given by the well known word error rate (WER), which is a good estimation of the user post-edition effort. It is defined as the minimum number of words to be substituted, deleted or inserted to convert the hypothesis into the reference, divided by the total number of reference words. Moreover, confidence intervals of 95 % were calculated by using the bootstrapping method with 10,000 repetitions [18].

## 3.5   Experimental Setup

Both the HTR and the ASR systems were implemented by using the iATROS recogniser [19]. All processes on language models (inference, interpolation, . . . ), the decoding output evaluation, and the transformation from WG to CN were done by using the SRILM toolkit [20].

# 4   Experiments

The performance of our multimodal crowdsourcing framework was tested with the 50 text line images of the Rodrigo corpus and the 350 speech utterances recorded from 7 different collaborators described in Subsect. 3.1.

First of all, the baseline values for both modalities were obtained. The baseline values were obtained by using the original LM in the decoding process of both modalities. As can be observed in Table 1, the HTR and ASR WER values are quite high due to the difficulty of the corpus.

**Table 1.** Baseline results.

| Modality | WER |
|----------|-----|
| HTR | 39.3 % ± 4.1 |
| ASR | 62.9 % ± 2.2 |

In a previous work [6] the speaker that best represented the average error rate of the speech set was selected for adjusting the multimodal combination ($\alpha$) and LM interpolation factors ($\gamma$). We observed as this crowdsourcing framework presents the highest reliability (for this test set) when the multimodal combination is a bit balanced to the speech output ($\alpha = 0.6$), and the LM interpolation to the original LM ($\lambda = 0.4$). The speaker order and the reliability verification did not show a significant impact on the results. Therefore, the configuration with best results was used in the next experiment, i.e. combination factor $\alpha = 0.6$, LM interpolation $\lambda = 0.4$, and speech decoding reliability threshold $R \geq 0.4$.

Finally, with the other 6 speakers the optimisation of the collaborator effort was tested. In this experiment we tested the influence of the number of collaborators and the number of lines to read. Figure 5 and Table 2 present the obtained results. As can be observed, the best results are obtained when all people collaborate with a full effort, i.e., giving the speech transcription of the whole set of text lines. In this case, the best result is 26.1 % ± 3.3 of WER, by using the 50 speech utterances of the 6 speakers. This result represents a statistically significant relative improvement of 33.6 % over the HTR baseline, which represents an important effort reduction for obtaining the final transcription.

However, similar statistically significant improvements can be achieved optimising the effort of the collaborators. As can be observed in Fig. 5 and Table 2, the optimal collaborator load is 30 lines (30.0 % ± 4.1 of WER for 6 collaborators). Besides, with this load, the obtained improvements are statistically significant after the collaboration of the 4th volunteer. In this case, the system output presented a WER of 30.5 % ± 4.2, which represents a relative improvement of 22.4 % over the baseline. Furthermore, the difference between this value and the obtained by using the 50 speech utterances of the 6 speakers is not statistically significant. However, it represents a collaborator effort reduction of 33.3 % in the number of collaborators and 40.0 % in the number of lines read by each collaborator.

The collaborators load optimisation allowed to reduce the number of global collaborations, given that with 120 collaborations (30 lines read by 4 collaborators) this crowdsourcing system improved significantly the transcription of 50 lines. Therefore, it can be expected that with 300 collaborations (50 lines read by 6 collaborators) this system could improve significantly the transcription of a test set of 125 lines.

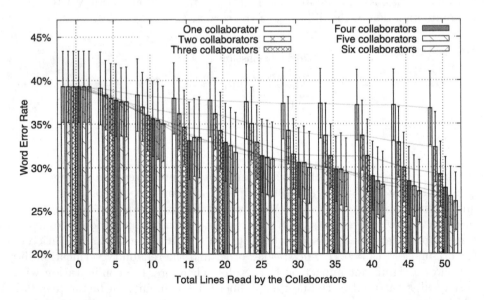

**Fig. 5.** Collaborator effort optimisation experiment results.

**Table 2.** Experiment results (WER).

| Lines | Collaborators | | | | | |
|---|---|---|---|---|---|---|
| | 1 | 2 | 3 | 4 | 5 | 6 |
| 5 | 39.1 % ± 4.2 | 38.3 % ± 4.0 | 37.9 % ± 4.0 | 37.7 % ± 4.2 | 37.6 % ± 3.9 | 37.6 % ± 4.0 |
| 10 | 38.3 % ± 4.2 | 37.0 % ± 4.0 | 36.0 % ± 4.1 | 35.6 % ± 4.4 | 35.4 % ± 4.5 | 35.0 % ± 4.3 |
| 15 | 37.9 % ± 4.1 | 36.2 % ± 4.0 | 34.6 % ± 4.3 | 33.1 % ± 4.5 | 33.5 % ± 4.5 | 33.5 % ± 4.6 |
| 20 | 37.7 % ± 4.2 | 36.2 % ± 4.1 | 34.2 % ± 4.4 | 32.9 % ± 4.5 | 32.5 % ± 4.4 | 31.7 % ± 4.6 |
| 25 | 37.6 % ± 4.3 | 35.0 % ± 4.2 | 32.9 % ± 4.3 | 31.3 % ± 4.2 | 31.1 % ± 4.3 | 30.9 % ± 4.3 |
| 30 | 37.4 % ± 4.1 | 34.2 % ± 3.9 | 31.5 % ± 4.1 | 30.5 % ± 4.0 | 30.5 % ± 4.2 | 30.0 % ± 4.1 |
| 35 | 37.4 % ± 4.0 | 33.7 % ± 3.7 | 31.3 % ± 3.7 | 29.8 % ± 3.7 | 29.8 % ± 4.2 | 29.4 % ± 4.0 |
| 40 | 37.2 % ± 4.1 | 33.7 % ± 4.0 | 31.3 % ± 4.2 | 29.0 % ± 4.0 | 28.4 % ± 3.9 | 28.0 % ± 3.8 |
| 45 | 37.2 % ± 4.1 | 32.9 % ± 4.1 | 30.0 % ± 4.0 | 28.4 % ± 3.9 | 27.8 % ± 3.5 | 27.2 % ± 3.6 |
| 50 | 36.8 % ± 4.2 | 32.3 % ± 4.0 | 29.2 % ± 3.8 | 27.6 % ± 3.5 | 26.7 % ± 3.4 | 26.1 % ± 3.3 |

## 5 Conclusions

In this work we have studied the optimisation of the work load in the side of collaborators in a multimodal crowdsourcing framework for transcribing historical manuscripts. The novelty presented in this work is the lines selection block that permits to ask the collaborators to read only those lines with lower reliability. This optimisation allows to obtain similar results reducing the number of collaborators and the number of lines that they have to read. Therefore, this crowdsourcing framework can be used to improve the transcription of a large amount of text line images.

In view of the obtained results, we believe that there is still room for improvement. We propose for future studies the use of sentences in the handwriting text corpus instead of lines as it could make multimodality more natural for speakers.

Finally, we plan to test this crowdsourcing framework publicly with the collaboration of a huge amount of speakers, and with other datasets. Another line to be explored is the use of this framework in the obtainment of alternative transcriptions (different from diplomatic transcriptions), such as modernised transcriptions.

**Acknowledgments.** Work partially supported by projects SmartWays - RTC-2014-1466-4 (MINECO) and CoMUN-HaT - TIN2015-70924-C2-1-R (MINECO/FEDER).

## References

1. Fischer, A., Wüthrich, M., Liwicki, M., Frinken, V., Bunke, H., Viehhauser, G., Stolz, M.: Automatic transcription of handwritten medieval documents. In: Proceedings of the 15th VSMM, pp. 137–142 (2009)
2. Plamondon, R., Srihari, S.N.: On-line and off-line handwriting recognition: a comprehensive survey. IEEE Trans. Pattern Anal. Mach. Intell. **22**(1), 63–84 (2000)

3. Doan, A., Ramakrishnan, R., Halevy, A.Y.: Crowdsourcing systems on the world-wide web. Commun. ACM **54**(4), 86–96 (2011)
4. Rabiner, L., Juang, B.H.: Fundamentals of Speech Recognition. Prentice Hall, Upper Saddle River (1993)
5. Hinton, G., Deng, L., Dong, Y., Dahl, G.E., Mohamed, A., Jaitly, N., Senior, A., Vanhoucke, V., Nguyen, P., Sainath, T.N., Kingsbury, B.: Deep neural networks for acoustic modeling in speech recognition: the shared views of four research groups. IEEE Sig. Process. Mag. **29**(6), 82–97 (2012)
6. Granell, E., Martínez-Hinarejos, C.D.: A multimodal crowdsourcing framework for transcribing historical handwritten documents. In Proceedings of the 16th DocEng, pp. 157–163 (2016)
7. Bellegarda, J.R.: Statistical language model adaptation: review and perspectives. Speech Commun. **42**(1), 93–108 (2004)
8. Xue, J., Zhao, Y.: Improved confusion network algorithm and shortest path search from word lattice. In: Proceedings of the 30th ICASSP, vol. 1, pp. 853–856 (2005)
9. Alabau, V., Romero, V., Lagarda, A.L., Martínez-Hinarejos, C.D.: A multimodal approach to dictation of handwritten historical documents. In: Proceedings of the 12th Interspeech, pp. 2245–2248 (2011)
10. Granell, E., Martínez-Hinarejos, C.D.: Combining handwriting and speech recognition for transcribing historical handwritten documents. In: Proceedings of the 13th ICDAR, pp. 126–130 (2015)
11. Rueber, B.: Obtaining confidence measures from sentence probabilities. In: Proceedings of the 5th Eurospeech, pp. 739–742 (1997)
12. Wessel, F., Schlüter, R., Macherey, K., Ney, H.: Confidence measures for large vocabulary continuous speech recognition. IEEE Trans. Speech Audio Process. **9**(3), 288–298 (2001)
13. Serrano, N., Castro, F., Juan, A.: The RODRIGO database. In: Proceedings of the 7th LREC, pp. 2709–2712 (2010)
14. Moreno, A., Poch, D., Bonafonte, A., Lleida, E., Llisterri, J., Mariño, J.B., Nadeu, C.: Albayzin speech database: design of the phonetic corpus. In: Proceedings of the 3rd EuroSpeech, pp. 175–178 (1993)
15. Dreuw, P., Jonas, S., Ney, H.: White-space models for offline Arabic handwriting recognition. In: Proceedings of the 19th ICPR, pp. 1–4 (2008)
16. Young, S., Evermann, G., Gales, M., Hain, T., Kershaw, D., Liu, X., Moore, G., Odell, J., Ollason, D., Povey, D., Valtchev, V., Woodland, P.C.: The HTK Book. Cambridge University Engineering Department, Cambridge (2006)
17. Kneser, R., Ney, H.: Improved backing-off for m-gram language modeling. In: Proceedings of ICASSP, vol. 1, pp. 181–184 (1995)
18. Bisani, M., Ney, H.: Bootstrap estimates for confidence intervals in ASR performance evaluation. In: Proceedings of ICASSP, vol. 1, pp. 409–412 (2004)
19. Luján-Mares, M., Tamarit, V., Alabau, V., Martínez-Hinarejos, C.D., Pastor, M., Sanchis, A., Toselli, A.H.: iATROS: a speech and handwritting recognition system. In: Procedings of the V Jornadas en Tecnologías del Habla, pp. 75–78 (2008)
20. Stolcke, A.: SRILM-an extensible language modeling toolkit. In Proceedings of the 3rd Interspeech, pp. 901–904 (2002)

# Assessing User Expertise in Spoken Dialog System Interactions

Eugénio Ribeiro[1,2](✉), Fernando Batista[1,3], Isabel Trancoso[1,2], José Lopes[4],
Ricardo Ribeiro[1,3], and David Martins de Matos[1,2]

[1] L$^2$F – Spoken Language Systems Laboratory, INESC-ID Lisboa, Lisbon, Portugal
`eugenio.ribeiro@l2f.inesc-id.pt`
[2] Instituto Superior Técnico, Universidade de Lisboa, Lisbon, Portugal
[3] ISCTE-IUL – Instituto Universitário de Lisboa, Lisbon, Portugal
[4] KTH Speech, Music, and Hearing, Stockholm, Sweden

**Abstract.** Identifying the level of expertise of its users is important
for a system since it can lead to a better interaction through adaptation techniques. Furthermore, this information can be used in offline
processes of root cause analysis. However, not much effort has been put
into automatically identifying the level of expertise of an user, especially
in dialog-based interactions. In this paper we present an approach based
on a specific set of task related features. Based on the distribution of the
features among the two classes – Novice and Expert – we used Random
Forests as a classification approach. Furthermore, we used a Support
Vector Machine classifier, in order to perform a result comparison. By
applying these approaches on data from a real system, Let's Go, we
obtained preliminary results that we consider positive, given the difficulty of the task and the lack of competing approaches for comparison.

**Keywords:** User expertise · Let's Go · SVM · Random Forest

## 1 Introduction

The users of a dialog system have different levels of expertise, that is, knowledge
of the system's capabilities and experience using it. Thus, identifying the level
of expertise of a user is important for a dialog system, since it provides cues for
adaptation which can improve dialog flow and the overall user satisfaction. For
instance, by identifying a novice user, the system may provide help on the first
signs of struggle and adapt its prompts to provide further information. Also,
user expertise information can be used to adapt the system's parameters, such
as Automatic Speech Recognition (ASR) timeout values, reducing the number
of misinterpretations and interruptions. Furthermore, it can be used in offline
processes to identify problems caused by lack of expertise, which is important
for the development of better dialog systems.

In this article we present an analysis of different features and how they
can be used to identify the level of expertise of a user on Let's Go [15] data.

© Springer International Publishing AG 2016
A. Abad et al. (Eds.): IberSPEECH 2016, LNAI 10077, pp. 245–254, 2016.
DOI: 10.1007/978-3-319-49169-1_24

The remaining sections are structured as follows: Sect. 2 presents related work on user expertise with dialog systems. Section 3 lists relevant feature classes for this task. Section 4 describes the datasets, the specific features extracted, and the classification approaches. Results are presented and discussed in Sect. 5, and, finally, Sect. 6 states the achieved conclusions and suggests paths for future work.

## 2    Related Work

A system that behaves the same way for all users, independently of their expertise, may not provide a truly usable interface for any of them. By knowing the level of expertise of its users, a system could improve the quality of the interaction through adaptation techniques based on that level [13]. However, not much effort has been put into identifying the level of expertise of a user, especially in dialog-based interactions.

Hjalmarsson [9] analyzed dialog dynamics and discussed the utility of creating adaptive spoken dialog systems and individual user models. She suggests that such models can be created using both rule-based and statistical approaches [8]. Given the correct set of rules, rule-based models have good performance on specific tasks. However, they must be handcrafted from the intuition of the designer or experts, which is a time-consuming process. Thus, when annotated data is available, statistical models are a better option. The author suggests Bayesian Networks, Reinforcement Learning, and Decision Trees as promising approaches for the task.

Hassel and Hagen [7] developed an automotive dialog system that adapts to its users' expertise. However, it does not attempt to identify each user's expertise, but rather assumes that every user is a novice and then adapts over time. The adaptation is task-based and controlled by the number of successful attempts and the time since the last execution of that task.

Jokinen and Kanto [10] used user expertise modelling to enable the adaptation of a speech-based e-mail system. They distinguish three levels of expertise – Novice, Competent, and Expert –, a subset of the five proposed by Dreyfus and Dreyfus [4] in their studies about the behaviour of expert systems. The developed models have two components – online and offline. The first tracks the current user session and provides cues for system adaptation, accordingly. The latter is based on statistical event distributions created from all sessions of a user and serves as a starting point for the next session. In terms of features, a small set is used, consisting on the number of timeouts, interruptions, and help requests, as well as the number of times a given task was performed, or a specific system dialog act was invoked.

## 3    Relevant Features

Since expertise depends on the task being performed, it cannot be identified by large sets of generic acoustic features such as the ones extracted by openSMILE [5]. Thus, a small set of task oriented features must be devised.

These features can be clustered into different categories, according to their origin and what aspects they intend to capture. In the following sections we describe each of these categories.

### 3.1   Interruptions

Expert users may interrupt the system when they are aware of the complete dialog flow. However, this is not a good approach when system utterances are confirmation prompts which only include the information to be confirmed in the end. In this case, interruptions usually signal a novice user. Furthermore, cases when the system interrupts the user can also reveal a novice user who uses long sentences or pauses that exceed the system's waiting times.

### 3.2   Delays

Negative delays between the system and user utterances mean that an interruption occurred, which has the previously described implications. On the other hand, long delays suggest that the user is still processing the system's utterance and is unsure about what to say and, thus, may reveal inexperience.

### 3.3   Durations

Long durations are typically more discriminative than short ones and may suggest inexperience. For instance, a long call usually means that something went wrong during the dialog. Long utterances also suggest inexperience, as they are more prone to recognition errors and interruptions by the system.

### 3.4   Speech Rate

Speech rate is also a possible indicator of the level of expertise of a user since both high and low speech rates may lead to communication problems. While high speech rates lead to higher error rates in recognition, low speech rates are related to paused speeches, which are more prone to be interrupted by the system. Thus, expert users usually keep a balanced speech rate.

### 3.5   Help Requests

When a user is new to a system and unsure how it works, he or she typically asks for help, revealing inexperience. This is especially clear in cases when the system offers help and the user immediately accepts it. Unfortunately, some systems do not provide help functionality or the user is not aware it exists.

## 4   Experimental Setup

This section describes our experimental setup, starting with the used datasets. Next, the used features and their distribution in the training dataset are thoroughly presented. After that, the used classification and evaluation approaches are described.

## 4.1   Datasets

We explored user expertise on data extracted from interactions with the Let's Go Bus Information System [15], which provides information about bus schedules, through spoken telephonic interaction with a dialog system. This system has been running for many years and has experienced changes over time. Thus, the characteristics of the data differ according to when it was obtained.

In our experiments we used the LEGO [16] corpus. This corpus is a subset of 347 Let's Go calls during the year of 2006. The corpus contains annotations relevant for the user level of expertise identification task, such as barge-in information and durations. In terms of the level of expertise, the original corpus is not annotated. Thus, we annotated each call with that information using two labels – Expert and Novice. Out of the 347 calls, 80 users were labeled as Expert and 235 as Novice. The remaining calls were impossible to annotate since the user did not interact with the system. We used this dataset for analyzing the distribution of different features and as training data for the classification task.

In addition to the 2006 data, we also looked into a small set of 80 calls from 2014 data of the Let's Go corpus. This set was annotated for expertise at KTH using the same two labels – Expert and Novice [11]. The audio files for all but one of calls are accompanied by the logs of the system, which provide important information for feature extraction. Of the 79 calls, 42 users were labeled as Expert and 37 as Novice. The reported Cohen's Kappa for the annotator agreement was 0.73, which is usually considered good. However, we also annotated the 79 calls, labeling 31 users as Expert and 48 as Novice, obtaining an agreement of 0.43 with the original annotation, which is usually considered moderate. We used the 56 calls with agreement to assess the generalization capabilities of our classifiers.

## 4.2   Features

In Sect. 3 we defined a set of feature classes that are relevant for identifying the level of expertise of a user. In this section we describe the specific features that we were able to extract from the datasets. Furthermore, for the training dataset, LEGO, we perform an analysis of the distributions of the features among the data, in order to perform a comparison with the previously defined expectations. Table 1 presents these distributions.

**Interruptions.** The LEGO corpus is annotated with user barge-in information. Thus, we were able to extract the number of user barge-ins per dialog. Table 1 shows that novice users are more prone to interrupt the system, with an average of 5 barge-ins per dialog. This was expected, since most of the system utterances in the corpus are of the kind that state information to be confirmed in the final words and, thus, should not be interrupted. However, these statistics did not take the length of the dialog into account. Thus, we calculated the user barge-in rate as the percentage of exchanges containing user barge-ins. The previous results were confirmed, as, on average, novice users barged-in on 16 % of the exchanges, while experts only barged-in on 10 % of the exchanges. The median

**Table 1.** Feature distribution among the LEGO dataset in terms of average ($\mu$), median($\tilde{x}$), and standard deviation($\sigma$).

| Feature | Novice | | | Expert | | |
|---|---|---|---|---|---|---|
| | $\mu$ | $\tilde{x}$ | $\sigma$ | $\mu$ | $\tilde{x}$ | $\sigma$ |
| Interruptions | | | | | | |
| # Barge-ins | 5.06 | 3.00 | 6.79 | 2.75 | 2.00 | 3.15 |
| Barge-in Rate | 16.2 | 15.4 | 9.9 | 10.3 | 9.5 | 6.9 |
| Delays (s) | | | | | | |
| 1$^{st}$ turn | 1.52 | 1.28 | 3.00 | 1.32 | 1.21 | 2.81 |
| 1$^{st}$ turn (Positive) | 2.82 | 2.18 | 2.79 | 1.90 | 1.49 | 2.72 |
| Durations (s) | | | | | | |
| Utterance | 1.81 | 1.44 | 3.14 | 1.19 | 1.20 | 0.43 |
| Call | 123 | 104 | 95 | 102 | 76 | 78 |
| 1$^{st}$ turn | 1.81 | 1.19 | 2.02 | 1.72 | 1.39 | 1.66 |
| # Exchanges | 28.0 | 23.0 | 23.4 | 23.8 | 20.0 | 13.8 |
| Speech rate (phones/s) | | | | | | |
| Global | 13.7 | 14.2 | 3.3 | 14.8 | 14.9 | 1.9 |
| 1$^{st}$ turn | 14.3 | 14.5 | 4.1 | 14.8 | 14.5 | 2.8 |
| Help requests | | | | | | |
| # Requests | 0.27 | 0.00 | 0.55 | 0.00 | 0.00 | 0.00 |

values of 15 % and 10 % for novice and expert users, respectively, also support the hypothesis. Furthermore, only novice users have barge-in rates over 30 %. Information extracted from the first turn is not as discriminative, as around 60 % of the users barged-in on the first turn, independently of the class. However, the first system utterance is a fixed introduction, which encourages expert users to barge-in, in order to skip to important parts of the dialog.

On Let's Go 2014, the barge-in information was extracted from the interaction logs.

**Delays.** LEGO annotations include the duration of each user utterance, as well as the time when each exchange starts. However, each exchange starts with the system utterance, for which the duration is not annotated. Thus, we were not able to obtain delay information for most exchanges. The only exception was the first exchange, since the system utterance is fixed and, thus, so is its duration $-10.25$ s. In this case, we calculated the delay as the difference between the time when the user utterance starts and the time when the system utterance ends. As expected, the results presented in Table 1 suggest that novice users take longer to answer than expert users. Furthermore, when only positive delay values are taken into account, the discrepancy between the two classes is even more evident.

On the 2014 data, we used a similar approach to obtain the first turn delay. In this case, the duration of the first system utterance is 13.29 s. The remaining information required to calculate the delay was obtained from the interaction logs.

**Durations.** The LEGO corpus is annotated in terms of duration of user utterances, as well of the whole call. However, a few of the utterances are wrongly annotated. Nonetheless, we were able to compute the average user utterance duration per dialog. As expected, novice users tend to use longer utterances and are much less consistent than expert users. There are no expert users with average utterance durations over 3 s. In terms of the whole call, the same conclusions can be drawn, both in terms of time duration and number of exchanges, as novice users have higher values for all the measures. While most calls by expert users last less than 2 min, calls by novice users have a wider distribution. As for the duration of the first utterance, on average, novice users still use longer utterances. However, that is not true in terms of median value. Nonetheless, standard deviation for novice users is higher than the average value, which suggests that novice users adopt unpredictable behaviors.

We obtained duration information from 2014 data directly from the audio files, using SoX [1].

**Speech Rate.** We extracted the speech rate in phones per second from each user utterance of the LEGO corpus and used those values to calculate the average speech rate for each dialog. The phones for each utterance were obtained using the neural networks included in the AUDIMUS [12] ASR system. Table 1 shows similar average and median values for both classes, around 15 phones per second. However, expert users are more steady, which leaves the tails of the distribution for novice users only. Looking only at the first user utterance, average and median values are even closer for both classes. Nonetheless, the tails of the distribution are still reserved for novice users only, although the expert users are slightly less steady. The same extraction procedure was applied on 2014 data.

**Help Requests.** From the existing information, we were able to extract the number of help requests detected by the system during each LEGO dialog. As expected, only novice users asked for help, with an average of 0.27 help requests per dialog. 23 % of novice users asked for help at least once and up to 3 times. Furthermore, 17 % of the novice users asked for help on the first turn.

On the 2014 data, we obtained the number of help requests from the dialog transcriptions, by looking for the help keyword or the zero key on user utterances.

### 4.3  Classification

Distinguishing between novice and expert users is a binary classification task. From the multiple classification approaches that could be used, we opted Support

Vector Machine (SVMs) [3], since it is a widely used approach and typically produces acceptable results, and Random Forest (RF) [2], an approach based on decision trees, which are indicated for this task, given the distribution of our features among the two classes.

To train our SVMs, we took advantage of the Sequential Minimal Optimization (SMO) algorithm [14] implementation provided by the Weka Toolkit [6]. We used the linear kernel and kept the C parameter with its default 1.0 value.

We opted for an RF approach due to its improved performance when compared to a classic decision tree algorithm. We also used the implementation provided by the Weka Toolkit to train our RFs. We used 1000 as the number of generated trees, since it provided a good trade-off between training time and classification accuracy.

### 4.4   Evaluation

Since there is no standard partition of the LEGO corpus into training and testing sets, we obtained results using 10-fold cross-validation. Furthermore, we used the data from 2014 to assess the generalization capabilities of our classifiers.

In terms of measures, we use Accuracy and the Kappa Statistic since they are the most indicated measures to evaluate performance and relevance on this task. Accuracy is given by the ratio between the number of correct predictions and the total number of predictions. The Kappa Statistic gives the weighted agreement between the predictions of the classifier and the gold standard, in relation to those of a chance classifier.

## 5   Results

Since the LEGO dataset is highly unbalanced, we balanced it using the Spread Subsample filter provided by the Weka Toolkit. Still, we performed experiments on both the balanced and unbalanced data. Table 2 presents the results obtained using each set of features independently, as well as different combinations. The **First Turn** set combines the features extracted from the first turn only, while the **Global** set combines the features extracted from the whole dialog. The **All** set combines the two previous sets. The **Selected** set is obtained by applying the Best First feature selection algorithm, provided by the Weka Toolkit, to the **All** set.

The SVMs classification approach performed poorly on the unbalanced dataset, never surpassing a chance classifier. However, the RF approach achieved 80 % accuracy using the **Selected** feature set, which represents an improvement of 6 % points. Given the difficulty and subjectivity of the task, the Kappa coefficient of 0.40 should not be disregarded.

On the balanced dataset, both the SVM and RF approaches were able to surpass the chance classifier. Still, similarly to to what happened on the unbalanced dataset, the RF approach performed better. Using all the available features, it achieved 79 % accuracy, which represents an improvement of 8 % points over the

**Table 2.** Results on the unbalanced (Chance = 0.741) and balanced (Chance = 0.500) versions of the LEGO dataset

| | Unbalanced | | Balanced | | | |
|---|---|---|---|---|---|---|
| | Random forest | | SVM | | Random forest | |
| Feature set | Accuracy | $\kappa$ | Accuracy | $\kappa$ | Accuracy | $\kappa$ |
| Interruptions | 0.702 | 0.140 | 0.600 | 0.200 | 0.613 | 0.225 |
| Delays | 0.693 | 0.168 | 0.494 | −0.013 | 0.519 | 0.038 |
| Durations | 0.790 | **0.403** | 0.594 | 0.188 | 0.744 | 0.488 |
| Speech rate | 0.686 | 0.037 | 0.513 | 0.025 | 0.525 | 0.050 |
| Help requests | 0.741 | 0.000 | 0.631 | 0.263 | 0.600 | 0.200 |
| First turn | 0.767 | 0.321 | 0.594 | 0.188 | 0.713 | 0.425 |
| Global | 0.783 | 0.377 | 0.681 | 0.363 | 0.769 | 0.538 |
| All | 0.793 | 0.385 | **0.706** | **0.413** | **0.794** | **0.588** |
| Selected | **0.796** | **0.403** | **0.706** | **0.413** | 0.781 | 0.563 |

SVM counterpart and 29 % points over the chance classifier. The Kappa coefficient of 0.59 is 50 % higher than the one obtained for the unbalanced dataset, in spite of facing the same concerns. In this version of the dataset, feature selection did not improve the results.

The **First Turn** feature set is the most relevant for expertise level identification in real time. Using this set, an accuracy of 77 % was achieved on the unbalanced dataset, which represents an improvement of 3 % points over the chance classifier. On the balanced dataset, the RF approach was able to improve the results of a chance classifier by 21 % points and achieve a Kappa coefficient of 0.42. However, the SVM classifier performed poorly. Overall, this means that it is not easy to identify the level of expertise of a user based solely on the first turn of the dialog. Still, a preliminary classification can be obtained to start guiding the system towards user adaptation, and improved as the dialog flows.

In terms of the individual feature sets, duration related features are the most important for the RF approach on both versions of the dataset. On the balanced dataset, interruption and help related features also provide important information. For the SVM approach, the important features remain the same but the order of importance is inverted.

Table 3 presents the results obtained on Let's Go 2014 data by the classifiers trained on the balanced LEGO corpus. We do not show the rows related to feature categories that did not provide relevant results. We can see that, in this case, the SVM approach surpassed the RF one, achieving 66 % accuracy and a Kappa coefficient of 0.33, using the **Selected** feature set. This represents an improvement of 11 % points over the chance classifier. As for the RF approach, although its accuracy using the **Selected** feature set is just two percentage points below the SVM approach, its Kappa coefficient of 0.22 is much lower and is surpassed, although only slightly, by the 0.23 obtained by using only help related features. Overall, this means that the RF classifiers, which performed better on the LEGO corpus, have less generalization capabilities than the SVM ones. This explains the negative results obtained by the RF classifier using the **Global** feature set, as the differences between both datasets are more noticeable when looking at the dialogs as a whole than when just looking at first turns.

**Table 3.** Results on Let's Go 2014 data (Chance = 0.554)

| Feature set | SVM | | Random forest | |
|---|---|---|---|---|
| | Accuracy | $\kappa$ | Accuracy | $\kappa$ |
| Help requests | 0.607 | 0.268 | 0.589 | **0.232** |
| First turn | 0.571 | 0.207 | 0.538 | 0.082 |
| Global | 0.589 | 0.153 | 0.538 | −0.018 |
| All | 0.643 | 0.283 | 0.589 | 0.103 |
| Selected | **0.661** | **0.327** | **0.643** | 0.217 |

# 6 Conclusions

In this article we presented an approach for automatically distinguishing novice and expert users based on a specific set of task related features. Given the distributions of the features, a classification approach based on decision trees was indicated. This was confirmed when the RF approach outperformed the widely used SVMs on both versions of the LEGO corpus.

Since this is a relatively unexplored task and the dataset was not previously annotated for expertise, we cannot compare our results with other work. Nonetheless, we believe that the obtained results are positive, since our approach focused on identifying the level of expertise from a single session, without previous information about the user, which is a difficult task.

Furthermore, we were also able to obtain relevant results using features extracted only from the first turn of each dialog. This is important for a fast adaptation of the system to the user's level of expertise, as it provides a preliminary classification of that level, which can be improved as the dialog flows, through the accumulation of the results of all turns.

On the downside, the results obtained on the data from Let's Go 2014 were not as satisfactory, with the RF classifiers revealing less generalization capabilities than the SVM ones

In terms of future work, we believe that it would be important to obtain more annotated data, in order to train more reliable classifiers, with improved generalization capabilities.

**Acknowledgements.** This work was supported by national funds through Fundação para a Ciência e a Tecnologia (FCT) with reference UID/CEC/50021/2013, by Universidade de Lisboa, and by the EC H2020 project RAGE under grant agreement No 644187.

# References

1. SoX - Sound eXchange, version 14.4.1. http://sox.sourceforge.net/
2. Breiman, L.: Random Forests. Mach. Learn. **45**(1), 5–32 (2001)
3. Cortes, C., Vapnik, V.: Support-vector networks. In: Machine Learning, pp. 273–297 (1995)
4. Dreyfus, H.L., Dreyfus, S.E.: Mind Over Machine: The Power of Human Intuition and Expertise in the Era of the Computer. The Free Press, New York (1986)
5. Eyben, F., Weninger, F., Gross, F., Schuller, B.: Recent developments in openSMILE, the Munich open-source multimedia feature extractor. In: Proceedings of the 21st ACM International Conference on Multimedia, pp. 835–838 (2013)
6. Hall, M., Frank, E., Holmes, G., Pfahringer, B., Reutemann, P., Witten, I.H.: The WEKA data mining software: an update. SIGKDD Explor. Newsl. **11**(1), 10–18 (2009)
7. Hassel, L., Hagen, E.: Adaptation of an automotive dialogue system to users' expertise and evaluation of the system. Lang. Resour. Eval. **40**(1), 67–85 (2006)
8. Hjalmarsson, A.: Adaptive Spoken Dialogue Systems (2005). http://www.speech.kth.se/~rolf/NGSLT/gslt_papers_2004/annah_termpaper_05.pdf. Accessed 18 Dec 2015
9. Hjalmarsson, A.: Towards user modelling in conversational dialogue systems: a qualitative study of the dynamics of dialogue parameters. In: Proceedings of INTERSPEECH 2005, pp. 869–872 (2005)
10. Jokinen, K., Kanto, K.: User expertise modeling and adaptivity in a speech-based e-mail system. In: Proceedings of the 42nd Annual Meeting of the Association for Computational Linguistics, pp. 87–94 (2004)
11. Lopes, J., Chorianopoulou, A., Palogiannidi, E., Moniz, H., Abad, A., Louka, K., Iosif, E., Potamianos, A.: The SpeDial datasets: datasets for spoken dialogue system analytics. In: Proceedings of the 10th International Conference on Language Resources and Evaluation (LREC) (2016)
12. Meinedo, H., Viveiros, M., Neto, J.P.: Evaluation of a Live Broadcast News Subtitling System for Portuguese. In: Proceedings of INTERSPEECH 2008, pp. 508–511 (2008)
13. Nielsen, J.: Usability Engineering. Morgan Kaufmann Publishers Inc., San Francisco (1993)
14. Platt, J.: Fast training of support vector machines using sequential minimal optimization. In: Advances in Kernel Methods - Support Vector Learning. MIT Press (1998)
15. Raux, A., Bohus, D., Langner, B., Black, A.W., Eskenazi, M.: Doing research on a deployed spoken dialogue system: one year of Lets Go! experience. In: Proceedings of INTERSPEECH 2006, pp. 65–68 (2006)
16. Schmitt, A., Ultes, S., Minker, W.: A parameterized and annotated spoken dialog corpus of the CMU Let's Go bus information system. In: Proceedings of the 8th International Conference on Language Resources and Evaluation (LREC) (2012)

# Automatic Speech Feature Learning for Continuous Prediction of Customer Satisfaction in Contact Center Phone Calls

Carlos Segura[1]([✉]), Daniel Balcells[1,2], Martí Umbert[1,3],
Javier Arias[1], and Jordi Luque[1]

[1] Telefonica Research Edificio Telefonica-Diagonal 00, Barcelona, Spain
{carlos.seguraperales,jordi.luqueserrano}@telefonica.com
[2] Department Signal Theory and Communications,
Universitat Politècnica de Catalunya, Barcelona, Spain
[3] Music Technology Group, Universitat Pompeu Fabra, Barcelona, Spain

**Abstract.** Speech related processing tasks have been commonly tackled using engineered features, also known as hand-crafted descriptors. These features have usually been optimized along years by the research community that constantly seeks for the most meaningful, robust, and compact audio representations for the specific domain or task. In the last years, a great interest has arisen to develop architectures that are able to learn by themselves such features, thus by-passing the required engineering effort. In this work we explore the possibility to use Convolutional Neural Networks (CNN) directly on raw audio signals to automatically learn meaningful features. Additionally, we study how well do the learned features generalize for a different task. First, a CNN-based continuous conflict detector is trained on audios extracted from televised political debates in French. Then, while keeping previous learned features, we adapt the last layers of the network for targeting another concept by using completely unrelated data. Concretely, we predict self-reported customer satisfaction from call center conversations in Spanish. Reported results show that our proposed approach, using raw audio, obtains similar results than those of a CNN using classical Mel-scale filter banks. In addition, the learning transfer from the conflict detection task into satisfaction prediction shows a successful generalization of the learned features by the deep architecture.

**Keywords:** Feature learning · End-to-end learning · Convolutional neural networks · Conflict speech retrieval · Automatic tagging

## 1 Introduction

Nowadays, call centers are one of the most used customer interaction channels. Beyond the actual content of the call, nonverbal communication in speech can be perceived and interpreted from a social and psychological point of view. Such social constructions influence and shape our perception for contentedness and

A. Abad et al. (Eds.): IberSPEECH 2016, LNAI 10077, pp. 255–265, 2016.
DOI: 10.1007/978-3-319-49169-1_25

perceived levels of engagement and cooperation over the contact interaction. Automatic understanding and retrieval of a person's social phenomena from speech is of special interest in multiparty conversations. Conflict is recognized as one of the dimensions along which an interaction is perceived and assessed. Having appropriate technology for speech mining and information retrieval is a prior step for understanding customers needs, their expectations and thus for the improvement of the service. Therefore, automatic estimation of customer satisfaction based on the audio of a phone contact is clearly of interest for any business.

Most of the approaches for task classification involving audio signals usually rely on traditional features, such as spectral based ones, and use a decoupled approach which comprises mainly two steps. In the first step, features are extracted from the raw audio signal, e.g., front-end processing, and then employed as an input for a second step that carries out the model learning. Usually, such features are designed by hand and strongly depend on a high expertise both on the knowledge of the addressed problem and on the audio signal itself.

In recent years, a trend has arisen in different research fields that aims at building architectures capable of learning features directly from the raw input data. For instance, in computer vision novel feature learning techniques are applied directly on the raw pixel representations of images avoiding the signal parameterization or any other prior preprocessing [15]. Budnik *et al.* [3] report an extensive comparison of the performance of CNN based features with traditional engineered ones, as well as with combinations of them, in the framework of the TRECVid semantic indexing task.

In speech processing, several successful DNN-based systems for extracting frame-by-frame speech features have been presented [4,9]. Novel proposed features, usually extracted from DNN topologies, are reaching the same level of proficiency and success as those from the image or video processing fields. Nevertheless, there are few works that address the processing in one single step and most of them rely on classical spectral representations of the speech signal from which they compute DNN-based features. Some recent works aim to directly handle the raw audio data in one single step. Jaitly *et al.* [12] modeled speech sound waves using a Restricted Boltzmann machine (RBM) and reported better phoneme recognition performance than methods based on Mel cepstrum coefficients. In [1,18] the authors show that CNNs can model phone classes from the raw acoustic speech signal, reaching performance on par with other existing feature-based approaches. Previous work in [6,10] has inspired our approach for end-to-end learning of salient features suitable for conflict detection in dyadic conversations. Hoshen *et al.* [10] trained a system end-to-end rather than manually designing the robust feature extraction for the multichannel input, jointly optimizing a noise-robust front-end along with the context-dependent phone state DNN classifier.

Additional work has applied computational analysis to recorded call center conversations. Park and Gates [19] and Zweig *et al.* [24] proposed machine learning techniques using linguistics and prosodic features to predict customer satisfaction. Emotion detection has also captured the attention of researchers within the call center domain. We can find other examples given by Devillers *et al.* in [5] where they report results on detecting emotional states by using acoustic features; or in [22] detecting negative emotions in call center conversations and its suitability for inferring customer satisfaction.

In this paper we propose a feature learning approach based on Deep Convolutional Neural Networks (DCNN) for continuous prediction of satisfaction in contact center phone calls. The network is initially trained on debates from French TV shows [21] aiming to find out salient information in raw speech that correlates with conflict level over the conversation. Then feature transfer is assessed on completely unrelated data, that is, phone calls from several contact centers. It is done by adapting the parameters of the ending layers with few samples in order to simulate a real low-resourced scenario. We analyse more than 18 thousand phone conversations made to the call center of a major company in a Latin American country. All the calls were made in Spanish. The proposed system should not only specifically tackle the conditions present in telephone channel, but also be able to discover suitable and robust descriptors from the raw audio data which at the same time are meaningful and both domain and task agnostic.

## 2    End-to-End Learning

### 2.1    System Description

The CNN architecture that we used as a basis for all our experiments is depicted in Fig. 1. CNN have reported great success achieving traslation invariance in image recognition tasks [14,16]. In the same sense, our deep CNN-based feature learning architecture makes use of local filtering and feature pooling. It comprises a total of 6 layers: four convolutional layers with different amounts of filters and lengths (see Fig. 1 for layer sizing) alternating with decimation and max pooling layers. The decimation value is 8 for the first two convolutional layers and 4 for the third one. Average pooling is used at the output of the fourth convolutional layer.

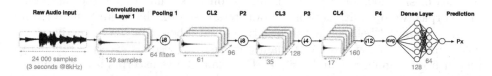

**Fig. 1.** The convolutional neural network architecture proposed. Filter sizes are in number of samples, and number of units are depicted in the scheme. Method and value for pooling layers using, decimation through max-pooling (↓) and averaging (avg) which compute some stats as the mean and standard deviation, are also reported. Training samples are randomly selected from 3 s excerpts from original raw data.

Let's assume the speech input to the CNN is a matrix, is $x$, whose columns are raw audio vectors $x = [x_n, x_{n+1} \ldots x_{n+N}]$ where $x_n$ is the audio sample vector shifted by a stride. In this work we used a value of 1 for time shifting and the $\boldsymbol{x_n}$ vectors range in size from 3 s to several minutes at 8,000 samples per second. The activations at the first convolutional layer comprise $J = 64$ filters and we denoted them as $\boldsymbol{h}_j = [h_1 \quad h_2 \cdots h_J]$. Therefore, the convolutional layer operation can be seen as a convolutional operation of each filter on the input raw audio,

$$h_j = \theta \left( \boldsymbol{w}_j \boldsymbol{x}^T + b_j \right),$$

where $\theta(x)$ is the activation function and $b_j$ the bias term for filter $h_j$. Note that it can be seen as a standard MLP network layer taking into account that filters are of the same size and input raw audio shifted accordingly. Successive convolutional filters are applied on two dimensions rather than only one as in the input layer. In addition to convolutional filters, max-pooling layers perform local temporal max operations over the input sequence, selecting the maximum in a window of decimation $d$ size, as ($\downarrow d$) in Fig. 1. More formally, the transformation at starting sample vector $n$, $\boldsymbol{c}_n^j$, corresponding to the filter output sequence of the first convolutional layer and $j$th filter is:

$$\max_{n-\frac{(d-1)}{2} \leq s \leq n+\frac{(d-1)}{2}} \boldsymbol{c}_s^j$$

Next, the average pooling output, see Fig. 1 at the CL4 output feeds two dense layers. Latter pooling stage compacts even more the original signal by computing some stats such as maximum, mean and variance from the CNN architecture output. The dense layer is employed as a back-end for the modeling of the salient features computed by previous convolutional steps. It comprises an input layer of 128 and an output one with 64 neuron units, respectively. In the first two convolutional layers no activation function $\theta$ is used, the subsampling/stride of the convolution being the only non-linearity. At the third and fourth layers, rectified linear units along with max-pooling are applied. Finally, both dense layers use maxout [8] as activation function and a dropout value of 0.5.

The network is trained using stochastic gradient descent (SGD) with mini batches of size 200. In the case of regression task, that is, for the $SC^2$ conflict corpus, we optimize network parameters based on the Mean Square Error (MSE) computed between network outputs and labels. We have experimented with different window sizes, but mainly we select $t$ seconds excerpts randomly picked from original raw audio signal. For example, 3 s excerpts lead to sample instances that amount for 24 thousand raw audio samples at 8 kHz sampling rate. Note that conflict scores are given for each 30 s excerpt within the $SC^2$ corpus (see Sect. 3.1) and thus our sampling procedure may extract training instances that are non-relevant regions within the 30 s excerpts, like silences or other non-speech related content such as background music. Nevertheless, we assume that the effect of training the network by using some of those 3 s "noisy" instances is mitigated by the mini batch size, the slice context and the number of epochs employed for the network training. Note that in the case of call center phone calls, audio recordings are stereo and at 8 kHz sampling rate, so we decided to downsample original $SC^2$ corpus to meet telephone channel bandwidth. This aims at mitigating sampling rate effects on the training and feature transferring between both systems. We also applied a simple speech detection algorithm based on energies for discarding likely non-speech samples.

## 2.2 Filter Learning and Spectogram Based Features

Figure 2 represents the normalized magnitude spectra taken from the first convolutional layer CL1 (see the Fig. 1). Filters of length 128 samples are sorted by the frequency bin containing the peak response.

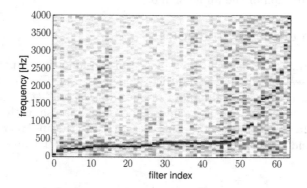

**Fig. 2.** Normalized magnitude spectra of the filters in the first convolutional layer CL1, see Fig. 1, ordered by frequency bin containing the peak response (black pixels).

It is worth to note that the filters response is almost linear in the range $[0, 1000]$ Hz, which concentrates almost 80 % of the convolutional filters. From this point on, normalized magnitude behaves more like a logarithm function, until it reaches 4 kHz frequency, after which filter peaks are more widely spaced. Similar filter bank responses are reported in previous works [6,10].

In order to compare previous end-to-end feature learning systems, we consider a second approach, that is, classical spectrogram "images" as the network input. To do so, we try to maintain the same network architecture and parameters, freezing the number of layers and units in each of them and the learned parameters, in order to have fair comparisons between both systems. The input to the network consists of the output of 128 MEL-scale log filter banks energies. Therefore, the convolution is only performed in the time dimension using filters of 5x128 coefficients at the first layer CL1, 5x1, 4x1 and 4x1 in the following CL layers. Latter average-pooling step and dense layers match the configuration used within the raw-audio based system.

## 2.3 Feature Transfer

Once network parameters are trained through the SSPNet Conflict Corpus ($SC^2$), we make use of the same network parameters as initialization but only for those in the dense layers. We are interested in adapting the network to a different task, as predicting self-reported customer satisfaction, but also in assessing the suitability of the filter banks learned in the convolutional steps. Therefore, we decide to keep frozen the parameters from all convolutional layers, that are more focus on the signal representation, at the same time we perform stochastic gradient descent (SGD) only on the parameters within the dense layers. The key idea is to avoid retrain the whole system from scratch, incorporating previous learning parameters as initialization values for the new network training and performing SGD with a small learning rate and lesser number of epochs. Thus speeding up the network training since we do not need to discover again a new feature representation of the audio signal.

## 3    Experimental Evaluation

Two different data sets have been employed in the following experiments. The former comprises a collection of political debates, from TV shows in French, manually labelled from several annotators in terms of conflict scoring. The second is a collection of phone call conversations in Spanish with self-reported customer satisfaction from several contact centers in a Latin American country. Experiments and simulations have been carried out using Theano library [2].

### 3.1    Corpus

The SSPNet Conflict Corpus ($SC^2$) was collected in the framework of the Social Signal Processing Network (SSPNet), the European Network of Excellence on modelling, analysis and synthesis of non-verbal communication in social interactions [23]. $SC^2$ corpus was used in the conflict challenge organized in the frame of the Interspeech 2013 computational paralinguistic challenge [13]. It contains 1,430 clips of 30 s extracted from a collection of 45 Swiss political debates (in French), 138 subjects in total (23 females and 133 males). The clips have been annotated in terms of conflict level by roughly 550 assessors, recruited via Amazon Mechanical Turk, and assigned a continuous conflict score in the range $[-10, +10]$. The binary classification task is created based on these labels, namely to classify into high ($\geq 0$) or low ($< 0$) level of conflict. The metrics used in the Conflict detection challenge were Unweighted Average Recall (UAR) and Correlation Coefficient (CC) that we also report in this work.

The call center data is composed of 19,360 inbound phone calls [17]. It represents a random subset of calls extracted from contact centers in one Latin American country. All the calls were made in Spanish. Data was collected throughout one month such that it comprises a huge variety of interactions between the customer and the call center's agent and different client's requests. At the end of each call, the customer is called back and gently asked to complete a survey related to the service:

*According to its previous call to our call center, how satisfied, overall, are you with the telephone service of X. Press 1–5 where 1 is very dissatisfied and 5 very satisfied.*

The Table 1 reports the distribution of customer satisfaction in our data set. Note that the distribution is significantly skewed towards 5 (64 %). Calls with low level of satisfaction, 1 and 2, are approximately 17 % of the data. For this data set, a binary classification task is created based on these labels, namely to classify into high satisfaction ($\geq 4$) or low satisfaction ($\leq 2$) level of satisfaction.

**Table 1.** Distribution of the self-reported satisfaction score in the call center data set.

|  | Self-reported customer satisfaction | | | | |
| --- | --- | --- | --- | --- | --- |
|  | 1 | 2 | 3 | 4 | 5 |
| Number of calls | 2651 | 648 | 1229 | 2412 | 12420 |

## 3.2 SSPNet Conflict Challenge

The baseline system provided by the organizers in the Conflict Sub-challenge, based on support vector regression, reached a remarkable performance around 80.8 % UAR on test conditions [21] for the binary classification task. Previous result was overcome by the conflict sub-challenge winner [20], using random K-nearest neighbors and reaching 82.6 % of accuracy and further improved at following reported works [11]. Latter paper reported 84.9 % accuracy based on an ensemble Nyström method for high-dimensional prediction of conflict. It aimed to model a set of $6,373$ features, comprising a variety of low-level descriptors and functionals, extracted per conversation basis using OpenSmile [7]. For further details, see the Table 2 in [11].

The Table 2 reports the results obtained with the proposed systems, raw-audio-based and spectrogram-based CNNs, in terms of the metrics initially proposed in the SSPNet challenge: Unweighted Average Recall (UAR) and Correlation Coefficient (CC). The estimation of the conflict level in each test audio file is performed running the trained network using windows of 3 s with an overlap of 50 % yielding to a time series of 19 conflict values. Finally, those conflict values are averaged to get the final score. The table shows that both systems perform similarly in the two conflict tasks, regression and classification, and that both are comparable to the baseline in the third row. It is worth to mention that we have

**Table 2.** Results on SSPNet conflict test database in terms of Unweighted Average Recall (UAR) and Correlation Coefficient (CC).

|  | CC | UAR |
| --- | --- | --- |
| Spectrogram CNN | 0.793 | 0.784 |
| Raw-audio CNN | 0.779 | 0.798 |
| SVR SMO [21] | 0.826 | 0.808 |
| Ensemble SPLS Nyström [11] | 0.849 | - |

not exhaustively tuned our CNN architecture to optimize CC and UAR metrics and that the original signal is downsampled from 48 kHz down to 8 kHz prior any further processing. The main conclusions from the table are (1) our end-to-end learning scheme is able to discover salient features directly from raw audio, (2) it performs comparable to reported systems based on traditional hand-crafted features and (3) there is no significant difference between using raw audio or Mel-like showing the ability of CNNs to learn from raw audio.

The main difference between the methods is the computational cost of the front-end. In the training phase of the spectrogram-based approach, the features are precomputed once to speed up the process. On the other hand, the raw-audio based front-end has more computational cost because it must run at each iteration, since it is trained jointly with the classifier in the CNN. However, in the testing phase, we see a speed increase of 1.64x in the case of the raw-audio approach due to the fact that it runs entirely on the GPU, while the spectrogram extraction step is computed in the CPU in our setup.

### 3.3   Feature Transfer and Satisfaction Prediction

The original $SC^2$ corpus is downsampled since one of the main purposes of this work is to validate that our learned features generalize to the task of estimating self-reported customer satisfaction, thus ensuring that the learned features can be applied to telephone channel conditions. Moreover, working with signals at 8 kHz also makes it easier to train the CNN with raw audio input. The proposed raw-audio CNN system is applied on the task of predicting the customer satisfaction from call center conversations. The main difference with respect to the SSPNet Conflict detection task is that the network will be trained for a binary classification problem using a logistic regression loss function. The training recordings consist of 200 conversations, with a balanced number of low and high satisfaction. Only the second half of the phone call is used for training the CNN. To assess the performance on held-out data, a balanced testing subset of 1000 conversations is prepared. In addition, aiming to study the effects on the duration of the analyzed time, we focus our analysis on the ending part of the phone call conversation.

Table 3 compares the performance in terms of AUC for the two considered approaches. In the first configuration, the network is trained from scratch using random weights initialization. In the second one, learned parameters from the whole $SC^2$ corpus are used as starting point, but only the weights of the dense layers are adapted to the new task. In this transfer learning step, a small learning rate is used along with less training epochs. Concretely, for training the network from scratch a learning rate of 0.002 and 1900 epochs are considered, whilst for the network adaptation a learning rate of 0.0002 and 900 epochs have been tested. Since the network provides a continuous satisfaction value for each time window, different functions are compared to aggregate those values and provide a single satisfaction score for the whole conversation.

The results reported in Table 2 show that the aggregation based on the median value of the satisfaction estimates reaches the best performance,

**Table 3.** Comparison of the performance of the continuous satisfaction estimation in terms of AUC metric using random weights initialization and using the weights learned from the SSPNet conflict data.

|  | Max | Min | Mean | Median |
|---|---|---|---|---|
| Random initialization | 0.56 | 0.553 | 0.585 | 0.600 |
| Transfer learning | 0.537 | 0.540 | 0.567 | 0.584 |

obtaining 0.60 AUC for the random initialization configuration and 0.584 AUC for the adapted network respectively. Table 4 details the performance of both networks on the satisfaction testing subset considering different audio segment duration and for the median aggregation. Results indicate that both systems obtain the best performance using as much data as possible, 4 minutes of each conversation, followed by the scores obtained considering only the last 30 s of the conversations. It is worth to note that the end-to-end system trained with no prior knowledge, *Random Initialization*, outperforms the proposed feature transfer system. Nevertheless, in both cases, learned filters by the convolutional layers are useful again even in a harder task as detecting satisfaction relying on self-reported labels per the whole conversation.

**Table 4.** Comparison of AUC scores for the raw-audio CNN systems tested only on the last 30, 60, 120 and 240 s of every call.

|  | 30 s | 60 s | 120 s | 240 s |
|---|---|---|---|---|
| Random initialization | 0.552 | 0.534 | 0.550 | 0.600 |
| Transfer learning | 0.520 | 0.516 | 0.542 | 0.584 |

## 4  Conclusions

The major contributions of our work are in the novel CNN architecture presented for extracting salient information directly from raw audio, together with the validation of such descriptors in a call center data set. Results reported on the SSPNet challenge data show that the proposed end-to-end architecture is able to learn features directly from structures in the time domain and having comparable results than those using classical Mel filter bank energies. Rather than that we show that the CNN based system performs comparable to the systems based on traditional hand-designed features and that the learned features are informative for the estimation of self-reported satisfaction.

**Acknowledgements.** We would like to thank the AVA innovation team members, among them, Roberto González and Nuria Oliver for interesting review. This project has received funding from the EU's Horizon 2020 research and innovation programme under grant agreement No. 645323. This text reflects only the author's view and the Commission is not responsible for any use that may be made of the information it contains.

# References

1. Abdel-Hamid, O., Mohamed, A.R., Jiang, H., Penn, G.: Applying convolutional neural networks concepts to hybrid NN-HMM model for speech recognition. In: 2012 IEEE International Conference on Acoustics, Speech and Signal Processing (ICASSP), pp. 4277–4280, March 2012
2. Bergstra, J., et al.: Theano: a CPU and GPU math expression compiler. In: Proceedings of the Python for Scientific Computing Conference (SciPy), Austin, TX, vol. 4, p. 3 (2010)
3. Budnik, M., Gutierrez-Gomez, E.L., Safadi, B., Quénot, G.: Learned features versus engineered features for semantic video indexing. In: 2015 13th International Workshop on Content-Based Multimedia Indexing (CBMI), pp. 1–6, June 2015
4. Deng, L., Li, J., et al.: Recent advances in deep learning for speech research at Microsoft. In: 2013 IEEE International Conference on Acoustics, Speech and Signal Processing (ICASSP), pp. 8604–8608. IEEE (2013)
5. Devillers, L., Vaudable, C., Chastagnol, C.: Real-life emotion-related states detection in call centers: a cross-corpora study. In: Eleventh Annual Conference of the International Speech Communication Association, vol. 10, pp. 2350–2353 (2010)
6. Dieleman, S., Schrauwen, B.: End-to-end learning for music audio. In: 2014 IEEE International Conference on Acoustics, Speech and Signal Processing (ICASSP), pp. 6964–6968, May 2014
7. Eyben, F., Wollmer, M., Schuller, B.: OpenEAR - introducing the Munich open-source emotion and affect recognition toolkit. In: 3rd International Conference on Affective Computing and Intelligent Interaction and Workshops, ACII 2009, pp. 1–6 (2009)
8. Goodfellow, I.J., Warde-Farley, D., Mirza, M., Courville, A.C., Bengio, Y.: Maxout networks. Int. Conf. Mach. Learn. (ICML) **28**, 1319–1327 (2013)
9. Hinton, G., et al.: Deep neural networks for acoustic modeling in speech recognition: the shared views of four research groups. IEEE Sig. Process. Mag. **29**(6), 82–97 (2012)
10. Hoshen, Y., Weiss, R.J., Wilson, K.W.: Speech acoustic modeling from raw multichannel waveforms. In: 2015 IEEE International Conference on Acoustics, Speech and Signal Processing (ICASSP), pp. 4624–4628. IEEE (2015)
11. Huang, D.Y., Li, H., Dong, M.: Ensemble Nyström method for predicting conflict level from speech. In: Signal and Information Processing Association Annual Summit and Conference (APSIPA), 2014 Asia-Pacific, pp. 1–5, December 2014
12. Jaitly, N., Hinton, G.: Learning a better representation of speech soundwaves using restricted Boltzmann machines. In: 2011 IEEE International Conference on Acoustics, Speech and Signal Processing (ICASSP), pp. 5884–5887. IEEE (2011)
13. Kim, S., Filippone, M., Valente, F., Vinciarelli, A.: Predicting the conflict level in television political debates: an approach based on crowdsourcing, nonverbal communication and Gaussian processes. In: Proceedings of the 20th ACM International Conference on Multimedia, pp. 793–796. ACM (2012)
14. Krizhevsky, A., Sutskever, I., Hinton, G.E.: Imagenet classification with deep convolutional neural networks. In: Advances in Neural Information Processing Systems, pp. 1097–1105 (2012)
15. Le, Q.V.: Building high-level features using large scale unsupervised learning. In: 2013 IEEE International Conference on Acoustics, Speech and Signal Processing (ICASSP), pp. 8595–8598, May 2013

16. LeCun, Y., Bengio, Y.: Convolutional networks for images, speech, and time series. Handb. Brain Theor. Neural Netw. **3361**(10) (1995)
17. Llimona, Q., Luque, J., Anguera, X., Hidalgo, Z., Park, S., Oliver, N.: Effect of gender and call duration on customer satisfaction in call center big data. In: Proceedings of 16th Annual Conference of the International Speech Communication Association, INTERSPEECH 2015, Dresden, Germany, 6–10 September (2015)
18. Palaz, D., Magimai-Doss, M., Collobert, R.: Convolutional neural networks-based continuous speech recognition using raw speech signal. In: 2015 IEEE International Conference on Acoustics, Speech and Signal Processing (ICASSP), pp. 4295–4299, April 2015
19. Park, Y., Gates, S.C.: Towards real-time measurement of customer satisfaction using automatically generated call transcripts. In: Proceedings of the 18th ACM Conference on Information and Knowledge Management, pp. 1387–1396. ACM (2009)
20. Räsänen, O., Pohjalainen, J.: Random subset feature selection in automatic recognition of developmental disorders, affective states, and level of conflict from speech. In: INTERSPEECH, pp. 210–214 (2013)
21. Schuller, B., et al.: The INTERSPEECH 2013 Computational Paralinguistics Challenge: Social Signals, Conflict, Emotion, Autism
22. Vaudable, C., Devillers, L.: Negative emotions detection as an indicator of dialogs quality in call centers. In: 2012 IEEE International Conference on Acoustics, Speech and Signal Processing (ICASSP), pp. 5109–5112. IEEE (2012)
23. Vinciarelli, A., Kim, S., Valente, F., Salamin, H.: Collecting data for socially intelligent surveillance and monitoring approaches: the case of conflict in competitive conversations. In: 2012 5th International Symposium on Communications Control and Signal Processing (ISCCSP), pp. 1–4, May 2012
24. Zweig, G., Siohan, O., Saon, G., Ramabhadran, B., Povey, D., Mangu, L., Kingsbury, B.: Automated quality monitoring for call centers using speech and NLP technologies. In: Proceedings of the 2006 Conference of the North American Chapter of the Association for Computational Linguistics on Human Language Technology: Companion Volume: Demonstrations, pp. 292–295. Association for Computational Linguistics (2006)

# Reversible Speech De-identification Using Parametric Transformations and Watermarking

Aitor Valdivielso[1], Daniel Erro[1,2(✉)], and Inma Hernaez[1]

[1] Aholab, University of the Basque Country (UPV/EHU), Bilbao, Spain
derro@aholab.ehu.es
[2] IKERBASQUE, Basque Foundation for Science, Bilbao, Spain

**Abstract.** This paper presents a system capable of de-identifying speech signals in order to hide and protect the identity of the speaker. It applies a relatively simple yet effective transformation of the pitch and the frequency axis of the spectral envelope thanks to a flexible wideband harmonic model. Moreover, it inserts the parameters of the transformation in the signal by means of watermarking techniques, thus enabling re-identification. Our experiments show that for adequate modification factors its performance is satisfactory in terms of quality, de-identification degree and naturalness. The limitations due to the signal processing framework are discussed as well.

## 1 Introduction

The exponential growth of the amount of multimedia data generated and shared over public networks everyday is increasing the interest in privacy protection issues [1]. In the particular case of speech, there is a wide variety of situations where it is convenient to hide the identity of the speaker: recordings from protected witnesses, phone calls recorded by companies, fair hiring processes with no discrimination by gender or age, medical recordings for diagnosis and rehabilitation, etc.

Previous works have tackled the de-identification problem using voice conversion technologies [2,3] or a recognition + synthesis approach [4]. However, no special care has been taken regarding the reversibility of the de-identification process, thus posing difficulties to a possible re-identification step. In more recent works, reversible voice transformation functions[1] based on frequency warping have been suggested [5,6]. Apart from showing the good performance of this type of functions, these studies have revealed the importance of the distortions due to the signal processing framework.

This work presents a speech de-identification method with the following characteristics. First, it applies a basic parametric voice transformation framework based on a wideband harmonic model and frequency warping and pitch scaling operations. This means the transformation can be expressed in terms of just two

---

[1] Voice conversion can be seen as a particular case of voice transformation where there is a specific target speaker.

© Springer International Publishing AG 2016
A. Abad et al. (Eds.): IberSPEECH 2016, LNAI 10077, pp. 266–275, 2016.
DOI: 10.1007/978-3-319-49169-1_26

floating-point factors. It also uses digital watermarking techniques to include the transformation parameters in the signal itself, thus facilitating re-identification. Experimental validation shows the effectiveness of this relatively simple approach.

The contents of the paper are the following: Sect. 2 describes the signal processing framework, namely the wideband harmonic model and its modification procedures; Sect. 3 describes the watermarking technique applied; Sect. 4 is devoted to the assessment of the different parts of the system; finally, conclusions and future works are listed in Sect. 5.

## 2    Signal Processing Framework

Among all possible signal models available in the literature, we have chosen a full-band harmonic model for the following reasons: (i) for an adequate $f_0$, it can model unvoiced frames as well as voiced frames; (ii) it is computationally less expensive than hybrid [7] or adaptive models [8]; (iii) it provides a solid and consistent framework for transformation, avoiding the need of transforming and combining different streams [9]. The harmonic model describes locally stationary signal segments as:

$$h[n] = \sum_{l=1}^{L} A_l \cos\left(l\omega_0 n + \phi_l\right) \tag{1}$$

where $\omega_0 = 2\pi f_0 / f_s$, $f_s$ is the sampling frequency, $L = \lceil \pi/\omega_0 \rceil - 1$ is the number of harmonics within the analysis bandwidth, and $A_l$ and $\phi_l$ are the amplitude and phase of the $l$th harmonic. In pitch-asynchronous approaches, phases can be decomposed into a linear term and a dispersion term [7]:

$$\phi_l = l\gamma + \theta_l, \quad 1 \le l \le L \tag{2}$$

The linear term $\gamma$ controls the "delay" of the waveform pulse onset with respect to the analysis/synthesis instant, and the terms $\{\theta_l\}$ determine the pulse shape.

### 2.1    Analysis

First, a pitch detection algorithm [10] is used to extract the $f_0$ value at every frame. Then, amplitudes and phases are calculated within short intervals:

$$\{A_l, \phi_l\}_{l=1...L} = \arg\min \sum_n w[n]^2 \left(s[n + n_a] - h[n]\right)^2 \tag{3}$$

where $w[n]$ is the analysis window (typically containing two signal periods) and $n_a$ is the analysis instant. In unvoiced frames we assume a fictitious $f_0$ of 100 Hz. This minimization is carried out by means of a least squares approach, as described in [9]. Then, phases are decomposed into the two terms mentioned in Eq. (2) according to the following criterion [7]:

$$\gamma = \arg\max \sum_{l=1}^{L} A_l \cos(\phi_l - l\gamma), \quad \theta_l = \phi_l - l\gamma \; \forall l \tag{4}$$

## 2.2  Modification

To perform modifications, we assume a simple signal model where a locally periodic impulse-like excitation (spectrally flat) passes through a filter that conveys the spectral information of speech. Thus, amplitudes and phases can be seen as uniformly-spaced discrete samples of the response of the filter. We suggest two basic modifications: (i) modifying the periodicity of the excitation and (ii) modifying the vocal tract length by manipulating the frequency scale of the filter, which is known as frequency warping). To implement both of them, we first need a strategy to recover the amplitude and phase response of the filter (henceforth named amplitude and phase envelopes) from their discrete samples. We follow the procedures in [7], based on linear interpolation:

$$
\begin{aligned}
A(\omega) &= \exp\left(\log A_l + (\log A_{l+1} - \log A_l)\frac{\omega - l\omega_0}{\omega_0}\right) \\
\theta(\omega) &= \arg\left(A_l e^{j\theta_l} + (A_{l+1}e^{j\theta_{l+1}} - A_l e^{j\theta_l})\frac{\omega - l\omega_0}{\omega_0}\right)
\end{aligned}
\quad,\quad l = \left\lfloor \frac{\omega}{\omega_0} \right\rfloor
\tag{5}
$$

For a complete definition of these envelopes, we assume $A_0 = A_1$, $A_{L+1} = A_L$, $\theta_0 = \theta_1$ and $\theta_{L+1} = \theta_L$. We now define $\lambda$ and $\alpha$ as the $f_0$ modification factor and the frequency warping factor, respectively. We assume the following frequency warping curve, which is frequently used in speech processing [11] (see Fig. 1):

$$
\text{warp}_\alpha(\omega) = \tan^{-1}\frac{(1-\alpha)^2 \sin\omega}{(1+\alpha)^2 \cos\omega - 2\alpha}
\tag{6}
$$

Positive values of $\alpha$ push spectral envelopes towards the Nyquist frequency (male-to-female) whereas negative ones push them towards zero (female-to-male). This warping function is reversible and it fulfills $\text{warp}_\alpha^{-1}(\omega) = \text{warp}_{-\alpha}(\omega)$. The amplitudes and phases of the modified signal are obtained by resampling the frequency-warped envelopes at multiples of the new fundamental frequency $\omega_0' = \lambda\omega_0$:

$$
\begin{aligned}
A_l' &= A\left(\text{warp}_{-\alpha}(l\omega_0')\right) \\
\phi_l' &= \theta\left(\text{warp}_{-\alpha}(l\omega_0')\right) + l\gamma'
\end{aligned}
\quad 1 \le l \le L'
\tag{7}
$$

where $L' = \lceil \pi/\omega_0' \rceil - 1$ and $\gamma'$ is adjusted in accordance with the new periodicity through the following recursion, in which $k$ denotes the frame index and $N$ denotes the frame shift (measured in samples):

$$
\gamma'^{(k)} = \gamma'^{(k-1)} + \lambda\left(\gamma^{(k)} - \gamma^{(k-1)} + 2\pi M\right)
$$

$$
M = \text{round}\left\{\frac{1}{2\pi}\left(\gamma^{(k-1)} + N\frac{\omega_0^{(k-1)} + \omega_0^{(k)}}{2} - \gamma^{(k)}\right)\right\}
\tag{8}
$$

In unvoiced frames, only the warping transform is applied, while the fictitious $f_0$ is kept unmodified. It is worth remarking that to recover the original signal from its modified version, the system should re-modify it by factors $1/\lambda$ and $-\alpha$.

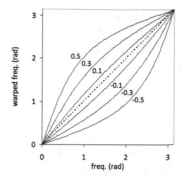

**Fig. 1.** Frequency warping curve given by Eq. (6) for different values of $\alpha$.

## 2.3  Synthesis

Waveforms are generated by means of the overlap-add technique using constant-length triangular windows with 50 % overlapping:

$$\hat{s}[n + kN] = \left(\frac{N - n}{N}\right) h'^{(k)}[n] + \left(\frac{n}{N}\right) h'^{(k+1)}[n - N], \quad 0 \leq n < N, \quad \forall k \quad (9)$$

where the contribution of each frame, $h'[n]$ (we now omit the frame index for clarity), is built from $\omega'_0$ and $\{A'_l, \phi'_l\}_{l=1...L'}$ similarly as in Eq. (1).

## 3  Watermarking

Watermarking is the process of inserting digital information inside a carrier signal in such a way that this information remains imperceptible for the user. In the particular case of speech signals, several watermarking methods have been proposed [12], which exploit signal characteristics such as spread spectrum [13], echoes [14], relative phase information [15], etc.

In this work we investigate an enhanced version of the intermediate significant bit (ISB) technique originally proposed in [16]. The watermark is hidden on the original signal interpreting it as a data stream rather than a waveform: instead of varying higher-level attributes such as amplitudes, phases, frequencies, etc., the message is encoded into an intermediate bit of the PCM samples of the signal. There is a trade-off between robustness and integrity of the signal: when the least significant bit (LSB) is used, the hidden information can be easily corrupted by noise or by the use of lossy compression formats, whereas for bits with higher significance the probability that signal alterations are perceived by the user increases. To enhance the performance of the system, we have taken two precautions:

– The watermark has been protected by means of an (11,7) Hamming code [17] (4 additional backup bits per every 7 bits of information), which enables reparation if one of these bits is erroneous, thus increasing the robustness against noise.

– Instead of inserting the watermark at the beginning of the signal, we search for the optimal watermark insertion point, defined as the segment which would require the lowest amount of bit toggles with respect to the original signal. Insertion points within segments at low-quantization levels (silences, etc.) are penalized.

Figure 2 illustrates the superiority of the enhanced watermark insertion method over random insertion in terms of bit error rate (BER). Thus, a watermark containing the values of the de-identification parameters $\alpha$ and $\lambda$ is inserted via biwise logical XOR, and its location and length are stored as metatada together with an encrypted password which is necessary to recover the hidden information.

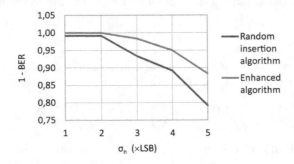

**Fig. 2.** Performance degradation at different levels of noise when a 120-bit watermark is inserted at the 7th ISB. $\sigma_n$: standard deviation of noise (mean $= 0$), measured in number of times the LSB.

## 4    Experiments and Discussion

Except where otherwise specified, the materials used in our experiments were taken from a database containing 10 short sentences, each recorded by 10 different non-professional speakers (5 male, 5 female). All recordings were made in a quiet room, and the signals were digitized at 16 kHz sampling frequency and 16 bits/sample. All the voices were used to compute objective measures. For subjective measures, we selected 2 voices per gender, specifically those who exhibited the highest contrast in terms of average pitch. These voices are referred to as M1, M2, F1 and F2.

For a more manageable experimental framework, we designed the system to be gender-dependent. To do this, we implemented a very simple gender detector based on $f_0$. More specifically, we established an empirical mean $f_0$ threshold equal to 154 Hz: for voices exhibiting a higher mean $f_0$, we applied modifications with $\alpha < 0$ and $\lambda < 1$ (as corresponds to female-to-male transformations); for lower mean $f_0$, $\alpha > 0$ and $\lambda > 1$ (as corresponds to male-to-female transformations). Informal listenings confirmed that the opposite modifications make modified speech more unnatural in most of the cases.

## 4.1   Validation of the Signal Processing Framework

To quantify the degradation produced by watermarking, we computed two types of objective measures: peak signal-to-noise ratio (PSNR) and PESQ[2] (ITU-T P.862) [18]. Average results are shown in Fig. 3 for a variable watermark length and for different ISBs. Both measures show that the length is not critical, at least for the typical values considered in this study, while the chosen bit insertion level has a clear impact on the signal. Nevertheless, for ISBs between 1 (noise-free scenario) and 7 (moderate additive noise) the PESQ scores remain close to the maximum (which means the watermark is imperceptible).

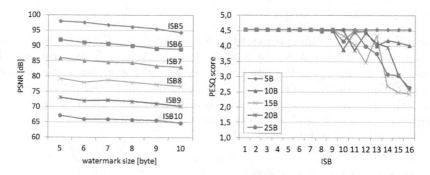

**Fig. 3.** Impact of watermark insertion for different ISB layers and watermark sizes in terms of PSNR (left) and PESQ score (right) for utterances of approximate length 5 s.

Another source of distortion is the harmonic model itself. For the voices under study, we compared the original signals with their harmonic resynthesis (without modification) and we observed PESQ scores between 3.7 and 4.2. However, in the target application it is more important to quantify the effect of the whole signal processing chain: harmonic modeling + modification + resynthesis + harmonic modeling of the de-identified signal + inverse modification + resynthesis. PESQ is not adequate for measuring the resulting distortions because it penalizes waveform differences even if they do not alter the perceptual quality. Therefore, we conducted a perceptual test in which 10 listeners were asked to rate on a 1–5 scale the quality of the re-identified signals in comparison with the harmonic resynthesis of the original ones. We considered several combinations of factors: $\alpha = \{0.05, 0.10, 0.15\}$ and $\lambda = \{1.2, 1.6, 2.0\}$ for male voices, and the opposite/inverse values for female voices. The test was carried out by means of a web interface and the evaluators were asked to use headphones. The results are shown in Fig. 4. Overall, we can observe that the quality mean opinion scores (MOSs) are high (close to 4) for most factor combinations. However, it is interesting to observe that deeper $\lambda$ modifications seem to degrade the quality of the

---

[2] PESQ predicts the mean opinion score of a distorted signal in comparison with its original clean version.

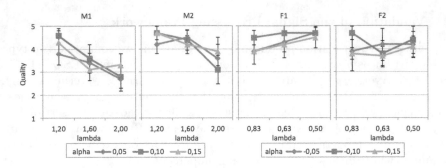

**Fig. 4.** Quality MOS at 95 % confidence intervals for different voices and factors.

re-identified signals for male voices while for female voices the trend is opposite. The reason is that when $\lambda > 1$, as happens for male voices, $f_0$ increases and the number of harmonics, i.e. the number of samples of the underlying envelopes, decreases. This reduction of the frequency resolution cannot be compensated just by applying the inverse transform. This is a limitation of the signal processing framework (in fact, it applies to any other speech model we could use) which should be addressed in future studies.

### 4.2   Degree of De-identification

De-identification is interesting not only from the point of view of human listeners but also of machines. We conducted two experiments. The first one was a listening test similar to the previous one in which 21 volunteers rated, on a 1–5 scale, the similarity between the original voice and the de-identified one and the naturalness of the latter (how "human" it sounds). The results are shown in Fig. 5. We can observe that for most of the considered factor combinations the de-identification is successful (MOS < 3). As for naturalness, in general it is moderately high (MOS > 3) for $\alpha \leq 0.1$, and there seems to be a logical relationship between $\alpha$ and $\lambda$: a deeper frequency warping should be accompanied by a deeper $f_0$ modification for a more natural output. Overall, a good performance balance can be expected for $\alpha$ near $\pm 0.1$ (possibly slightly lower) and $\lambda$ near $1.6^{\pm 1}$.

Our second experiment aimed at assessing the performance of the system when judged by a machine. We used the trial version of a commercial speaker identification system called Phonexia [19], which is based on state-of-the-art technologies (it builds voiceprints using Gaussian mixture models and iVectors [20]). Given the training requirements of the system, we used a different database for evaluation, namely Eustace [21], which contains recordings from 6 different speakers (3 male, 3 female). We used 31 utterances per speaker for training (enrollment) and another long utterance for evaluation. Figure 6 shows the scores (between 0 and 100 %) returned by Phonexia. We can see that in this case $\lambda$ is much less relevant than $\alpha$ and for $|\alpha| > 0.05$ the system was never

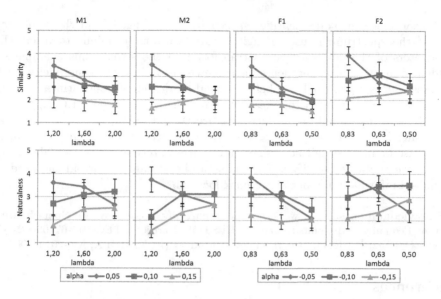

**Fig. 5.** Similarity and naturalness MOS at 95 % confidence intervals for different voices and factors.

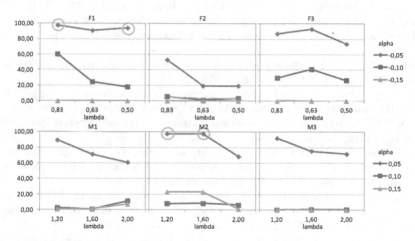

**Fig. 6.** Phonexia scores for different voices and factors. Yellow circles indicate a correct identification of the speaker. (Color figure online)

able to recognize the speaker, which confirms the effectiveness of the suggested modification despite its simplicity.

## 5   Conclusions

We have presented a speech de-identification system with the following characteristics: it uses a wideband harmonic model for signal analysis, modification and reconstruction; it de-identifies speech by modifying $f_0$ and the frequency axis of the spectrum; it uses a digital watermarking technique to insert the parameters of the de-identification transforms in the signal, thus enabling its re-identification. Our experiments have shown that, despite its simplicity, such a system offers a good balance between quality, degree of de-identification and naturalness for warping factors near $\pm 0.1$ and pitch factors near $1.6^{\pm 1}$.

Future works should be conducted to overcome the limitations of the signal processing framework for male voices. To widen the scope of the method, it would also be interesting to design an automatic watermark detection algorithm so that we could de-identify a continuous audio stream and avoid the need of privileged information about watermark location.

**Acknowledgements.** This work has been partially funded by the Spanish Ministry of Economy and Competitiveness (RESTORE project, TEC2015-67163-C2-1-R MINECO/FEDER,UE) and the Basque Government (ELKAROLA, KK-2015/00098).

# References

1. Ribaric, S., Ariyaeeinia, A., Pavesic, N.: De-identification for privacy protection in multimedia content: a survey. Signal Process. Image Commun. **47**, 131–151 (2016)
2. Jin, Q., Toth, A.R., Schultz, T., Black, A.W.: Voice convergin: speaker de-identification by voice transformation. In: Proceedings of ICASSP, pp. 3909–3912 (2009)
3. Pobar, M., Ipsic, I.: Online speaker de-identification using voice transformation. In: Proceedings of MIPRO, pp. 1264–1267 (2014)
4. Justin, T., Struc, V., Dobrisek, S., Vesnicer, B., Ipsic, I., Mihelic, F.: Speaker de-identification using diphone recognition and speech synthesis. In: Proceedings of 11th IEEE International Conference on Automatic Face and Gesture Recognition, pp. 1–7 (2015)
5. Magariños, C., Lopez-Otero, P., Docio, L., Erro, D., Rodriguez-Banga, E., Garcia-Mateo, C.: Piecewise linear definition of transformation functions for speaker de-identification. In: Proceedings of SPLINE (2016)
6. Magariños, C., Lopez-Otero, P., Docio, L., Rodriguez-Banga, E., Erro, D., Garcia-Mateo, C.: Reversible speaker de-identification using pre-trained transformation functions. IEEE Signal Process. Lett. (2016, submitted)
7. Erro, D., Moreno, A., Bonafonte, A.: Flexible harmonic/stochastic speech synthesis. In: Proceedings of 6th ISCA Speech Synthesis Workshop, pp. 194–199 (2007)
8. Degottex, G., Stylianou, Y.: Analysis and synthesis of speech using an adaptive full-band harmonic model. IEEE Trans. Audio Speech Lang. Process. **21**(10), 2085–2095 (2013)
9. Stylianou, Y.: Harmonic plus noise models for speech, combined with statistical methods, for speech and speaker modification. Ph.D. thesis, ENST, Paris (1996)
10. Boersma, P.: Accurate short-term analysis of the fundamental frequency and the harmonics-to-noise ratio of a sampled sound. In: Proceedings of Institute of Phonetic Sciences, University of Amsterdam, pp. 97–110 (1993)
11. Tokuda, K., Kobayashi, T., Masuko, T., Imai, S.: Mel-generalized cepstral analysis - a unified approach to speech spectral estimation. In: Proceedings of ICSLP, vol. 3, pp. 1043–1046 (1994)

12. Nematollahi, M.A., Al-Haddad, S.A.R.: An overview of digital speech watermarking. Int. J. Speech Tech. **16**(4), 471–488 (2013)
13. Kirovski, D., Malvar, H.S.: Spread-spectrum watermarking of audio signals. IEEE Trans. Signal Process. **51**(4), 1020–1033 (2003)
14. Korzhik, V.I., Morales-Luna, G., Fedyanin, I.: Audio watermarking based on echo hiding with zero error probability. Int. J. Emerg. Technol. Adv. Eng. **10**(1), 1–10 (2013)
15. Hernaez, I., Saratxaga, I., Ye, J., Sanchez, J., Erro, D., Navas, E.: Speech watermarking based on coding of the harmonic phase. In: Navarro Mesa, J.L., Ortega, A., Teixeira, A., Hernández Pérez, E., Quintana Morales, P., Ravelo García, A., Guerra Moreno, I., Toledano, D.T. (eds.) IberSPEECH 2014. LNCS (LNAI), vol. 8854, pp. 259–268. Springer, Heidelberg (2014). doi:10.1007/978-3-319-13623-3_27
16. Zeki, A.M., Manaf, A.A.: A novel digital watermarking technique based on ISB (Intermediate Significant Bit). Int. J. Comput. Electr. Autom. Control Inf. Eng. **3**(2), 444–451 (2009)
17. Moon, T.K.: Error Correction Coding: Mathematical Methods and Algorithms. Wiley, New York (2005)
18. Rix, A., Beerends, J., Hollier, M., Hekstra, A.: Perceptual evaluation of speech quality (PESQ) - a new method for speech quality assessment of telephone networks and codecs. In: Proceedings of ICASSP, vol. 2, pp. 749–752 (2001)
19. Phonexia speaker identification. https://www.phonexia.com/technologies/sid
20. Dehak, N., Kenny, P., Dehak, R., Dumouchel, P., Ouellet, P.: Front-end factor analysis for speaker verification. IEEE Trans. Audio Speech Lang. Process. **19**(4), 788–798 (2011)
21. White, L., King, S.: The EUSTACE speech corpus (2003). http://www.cstr.ed.ac.uk/projects/eustace

# Bottleneck Based Front-End
# for Diarization Systems

Ignacio Viñals[1]([⊠]), Jesús Villalba[2], Alfonso Ortega[1],
Antonio Miguel[1], and Eduardo Lleida[1]

[1] ViVoLAB, Aragón Institute for Engineering Research (I3A),
University of Zaragoza, Zaragoza, Spain
{ivinalsb,ortega,amiguel,lleida}@unizar.es
[2] Cirrus Logic, Madrid, Spain
jesus.villalba@cirrus.com

**Abstract.** The goal of this paper is to study the inclusion of deep learning into the diarization task. We propose some novel approaches at the
feature extraction stage, substituting the classical usage of short-term
features, such as MFCCs and PLPs, by Deep Learning based ones. These
new features come from the hidden states at bottleneck layers in neural
networks. Trained for ASR tasks.

These new features will be included in the University of Zaragoza
ViVoLAB speaker diarization system, designed for the Multi-Genre
Broadcast (MGB) challenge of the 2015 ASRU Workshop. This system,
designed following the i-vector paradigm, uses the input features to segment the input audio and construct one i-vector per segment. These
i-vectors will be clustered into speakers according to generative PLDA
models.

The evaluation for our new approach will be carried out with broadcast audio from the 2015 MGB Challenge.

**Keywords:** Diarization · Deep Neural Networks · Bottlenecks

## 1 Introduction

Speaker diarization is the problem of determining who and when, in a set of
speakers, is active at each time, given some audio. Therefore, it is closely related
to the speaker recognition problem. Traditionally, diarization has been applied
to telephone conversations, broadcast news, meetings, etc. Recently, the Internet
has provided a new milestone, with an immense growth of availablemultimedia

This work has been supported by the Spanish Ministry of Economy and Competitiveness and the European Social Fund through the 2015 FPI fellowship, the project
TIN2014-54288-C4-2-R and by the European Unions FP7 Marie Curie action, IAPP
under grant agreement no. 610986. Besides, we gratefully acknowledge the support of
NVIDIA Corporation with the donation of the Titan X GPU used for this research.

© Springer International Publishing AG 2016
A. Abad et al. (Eds.): IberSPEECH 2016, LNAI 10077, pp. 276–286, 2016.
DOI: 10.1007/978-3-319-49169-1_27

content requiring automatic indexation. Detailed reviews about the evolution of diarization are available in [1, 2].

The first successful diarization systems were approaches based on a segmentation of the audio into acoustically uniform segments, by using Bayesian Information Criterion [3], and an Agglomerative Hierarchical Clustering (AHC) [4]. Later on, with the advent of JFA [5], new approaches appeared: The stream-based strategy [6] constructs speaker-factors in terms of a sliding window. These speaker-factors are clustered afterwards according to different metrics and algorithms, such as PCA or K-means. Other options rely on Variational Bayes theory [7], considering both the speaker-factors and the speaker labels to be latent variables, jointly estimated to maximize a lower bound of the likelihood on the dataset.

The interest in adapting Deep Neural Networks to speaker recognition has recently increased, due to their performance gains obtained in ASR tasks [8]. Two main strategies have shown to be effective for this purpose: On the one hand, we can consider the "direct" methods, using the DNNs as classifiers for the speaker recognition. On the other hand, we can apply the "indirect" methods, in which the DNNs are trained for completely different purposes, but letting users extract some discriminative information, used by another classifier which performs our desired job. The nature of the extracted data can include frame-level features, also known as bottlenecks [9, 10], and multi-modal statistics [11] to be applied in i-vector systems [12].

In this paper, our goal is to study the inclusion of Deep Learning in diarization. We make use of DNNs according to the indirect methods described before, obtaining frame-level features from their bottleneck layer. These new features will serve to generate streams of i-vectors, which are clustered into speakers by Bayesian PLDA. The bottleneck features will be analysed on their own and complementing the original MFCC features by concatenation.

In order to proceed with this analysis, we have utilized the data provided for the 2015 Multi-Genre Broadcast (MGB) diarization challenge. The challenge evaluated speaker diarization systems in a longitudinal setting, across multiple episodes from the same shows. The dataset is composed of BBC TV recordings [13], which belong to multiple shows from different genres.

The paper is organized as follows. The description of the ViVoLAB diarization system is presented in Sect. 2. Section 3 discusses about DNNs and bottleneck features. Our experiments can be found in Sect. 4. Finally, Sect. 5 presents the conclusions.

## 2 The ViVoLAB Diarization System

The ViVoLAB diarization system is a PLDA-based architecture carried out for the 2015 MGB Challenge [13, 14]. Its schematic is illustrated in Fig. 1.

The system receives the episode audio to diarize $s_i(t)$, and information about the diarization of previous episodes, the set $\Phi_{i-1}$. This set includes i-vectors per speaker and episode. From the episode audio, MFCC features are extracted and an initial segmentation is performed. A stream of i-vectors is created in terms

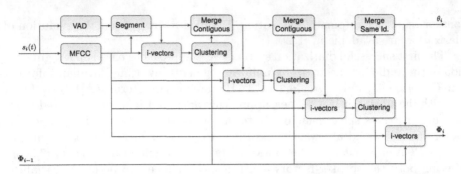

**Fig. 1.** Block diagram of the ViVoLAB speaker diarization system.

of the resultant segmentation. These i-vectors are clustered, and consecutive segments with a common speaker are merged. During the clustering process we take into account the information from previous episodes $\Phi_{i-1}$. The i-vectors are recalculated according to the new segments. We repeat this process twice to create longer segments with more robust i-vectors. Finally, a last clustering stage creates the final labelling $\theta_i$ for the episode. Before leaving the episode, we extract i-vectors per speaker from the final labelling and append them to the received set $\Phi_{i-1}$, composing the set $\Phi_i$ for posterior episodes diarization.

## 2.1    Segmentation

Bayesian Information Criterion (BIC) [3] obtains the speaker boundaries location during the initial segmentation. This method opposes two hypotheses for an analysis window: $H_0$, in which the audio comes from two different speakers, and $H_1$, defending the presence of only one speaker. The final measure is the difference between the BIC values for each hypothesis,

$$\Delta\mathrm{BIC} = \log(R) - \lambda P \tag{1}$$

where $R$ is the likelihood ratio of hypotheses and $P$ a penalty term so as to compensate the model complexity capabilities of $H_0$ compared to $H_1$, adjusted by a scaling hyperparameter $\lambda$. Full covariance Gaussian distributions are considered.

## 2.2    I-vector Extraction

According to the i-vector paradigm [12], a speech segment $s$ can be modelled by a Gaussian Mixture Model (GMM), whose super-vector mean $\mathbf{M}$ is defined as

$$\mathbf{M} = \mathbf{m} + \mathbf{T}\phi \tag{2}$$

where $\mathbf{m}$ is the UBM means super-vector, $\mathbf{T}$ is a low-rank matrix and $\phi$ a standard normal distributed vector. $\mathbf{T}$ describes the total variability space, i.e. it spans the subspace containing important inter and intra-speaker variability in the super-vector space

The posterior distribution of $\phi$ given the segment data is a Gaussian distribution whose mean is referred as i-vector in the bibliography. By this method, our previously variable-length segments are represented by a fixed-length vector.

The obtained i-vectors are normalized following [15], in which normalizing i-vectors by their magnitude improves their discriminant effects. Before length normalization, centering and whitening are applied on the i-vectors to evenly distribute them in the unit hypersphere.

## 2.3   Unsupervised PLDA Clustering

Our clustering process is based on the Fully Bayesian Unsupervised PLDA model, introduced in [16]. The system, constructed around the Simplified PLDA (SPLDA), assumes each i-vector $\phi_j$ from a speaker $i$ is defined according to a generative model like

$$\phi_j = \mu + \mathbf{V}\mathbf{y}_i + \epsilon_j \tag{3}$$

being $\mu$ a speaker independent term, $\mathbf{V}$ a low rank eigenvoices matrix, $\mathbf{y}_i$ the speaker factor vector and $\epsilon_j$ the within class variability term. The priors for $\mathbf{y}_i$ and $\epsilon_j$ are a standard normal and a normal with zero mean and precision $\mathbf{W}$ respectively. The model parameters ($\mu$, $\mathbf{V}$, $\alpha$ and $\mathbf{W}$) are hidden variables whose priors ($P(\mu)$, $P(\mathbf{V}|\alpha)$, $P(\alpha)$ and $P(\mathbf{W})$) are described in [16].

The distribution of each speaker is assumed to be Gaussian with mean $\mu + \mathbf{V}\mathbf{y}_i$, and precision $\mathbf{W}$. However, speaker labels are not provided but considered hidden variables $\theta$. Therefore, $\theta$ divides $N$ i-vectors into $M$ speakers. Figure 2 illustrates the Bayesian Network of this model.

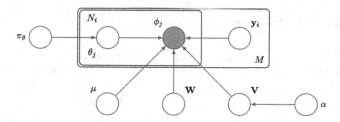

**Fig. 2.** BN for unsupervised SPLDA.

These $\theta$ latent variables depend on a categorical distribution defined by the weights of $\pi_\theta$

$$P(\theta|\pi_\theta) = \prod_{j=1}^{N} \prod_{i=1}^{M} \pi_{\theta_i}^{\theta_{ji}} . \tag{4}$$

These weights have been defined in terms of a Dirichlet prior

$$P\left(\pi_\theta|\tau_0\right) = \mathrm{Dir}(\pi_\theta|\tau_0) = C(\tau_0)\prod_{i=1}^{M}\pi_{\theta_i}^{\tau_0-1} \tag{5}$$

being $\tau_0$ equal for all components, and $C(\tau_0)$ a normalization constant

$$C(\tau_0) = \frac{\Gamma(M\tau_0)}{\Gamma(\tau_0)^M} \tag{6}$$

representing $\Gamma$ the Gamma function.

The high complexity of the model makes impossible its close form resolution, so we presented its solution by Variational Bayes. By this way we approximated the joint posterior to a product of factor distributions of the form:

$$P\left(\mathbf{Y}, \theta, \pi_\theta, \mu, \mathbf{V}, \mathbf{W}, \alpha|\mathbf{\Phi}\right) \approx$$

$$q\left(\mathbf{Y}\right)q\left(\theta\right)q\left(\pi_\theta\right)\prod_{r=1}^{d}q\left(\tilde{\mathbf{v}}_r'\right)q\left(\mathbf{W}\right)q\left(\alpha\right) \tag{7}$$

During training, we iteratively update the variational factors of the model parameters ($\mu$, $\mathbf{V}$, $\mathbf{W}$ and $\alpha$), the speaker factors for both reference data $q\left(\mathbf{Y}_{\mathrm{REF}}\right)$ and the adapted $q\left(\mathbf{Y}_{\mathrm{ADAPT}}\right)$, as well as their label $q\left(\theta_{\mathrm{ADAPT}}\right)$ and label priors $q\left(\pi_{\theta_{\mathrm{ADAPT}}}\right)$. Nevertheless, in the online diarization steps, all PLDA parameters ($\mu$, $\mathbf{V}$, $\mathbf{W}$ and $\alpha$) remain unmodified, being only updated those related with the labelling: the speaker factors $q\left(\mathbf{Y}\right)$, the speaker labels $q\left(\theta\right)$ and the label priors $q\left(\pi_\theta\right)$. The speaker labels $q\left(\theta\right)$ will be considered the diarization labelling $\theta_i$ for an audio session.

## 3    DNNs and Bottlenecks

Deep Neural Network is a denomination for certain neural networks characterized by their high computational complexity. A relevant contribution in speech technologies was [8], significantly improving the ASR tasks. This work calculated triphone posteriors with a DNN trained to classify them.

The inclusion of DNNs in speaker recognition tasks is more complicated. While the direct classification methods have suffered from problems such as overtraining and out-of-domain data, the indirect use of DNNs has gained popularity. Certain ideas have shown to boost the performance, such as extracting bottleneck features from a DNN [9,17], or substituting the traditional GMM-UBM by a DNN-UBM in the i-vector front-end [10,11]. In both cases, the DNNs were trained for ASR tasks.

Bottleneck neural networks are DNNs characterized by having one layer with significantly lower dimensionality compared to its surroundings. In consequence, this layer compresses the information propagated from the neural network input, gaining robustness to noise and protection from overfitting. The layers before the bottleneck are expected to produce robust features, whereas the posterior ones are mostly dedicated to discriminate among the target classes.

The bottleneck features are considered to be the output of the compressive layer, mapping the information at the input of the neural network. Once the network is trained, all the layers after the bottleneck lose their necessity, being truncated from the original architecture for evaluation purposes.

For ASR purposes the bottleneck compression and decompression is commonly located right before the softmax layer [8]. By contrast, in speaker verification this idea has been questioned [9,17], showing the earlier the bottleneck is, the better performance is obtained.

## 4   Experiments

The chosen data for our experiments is the provided dataset for the 2015 MGB challenge [13]. It is divided in three parts: training (composed of 1600 h of audio), development and evaluation. The training metadata includes the BBC subtitles, time stamps and a Matched Error Rate (MER) score, a measure about the labels quality for speech alignment, per speaker utterance. The training set metadata was obtained using a slightly supervised alignment. Regarding the other sets metadata, it includes VAD and speaker segmentation information for each set. Whereas the development metadata is accurate enough to be considered ground truth, the test one is an approximation obtained by automatic unsupervised methods, and significantly less accurate. This approximation constitutes the baseline information for the test set.

Being restricted the data to only those provided by the organization, we did not have enough to train our model-based approaches for a voice detector system. In consequence, using the provided metadata, we have performed two analyses: the results of our system with ground truth metadata for both development and test sets, and the test set evaluated under competition conditions (baseline metadata). In both cases a BIC segmentation is tested apart from the provided segmentation, seeking more realistic results.

### 4.1   Bottleneck Features Extraction

Our bottleneck features have been obtained using a DNN constructed in terms of a monolithic architecture: 7 hidden layers, 6 of them of 1024 neurons, having a 90 neuron linear bottleneck layer in the second position. The neural network finishes with a softmax layer. This configuration, adjusted to optimize the final DER results, highlights the relevance of the bottleneck position placing it close to the neural network input, agreeing with other authors [9,17]. The layer before the bottleneck has been pretrained with a Restricted Boltzmann Machine (RBM) layer.

In order to train the bottleneck network, a subset extracted from the train set has been used, considering only the utterances with less than 10 % MER. The input samples are the output of 40 Mel Filter bank, analysing a 25 ms window with a 10 ms window shift, with a context of ±5 frames. Regarding the targets, the network tries to discriminate among context-dependent cross-word triphone senons. The labels have been created with Kaldi [18], based on the MGB Kaldi recipe, provided during the challenge. Kaldi neural network software has been used as well.

Apart from working exclusively with bottleneck features, we have also considered the option of appending them with the classical short-term features, in our case, the MFCCs used along the original experiment.

## 4.2   Simplified MGB System

The previously described bottleneck features are retrieved for the already mentioned sets (train, development and evaluation, respectively). The obtained features are used by the ViVoLAB diarization system, alone or complementing the original 20 ETSI standard [19] MFCCs. Short time CMVN is applied, not mattering the input features.

The resultant features are used for the offline training as follows. A 256-Gaussian UBM-GMM and a 100-dimension i-vector extractor are trained with the train set. In order to train the PLDA, the development set is chosen [14] because it is the only set with reliable labelling. Its short length motivates the option of training two different PLDAs. Both of them are supervisedly trained with the development set, but only the second one is trained unsupervisedly afterwards with the train set. The speaker factor dimensions are 50 and 60 respectively.

Regarding the online diarization process, we make use of a ground truth VAD (GTVAD). In terms of segmentation, we consider the provided ground truth segmentation (GTS) and a BIC-based speaker-change-point detector. The latter is exclusively performed on MFCC for comparison reasons. The obtained results with the development set are presented in Table 1.

**Table 1.** DER (%) for different systems, evaluated on dev. set. SCPD stands for Speaker Change Point Detection, GTS means Ground Truth segmentation, BIC denotes BIC Speaker Change Point Detection with MFCC and ground truth VAD, PLDA was trained on the dev. set for one system and on the train and dev. sets for the other one.

| SCPD | PLDA train | MFCC | BN | BN + MFCC |
|------|-----------|------|-----|-----------|
| GTS | dev. | 24.32 | 24.08 | **22.34** |
| BIC | dev. | 28.05 | 27.52 | **23.89** |
| GTS | dev. + train | 22.8 | 22.91 | **20.99** |
| BIC | dev. + train | 27.41 | 26.53 | **24.45** |

According to the mentioned results, bottleneck features acting alone are, at least, performing as good as the original MFCCs. Besides, for those cases whose segmentation is based on BIC, the improvement is slightly more noticeable in terms of DER. If the concatenation of the bottleneck features and MFCCs is performed, the DER term drastically decreases for all the experimental conditions compared with both MFCCs and simple bottleneck features.

Moving the analysis to the evaluation set, the equivalent results under the same conditions are shown in Table 2.

**Table 2.** DER (%) for different systems, evaluated on test set. SCPD stands for Speaker Change Point Detection, GTS means Ground Truth segmentation, BIC denotes BIC Speaker Change Point Detection with MFCC and ground truth VAD, PLDA was trained on the dev. set for one system and on the train and dev. sets for the other one.

| SCPD | PLDA train | MFCC | BN | BN + MFCC |
|---|---|---|---|---|
| GTS | dev. | **33.01** | 33.24 | 35.73 |
| BIC | dev. | **34.39** | 36.14 | 36.65 |
| GTS | dev. + train | 32.96 | 34.77 | **31.68** |
| BIC | dev. + train | 34.43 | 36.43 | **32.59** |

These results reveal that bottleneck features combined with MFCCs perform better than the original MFCCs as long as the training set contains enough data to conduct a proper generalization (development + train PLDA). If only limited data is available (development PLDA), the bottleneck based features suffer from a reduction in performance, caused by a high adaptation to the training set. This is more noticeable regarding bottleneck features, because they cannot maintain the small improvement respect to MFCCs by themselves.

### 4.3   Competition MGB System

Regarding competition conditions, the ground truth information has been substituted by the approximate baseline information, also provided by the organization. Therefore our experiments work with the baseline VAD, and cover both the baseline segmentation (BLS) and the BIC segmentation computed on MFCCs. In terms of VAD, its accuracy causes a 10.1 % DER degradation, divided into a 6.10 % Missed Speech term and a 4.00 % False Speech term. About the segmentation quality, impurity tests on the different segmentations have been carried out, being BIC significantly much purer than the baseline in terms of clustering impurity (72 % to 5 %). Under these premises, the obtained results are illustrated in Table 3.

With test data, the concatenation of bottleneck features with MFCCs keeps on performing better than simple bottleneck features in most cases, but they are not as accurate as MFCCs. Although the baseline VAD provokes a reduction in performance, it is more severe while working with the bottleneck-based features. Nevertheless, we manage to keep improving the original features with a

**Table 3.** DER (%) for different systems. SCPD stands for Speaker Change Point Detection, BLS stands for baseline segmentation, BIC denotes BIC segmentation with MFCC and baseline VAD provided by the organizers, PLDA was trained on the dev. set for one system and on the train and dev. sets for the other one.

| SCPD | PLDA train | MFCC | BN | BN + MFCC |
|------|-----------|------|------|-----------|
| BLS | dev. | **44.67** | 46.45 | 45.40 |
| BIC | dev. | 42.77 | 43.85 | **41.08** |
| BLS | dev. + train | **42.96** | 43.87 | 44.32 |
| BIC | dev. + train | 39.86 | 41.92 | **39.68** |

BIC MFCC segmentation, if the posterior clustering is performed with i-vectors obtained from bottlenecks concatenated with MFCCs.

Besides, the baseline segmentation experiments show a higher degradation while working with bottlenecks, compared to MFCC features.

Finally, comparing our competition results with those presented to the MGB evaluation ([13] Table 4 Task 4), we manage to improve our own previous results (43 %) and perform slightly better than the best known results at the competition (40.2 %).

## 5   Conclusions

Along the experiments we have confirmed the potential of bottleneck features concatenated with MFCCs applied to diarization. However, we need a significant amount of training data. Otherwise, these features become quite sensitive, losing their boost in performance.

Moreover, our combined features have successfully worked in the presence of short-length segments, provided by the ground truth and BIC segmentation, and improving the MFCCs counterpart. Therefore, any possible degradation caused by short-length segments is compensated by the long-length segments boost in performance, improving the DER score in general terms.

Besides, the combination of features is robust enough to work with a noisy VAD, performing at least slightly better than the MFCC reference, and a better performance is available by independently improving the voice detection system.

By contrast, the Baseline Segmentation experiments illustrate the weakness of bottleneck-based i-vectors if the segments contain information from various speakers. However, simple segmentations (BIC) are good enough to start performing better than the MFCC reference.

Future work will investigate in detail each strength and weakness, in order to maximize the bottlenecks revealed potential.

# References

1. Miro, X.A., Bozonnet, S., Evans, N., Fredouille, C., Friedland, G., Vinyals, O.: Speaker diarization: a review of recent research. IEEE Trans. Audio Speech Lang. Process. **20**(2), 356–370 (2012)
2. Tranter, S.E., Reynolds, D.: An overview of automatic speaker diarization systems. IEEE Trans. Audio Speech Lang. Process. **14**(5), 1557–1565 (2006)
3. Chen, S., Gopalakrishnan, P.: Speaker, environment and channel change detection and clustering via the Bayesian information criterion. In: Proceedings of DARPA Broadcast News Transcription and Understanding Workshop, vol. 6, pp. 127–132 (1998)
4. Reynolds, D., Torres-Carrasquillo, P.: Approaches and applications of audio diarization. In: ICASSP, IEEE International Conference on Acoustics, Speech and Signal Processing - Proceedings, vol. V, pp. 953–956 (2005)
5. Kenny, P.: Joint factor analysis of speaker and session variability: theory and algorithms. (Report) CRIM-06/08-13, CRIM, Montreal, pp. 1–17 (2005)
6. Vaquero, C., Ortega, A., Miguel, A., Lleida, E.: Quality assessment of speaker diarization for speaker characterization. IEEE Trans. Acoust. Speech Lang. Process. **21**(4), 816–827 (2013)
7. Reynolds, D., Kenny, P., Castaldo, F.: A study of new approaches to speaker diarization. In: Interspeech, pp. 1047–1050 (2009)
8. Hinton, G., Deng, L., Dong, Y., Dahl, G., Mohamed, A., Jaitly, N., Vanhoucke, V., Nguyen, P., Sainath, T., Kingsbury, B.: Deep neural networks for acoustic modeling in speech recognition. IEEE Sig. Process. Mag. **29**(6), 82–97 (2012)
9. Ghalehjegh, S.H., Rose, R.: Deep bottleneck features for I-vector based text-independent speaker verification. In: 2015 IEEE Workshop on Automatic Speech Recognition and Understanding (ASRU), pp. 555–560 (2015)
10. Richardson, F., Reynolds, D., Dehak, N.: A unified deep neural network for speaker and language recognition. In: Interspeech, pp. 1146–1150 (2015)
11. Lei, Y., Scheffer, N., Ferrer, L., McLaren, M.: A novel scheme for speaker recognition using a phonetically-aware deep neural network. In: IEEE International Conference on Acoustics, Speech and Signal Processing (ICASSP), pp. 1714–1718 (2014)
12. Dehak, N., Kenny, P., Dehak, R., Dumouchel, P., Ouellet, P.: Front-end factor analysis for speaker verification. IEEE Trans. Audio Speech Lang. Process. **19**(4), 788–798 (2011)
13. Bell, P., Gales, M.J.F., Thomas Hain, J., Kilgour, P Lanchantin Liu, X., McParland, A., Renals, S., Saz, O., Wester, M., Woodland, P.C.: The MGB challenge: evaluating multi-genre broadcast media recognition. In: Proceedings of IEEE Workshop on Automatic Speech Recognition and Understanding, ASRU 2015S, Scottsdale, Arizona, USA, December 2015, vol. 1, no. 1. IEEE (2015)
14. Villalba, J., Ortega, A., Miguel, A., Lleida, E.: Variational Bayesian PLDA for speaker diarization in the MGB challenge. In: 2015 IEEE Workshop on Automatic Speech Recognition and Understanding (ASRU), pp. 667–674 (2015)
15. Garcia-Romero, D., Espy-Wilson, C.Y.: Analysis of i-vector length normalization in speaker recognition systems. In: Proceedings of Annual Conference of the International Speech Communication Association, INTERSPEECH, pp. 249–252 (2011)
16. Villalba, J., Lleida, E.: Unsupervised adaptation of PLDA by using variational Bayes methods. In: ICASSP, IEEE International Conference on Acoustics, Speech and Signal Processing - Proceedings, pp. 744–748 (2014)

17. Liu, Y., Qian, Y., Chen, N., Fu, T., Zhang, Y., Yu, K.: Deep feature for text-dependent speaker verification. Speech Commun. **73**, 1–13 (2015)
18. Povey, D., Ghoshal, A., Boulianne, G., Burget, L., Glembek, O., Goel, N., Hannemann, M., Motlicek, P., Qian, Y., Schwarz, P., Silovsky, J., Stemmer, G., Vesely, K.: The Kaldi speech recognition toolkit. In: Proceedings of ASRU (2011)
19. ETSI. ETSI ES 202 050 Speech Processing, Transmission and Quality Aspects (STQ); Distributed Speech Recognition; Advanced Front-end Feature Extraction Algorithm; Compression (2002)

# Author Index

Printed in the United States
by Bookmasters

Printed in the United States
By Bookmasters